Global Stage

Teacher's Book 6

Katie Foufouti

macmillan education

Macmillan Education
4 Crinan Street
London N1 9XW
A division of Springer Nature Limited

Companies and representatives throughout the world

Teacher's Book ISBN 978-1-380-00271-6
Teacher's Blended Pack ISBN 978-1-380-00268-6

Written by Katie Foufouti

First published 2019

Designed by emc design ltd
Front cover design and concept by 3CD
Cover adaptation by Roberto Martinez

The authors and publishers would like to thank the following for permission to reproduce their photographs: Matthew Hayes (p. 16), Lina Acosta Sandaal (p. 18)

The authors and publishers are grateful for permission to reprint the following copyright material: p. 11. Extract from 'Framework for 21st Century Learning' © 2017 Partnership for 21st Century Skills. Reprinted with permission; p. 17 Extract from 'Collaborative for Academic, Social, and Emotional Learning' © 2017 CASEL. Reprinted with permission.

Full acknowledgements for illustrations and photographs in the facsimile pages can be found in the **Language Book** ISBN: 978-1-380-00270-9 and **Literacy Book** ISBN: 978-1-786-32595-2.

Printed and bound by CPI Group (UK) Ltd, Croydon, CR0 4YY

2023 2022 2021 2020 2019
10 9 8 7 6 5 4

Contents

Scope and Sequence 4
Introduction 10
Review Unit 28
Unit 1 Keep in Touch and Unit Walkthrough 32
Unit 2 Time for a Change 62
Unit 3 Dream Big 78
Unit 4 How's That Possible? 94
Unit 5 What Is Art? 110
Unit 6 It's Your Turn 126
Unit 7 All About Ads 142
Unit 8 What Are the Odds? 158
Unit 9 Make Up Your Mind 174
Unit 10 Take the Lead 190
Put It Together Review Games 206
Process Writing 211
Audio Scripts 215
Video Scripts 239

macmillan education

Unit	Vocabulary	Explore Language	Global Citizenship
Language Review	**Vocabulary** *Emotions; Crime; Nature; Being Eco-Friendly; Storytelling; Work and Skills* **Grammar** *Present Perfect; Tag Questions; Present and Past Passive; Too and Enough; Agreeing with Too, So, Either, and Neither; Reported Speech; First and Second Conditional*		
1 Keep in Touch page 10	**Technology** *blog, blog post, comment, crash, download, email, message, save to favorites, search history, upload* **Online Safety** *create a profile, devices, lowercase letters, online privacy, online safety, password, personal information, register, secure, special characters, uppercase letters, username* **Chant** *Search the Net*	Verbs of Thinking Simple and Progressive Forms	How does technology help us learn? **Listening Skills** Listening for gist and details
2 Time for a Change page 22	**Lifestyle and Habits** *argue, be late, healthy diet, junk food, messy, polite, punctual, workout, rude, sleep late* **Healthy Food** *convenience food, high in fiber, high in salt and sugar, in season, local produce, packaging, processed food, red meat, saturated fat, white meat, whole grains* **Poem** *You Can Do Better*	Present Perfect Present Perfect Progressive	How do eating habits affect our lives? **Listening Skills** Listening for gist and details
Put It Together	Review Units 1 and 2 *Know It, Win It*		
3 Dream Big page 36	**Dreams and Ambitions** *ambition, confidence, determination, happiness, health, pride, success, wealth* **Persevering to Succeed** *be the hero, do things for fun, experience failure, fear of the unknown, find joy in, fresh start, notice the small things, nurture friendship* **Poem** *My Dreams*	Second Conditional *Wish* + Past Forms	How can children help solve the world's problems? **Listening Skills** Listening for gist and details
4 How's That Possible? page 48	**Facts, Mysteries, and Illusions** *evidence, fact, have a feeling, make up, optical illusion, play a trick, puzzle, see things* **Historical Discoveries** *ancient monument, archaeologist, clue, expert, legend, prehistoric times, solve, theory* **Poem** *My Friend Oscar*	Modals of Deduction: Past Forms Modals of Obligation: Past Forms	Why is it important to explore things we don't understand? **Listening Skills** Listening for gist and details
Put It Together	Review Units 3 and 4 *Chatter Boxes*		
5 What Is Art? page 62	**Describing Paintings** *abstract shapes, complex, doodles, dots, lines, playful, powerful, serious, simple, squiggles* **Artistic Elements and Features** *contrast, creativity, depict, iconic, large-scale, masterpiece, style, symbolize* **Poem** *The More I Look—A Poem Inspired by Kandinsky*	Past Perfect and Past Perfect Progressive Narrative Tenses	What can art tell us about different countries and periods of time? **Listening Skills** Listening for gist and details

Writing	Speaking	International English	Literacy Book
			Literacy: *Making Predictions; Sequence of Events; Sensory Details; Synonyms; Making Inferences; Understanding the Main Idea and Details; Transition Words*
Paragraph and Sentence Building Presenting Facts and Giving Details, Examples, and Opinions **Product** A Fact-Based Article	**Conversation** Asking for Clarification and Confirming Understanding **Pronunciation** Sentence Stress: Content Words	**US** *I forgot; take a look* **UK** *I've forgotten; have a look*	**Story** *Urgent Message* **Informational Text** *Communication Time* **Reading Skill** Understanding Chronology
Function Making Connections Between Entries **Word Study** Using Informal and Emotive Language **Product** A Diary Entry	**Presentation** Supporting an Argument and Being Persuasive **Pronunciation** Sentence Stress: Weak Forms	**US** *messy; we've gotten better* **UK** *untidy; we've got better*	**Diary** *My Stay at Camp Karma* **Informational Text** *Why Do We Sleep?* **Reading Skill** Analyzing and Evaluating
Paragraph Building Describing Causes and Effects, and Suggesting Solutions **Word Study** Positive and Negative Adjectives **Product** A Cause and Effect Article	**Conversation** Asking for Ideas and Summarizing Points **Pronunciation** Connected Speech: Consonant-Vowel Linking	**US** *soccer uniform* **UK** *football kit*	**Creative Nonfiction** *Communities Making Dreams Come True* **Poem** *Dreams* **Reading Skill** Understanding Author's Word Choice
Paragraph Building Including and Omitting Information **Word Study** Review: Time Phrases and Adjectives about Feelings and Reactions **Product** A Story Beginning	**Presentation** Asking Questions and Pausing for Effect **Pronunciation** Connected Speech: Elision, Dropping the *t*		**Informational Text** *The Sci-Files* **Fantasy** *An Enlightening Journey* **Reading Skill** Making Inferences
Paragraph Building Linking the Beginning, Middle, and End of a Story **Word Study** Using Descriptive Language **Product** A Mini Saga	**Presentation** Organizing and Summarizing Points **Pronunciation** Sentence Stress: Content Words	**US** *leaned* **UK** *leant*	**Creative Nonfiction** *Cave Painting* **Folk Tale** *The Boy Who Drew Cats* **Reading Skill** Recognizing Genres

Unit	Vocabulary	Explore Language	Global Citizenship
6 It's Your Turn page 74	**Playing Traditional Board Games** *board game, chance, land on, lose, miss a turn, pieces, players, strategy, throw the dice, win* **Playing Video Games** *avatar, collaborate, collect points, gaming, graphics, instructions, level up, multiplayer, role-playing game, virtual* **Poem** *Fun and Games*	Indirect Questions; Defining and Non-defining Relative Clauses	How can games help you learn about other ways of life? **Listening Skills** Listening for gist and details
Put It Together	Review Units 5 and 6 *Yesterday's Vacation Fun*		
7 All About Ads page 88	**Advertising** *advertisement, bargain, billboard, customer, discount, persuade, products, profit, quality, value* **Branding in Advertising** *brand, claims, false impression, image, promote, slogan, small print, target market* **Chant** *Why Buy?*	Reported Speech: Statements and Commands; Reported Speech: Questions	What do advertisements sell, other than products? **Listening Skills** Listening for gist and details
8 What Are the Odds? page 100	**Numbers, Shapes, and Symmetry** *angle, divide, even number, hexagon, multiply, odd number, prime number, sequence, spirals, symmetry* **Statistics Descriptors** *average, chart, data, fall, percentage, reach a peak, rise, statistics, stay stable, trend* **Poem** *I Love Numbers*	Passives: Present and Past; Passives: Future Forms *Will, Going to*	How does math link to different aspects of our lives? **Listening Skills** Listening for gist and details
Put It Together	Review Units 7 and 8 *Word Scramble Race*		
9 Make Up Your Mind page 114	**Decision-making** *brainstorm the options, consider the consequences, decide on a solution, define the problem, evaluate your ideas, learn from your mistakes, make a decision, regret* **Collaborative Decision-making** *be fair, control your emotions, fit in with, get your own way, have your say, independence, individual identity, peer pressure, pros and cons* **Poem** *Make Up My Mind*	Third Conditional: Statements; Third Conditional: Questions	How do the decisions we make affect other people? **Listening Skills** Listening for gist and details
10 Take the Lead page 126	**Positive Values** *can-do attitude, encourage, gut feeling, inspire, mentor, positive influence, respect, role model* **Influencing and Leading** *commitment, focus, honest, motivate, organizational skills, passionate, set a good example, support* **Poem** *Let's Look to the Future*	Future Progressive; Review: Future Forms	Can anyone be a leader? **Listening Skills** Listening for gist and details
Put It Together	Review Units 9 and 10 *Solve a Problem!*		
Process Writing page 140	Generating Ideas Step 1; Planning Step 2	Drafting Step 3; Editing and Publishing Step 4	

Writing	Speaking	International English	Literacy Book
Function Introducing Ideas and Making Comparisons **Word Study** Using Adverb and Adjective Collocations **Product** A For and Against Article	**Conversation** Giving Opinions and Disagreeing **Pronunciation** Intonation in Exclamations		**Informational Text** *The History of Board Games* **Story** *The Game of Life* **Reading Skill** Understanding Denotation and Connotation
Paragraph Building Giving Reasons and Summarizing Ideas **Word Study** Using Adjectives to Reinforce Opinion **Product** An Opinion Essay	**Conversation** Preparing for an Interview; Describing Qualities, Skills, and Experience **Pronunciation** Intonation	**US** *donut, advertisement* **UK** *doughnut, advert*	**Science Fiction** *Commercial Break* **Persuasive Text** *Ad Smart* **Reading Skill** Identifying Text and Graphic Features
Paragraph Building Writing Chronologically and Supporting a Point with Examples **Product** A Biography	**Presentation** Engaging and Motivating Your Audience; Using Visuals **Pronunciation** Consonant clusters	**US** *analyzed* **UK** *analysed*	**Biography** *Ada Lovelace* **Story** *The Binary Life* **Reading Skill** Recognizing Story Structure
Function Organizing Information and Engaging the Reader **Product** An Instructional Article	**Conversation** Inviting Contributions to a Conversation **Pronunciation** Connected Speech: Linking	**US** *middle school/high school; schedule* **UK** *secondary school; timetable*	**Instructional Text** *Making Decisions* **Story** *It's Not OK* **Reading Skill** Identifying Internal and External Conflict
Function Features of a Blog **Word Study** Informal Language and Ellipsis **Product** A Blog Post	**Presentation** Using Cause-and-effect Reasoning; Sounding Positive **Pronunciation** Sentence Stress: Influencing Meaning	**US** *regular people; buddy* **UK** *ordinary people; mate*	**Play** *Click to Follow* **Informational Text** *Recycle Runway* **Reading Skill** Summarizing Readings

Unit	Reading 1	Reading 2	Reading Skill	Content Area	Social and Emotional Learning	Key Concept	Language Book
Literacy Review	Making Predictions; Sequence of Events; Sensory Details; Synonyms Making Inferences; Understanding the Main Idea and Details; Transition Words						
1 Keep in Touch page 8	**Fiction** *Urgent Message* Story **Literary Term** register	**Nonfiction** *Communication Time!* Informational Text	Understanding Chronology	Science: Technology	Self-Management: Display grit, determination, or perseverance	What are the benefits of communication technology?	**Vocabulary** technology and online safety **Grammar** verbs of thinking, and simple and progressive forms
2 Time for a Change page 24	**Fiction** *My Stay at Camp Karma* Diary **Literary Term** dropped subjects	**Nonfiction** *Why Do We Sleep?* Informational Text	Analyzing and Evaluating	Science: Health	Responsible Decision-Making: Become self-reflective and self-evaluative	Why is it important to have good lifestyle habits?	**Vocabulary** lifestyle and habits, and healthy food **Grammar** present perfect and progressive
3 Dream Big page 40	**Nonfiction** *Communities Making Dreams Come True* Creative Nonfiction **Literary Term** prefix	**Fiction** *Dreams* Poem	Understanding Author's Word Choice	Social Studies: Communities	Self-Management: Exhibit positive motivation, hope, and optimism	Why is it important to have dreams?	**Vocabulary** dreams and ambitions, and persevering to succeed **Grammar** second conditional and *wish* + past forms
4 How's That Possible? page 56	**Nonfiction** *The Sci-Files* Informational Text	**Fiction** *An Enlightening Journey* Fantasy **Literary Term** personification	Making Inferences	Science: Environmental Science	Relationship skills: Prevent interpersonal conflict, but manage to resolve it when it does occur	Why are mysteries so fascinating?	**Vocabulary** facts, mysteries, and illusions, and historical discoveries **Grammar** modals of deduction and obligation: past forms
5 What Is Art? page 72	**Nonfiction** *Cave Painting* Creative Nonfiction	**Fiction** *The Boy Who Drew Cats* Folk Tale **Literary Term** synonym	Recognizing Genres	Arts and Humanities: Art History	Self-Awareness: Identify what triggers our own emotions	What would our world be like without art?	**Vocabulary** describing paintings and artistic elements and features **Grammar** past perfect simple and progressive, and narrative tenses

Unit	Reading 1	Reading 2	Reading Skill	Content Area	Social and Emotional Learning	Key Concept	Language Book
6 **It's Your Turn** page 88	**Nonfiction** *The History of Board Games* Informational Text **Literary Term** antonym	**Fiction** *The Game of Life* Story	Understanding Denotation and Connotation	History: Civilizations	Social Awareness: Respect others	Why do people play games?	**Vocabulary** playing traditional board games and video games **Grammar** indirect questions, and defining and non-defining relative clauses
7 **All About Ads** page 104	**Fiction** *Commercial Break* Science Fiction **Literary Term** alliteration	**Nonfiction** *Ad Smart* Persuasive Text	Identifying Text and Graphic Features	Social Studies: Communication	Responsible Decision-Making: Discuss strategies used to resist peer pressure	Does advertising influence the way we think?	**Vocabulary** advertising and branding in advertising **Grammar** reported speech
8 **What Are the Odds?** page 120	**Nonfiction** *Ada Lovelace* Biography **Literary Term** open compound	**Fiction** *The Binary Life* Story	Recognizing Story Structure	History: Computer Science	Responsible Decision-Making: Make decisions based on moral, personal, and ethical standards	Why are numbers important in our lives?	**Vocabulary** numbers, shapes, and symmetry, and statistics descriptors **Grammar** passives
9 **Make Up Your Mind** page 136	**Nonfiction** *Making Decisions* Instructional Text	**Fiction** *It's Not OK* Story **Literary Term** oxymoron	Identifying Internal and External Conflict	Social Studies: Ethics	Responsible Decision-Making: Reflect on how current choices affect future	How do we handle difficult choices?	**Vocabulary** decision-making and collaborative decision-making **Grammar** third conditional
10 **Take the Lead** page 152	**Fiction** *Click to Follow* Play **Literary Term** assonance	**Nonfiction** *Recycle Runway* Informational Text	Summarizing Readings	Science: Ecology	Relationship Skills: Resist inappropriate social pressures	How are we influenced by things around us?	**Vocabulary** positive values, and influencing and leading **Grammar** future progressive and future forms review

Welcome to *Global Stage*

You have in your hands a complete language and literacy course that will support you and your students in developing their English skills, and their love of reading and the English language.

The **Language Book** contains the building blocks of language skills and systems. Students will focus on learning the language and how it works. Beautiful picture dictionary scenes, lively poetry, and contextualized grammar sections support them in figuring out and learning new language. Photos and texts about children around the world will inspire them to explore thought-provoking questions about what it means to be a Global Citizen. Live-action videos will expose learners to other children using the language they are learning before they take their turn.

The **Literacy Book** contains a variety of fictional and nonfictional texts, as well as activities for learners to explore literacy concepts, develop reading skills, and respond to the texts they have read. As they work through the course, students will further develop their thinking skills, and they will build self-reflection skills, which will allow them to become increasingly more effective and independent learners.

Together, the **Language** and **Literacy Books** explore topics across the curriculum while exposing students to differences in American and British English through the International English feature.

How to Use the Books Together

The **Language Book** and **Literacy Book** units are designed to provide a complete English language learning experience. There is no prescribed order for teaching the books: You may start with either book. You can choose to work through a whole unit and then move to the other book. Alternatively, you can start with the first **Literacy Book** reading, then move to the **Language Book**, then back to the second **Literacy Book** reading.

Used together, the two books cover the four skills, provide a solid foundation in vocabulary and grammar, and help train your learners to become competent users of English and independent thinkers.

Pedagogical Philosophy

The goal of ***Global Stage*** is to support children in becoming competent and confident English speakers while also developing as self-directed, inquisitive learners and responsible global citizens.

Global Stage starts with the child and looks out towards the world.

Global Stage assumes that every learner comes to school with a wealth of knowledge, thoughts, and opinions about their lives and the world, and that this is the starting point for their continued learning. All units include moments for students to consider and share their experiences, as well as consider others' points of view. This not only validates their thoughts, priming them to be open to learning, but is also the basis for learning empathy, which is one of the goals of our Global Citizenship lesson.

We know that children learn best when they feel safe to express their emotions. This is why we have carefully interwoven a social and emotional learning strand into the course. When you read the texts with your class, you will find opportunities to pause and reflect on how the characters feel and why, as well as opportunities for the students to think about how they feel in their lives when they encounter similar situations. Building and strengthening the ability to reflect will support students in becoming considerate, thoughtful citizens of the world.

Global Stage encourages self-reflection and a growth mindset to support children in increasing their academic achievement.

Every child has strengths they can build on, as well as areas they should develop and strengthen. We also know that what students and their teachers believe about intelligence influences academic achievement. A growth mindset is the belief that intelligence is not fixed, but rather can grow and continue to develop. Carol Dweck, who coined this term, and her colleagues demonstrated that a growth mindset empowers children to increase their academic achievement.

Global Stage supports students by helping them learn to reflect on their learning. Teachers can further support their students by focusing their praise on children's effort and improvement from where they start on their learning journey. This kind of feedback that focuses on growth reinforces the notion that children have the power to make progress by working toward it, encouraging students to view their progress and skills as something they can improve, rather than purely the result of their static abilities.

Global Stage includes various forms of review to support children in improving self-reflection skills: Our **Language Book** reviews, the Think It Over pages, are always open-ended, prompting students to think about what they have learned, how they have learned it, how they think they might learn better, and what they think they should continue to work on. When you do these lessons in class, you can take advantage of this social moment for students to hear from each other. One child may mention that they learned the most with the unit poem, while another might recall a game or a story. Children will benefit from considering what has worked for them and for others, while also planning for how to continue to learn. These are also moments for you to praise the class for their effort, pointing out where they've made progress.

Our **Literacy Book** includes Think Together pages, a space for students to get used to reflecting on how they respond to texts, and how working with those texts might have enriched what they think about the Key Concept questions at the top of the page.

Finally, our **Student's App** on **Navio** allows learners to review the language and skills they have studied and receive instant feedback, as well as increasing challenges as they progress. Students will be supported in learning and improving their English, while having fun and working at their own pace.

Helping children notice where they are making progress will help them build their self-reflection skills and also encourage them to seek further challenge.

Global Stage helps you teach beyond the test.

In ***Global Stage*** you will find a robust and engaging course. With its dual-book approach to language and literacy, and its focus on engaging the students and allowing them to develop their thinking and self-management skills, ***Global Stage*** supports children in learning beyond the language needed for doing well on tests.

Students are challenged to learn at a stimulating pace. They encounter a variety of topics and language points, as well as texts and ideas. But you and they have strong support every step of the way. Whether it is the way the **Language Book** sets up a speaking or writing task in incremental steps so the learner knows what to work on and the teacher can see where they need help, or the way thinking opportunities are woven into the two books, encouraging children not only to learn information but also get better at analyzing it, ***Global Stage*** supports students' long-term development. For example, throughout the six levels of ***Global Stage***, learners will be developing the ability to figure out the meaning of Words in Context. They will learn that words have many layers of meaning, and they will learn to develop strategies to figure out aspects of the meaning themselves, from the context in each text. Their goal won't be to learn the word, but rather to understand the overall meaning of the text, and to make an educated guess about what the word may mean in that context. This skill will help them become better readers, learners, and test takers throughout their academic lives in English and in whatever other language they happen to be studying.

Global Stage supports children in developing 21st Century Skills.

In their widely accepted *Framework for 21st Century Learning*, which outlines their vision for student success in the new global economy, the Partnership for 21st Century Skills says that:

> *Learning and innovation skills increasingly are being recognized as the skills that separate students who are prepared for increasingly complex life and work environments in the 21st century, and those who are not. A focus on creativity, critical thinking, communication, and collaboration is essential to prepare students for the future.*

Global Stage infuses these important skills into every unit in a way that challenges the children and enhances the learning objective in each lesson. Students are consistently given opportunities to think and discuss everything from readings and skills to grammar points and writing mechanics. This ensures they are actively communicating to form a solid and personalized understanding of English. Our Think Together lesson, in the **Literacy Book**, includes a cooperative learning activity where learners can practice collaborating in a structured way, building the skills to listen to others, participating responsibly, and contributing equally to the activity outcome. Finally, lessons like Take the Stage and Write About It encourage creativity as students plan and produce individual presentations, conversation role-plays, and texts and critical thinking as they are supported to organize their thoughts.

Course Components

Language Book

The **Language Book** contains seven lessons per unit:

- Two Vocabulary lessons. One includes spoken word poetry and work on pronunciation and features of connected speech. The other lesson is linked to Global Citizenship themes and includes listening activities.
- Two Explore Language lessons with grammar presentation and practice.
- A writing lesson (Write About It) that explores different genres of writing linked to one of the texts in the **Literacy Book** unit. Carefully staged activities take students through the steps of Process Writing, helping them develop good habits and strategies to use with any writing task now and in the future. Four additional Process Writing lessons at the back of the book explore different techniques which students can try out in the different units.
- A speaking lesson (Take the Stage / Talk About It) that presents either a presentation or conversational skill and functional language for different situations.
- A Think It Over lesson that encourages self-reflection: getting students to think about what they've learned, how they learn, and setting goals.

Inductive Approach

Throughout ***Global Stage***, students are exposed to a simplified inductive approach to grammar, vocabulary, and skills. They are guided to look at language in context so that they can discover concrete patterns. When students are given an opportunity to figure out a concept for themselves, they are much more likely to develop a deeper understanding, appreciation, and retention of knowledge.

Recycling

Opportunities to review and recycle what they have learned are built into the course as language is reused in new contexts in later units within the **Language Book** as well as in the **Literacy Book**. In addition, a Put It Together review after every two units allows students to revisit and practice the target language in a communicative game. These fun games can be played again and again, thereby maximizing the opportunities for recycling and practice.

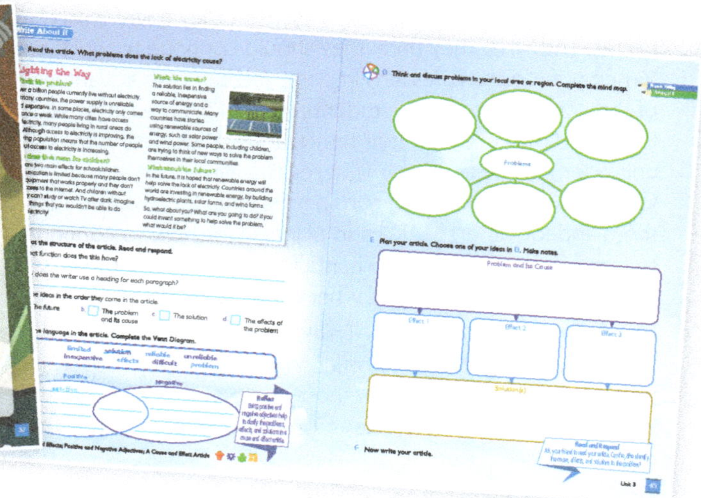

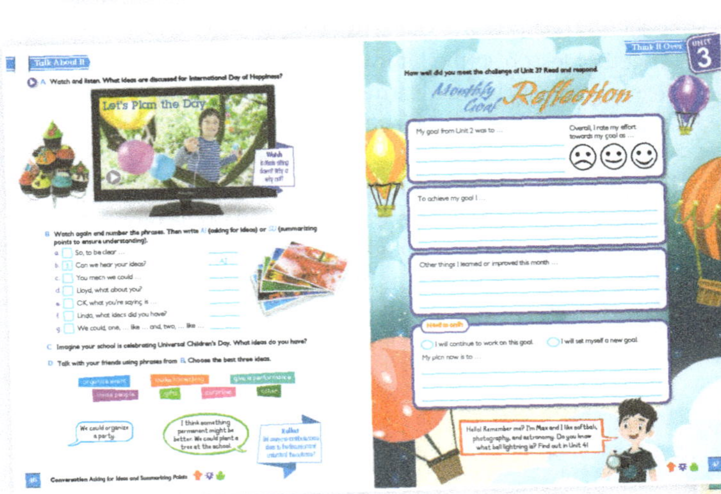

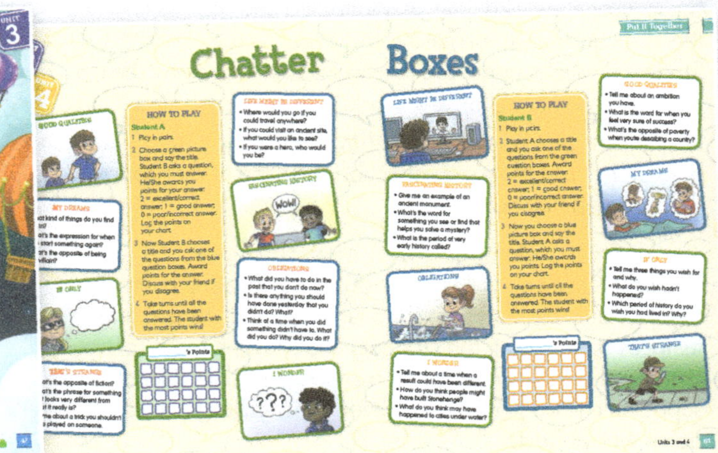

Literacy Book

There are two texts in each unit of the **Literacy Book**, which are fully explored in a series of lessons:

- A Get Ready to Read lesson introduces the unit topic and creates interest. It also includes the reading skill focus.
- A Reading lesson presents a fictional or nonfictional text.
- An Explore the Reading lesson includes post-reading comprehension and analysis activities. A focus on Literary Terms explores how different techniques and writers' choices enhance the reader experience.
- Each unit ends with a Think Together lesson that draws the two readings together and explores the Key Concept for each unit.

In each unit, students encounter a reading skill and learn the use of the skill through practice in context. Learning these skills helps students read more quickly and effectively, and gives them greater confidence, which in turn means they get more enjoyment from reading.

Each text includes a Words in Context feature in which students are encouraged to figure out the meaning of words from their context, rather than learn the words as vocabulary.

The **Literacy Book** develops Social and Emotional Learning (SEL) and Content and Language Integrated Learning (CLIL), while also including Visible Thinking Routines (VTR) and opportunities for Critical Literacy. Students are encouraged to work collaboratively by discussing and exploring ideas through Cooperative Learning Routines.

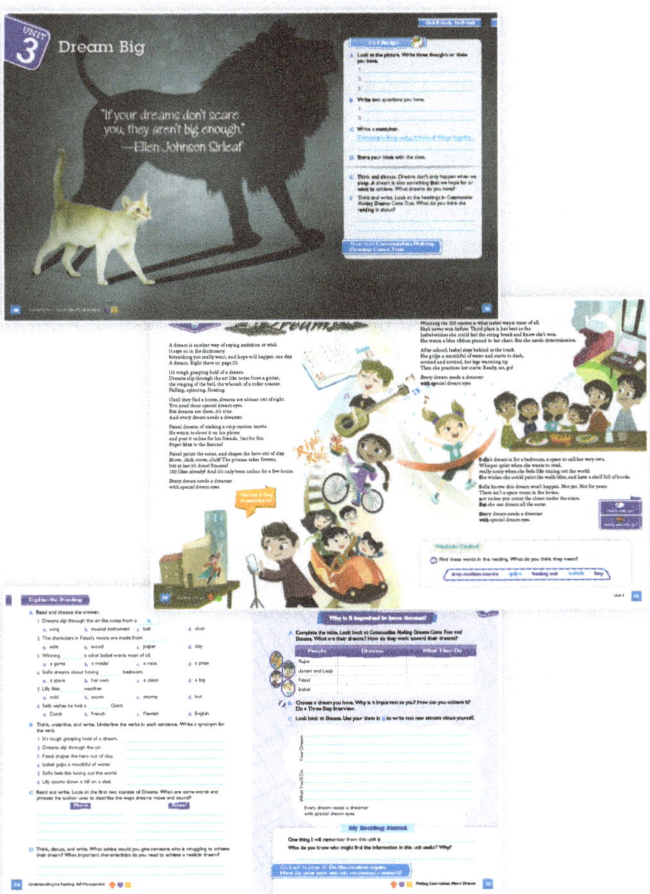

Three-Stage Reading Approach

The goal of the reading lessons is to get students reading for pleasure and to absorb information, rather than focusing on the mechanics of language in the text. The teaching notes suggest a three-stage approach to achieve this:

- Stage 1 **Engage with the Text.** This stage should be purely about reading for enjoyment and might include a prediction question to keep students motivated to find the answer.
- Stage 2 **Analyze the Text and Features.** In this stage, students read the text once again, while you help them analyze the text through the embedded callout questions. These questions will strengthen students' ability to make sense of the text and encourage them to begin thinking critically about what they are reading.
- Stage 3 **Interact with the Text.** This stage is about encouraging students to become actively involved in the learning process. They may be asked to act out a part of the reading or do reconstruction or analysis activities. When students interact more deeply with the text, their reading comprehension and writing skills improve, as they develop a greater understanding of how texts are constructed.

Literary Terms

Becoming a competent reader means understanding not only the words in a text, but also being able to analyze, interpret, and appreciate why the writer chose specific words and phrases. Learning to recognize literary terms and how they are used in different genres of text helps students understand more about the details and emotions in a text and develop a deeper connection with the author's intent, which helps them build more tools to tackle and create all kinds of texts now and in the future.

The **Literacy Book** helps students learn about the techniques, styles, and formatting used by authors. Each term has been selected from curricula used in US and UK schools. Each Literary Term section is linked to one reading in each unit as part of an Explore the Reading lesson, with further practice in the **Student's App** on **Navio**.

Literary Term Prefix

A **prefix** is a group of letters that is added to the beginning of a word to change its meaning.

Think, read, and write. What do you think the prefixes *micro–*, *inter–*, and *un–* mean?

1. The computer microchip was tiny. *Micro–* means ______
2. The world's longest international flight is from Qatar to New Zealand. *Inter–* means ______
3. Your room is so messy, it's very untidy. *Un–* means ______

Now find more words with the prefixes *micro–*, *inter–*, and *un–* in the reading.

Together, the two books lay the foundation for an inductive approach to learning, encouraging students to recognize patterns and think critically through ordering, analysis, and categorization tasks.

The Unit 1 Walkthrough notes give more in-depth information about the purpose and learning outcomes for each activity, as well as further guidance on addressing core features such as visualization, inductive grammar, international English, reading skills, Words in Context, and learning reflections.

Student's App on Navio

The **Student's App** on **Navio** is where students find their practice activities for the course. It expands on the topic and objectives found in the **Language Book** and **Literacy Book**. It includes automatically graded interactive exercises for each unit, which can be done in class or for homework, so that children receive immediate feedback. These exercises cover reading and listening skills, spelling and literary terms, speaking skill and pronunciation practice, extended writing practice, as well as grammar and vocabulary.

The **Student's App** on **Navio** world also provides support and guidance for more introspective objectives such as reading comprehension, SEL, and CLIL activities. It transforms the classroom-based lessons found in the **Language Book** and **Literacy Book** into an immersive, self-directed, game-like experience that students can do alone.

Using the **Student's App** on **Navio** with your students can take different forms:

Classroom study with **Language** and **Literacy Books** and Tap & Teach lessons.

- Study and practice alone in a computer lab with **Student's App**.
- Study and practice alone at home with **Student's App**.
- Study and practice with parents with **Student's App**.

Each gameplay produces data which is then sent to the teacher's gradebook, providing deeper insight into each student's strengths and weaknesses, and concrete data that can be quickly accessed to create more insightful feedback.

The activities on the **Student's App** on **Navio** are benchmarked to Cambridge English online practice, ranging from *Starters* for the lower levels to *Preliminary for Schools* for Level 6. This benchmarking covers both content and web app functionality, preparing students academically and equipping them for the practical experience of online testing.

Teacher's Book

This Teacher's Book provides all the steps you need to bring each lesson of the **Language** and **Literacy Books** to life, including lesson objectives, warm up and cool down activities, and full answer keys. Audio and video scripts are at the back of the book, and Unit 1 contains a comprehensive walkthough, with clear explanations of the purpose of each activity and tips on how to make the most of them in class. The notes also remind the teacher of the additional support available through the Tap & Teach Lessons (TTL) for heads-up learning, the supplementary printouts in the Resource Bank, and extra practice students can do in class or at home.

Teacher's App on Navio

The **Teacher's App** on **Navio** is your primary source for classroom resources and supplements, and is designed to work on both laptops and tablets. It includes Tap & Teach Lessons (projectable classroom lessons), the Resource Bank, the Test Generator, Student's Progress Tracker, the **Enhanced Teacher's eBook**, as well as access to the **Student's App**.

Tap & Teach Lessons (TTL)

Tap & Teach Lessons (TTL) are the course projectables. They contain tools for delivering dynamic and stimulating lessons, including class audio, videos, and interactive activities.

Every reading in the **Literacy Book** can be accessed through the Story Player in the TTL, which allows you to project the reading in *Read* (text only), *Listen* (audio only), or *Listen and Read* (audio and text) modes. If you use the TTL with an interactive whiteboard, you will be able to use all the standard features, such as highlighting and hiding content.

There are two types of video in ***Global Stage***:

- **Spoken Word Poetry Videos** (optional). These appear in Lesson 1 of the **Language Book** and feature a child or children performing the poem. Watching the performances on video offers another way to practice some of the vocabulary from the first lesson, and also to work on on features of rhythm and stress patterns in English.
- **Speaking Videos** (essential). These appear in Lesson 6 of the **Language Book** and feature a child or children modeling a presentation or conversation, which includes functional language. Students will analyze the language and use the video as a model when planning and preparing for their own presentation or conversation.

Videos at Home: The Flipped Classroom Approach

If you are unable to watch the videos in class or you want to provide students with additional support, consider asking them to watch the videos at home before the lesson. This allows students to engage with the content in a way that suits them, pausing and rewatching it as many times as they want. It also offers parents the opportunity to watch the video with their child and support their learning.

Give students a question or task to think about while they are watching: they will come to class feeling relaxed, confident, and prepared with ideas and observations to share. If students watch the speaking video at home, you could also have them do activities A and B from Take the Stage / Talk About It before the lesson. Watching the videos at home also frees up class time for collaborative and communicative activities.

Resource Bank

The Resource Bank is where you can find:

- **Literary Terms Printouts**. Extra practice of the literary terms covered in each unit of the **Literacy Book**.
- **Writing Support and Extension**. Attractive "Support" writing templates for the Write About It lessons in the **Language Book** for students who need them, as well as Writing Games printouts which add some fun and give students more opportunities to experiment and work with the language learned.
- **Review Unit Support**. Extra practice for the review units at the start of each student book. These cover grammar, vocabulary, reading skills, and literacy activities.
- **Grammar Printouts**. Extra practice for each grammar lesson in the **Language Book**.
- **Tests**. Unit, mid-year, and end-of-year tests.
- **Cambridge English Exam Materials**. Practice for students preparing for *Starters*, *Movers*, or *Flyers*, as well as *Key for Schools*, and *Preliminary for Schools*.
- **Letters to Parents**.
- **Other Printouts**. Graphic organizers to aid Visible Thinking Routines and reading skills in the **Literacy Book**, as well as extra materials for some of the Put It Together games and extension activities in the **Language Book**.
- **Videos and audio tracks** to support the course.
- **Curricula and Framework mapping documents.**

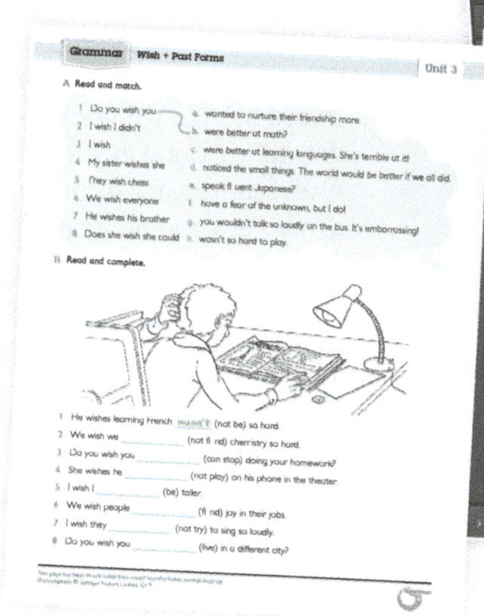

Grammar Wish + Past Forms Unit 3

A Read and match.

1 Do you wish you
2 I wish I didn't
3 I wish
4 My sister wishes she
5 They wish chess
6 We wish everyone
7 He wishes his brother
8 Does she wish she could

a. wanted to nurture their friendship more.
b. were better at math?
c. were better at learning languages. She's terrible at it!
d. noticed the small things. The world would be better if we all did.
e. speak fluent Japanese?
f. have a fear of the unknown, but I do!
g. you wouldn't talk so loudly on the bus. It's embarrassing!
h. wasn't so hard to play.

B Read and complete.

1 He wishes learning French wasn't (not be) so hard.
2 We wish we ________ (not find) chemistry so hard.
3 Do you wish you ________ (can stop) doing your homework?
4 She wishes he ________ (not play) on his phone in the theater.
5 I wish I ________ (be) taller.
6 We wish people ________ (find) joy in their jobs.
7 I wish they ________ (not try) to sing so loudly.
8 Do you wish you ________ (live) in a different city?

Test Generator

The Test Generator contains the pre-written unit, mid-year, and end-of-year test activities, as well as extra activities that allow teachers to generate and edit new tests.

Student's Progress Tracker

The Progress Tracker is an interactive gradebook that allows you to track your students' progress within ***Global Stage*** and the **Student's App** on **Navio**.

Student's App on Navio

As the teacher, you have full access to the **Student's App** on **Navio** so you can assign homework and activities for your students, and explore the digital world yourself.

Enhanced Teacher's eBook (ETB)

The digital **ETB** is an extended version of this **Teacher's Book**. In addition to teaching notes, it provides classroom management tips; ideas for differentiating activities; projects to support the Global Citizenship lessons; plus a range of activity and lesson extension ideas to develop, among others, Social and Emotional Learning (SEL), Discussion, Genre, Video Focus, Critical Thinking, Creative Thinking, and Collaboration. The **ETB** also highlights key links between the **Language Book** and the **Literacy Book**.

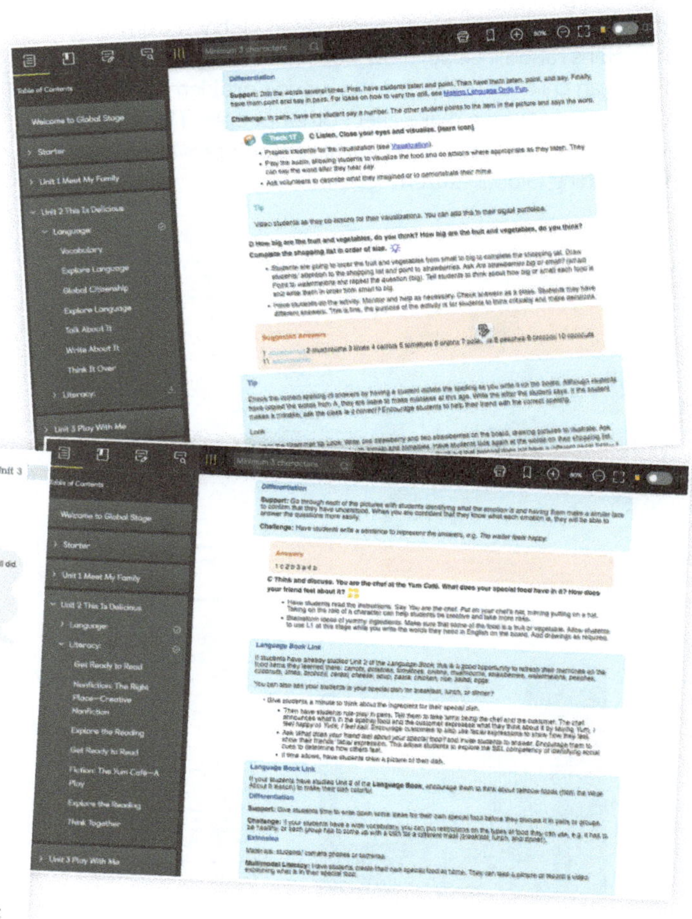

Holistic Learning

While the success of students and schools may be measured in terms of tests and grades, ***Global Stage*** believes in taking a holistic approach by developing the whole child and preparing him/her to take on the challenges of global living. Through its subject matter and in its activity types, the course encourages students to develop thinking skills, engage in cooperative learning activities, develop social and emotional learning (SEL) skills, and gain an awareness of global citizenship.

Global Citizenship Education

> *Global Citizenship Education (GCE) aims to empower learners to assume active roles, to face and resolve global challenges, and to become proactive contributors to a more peaceful, tolerant, inclusive and secure world.*
>
> —United Nations Educational, Scientific and Cultural Organization

The **Language Book** includes a Global Citizenship lesson in each unit, which has been designed to teach students about the lives of other children through the context of a listening activity. Discussion questions help them explore ideas and make connections to their own lives. The long-term objective is to prepare students for experiences outside of their everyday world and to fulfil aspirations to travel and study abroad.

In Level 6, lessons raise awareness about global issues through interesting and engaging topics designed to get students thinking about the things they can do as global citizens. Key questions raised include: How does technology help us learn?; How can children help solve the world's problems?; and How do the decisions we make affect other people? The Unit 1 Walkthrough notes for the **Language Book** provide guidance for teaching Global Citizenship lessons.

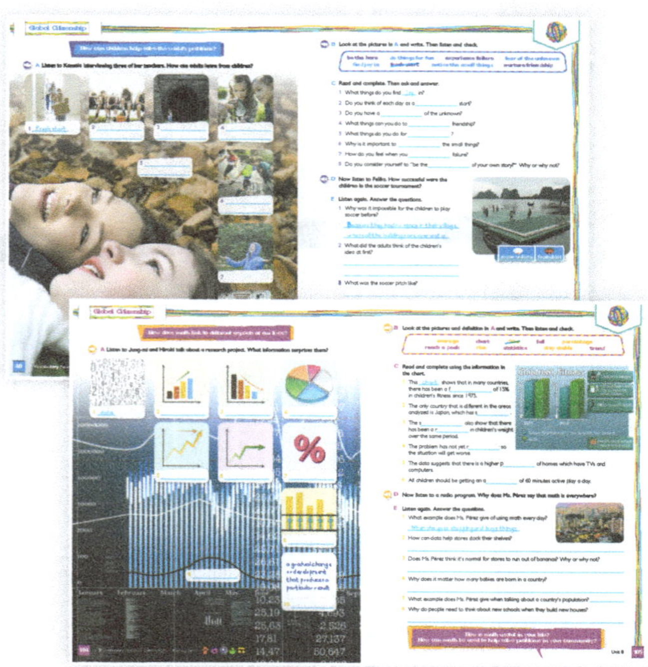

Matthew Hayes is a doctoral researcher at the Institute of Education in London under Douglas Bourn, Professor of Development Education. His research concerns Global Citizenship Education in English language textbooks.

What is GCE?

What does the future hold for your students, many of whom will graduate well into the 2030s? From the environment to the economy, poverty to jobs, challenges abound. But whatever the future holds, there is one thing we can be certain of: the biggest challenges facing humanity are not constrained by national borders or language but are truly global in scale and character. These are global problems requiring global solutions, and those of us working in education have a unique responsibility and opportunity to prepare the next generation for these challenges. GCE offers a solution to these challenges and has emerged in recent years as a high-profile policy agenda in education systems all over the world.

With this in mind, GCE can be an effective toolkit for teachers wishing to prepare their students for the challenges and opportunities of the 21st century. The skills and values it espouses are essential if our students are to successfully navigate all the future holds. GCE is too important to languish on the fringes of the curriculum, competing for space as an arbitrary additional subject in an already overcrowded timetable or sandwiched into one-off school events. Just as Digital Literacy is moving beyond ICT (information and communication technology) and into every corner of the curriculum, GCE thrives best where it is embedded in mainstream curriculum subjects. Few subjects better provide the context and aspiration called for by GCE than the teaching of English as a second language.

There is much scope for creativity too. Although GCE is a declared target of the United Nations' Sustainable Development Goals, one of its virtues is that it is not owned or prescribed by any supranational organization. There is no mandated curriculum and no accreditation body. The core concepts underpinning GCE have been traced back to some of our earliest history and are not only to be found in Western culture and philosophy. Arab scholars, for example, have written of the influence of medieval Muslim thinkers on GCE theory.

This democratic quality to GCE enables a wide variety of policy and practice, as GCE can be adapted to local contexts and cultures, and to your classroom. There are three broad themes in current GCE thinking and practice and as you work through this textbook, you will see these throughout the exercises and subject matter.

Global orientation: Often referred to as cosmopolitanism, this area of GCE cultivates a student's awareness of the world—its structures, cultures and politics—with a positive "orientation." Its focus is on tolerance and understanding, developing citizens that can comfortably and successfully navigate the world in all its variety.

Global skills: This area is about the competencies aspired to by global citizens. You may recognize it as closely related to "21st Century Skills" and "Life Skills," and it cultivates skills such as collaboration, creativity, critical literacy, and communication. This not only prepares students for success in a competitive global knowledge economy, but for lives as contributing global citizens able to identify and solve problems that are both local and global.

Global conscientiousness: This third theme runs through all aspects of GCE and is its most distinguishing feature. It is signalled through the word "citizenship," denoting an individual's legal status as a member of a given community, with this status granting them certain rights and responsibilities. While historically this community has been restricted to the nation-state, *global* citizenship looks beyond the national to the global community of which we are all a part. Its rights and responsibilities are global in nature, calling each of us to action. This can take many forms and there should be no universal prescription of actions to be taken. It is being an *active* global citizen which is required of us. This means listening to our conscience and, when it identifies global injustice, being motivated by this to act.

Your selection of this high-level English language textbook means English is a leading subject in your curriculum and timetable. No doubt you acknowledge the English language as the *lingua franca* of the modern era, enabling your students to participate on a global scale—whether in work or life. As educators, then, what better context in which to use GCE to encourage your students to think beyond their immediate community, and be globally oriented, competent and conscientious. The English language may have an historical affinity to the West, but GCE recognises that it should not be a pedestal to promote one culture and education above any other. On the contrary, through embedding GCE in English language teaching we can encourage our students to question an unjust world and its imbalanced perspectives.

By using this textbook to teach English in a creative, forward-thinking and global way you will be providing your students with the skills and values to go out into the world and be truly active global citizens.

Social and Emotional Learning (SEL)

> *Social and emotional learning (SEL) is the process through which children and adults acquire and effectively apply the knowledge, attitudes, and skills necessary to understand and manage emotions, set and achieve positive goals, feel and show empathy for others, establish and maintain positive relationships, and make responsible decisions.*
>
> —Collaborative for Academic, Social, and Emotional Learning

Research shows that SEL can positively affect students' connection to school, promote positive behavior, and lead to academic achievement. Helping students develop social and emotional skills lays the foundation for behaviors that will lead to positive personal development and professional success.

The five SEL areas are shown below.

Self-Awareness
The ability to recognize emotions, thoughts, strengths, and weaknesses. This includes having confidence and optimism.
Self-Management
The ability to regulate emotions, thoughts, and behaviors in different situations. This includes managing stress and working toward goals.
Social Awareness
The ability to empathize with others, to understand social norms, and to recognize resources and support in family, schools, and community.
Relationship Skills
The ability to establish and maintain healthy relationships. This includes active listening, cooperating, and handling conflict well.
Responsible Decision-Making
The ability to make good choices based on ethics, safety, and social norms. This includes considering the well-being of oneself and others.

SEL is integrated into the **Literacy Book** and a key concept area is addressed throughout the fictional text in each unit. As part of the reading strategy, students are guided to make connections between the SEL concept and the people and events in the text and, ultimately, to their own lives.

Lina Acosta Sandaal, MA, LMFT is the founder of Stop Parenting Alone, a parenting and therapy center in Miami in the USA. She is the parenting expert of a national morning show, and consults for MomsRising, a lobbying organization for family rights.

What is SEL?

Your mouth is dry, and your heart is in your ears. Some of your students look frozen, while others wriggle in their chairs. No one is truly into the day's well-planned discussion. What is happening? Why is the lesson failing? The lesson is suffering the effect of emotions, social awareness, and self-judgment in the classroom. In every moment of a teacher's day, the mind, brain, and body flow through the interactions between the external information and the internal understanding and reflecting of the environment. So when I am asked what is SEL and why do we need it, my response is whether you intentionally teach it or not, you have been a model for SEL from the first day you stepped into a classroom.

The goal of integrating and implementing social and emotional learning into the curriculum is to build students' ability for self-awareness, self-management, social awareness, relationship skills, and decision making. Students attain these competencies by practicing ways to understand and manage emotions, build and manage relationships, and show care and concern for others. The Fetzer Group coined the term, and the word "learning" was intentional. Social emotional skills and development are not stagnant; they continue to grow and expand with each experience students have with caregivers, teachers, friends, and the culture/community at large. If you hold this in mind, that your students are learning through repetition how to be self-aware, how to manage emotions and focus, how to continue to build and manage relationships and practice decision making, then the task of social and emotional learning in your curriculum will not feel so difficult.

Why SEL Is Important to Your Classroom

It is an absurd task to attempt to separate what happens socially and emotionally to a student from what they are cognitively learning from your lesson. When you ignore how SEL and academic achievement work together you are only teaching a percentage of your student, and not the whole child. A majority of teachers understand that their students walk into the classroom full of emotions, thoughts, and experiences that hinder their academic achievement. Deficits in social and emotional development hamper students' ability to learn, which leads to them disrupting the classroom. A student who cannot manage their emotional state will become overwhelmed with fear and embarrassment if you ask them to speak to you in a language in which they are not fluent. Focus, cognitive flexibility, and decision-making are impacted when we have low self-awareness and management of our emotional states.

Recall the difficulty of writing emails at work when you have just had a fight with a loved one on the phone. When we have a strong emotional and social response, it is hard to focus on the task at hand. If it is difficult for an adult, imagine a young student. If your curriculum includes social and emotional learning, your students will be practicing skills to make those daily stressors less intrusive to their learning. Research supports this. Children in the HighScope Perry Preschool Study showed how social and emotional skills attained in preschool continued to bring positive outcomes to those students through age 40. HighScope moved "non-cognitive" skills to the forefront of their curriculum. Conversely, the Adverse Childhood Experiences Study (ACEs) showed that children who suffer adverse experiences and do not process those emotions fare poorly both in their mental and physical health. Social and emotional learning helps students thrive throughout their entire lives.

What Well-Accomplished SEL Looks Like

Now, stop and imagine your classroom in a group discussion: one of the students is playing with his lip while rocking slightly, another student is raising her hand as high as possible, hoping you will see that she wants to speak next, and another student is mumbling in response to the story you just read together. In a classroom that prioritizes SEL, all of these examples of self-management and relationship skills are accepted. Why? Because you understand that the student who is playing with his lips and rocking regulates his emotional and physical states this way, instead of standing up and disrupting the class. The student who knows to raise her hand and contain her emotions is making a responsible, self-aware decision in managing her excitement as to not interrupt her friend who is speaking.

Finally the student who is speaking slowly, quietly and under his breath is at last risking to discuss in a group because you have spoken to your students about what it means to feel scared, how to tolerate that fear, and how to work through it. Today you reap the benefit of that continued social-emotional message. How amazing that your quiet, observant student has made the decision to speak, experiences the safety to manage his fear and the opportunity to strengthen his relationships with his friends and you, his teacher.

Content and Language Integrated Learning (CLIL)

Research has shown that content-based learning increases motivation as students see language being used in real-life contexts. The nonfictional texts in the **Literacy Book** include content from a range of different subject areas. They feature engaging topics and provide opportunities for thinking and discussion.

In Level 6, students will learn through science, social studies, arts and humanities, and history.

Competencies

Global Stage incorporates five competencies that have been identified and linked to outcomes such as better academic performance and positive peer relationships. Relevant icons appear in the footers of each lesson, and the teaching notes in this Teacher's Book and **ETB** highlight which activities are connected to each competency to allow for further exploration in the classroom.

Me
Activities that develop social and creative skills and consider lifestyle choices.
Act
Activities that help develop a sense of social responsibility, mutual understanding, tolerance, and ethical behavior.
Think
Activities that develop thinking skills to explain, infer, classify, discuss, notice, and discover.
Learn
Activities that foster learning autonomy and help develop learning strategies.
Communicate
Activities that promote interpersonal and collaborative skills to develop teamwork, leadership, empathy, and responsibility.

Self-Reflection

Self-reflection is an important part of any learning process. Research shows that without regular review and reflection time, much of a lesson can be forgotten. Self-reflection increases students' understanding of how they learn best, making future learning more effective and leading to improvements in achievement.

Self-reflection is a critical feature of ***Global Stage***. Students are asked to reflect on their performances and written work in the Writing and Speaking lessons in the **Language Book** and to reflect more deeply about their learning in the end-of-unit lessons in both the **Language Book** and **Literacy Book**.

The Think It Over lessons in the **Language Book** provide a series of graphic organizers, guiding students to focus on different aspects of their learning journey: what went well, what they enjoyed, and what goals they have for the next units or weeks. The purpose of these questions is to get students into the habit of self-reflection from an early age, helping them begin to learn how to learn and to take responsibility for their learning.

In the My Reading Journal section of the Think Together lesson in the **Literacy Book**, students are asked to give a personalized response to the readings and reflect on the unit as a whole. They are encouraged to think critically about what they enjoyed and why, what they would like to learn more about, and to identify strengths and weaknesses.

In Level 6, the **Language** and **Literacy Book** encourage students to start making connections between what they enjoyed and what they learned, which will help them understand how successes were achieved, how less successful experiences can be turned into learning experiences, and how to find strategies for working through activities they find less enjoyable.

The Unit 1 Walkthrough notes for both books provide more information on making these lessons a valuable and successful experience.

Learning Techniques

Visible Thinking

Visible Thinking is a flexible research-based framework developed out of Harvard University for enriching classroom learning and fostering students' intellectual development. Some of its key goals are:

- To develop deeper understanding of content.
- To encourage greater motivation for learning.
- To develop learners' thinking and learning abilities.
- To develop learners' attitudes toward thinking and learning and their alertness to opportunities for thinking and learning.
- To create a shift in classroom culture toward a community of enthusiastically engaged thinkers and learners.

Visible Thinking employs thinking routines—short, easy-to-learn strategies that help extend and deepen students' thinking. These routines make it easier for you to see how the students are thinking and interpreting content: *Are students explaining things to one another? Are they offering creative ideas? Are they brainstorming and debating plans?* Visible Thinking encourages students to develop discussion skills and to find personal meaning in the content. This stimulates their continued interest and commitment to their own learning in the classroom.

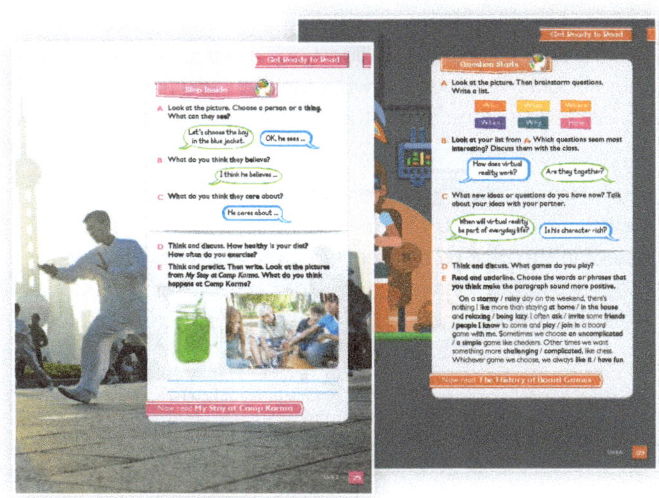

In Level 6, each opening lesson in the **Literacy Book** features one of six Visible Thinking Routines (VTR): See, Think, Wonder; Think, Pair, Share; Question Starts; Step Inside; Explanation Game; and 3-2-1 Bridge. These routines stimulate students' curiosity and encourage them to make predictions, observations, and interpretations about the picture. They provide an opportunity for students to think about the overarching theme/topic of each **Literacy Book** unit and tie into a pre-reading activity to prepare students cognitively for what they are about to read.

See, Think, Wonder

Students are asked what they see in the picture, then what they think about it, and finally what they wonder about it. This routine works best when students have time to think of ideas individually before sharing them with the class. In this way, students begin to use English meaningfully, although it is acceptable to use L1 to express more complex ideas.

Think, Pair, Share

This routine encourages individual participation and can be used with all abilities and class sizes. It is also used as a cooperative learning routine.

Think. Students first think independently about the question, forming ideas and questions of their own.

Pair. Students discuss their thoughts in pairs. This step allows students to articulate their ideas and to consider those of others. They are encouraged to listen to each other and use phrases like *I agree/disagree* and *Me, too.*

Share. Student pairs share their ideas with the whole class and give their reasons. The benefit of using this routine for discussion questions is that students get to try out their ideas in a safe setting (a pair), refining their thoughts and learning from others before presenting to a bigger group.

Question Starts

This routine encourages students to get into the habit of questioning things beyond what they see on the page. Students look at the picture and think of some questions they would like to ask about it, using the prompts Who? What? Where? When? Why? How? They then practice negotiation skills by deciding in groups on the three they think are the most interesting or would most like to know the answer to, before discussing the answers as a class. Finally, students work in pairs to discuss any new questions or ideas. At this point, they should move beyond what they see and think of ideas connected to some of the themes suggested by the picture.

Step Inside

Students are asked to explore different perspectives and viewpoints as they try to imagine what a person, animal, or object in the picture can see, what they believe, and what they care about. As well as developing social and emotional skills, this routine encourages creative thinking.

Explanation Game

This routine focuses students on individual aspects of a picture and encourages them to explore all manner of explanation. First, students are asked to choose something in the picture. Then, working in pairs, they say everything they notice about it, before suggesting reasons why it's like it is. Finally, they expand on these reasons as a class, explaining further their thought processes, ideas, and explanations. The routine can be repeated with different things/ideas, and different pairs.

3-2-1 Bridge

In this routine, students share three initial thoughts, two questions, and one metaphor about a picture. They will repeat this same process in the Think Together lesson, coming up with new thoughts, questions, and metaphors, based on their new understanding of the unit topic. They will then explore and discuss the ways their new ideas connect with their initial ones. This helps students to see the way their learning evolves and to form "bridges" between their first impressions and new ideas after exploring concepts more deeply.

For all six routines, it is important to scaffold student responses by asking follow-up questions, e.g. *What makes you say that?* and to encourage students to do the same, so that they begin to lead the discussion. Keep students' thinking visible by noting and displaying their ideas to return to in the Think Together lesson.

VTRs provide a great way to engage learners at the start of a topic, but they can also be used at different points in the unit to keep students connected to the topic or as a way to reflect on what they have learned in a meaningful way.

Cooperative Learning Routines

Using Cooperative Learning Routines provides opportunities for multiple students to participate in class. Along with higher academic achievement, you will see a reduction in the gap between high- and low-achieving students, improved social skills, higher self-esteem, and more enthusiasm for learning. You will also see the emergence of leadership and conflict-resolution skills.

The following routines are used in Level 6 in both the **Literacy Book** and **Language Book**:

Round Robin. In groups of four, students take turns brainstorming orally as many different answers to a discussion question as they can within a limited time frame (e.g. one minute). A **Rally Robin** is the same but with pairs.

Roundtable. Similar to a **Round Robin**, but students take turns within their groups writing or drawing their ideas on paper.

Three-Step Interview. Students work with a student from a different group to interview each other about a topic (steps 1 and 2). Then, they return to their original groups to share what they learned from their partners (step 3). This way, everyone is responsible for producing, receiving, and sharing information.

Chalk Talk. Write different words on large sheets of paper and have groups of students brainstorm everything they can think about that word. This is a chance to generate new ideas, review language, and bring a topic into focus.

Four Corners. Write four topics or questions on sheets of paper and post each one in a corner of the room. Students choose for themselves which topic they'd most like to explore and move to that corner. They then discuss the topic with the others in their corner. After the four groups discuss, they can share what they talked about with the rest of the class.

Inside–Outside Circle. You will need to make some space in the classroom for this routine. Students stand in concentric circles facing each other. Students in the outside circle ask questions, and those who are inside answer the question. On a signal, students rotate to create new partnerships. On another signal, students trade inside/outside roles. Talking one-on-one with a variety of partners gives extensive practice in speaking and active listening skills. Interactions can be structured to focus on specific skills and/or target language.

Option Explosion. Students discuss and share ideas to think of solutions to a problem or to generate new ideas, e.g. for a story. Use questions to help guide them, e.g. *What happens next? What about other characters? What if that solution doesn't work? How will that help?* Working in groups, they can appoint a scribe who writes down all the problems/solutions suggested. Then split the groups into pairs to think again, going beyond the obvious and really using their imaginations: all ideas are valid; nothing is too crazy! They can use the groups' ideas as a springboard, or think of new ideas. You can help them explore different aspects by asking more questions based on their discussion.

Tips for Setting Up Class Discussions

- Display the question(s) on the board, and give students a minute to reflect in silence.
- If there is more than one discussion question, deal with each in turn, giving students time to think and discuss in pairs or small groups. Allow the use of L1 for more complex ideas.
- Help students structure their discussions by using graphic organizers such as mind maps, or providing slips of paper to help build up a graphic organizer.
- You will not always be able to ask everyone for their ideas. Be sure you choose different students each time, so no one feels left out.
- Have students share their ideas in teams. Have each team choose a name or color. During each lesson or activity, one person will give the team's answers and responses. Record who the speaker is for each activity so everyone gets a turn.
- Use the Cooperative Learning Routines to structure the discussions and share information discussed.
- When sharing ideas as a class, Group Time can provide a relaxed atmosphere, which may encourage students to contribute more. See the **Group Time** box for more suggestions.

Group Time

Designate a particular area of the classroom for Group Time, free from distractions. Set out a circle of chairs, with no desks, so students can see each other clearly. You should also sit on a chair as part of this circle, so that it is clear your role is to encourage and facilitate discussion, rather than to lead it. At the beginning of the year, have students discuss and agree on some rules for Group Time, e.g. one person speaks at a time; everyone listens to each other; students can disagree with each other, but must do so respectfully; Group Time is fun! Nominate a student to be the scribe and write up the rules the class decides on.

During Group Time, ask open-ended questions and encourage students to give reasons for their answers. Pass an object, such as a cardboard microphone, around so it is clear who is speaking. Encourage everyone to join in the discussion, but give students a safe word to use, such as "pass," if they need more thinking time. Let them know it's OK to need time to think and that you will come back to them. At the end of the Group Time discussion, praise students for their ideas.

Visualization

Visualizations are used in the vocabulary lessons of each unit to encourage students to create mental images of the new words using their senses, previous experiences, and imaginations. Visualizations provide a different way for students to engage personally with the language and help them learn new words.

Set up a visualization activity as follows:

- Take several deep breaths with students, slowly saying *breathe in, breathe out.*
- Count down slowly from ten to one using a calm voice.
- Say *Close your eyes and visualize*, pointing to your temples to demonstrate *imagining*. If students prefer to keep their eyes open, that's fine, too. The key is for them to feel calm and relaxed, so avoid using phrases like *You must keep your eyes closed* or *Don't look!* which will restrict students.
- Play the audio and encourage students to imagine or act out as prompted. Pauses have been included in the audio to give time for reflection. They then repeat the word.
- At the end of the audio, give students time to reflect and share their ideas in pairs. At this level, they should be able to discuss the ideas, but they could use drawings if it helps.
- Emphasize that everyone's visualizations will be different and that all ideas are valuable.

The first few times you do a Visualization activity, you may want to play each prompt twice to give students time to understand the prompt and then think.

The more regularly you do this, the more comfortable students will feel and the more they will get out of the activity. A visualization track for the vocabulary in the Global Citizenship lesson is available in the TTL, though it is not highlighted on the **Language Book** page.

Words in Context

Successful readers of English need to have a bank of strategies for dealing with words they don't yet know, just as they do in their L1. Understanding a word fully builds up over time so ***Global Stage*** is designed to give extensive exposure to words in different contexts, thereby encouraging students to revisit and revise assumptions as they read. In Levels 5 and 6, the approach to Words in Context in the **Literacy Book** builds on previous levels as students actively choose and try out different strategies. In this way, they will come to recognize that different words will need different strategies depending on the contextual clues provided. Having students experiment and take responsibility for their learning prepares them for dealing with unknown words in all manner of texts they come across in the future.

In Level 6 this feature is developed in three ways:

- Students are given a selection of strategies to use and they figure out which strategies work best for each of the words/phrases. In all cases, more than one strategy may be used, and you can encourage students to explain their choices.
- Students are given a selection of strategies to use, but one of them can't be used effectively (a red herring). This way, students have to analyze how the strategies work, which will highlight why some don't, and encourage them to use a variety of strategies, and not to rely on just one or two.
- Students brainstorm different strategies to use. This helps students begin to take responsibility for their choices and become more independent in the reading and learning.

The strategies can be roughly categorized as using the text, knowledge of English, and general knowledge. Students should be encouraged to notice what kind of word it is (noun, adjective, verb, etc.) and to look for all instances within the text, as key words will often appear more than once and each entry gives more clues. The following strategies are suggested for the texts in this level, but others could also be used:

Using the text

- **Pictures:** use any visuals (illustrations, photos, graphics) which may provide a context or actually show the word.
- **Surrounding words/phrases/sentences/paragraphs:** the words and sentences before and after the key word will give clues about what kind of word it is (noun, adjective, plural, singular), and what would make sense in the context. There might be an explanation, definition, or the same idea phrased in a different way.
- **Positive/negative:** noticing the tone can help narrow down the options of meaning. Looking at the grammar, as well as the surrounding words/phrases will help with this.
- **Contrasting ideas:** a writer may compare different ideas to make their point stronger. Contrasting ideas can help determine what a word *isn't*, which helps lead to what it is.

Knowledge of English

- **Word building/families:** recognizing what kind of word it is can help narrow down ideas, e.g. plural/singular, compound nouns. Words may also appear several times in in different forms, providing more clues in different sentences.
- **Prefixes/Suffixes:** looking at the beginning and ends of words not only helps us identify the kind of word, but may also provide contrasting information, positive/negative, opposite ideas, etc.
- **Sentence structure / grammar:** recognizing grammar, sentence features such as quotation marks, and how sentences are constructed can give more context.
- **Word sounds:** occasionally thinking about how a word sounds and noticing the style of the writing can also help.
- **Making connections (cause & effect):** using textual clues such as conjunctions (e.g. *so*) show what relation an idea has to the previous/next one.

General knowledge

- **World knowledge:** thinking logically and drawing on the knowledge they already have about the world is a really important strategy to use. Students should always be encouraged to guess based on what they already know.
- **Personal experience:** drawing on their own experiences is another invaluable strategy to use. However, they should be sure to read the text carefully to check if the writer's experience is the same or different.

Multimodal Literacy

To become fully literate in today's world, students must become as proficient with the new literacies of search engines, web pages, email, instant messages, blogs, podcasts, e-books, wiki pages, digital photos, videos, and apps as they are with the traditional literacies of paper, pencil, and books. To do this, students need to develop skills to use each of these technologies effectively, e.g. searching for key words, navigating a nonlinear reading pathway via hyperlinks, and utilize critical-thinking skills for online reading. In an age when anyone can publish anything on the internet, it is more important than ever to equip students with the tools to evaluate source material.

Both the **Language Book** and the **Literacy Book** provide opportunities for developing higher-order thinking skills through activities that teach students to analyze, question, and to foster thoughtful discussion. In addition, the digital **ETB** includes Multimodal Literacy ideas for taking lessons beyond the book and integrating them with the students' own technologies, e.g. for a research project, students can find more information about a topic by using both print and digital resources. Projects can be researched at home with parental support, or teachers can set up small groups to collaborate together, culminating in a class presentation.

Students can also create using different technologies (e.g. digital cameras, videos, apps) and choose work to upload to a digital portfolio, which can be shared with parents.

Ideas for Introducing Multimodal Literacy Skills and Concepts

- **Encourage students to use *Global Stage's* digital resources.** The **Student's App** provides important early experiences of navigating an online interface in a controlled and safe environment.
- **Show how putting precise keywords into search engines can help you find better information.** If you have access to computers and the internet in school, give students a question to answer in pairs, but tell them they can only use one keyword. Discuss how successful they were, then have them repeat the activity with two and then multiple keywords. Elicit that using more keywords helps us be more specific and yields better information.
- **Highlight the importance of scanning for key information.** Before having students research online, elicit what they need to look out for to scan effectively. Scanning is a core reading skill in the **Literacy Book**, so you can make the connection with online research.
- **Have less-confident readers teach more-confident readers.** When you introduce a new technology or skill in class, differentiate by teaching it to less-confident readers first so that they become the experts, and then empower them to teach others. That way, everyone is given the chance to be good at something and no one gets left behind.
- **Use digital portfolios.** Digital portfolios replace traditional folders as a way to capture and store students' work. You can put students in charge of what gets included in their portfolio as a way to encourage independence, responsibility, and reflection. They enable you to:
  - Demonstrate oral skills through videos and audio recordings, alongside on-paper tasks.
  - Empower students struggling with writing and reading by giving them alternative ways to express themselves and demonstrate learning.
  - Share students' learning easily and frequently with parents.

Digital portfolios also allow students to view their learning journey and become a valuable tool for self-reflection. The digital **ETB** provides suggestions for digital portfolios.

Classroom Management

Making Language Drills Fun

The **Language Book** audio contains language drills to practice the new language presented in each Vocabulary and Explore Language lesson. Drilling helps familiarize students with the language and encourages them to notice the correct pronunciation and rhythm, which gives them confidence when they speak in freer activities.

Drilling works by being repetitive, but you can add some variations to make it fun and keep students engaged:

- **Volume**. Have students whisper and then get progressively louder, and then quieter again.
- **Emotion**. Have students use a happy voice and then repeat with sad, angry, tired, and excited voices.
- **Speed**. Have students speak very slowly, then get progressively faster, and then slower again.
- **Voices**. Have students imagine they are different people or animals, e.g. a lion, a mouse, a robot, a famous character/actor. Even when speaking in these different styles, students must use the correct pronunciation and intonation.

Play the audio several times so students can focus first on copying the pronunciation of the individual words and sounds accurately, and then intonation for phrases/sentences. For grammar drills, focus on rhythm and chunks of language, not just individual words. After practicing the recorded sentences, have the students build a substitution drill on the board from prompts you give, e.g. *I've already* ____________ *(bus/lunch)*. Students could suggest *seen three buses, eaten my lunch*, etc. Then have them practice saying the new sentences in pairs.

Role-play in the Classroom

Performing role-plays in class is a great way for students to interact with the new language or stories and gain confidence using the language in a more informal way. Both the **Language** and **Literacy Books** offer many opportunities for role-play, such as the presentation dialogues in the Explore Language lessons and the stories in the **Literacy Book**.

Five Stepping Stones to Performance

- **Step 1** Put students into groups according to how many parts there are in the dialogue or story. Vary the groups so students work with classmates they don't normally work with. Pair confident students with less-confident classmates. Allow students to assign themselves roles within their groups, as this will allow them to practice negotiating skills.
- **Step 2** Play any audio or video tracks first for students to follow along. Encourage students to think about how the characters are feeling at key moments in the story. Have students notice sound effects and ask them what these add to the overall effect. Play the audio/video again for students to say their lines out loud along with their character, copying intonation and rhythm.
- **Step 3** Give students time to practice their role-play on their own, focusing not only on delivering the correct lines, but also what's being said, their character's personality, and how he/she feels. At this point they can start to include some suitable facial expressions and actions. You can challenge stronger students to continue the conversation or add embellishments to their character.
- **Step 4** Have pairs or groups come to the front and perform their role-play for the class. Make sure everyone gets a chance to perform at some point during the course. Encourage students to video record each other's performances and to add them to their digital portfolios.

- **Step 5** Organize an open event for parents or other classes in the school. Students can prepare and act out different stories from the **Literacy Book** or the situations from the **Language Book**. Give students extra practice time to give them confidence to perform in front of an audience. Encourage them to think about suitable props, costumes, and sound effects to use in their performance (e.g. rustling paper for rain), or to source these through sound-effect apps.

Tip At an open event, you can bring together a variety of performance pieces including spoken word poems/chants (with or without choreography), presentations from Take the Stage lessons, oral storytelling using part of a story, or a role-play.

Differentiated Learning

Even across one class, students differ in many ways; from age, energy, interests, adaptability, experience, and familiarity with the world outside the home, to emotional maturity, linguistic aptitude, and physical development. As a way of targeting learning to meet individual students' needs, the **ETB** lesson notes include below-level *Support* differentiation ideas to help students achieve the activity goal and above-level *Challenge* ideas to extend activities. For print users, the following are ways you can differentiate activity types:

Vocabulary

Support: Ask questions to guide and help confirm understanding.

Challenge: Have students think of synonyms and antonyms. Establish if the synonyms are "true" or have specific uses and contexts.

Language Drills

Support: Play the audio several times before having students repeat. Break down the phrases into smaller chunks and build them up until students have the full sentence.

Challenge: Have students substitute words in the drill to make new questions and statements. Ask them to come up with wild and funny ideas!

Conversations

Support: At this level, conversations should be spontaneous, but students can make notes about what they want to say. Have them select a few functional phrases, writing each one on a different piece of paper. They turn it over when they've used it.

Challenge: Encourage students to take the lead in ensuring the conversation is balanced, encouraging all speakers to participate.

Writing

Support: Have students discuss their ideas with a partner before completing their plan. This will help them organize their thoughts into writing.

Challenge: Students should challenge themselves to use complex sentence structure and longer sentences including conjunctions, and a show a rich range of vocabulary.

Question Starts Visible Thinking Routine

Support: Suggest example questions using each question word and write them on the board. Also ask students what they think they know about the picture, which will lead into an interesting discussion and should generate more questions.

Challenge: For every question generated, encourage students to provide a secondary question that links to the previous one; e.g. *Who's the girl? And where's she from?*

Step Inside Visible Thinking Routine

Support: Write prompts on the board to help students phrase their answers, e.g. *I think he/she/it can see ... / I think he/she/it believes that ... / He/she/it probably cares about ....*

Challenge: Encourage students to link their ideas for what they care about to what they are looking at and what they believe, e.g. *I think he cares about (x) because he's looking at (y), and I think he believes that (z).* or *He's looking at (y), and I think he believes (z), so I think he cares about (x).*

Reading Comprehension

Support: Have students work in pairs to answer questions. Both students should look back at the reading to find the answer. They can then compare their answers before writing them in their books.

Challenge: Encourage students to answer the questions in their own words and with full sentences when appropriate, rather than just copying from the text.

Discussion

Support: Give students a list of questions to think about and answer before they talk. Writing notes or answers first can help shy students or those lacking confidence to join in.

Challenge: Encourage students to respond to a point made by someone else, summarizing it before giving their opinion.

Role-plays (in the **Literacy Book**)

Support: Play the audio while students perform the story. This way, students don't have to worry about their lines and can focus on interpreting each scene.

Challenge: Have students improvise the story, making their own changes to the dialogue.

Games Bank

60 Seconds

Put students in groups of three or four. Each student has 60 seconds to say as many things as they can that they learned in the lesson. They can mention anything they have learned, including vocabulary and facts. Use the timer on the TTL and call out *Time!* when the time is up.

Board Race

Divide the class into two teams and divide the board vertically in two halves. Give a board pen to one of the students on each team. Tell students the theme and give teams two minutes to write as many words connected to that theme as they can. Each word must be written by a different student on the team, and only one student is allowed to be standing from each team at any time. When finished, have the teams check each other's spelling and count how many correct words each team had.

Chain Game

Use chain memory games to practice the target language or lesson concepts. Have students sit in a circle. One student says a sentence, e.g. about one of the characters in a story: *I think Pia is clever.* The next student adds another adjective to the sentence, e.g. *I think Pia is clever and determined.* This continues until someone gets mixed up or can't remember what the last person said. That student says a new sentence and starts the chain again. Make sure students know that sentences don't have to be true; they can use their imaginations!

You can vary this game to practice the third person, e.g.

Student A: *If I were someone famous, I'd be a sports star.*

Student B: *If he were someone famous, he'd be a sports star and I'd be a basketball player.*

You can play this game in teams. The team that continues one chain for the longest time wins!

Change Places

Have students place their chairs in a big circle and sit down. Remove one chair so that one student is standing. Call out yes/no questions and have students stand up and change places with another student if the answer is *yes*. The student who doesn't find a chair stands in the middle and asks the next question (if the answer is *yes* for them, they should also move).

Correct the Teacher

Call out lines from songs, stories, or dialogues but make mistakes. When students hear a mistake, they raise their hands and call out *No!* Choose a student to correct the mistake.

Disappearing Sentences

Choose four reasonably simple sentences from the text. Write the sentences on the board and have students read them aloud. Then erase two or three words from each sentence and have students say them again, including the missing words. Erase more words and repeat until students are saying the complete sentences from a (nearly) empty board.

You can also use this game to practice the target grammar using the structure in the sentence.

Disappearing Words

Ask students to choose what they consider to be the most important words in a text and write them on the board (up to about 15 words). Have them turn away and then erase one word from the board. Have students turn back and identify which word is missing. Ask them how the word was used in the text. Continue until you have an empty board.

You can also play this game with key vocabulary words from a unit. Each time a word disappears, ask students to remember why it was important in the unit.

Draw It!

Have a volunteer come to the front and show him/her a word from the vocabulary set you wish to practice, or whisper it into his/her ear. The student draws the word on the board. Have students raise their hands and guess the word. You can also set this up in teams. Students have a time limit (e.g. 30 seconds or a minute) to draw a picture for their team to guess the word or phrase. If they can't guess it, the other team(s) gets a chance to guess and win a point.

Find Someone Who

Have students mingle, asking and answering questions to find someone with the same (or a similar) answer to them. You can have them write down the questions and their own answer, and then note down the people who match them, or it can be more of a memory test where they recall at the end who they matched with. They should find one person for every question asked. The first person to find matches for all the questions is the winner.

This can be a good way for students to get to know each other better, beyond what they already think they know. It can also be used to create pairings: students find a match and then they do the next activity with that person.

You can provide the prompt questions or have students write their own based on a topic.

How Many Words?

Read some sentences and have students count the words in each sentence. (Point out that contractions, e.g. *wasn't*, count as one word in this game.) When students think they know the number of words, they raise their hands. Invite a student to say the number. Ask if the others agree, and then count the words together to see if they were correct. This game helps consolidate target grammar.

Pass the Whisper!

Have students stand in a line. Whisper a sentence or question using the target language to one student and have him/her pass it on until it reaches the student nearest the door. That student must say the sentence or question aloud or write it correctly on the board. Repeat as required.

Running Spelling

Divide the class into two teams. Give one student in each team a board pen. Divide the board in two. Say a word twice. The students with the pens run to the board and write the first letter of the word. Then they hand the pen to the next student on their team, who writes the next letter. Both teams stop writing when one team finishes the word. Check the spelling. Then play again with a different word. The team with the most correctly spelled words at the end of the game wins.

Shark

Before the game starts, draw on the board a simple series of ten steps leading down to water. On the top step, draw a stick figure. In the water, draw a shark waiting with an open mouth.

Use words from the lesson and draw a series of lines on the board, one for each letter. Have students raise their hands to guess the letters. For each correct guess, write the letter on the line. For each incorrect guess, erase the stick figure and draw it again one step nearer the shark. Write the wrong letters on the board so they are not repeated.

Students win if the word is completed before the stick figure reaches the shark—but they must continue saying letters, not shout out the word!

Snowballs

Students write down something they learned on a piece of scrap paper and make it into a ball. On your signal, they throw their paper snowballs in the air. Then each student picks up a ball, opens it, and reads it aloud.

Stand Up, Sit Down

Call out statements that practice the target language or statements related to a text, e.g. *I've lived in this city for 5 years.* If the statement is true for students, they stand up. If it is not true, they stay sitting down. Alternatively, you can have students put their hands on their heads for true statements and keep their hands by their sides for false ones. You can play this game for true/false statements.

Test the Teacher

Students work in groups to write questions about information from a text. Make sure students write the answer next to the question. Each group then takes turns asking the teacher a question. The teacher must answer the question from memory! If the teacher answers correctly, he/she gets one point. If the answer is incorrect, the group gets one point.

Versus

Have students stand in a line in the middle of the classroom or in the hallway. Call out a series of two-option questions using words from the vocabulary set you want to practice, pointing to the left or right for each option. Students choose their favorite by stepping to the left or right, according to their preference. Nominate students to give reasons and examples for their preferences.

What's the Next Word?

Divide the class into small groups. Read sentences from a story, dialogue, or presentation and stop before key words. Have students decide in their groups what the next word is and raise their hands to answer.

What Was the Last Word?

Divide the class into two teams and give each team a board pen. Play the audio or video and stop after key vocabulary. One member of each team runs to the board and writes the last word heard.

Who Said It?

Review dialogue and characters from readings. Make handwritten cards with a quotation from the reading. First, check that students remember the names of the characters in the target reading. Then hold up one of the cards, saying *What does it say?* and have students read it aloud altogether. Say *Who said it?* When they have answered for each sign, play the reading audio or use the Story Player in the TTL to check answers. Alternatively, say the quotations aloud without writing them down.

Word Tennis

In this game, pairs of students will pass words or sentences between them. Students take turns saying words connected to a particular topic, e.g. *advertisements*: Student A: *billboard*, Student B: *persuade*, Student A: *slogan*, Student B: *products*.

Yes/No Game

Write a big *Yes* on the left of the board and a big *No* on the right. Tell students you will say sentences. If they agree with the sentence or think it is true, they point left and say *Yes!* If they disagree or think it is false, they point right and say *No!*

Alternatively, make the game into a Total Physical Response (TPR) game by assigning *Yes* to one side of the room and *No* to the other and having students move from one side to the other as you say each item. Where appropriate, nominate students to explain their choice.

Language Review

Vocabulary

Lesson Objectives

- to review and practice vocabulary about emotions, crime, nature and the environment, storytelling, and work and skills

Materials
Audio Track 1

Warm Up

Have students look at the pictures on pp. 6–7 for 30 seconds and then close their books. Alternatively, display them using the Tap & Teach Lessons (TTL). Then have students call out words related to the pictures they remember. Write these on the board and group them into categories as far as possible.

A TRACK 1 TB p. 215 **Listen and write. How did all the children feel?**

- Have students look at the first picture on p. 6 again. Elicit any other words that come to mind and add them to the board.
- Tell students they are going to listen to Daniel talking to his mom about his friends in the picture. Ask *Who's feeling good, and who's feeling bad?* Elicit ideas by looking at the picture. Play the audio and have students listen. Then check the answer. (Leila and Daniel felt good. Giulia, Jane, and Amari felt bad. Chen was confused so he may have felt bad. Michael learned how to dive so he probably felt good.)
- Refer students to the example on the page and point out that this is the adjective that describes that person's feelings. Play the audio again and pause it for students to write the adjectives. Display the answers on the board for students to check.

Answers
1 *confused* 2 enthusiastic 3 upset 4 worried
5 furious 6 delighted

B Unscramble and write the crime words.

- Have students discuss what is happening in the picture at the bottom of the page. Elicit ideas.
- Refer students to the example answer and point out that all the words are crime-related. Tell them that the image provides some clues. Have students unscramble the words on their own or in pairs.
- To check answers, ask students to spell out a word and write it on the board. Ask further questions to check comprehension (see **ETB**).

Answers
1 *thief* 2 detective 3 fingerprint 4 suspicious
5 clue 6 witness

C Find and write five positive words and five negative words about nature and the environment.

- Students are going to find and categorize the vocabulary. Refer students to the word search and the example. Point out that after finding the words, they must decide whether they are positive or negative. Have students complete the activity individually and then compare answers with a partner. You may want to remind them that some words will appear in the word search backwards.
- To check answers, copy the categories on the board and invite students to write a word in one of the two categories. Alternatively, you can display them using the TTL.

Answers
Positive: 1 *eco-friendly* 2 conservation 3 organic
4 sustainable 5 recycle
Negative: 6 pollution/poison 7 poison/pollution
8 damage 9 harm 10 endangered

D Read and complete.

- Have students look at the words in the box and say what they think the text is going to be about. Ask them to read the text once to find out (a movie).
- Have students complete the text individually and compare answers in pairs.
- Check the answers and write or project them on the board.

Answers
1 *character* 2 hero 3 enemy 4 villain 5 imagination
6 empathize 7 fascinating 8 suspense 9 moral

E Look, read, and choose.

- Have students look at the pictures and say in pairs which one they like best.
- Refer students to the example. Explain that the sentence refers to the first picture. Have students choose the correct words individually and compare answers in pairs.
- To check answers, choose students to read a sentence aloud.

Answers
1 *talented* 2 rewarding 3 observant 4 challenging
5 skills 6 degree

Cool Down

Play *Running Spelling* (see TB p. 26) with key vocabulary from this lesson.

Practice **Resource Bank:** Language Review; Vocabulary Printouts
Student's App: Language Review; Vocabulary Practice

Grammar

Lesson Objectives

- to review grammar from previous levels: present perfect; tag questions; present and past passive; *too* and *enough*; agreeing with *too*, *so*, *either*, and *neither*; reported speech; first and second conditional

Materials
Audio Track 2

Warm Up

Ask students if they or a family member have ever bought or received something from abroad. Ask *What was it? Where did you/they buy it? Why do people buy things from other countries?* Have them discuss their answers in pairs and then share their ideas with the class.

A TRACK 2 TB p. 215 **Listen and complete.**

- Have students look at the picture and say what they can see happening and where the people are. Elicit that they're at a type of international fair.
- This activity reviews present perfect and tag questions. Refer students to the example answer. Elicit the form (present perfect) and why it is appropriate (the woman is asking about the boy's experiences). Ask students to look at what the rest of the people are saying and guess what's missing. Play the audio and have students check and complete the sentences and questions.
- Check answers. Elicit when we use tag questions (to confirm something or find out if someone agrees with us).

Answers
1 *Have; tried* 2 aren't they 3 've/have; eaten
4 wasn't it 5 Have; seen 6 haven't you

B Read and complete.

- Have students read the first sentence and identify the verb form of the example (simple past passive). Elicit when we use the passive (when we don't know / aren't interested in who did the action).
- Encourage students to read the sentences first and look for clues that indicate whether they need to use the present or past. Have them complete the sentences individually before comparing in pairs.
- Invite students to read a sentence each and ask if everyone agrees.

Answers
1 *were made* 2 was taught 3 were built 4 is eaten
5 was taken 6 is played 7 were written
8 was prepared

C Match the sentences to the responses.

- This activity reviews *too*, *enough*, and ways of agreeing. Have two students read the first exchange. Then give them time to match the rest individually and compare answers in pairs.
- To check answers, nominate students to read an exchange aloud. Encourage them to respond with feeling.

Answers
1 *b* 2 d 3 f 4 e 5 a 6 c

D Read and choose.

- This activity reviews relative clauses and reported speech. Ask students to read the first exchange and say what grammar points they are going to practice (relative clauses and reported speech).
- Have students complete the activity and compare with a friend. Invite students to read an exchange in pairs. Write the answers on the board and ask if everyone agrees.

Answers
1 a *who*; b loved 2 a who; b weren't
3 a where; b too small 4 a that; b enough

E Complete with the correct form of the verbs.

- This activity reviews verb forms and conditionals. Ask students to read the dialogue once and say what it's about (a guitar club). Ask *Who's interested in joining the club?* (Caleb) *Who's already a member?* (Ethan)
- Have students complete the dialogue with the correct form of the verbs and then compare in pairs.
- Invite students to read parts of the dialogue aloud and explain why they used the specific verb form. Discuss the conditional sentences and what type they are (2 and 8 = first conditional; 5, 6, and 7 = second conditional).

Answers
1 *was thinking* 2 join 3 saw 4 wanted 5 were
6 'd/would be 7 wouldn't be 8 arrive
9 don't have to

Cool Down

Play *Disappearing Sentences* (see TB p. 25) with key sentences from this lesson.

Practice **Resource Bank:** Language Review; Grammar Printouts
Student's App: Language Review; Grammar Practice

Fiction

Lesson Objectives

- **to review making predictions, sequence of events, and sensory details**
- **to review literary terms: synonyms**

Materials

Audio Track 1; picture(s) of Petra in Jordan (Activity A)

Warm Up

Have students do a Think, Pair, Share (see TB p. 20) to think about the last story they read, what it was about, and where it was set.

A TRACK 1 TB p. 229 **Think and write. Predict from the pictures and the title. Where do you think the story is set? Then read.**

- This activity reviews making predictions. Have students look at the pictures and the title of the story extract. Have students discuss the prediction question in pairs and then write their answer.
- Invite students to share their ideas with the class.
- Play the audio and have students follow along in their books. Elicit whether their predictions were right. Then have students see if they can find Petra on a map. You could also show students photos of Petra.

Suggested Answers

in Petra / at an ancient site / in the desert / in a hot country / in Jordan

B Answer the questions. Then discuss how you know.

- These comprehension questions review the reading skills of inference, drawing conclusions, and understanding main ideas and details. Ask students to read the questions and refer to the text again to answer them. Have them do this individually and then compare answers in pairs, discussing the evidence in the text. Point out that for some questions there is no evidence in the text, so they will need to infer or think logically.
- To check answers, read a question and invite different students to answer and quote evidence from the story where appropriate.

Answers

1 He comes from near/around Petra. (because he knows a secret way in) 2 He was curious. / to get out of the heat and away from the crowds (I was cool and quiet in the tunnel.) 3 It was hidden for a long time. / Nobody knew it was there for many years. 4 He was surprised because it doesn't often rain in the desert. (He says, "I didn't know it rained in the desert.") 5 The passage filled up quickly with rain. (The boy said that the water tunnel floods.) 6 It was for controlling/directing water into/around the Lost City. (The boy says it's an old water tunnel.)

C Read and sequence the events. Then predict what will happen next.

- This activity reviews understanding a sequence of events. Ask students to put the events from the story in A in order. Explain that for number 7, they should write their own idea about how the story continues.
- Have students compare their answers in pairs and share their continuations. Then check and share as a class.

Answers

6; 3; 5; 1; 2; 4
7 Students' own answers

D Think and write. Then discuss. Complete the table with sensory details from the story. Which sense doesn't have an example?

- This activity reviews the skill of identifying sensory details. Look at the senses together and elicit which body part each one refers to. Elicit an example of a sight from the story.
- Have students read the story again and complete the table with sensory details. Point out that there's a sense that hasn't been covered in the story.
- Have students compare answers in pairs. Then check.

Answers

Sight: "disappearing around corners"; "beautiful ancient carvings"
Sound: "it was cool and quiet"; "Zac's voice echoed"
Touch: "it was cool and quiet"; "hot desert sun"; "smooth pink and red rocks"; "water splashed around his ankles"
Smell: "I smell rain!"
Taste: (no example)

Literary Term: Synonyms

Think and write. What are the synonyms for the underlined words?

- Read the example and, if necessary, review what a synonym is. Then ask students to match the rest of the words in the box to their underlined synonyms. Check answers.

Now find five pairs of synonyms in the reading.

- Give students time to find the pairs of synonyms in the reading. They can do this individually or in pairs. Check answers as a class.

Answers

1 *discover* 2 brothers and sisters 3 yell 4 simple
Synonyms in the reading: ran off / dashed off; entrance / way in; stone/rock; tunnel/passage; called/shouted

Cool Down

Ask students to act out the story in groups of three. One of the students reads the narration aloud.

Practice **Resource Bank:** Literacy Review; Reading Skills Printouts
Student's App: Reading Skills Practice; Literary Terms Practice

Nonfiction

Lesson Objectives

- to review making inferences and understanding the main idea and details
- to review literary terms: transition words

Materials
Audio Track 2

Warm Up

Ask students to think of places they would like to visit around the world. Elicit places on the board and invite students to say why they would like to go there.

A TRACK 2 TB p. 239 **Look at the pictures of Machu Picchu. What do you think the big steps are for? Do you think the reading is about the past, the present, or the future?**

- Draw students' attention to the title and the pictures. Elicit what they know about Machu Picchu.
- Ask students to look at the pictures again and discuss the two questions in pairs. Then elicit ideas.
- Play the audio and have students follow along in their books. Ask them whether their guesses were correct.

Example Answers
I think the big steps are for farming. I think the reading is about the past.

B Read and match the two parts of the sentences.

- This activity reviews the skills of skimming and scanning. Refer students to the example and point out that the sentences explain cause and effect.
- Have students complete the activity, checking the information in the text. Check answers as a class.

Answers
1 *b* 2 d 3 a 4 c 5 f 6 e

C Choose one of the three main ideas in the reading and complete the graphic organizer. Write three details for the main idea.

- This activity reviews the main idea and details. Ask students to discuss in pairs what the main ideas of the paragraphs are. Elicit ideas and agree on them as a class.
- Then ask students to choose one main idea and work on their own to find three details in the text that support it.
- Let them compare answers in pairs. Then check as a class.

Example Answers
Main Idea: The Incas built Machu Picchu.
Details: They made huge steps in the mountains for farming and making their homes. / Their engineering skills were good. / They developed ways to transport water to the fields and houses.

D Think, discuss, and write. Why do you think Machu Picchu is a UNESCO World Heritage Site? Write three reasons.

- This activity invites students to engage personally with the text. Elicit what a UNESCO World Heritage Site is and any examples. Ask the question and elicit ideas.
- Have students discuss more ideas in pairs, choose three, and write them. Invite them to share new ideas as a class.

Suggested Answers
It was created by an ancient civilization that no longer exists. / It shows how people lived in the past. / It teaches us about history and ancient architecture. / It's well preserved.

My Reading Journal

What else would you like to learn about Machu Picchu?

Have students look back at the reading and think about other things they would like to learn about Machu Picchu. Ask them to discuss ideas in pairs.

Then have students choose one of the ideas and complete the sentence.

Have students share their ideas with the class.

Example Answers
I want to learn what tools they used to build it / how many people used to live there / if I can hike up Machu Picchu / how much it costs to fly to Peru.

Literary Term: Transition Words

Read and complete.

- Read the words and phrases in the box. Explain that these are transition words (words that helps us tell a story and order the events). Ask students to read the first two sentences and say which transition word fits. They should then complete the task individually or in pairs. Then check answers.

Now find more transition words in the reading.

- Ask students to read the text again and find more transition words.

Answers
Of course; Meanwhile; Suddenly; Eventually; as a result
Transition words in the reading: Then, Consequently, Eventually

Cool Down

Ask *Which of the two places would you like to visit—Petra or Machu Picchu? Why?* Ask students to compare ideas in pairs. Then invite them to share with the class.

Practice **Resource Bank:** Literacy Review; Reading Skills Printouts
Student's App: Reading Skills Practice; Literary Terms Practice

UNIT 1

Keep in Touch

Unit Overview

Themes

The importance of online safety

The history of communication technology and how it impacts our lives

Synopsis

In this unit, students will explore the importance of technology in our day-to-day lives. They will learn about online safety and fake news. They will discuss how children their age use the internet and learn how communication technology has evolved over time. Students will write a fact-based article and plan and prepare a conversation discussing a blog post.

Language Book

Vocabulary

blog, blog post, comment, crash, download, email, message, save to favorites, search history, upload

Pronunciation: Sentence Stress: Content Words

p. 35

Explore Language

Verbs of Thinking

p. 37

Global Citizenship

How does technology help us learn?

create a profile, devices, lowercase letters, online privacy, online safety, password, personal information, register, secure, special characters, uppercase letters, username

p. 39

Explore Language

Simple and Progressive Forms

p. 41

Write About It

A Fact-Based Article

Paragraph and Sentence Building: Presenting Facts and Giving Details, Examples, and Opinions

p. 43

Talk About It

Conversation: Asking for Clarification and Confirming Understanding

p. 45

Think It Over

Review and Reflection: My Planning Sheet

p. 47

Think Together

What are the benefits of communication technology?

p. 61

Visible Thinking

Think, Pair, Share

p. 49

Nonfiction

Informational Text: *Communication Time!*

Words in Context: *wireless, telegraph, patents, reverses, demonstration, wi-fi*

p. 57

Literacy Book

Fiction

Story: *Urgent Message*

Words in Context: *instant message, weird, coast guard, prank, enlarged*

p. 51

Reading Skill

Understanding Chronology

p. 55

Literary Term

Register

p. 53

Language and Literacy Connections

The connecting theme for Unit 1 is using technology in our everyday lives.

	Language	Literacy
Vocabulary	**Set 1:** technology **Set 2:** online safety	**Fiction:** email, personal information, search for, username **Nonfiction:** message
Grammar	**Verbs of Thinking** I wonder if he always wakes up on time. I don't remember if the children play them. I forgot which website it was. I don't understand why they have drums. **Simple and Progressive Forms** It says here that the reports are fake. Daniel told me about it. I'm taking a look right now. He was looking for information yesterday. Is anyone else reporting it?	**Fiction** She started to wonder if this was someone's bad idea of a joke. Pia lifted her head off the pillow. Somehow Helen was sending messages. **Nonfiction** Marconi wins the Nobel Prize. People are always looking to improve the way they communicate.
Skills	**Pronunciation:** sentence stress: content words **Process Writing:** generating ideas	**Reading:** understanding chronology **Literary Term:** register
International English	I forgot / I've forgotten take a look / have a look	the heebie-jeebies / the chills

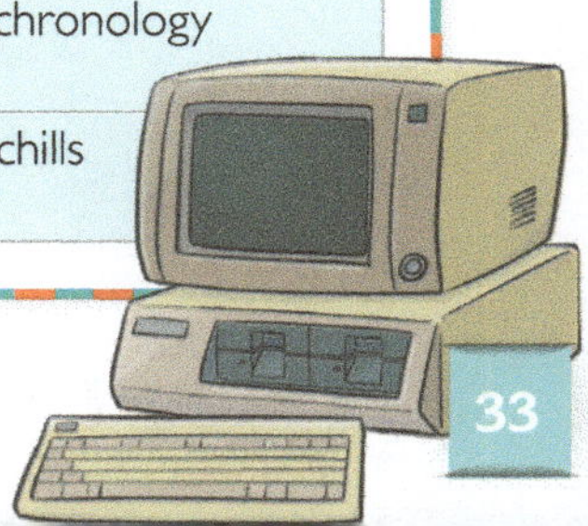

Lesson 1 Walkthrough Vocabulary

This lesson introduces the theme of the unit, and presents and practices the first vocabulary set.

The teaching notes provide **Warm Up** and **Cool Down** ideas to help set the tone for the lessons, often in the form of games or discussion points.

In the **Enhanced Teacher's eBook (ETB)**, there is also a **Two-Minute Review** which looks back at language from previous lessons.

D Controlled Practice & Critical Thinking

A critical thinking activity provides controlled written practice of the new words. By having to think and at times discuss and justify their choices, students engage actively with the new words. Practice of the written forms will also help cement them in the mind.

A Contextualized Presentation: Picture Dictionary Scene

The unit starts with a dynamic dialogue set in the context of a picture dictionary scene which helps students activate their world knowledge and ignites their interest in the topic. Several of the new words for the unit are contextualized in this audio.

Unit Topic

The unit title is the same in the **Language Book** and the **Literacy Book**, with the topic explored in different ways across the two books.

Characters

One character in each unit travels to the next, helping to reinforce the idea of Global Citizens and how we're connected.

A character or element from the same unit in the **Literacy Book** is part of the picture dictionary scene in the **Language Book**.

B Drill & Controlled Vocabulary Practice

The vocabulary presentation and drill of up to 12 words/phrases has the students look at the picture (including as definitions) and number the words in the list, before checking with the audio. This can also be used as a pronunciation drill.

Encouraging students to make educated guesses and engage with the image helps them to start thinking actively about the words and meanings.

C Visualization

A visualization activity supports the students to assimilate the new words by making them their own. They are guided to build images, memories, or word-associations via an audio track.

E Spoken Word

A spoken word rap, chant, or poem provides a new context for the vocabulary by exploring SEL competencies or other aspects of the topic. It also gives students the chance to practice saying the words in connected speech. There are audio and videos to support this activity.

F Pronunciation

Features of connected speech are pulled from the spoken word activity to analyze and practice. This builds on the individual sounds work from previous levels.

Vocabulary

Lesson Objectives

- to learn technology-related vocabulary: *blog, blog post, comment, crash, download, email, message, save to favorites, search history, upload*
- to say a chant about searching for information online
- to recognize and practice sentence stress: content words

Materials
Audio Tracks 3 to 7; Video

Warm Up

To introduce the theme of the unit, have students discuss how they keep in touch with their family and friends. Do they talk to them face-to-face or use technology? Why?

A TRACK 3 TB p. 215 **Listen. What information does Daniel want? How does he find it?**

- Have students look at the picture and ask them to find Daniel from the Review Unit (he is at the bottom of the illustration). Then ask students to say what they see. Ask questions to prompt discussion: *What are the students doing? What lesson do you think they are in? Is the teacher happy that a student is arriving late?*
- Have students listen to Daniel and Kate chatting in the computer lab. Ask *What information does Daniel want? How does he find it?* Play the audio and check answers.

Answers
Daniel wants to find the good website he and Sofia found the day before (with information on the school day in Ghana). Kate helps him find it in his search history.

B TRACK 4 TB p. 215 **Find and number the words in A. Then listen and check.**

- Have students look at the list of words and phrases. Point out the example and have students find *crash* in the picture. Tell students to find the other words and to write the numbers in their books. Play the audio for them to listen and check. Check answers with the class.

Answers
1 *crash* 2 upload 3 email 4 message
5 search history 6 blog 7 blog post 8 comment
9 save to favorites 10 download

C TRACK 5 TB p. 215 **Close your eyes. Listen, visualize, and say.**

- Prepare students for the visualization (see TB p. 21).
- Play the audio for students to visualize the ideas as they listen. Tell them not to speak until they hear the word *say*.
- Have students share what they imagined in pairs. Then have some students share their ideas with the class, e.g. *My blog's going to be about my favorite music.*

D Look and write. There is more than one possible answer.

- Point to the table and headings. Elicit the difference between *getting* and *writing* information. Look at the two examples and elicit why they go in the second column.
- Tell students to write the words and phrases from A in the table. Then check answers as a class. You could project the answers using the TTL.

Suggested Answers
Getting information, photos, and videos: download; save to favorites; search history
Writing information and showing pictures and videos: *blog, blog post*; comment; email; message; upload
Having a problem: crash

E TRACK 6 TB p. 215 **Listen and write. Then watch and say.**

- Point to the title *Search the Net*. Ask students what they search the net for. Play the audio or video.
- Have students look at the lyrics and complete the blanks, using the initial letters to help. Remind students all the words can be found in A. Play the audio or video and have students check their answers.
- Play the audio or video again and have students join in with the chant. Encourage students to copy the rhythm and pronunciation.

Answers
1 *blog post* 2 Save 3 Upload 4 download 5 crash

F TRACK 7 TB p. 215 **Pronunciation. Listen and say. Copy the sentence stress. Find other sentences in the poem and notice the stress patterns.**

- Display the examples from the chant. Play the audio and show that the dots show the stressed words. Play the audio again and have students clap the sentence stress and repeat the sentences chorally as they clap.
- Elicit that content words are stressed (nouns, verbs, adverbs, adjectives). Unstressed words are function words (auxiliary verbs, pronouns, determiners, articles). Note: *My* in the first sentence is an exception, because the speaker uses stress to show whose turn it is.
- Have students work in pairs to identify the stress in the other sentences. Then have students say them out loud.

Answers
Search the net, search the net. / Facts—who can find the most? / Upload your photos—wow! / Don't download that—it's trash!

Cool Down

With books closed, play *Board Race* (see TB p. 25) by having students write as many technology-related words as they can.

Practice **Student's App:** Vocabulary Practice; Spoken Word Video

Lesson 2 Walkthrough Explore Language

This grammar lesson presents and practices the first target structure using a simplified inductive approach.

A Contextualized Presentation

The target grammar structures are presented in context through a comic strip cartoon story, dialogue, or monologue and have an accompanying audio recording.

B Grammar Analysis Table

Students fill in the grammar table by finding the examples in the story in Activity A, focusing on form. The key language is highlighted to help students spot patterns in how the structure is constructed. In this level, a noticing question draws students' attention to a particular aspect, encouraging students to start to question and think about grammar for themselves.

C Inductive Analysis

Concept questions help focus students on the meaning and when to use the target grammar. This simplified inductive approach encourages students to make assumptions, discuss, and verify ideas using the examples in Activity A. By taking an active role in their learning, they will gain a better understanding of language, and will be better equipped for new ideas in the future.

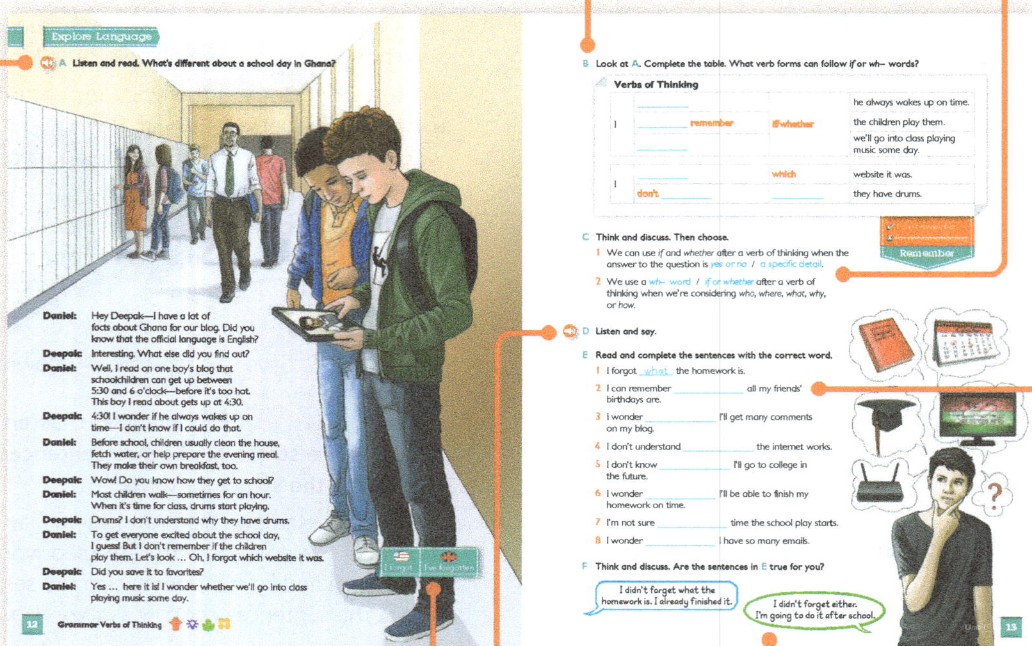

International English

Regular *International English* features highlight differences between American and British English, helping raise awareness of different Englishes around the world. Audio for these words is available on the Tap & Teach Lessons (TTL).

D Drill: Sentence Level

An audio recording provides example sentences and questions for pronunciation practice. Drilling new grammar structures helps students become comfortable with how they sound before using them in a freer context. (See also TB p. 23)

E Controlled Practice: Written

Controlled written practice helps consolidate the grammar.

F Freer Practice: Communication

The lesson ends with an activity which allows students to use the grammar in a freer context. There is always a speaking task, and it may also include some writing.

Explore Language

Lesson Objectives

- to learn how to use verbs of thinking
- to practice vocabulary related to technology

Materials
Audio Tracks 8 and 9

Warm Up

Elicit which African country was mentioned in the previous lesson (Ghana) and brainstorm ideas. If appropriate, have students do some research on the internet under the following categories: location, flag, language, animals, food, and weather.

A TRACK 8 TB p. 215 **Listen and read. What's different about a school day in Ghana?**

- Tell students that they are going to listen to Daniel talking to a boy named Deepak. Have students look at the picture and identify where the boys are (at school) and what they are looking at (Daniel's tablet). Play the audio and have students follow the dialogue in their books.
- Ask the question *What's different about a school day in Ghana?* and elicit answers. Play the audio again for students to check.

Answers
In Ghana, children get up between 5:30 and 6:00. / They do household chores before school (and the types of chores they do). / They walk to school (sometimes for an hour). / Drums play when it's time for class.

International English

Point to the flags and elicit which countries they represent (the USA and UK). Tell students that they will see American English words used in this course, but that British English is also correct. If appropriate, you could also ask them to choose whether they want to use American or British English, but let them know they have to be consistent.

Ask them to look at the phrases and identify the forms (simple past and present perfect). Explain that speakers of American English tend to use the present perfect far less than British English speakers.

B Look at A. Complete the table. What verb forms can follow *if* or *wh–* words?

- Display the table using the TTL. Tell students that the words they need to complete the table are all in A. Have them complete the table individually. Check answers as a class.
- Point out the *wh–* words in the table and elicit more examples. Make a list of other *wh–* words and when they are used, e.g. *when* = time, *why* = reason, *who* = person.
- Ask the noticing question *What verb forms can follow "if" or "wh–" words?* Discuss answers and have students underline the verb form in each case.
- Refer students to the Grammar tip *Remember*. Ask why we can't say *I'm not remembering* (*remember* is a thinking verb, not an action verb). If you feel students need more guidance, the **ETB** provides a differentiation activity.

Answers
wonder; don't; wonder; forgot; understand; why
If and *wh–* words are usually followed by a simple present, a simple past, or future form.

C Think and discuss. Then choose.

- Refer students to the table in B and encourage them to try making questions out of the sentences. What sorts of questions are they? What sorts of answers would they expect? Have students work in pairs to discuss the sentences and answer options. Check answers.

Answers
1 *yes* or *no* 2 *wh–* word

D TRACK 9 TB p. 216 **Listen and say.**

- This activity helps with pronunciation in fluent speech so students can begin to internalize the structure. Play the audio and have students repeat each example chorally. (See TB p. 23, Making Language Drills Fun.)

E Read and complete the sentences with the correct word.

- This activity provides controlled practice of verbs of thinking and *if* or *wh–* words. Look at the example together. Elicit that *what* refers to the homework, and we use it because homework is a thing.
- Have them complete the sentences individually or in pairs.
- To check answers, invite students to read a sentence aloud and encourage the rest of the class to say whether they agree. Ask them to explain why if they disagree.

Answers
1 what 2 when 3 if/whether 4 how 5 if/whether
6 whether/if 7 what 8 why

F Think and discuss. Are the sentences in E true for you?

- This activity provides freer practice of verbs of thinking and *if* or *wh–* words. Have two students read the example exchange. Then give students time to read through the sentences again and think how they feel about each one.
- Have students discuss the sentences in pairs or groups.

Cool Down

With books closed, play *How Many Words?* (see TB p. 26) using the sentences from B and E on p. 13.

Practice **Resource Bank:** Grammar Printout
Student's App: Grammar Practice

Lesson 3 Walkthrough Global Citizenship

This lesson presents and practices the second vocabulary set, and explores the Global Citizenship topic through listening and discussion.

A Contextualized Vocabulary

A dialogue, discussion, or monologue provides initial input on the Global Citizenship theme and contextualizes some of the new vocabulary for the lesson.

Comprehension questions are provided in the **ETB**.

Opening Question

The lesson starts with an Opening Question to get students thinking about the lives of other children around the world and issues which affect us globally. There are no right or wrong answers for this as the focus is on raising awareness and provoking thought and discussion.

B Drill & Controlled Vocabulary Practice

The second vocabulary set of up to 12 words/phrases is presented and practiced through a matching activity, which is then checked with an audio recording. The vocabulary items are represented in photos or as definitions.

A Visualization recording is available on the TTL for this vocabulary set.

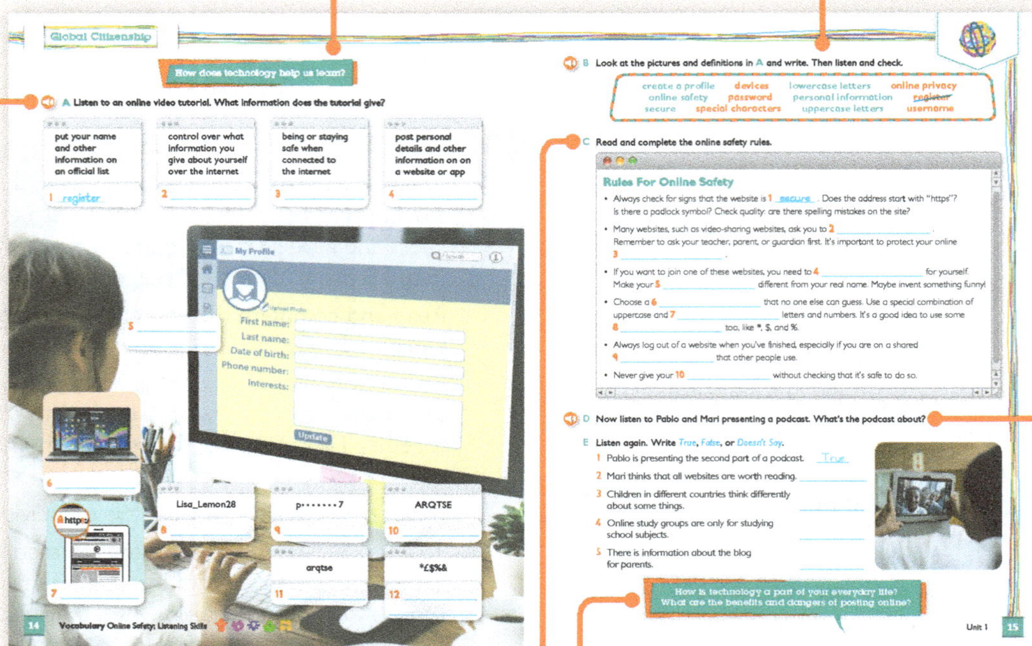

Global Citizenship

How does technology help us learn?

A Listen to an online video tutorial. What information does the tutorial give?

put your name and other information on an official list 1 register

control over what information you give about yourself over the internet 2

being or staying safe when connected to the internet 3

post personal details and other information on on a website or app 4

Lisa_Lemon28 p•••••••7 ARQTSE arqtse *£$%&

14 Vocabulary Online Safety; Listening Skills

B Look at the pictures and definitions in A and write. Then listen and check.

create a profile, devices, lowercase letters, online privacy, online safety, password, personal information, ~~register~~, secure, special characters, uppercase letters, username

C Read and complete the online safety rules.

Rules For Online Safety

- Always check for signs that the website is 1 secure. Does the address start with "https"? Is there a padlock symbol? Check quality: are there spelling mistakes on the site?
- Many websites, such as video-sharing websites, ask you to 2 ______. Remember to ask your teacher, parent, or guardian first. It's important to protect your online 3 ______.
- If you want to join one of these websites, you need to 4 ______ for yourself. Make your 5 ______ different from your real name. Maybe invent something funny!
- Choose a 6 ______ that no one else can guess. Use a special combination of uppercase and 7 ______ letters and numbers. It's a good idea to use some 8 ______ too, like *, $, and %.
- Always log out of a website when you've finished, especially if you are on a shared 9 ______ that other people use.
- Never give your 10 ______ without checking that it's safe to do so.

D Now listen to Pablo and Mari presenting a podcast. What's the podcast about?

E Listen again. Write *True*, *False*, or *Doesn't Say*.

1 Pablo is presenting the second part of a podcast. True
2 Mari thinks that all websites are worth reading. ______
3 Children in different countries think differently about some things. ______
4 Online study groups are only for studying school subjects. ______
5 There is information about the blog for parents. ______

How is technology a part of your everyday life? What are the benefits and dangers of posting online?

Unit 1 15

C Controlled Vocabulary Practice: Written

Students practice at least six of the new vocabulary in a written context related to the lesson topic.

D & E Listening for Gist and Details

A second audio recording delves further into the Global Citizenship topic, as a monologue or interview. The speakers may be from different countries, or have a particular interest or expert knowledge to share.

The first listening focuses on understanding the gist, while the second looks at the details, using a variety of activity types often seen in exams.

Discussion Questions

The lesson ends with Discussion Questions to stimulate thought and conversation about what students have learned from the lesson. One question focuses on their personal experience, while the other encourages them to think more globally. Further notes on developing this discussion and ideas for project work are given in the **ETB**.

Global Citizenship

Lesson Objectives

- to learn vocabulary related to online safety: *create a profile, devices, lowercase letters, online privacy, online safety, password, personal information, register, secure, special characters, uppercase letters, username*
- to explore the importance of online safety
- to practice listening for gist and details

Materials

Audio Tracks 10 to 12; Audio Track A

Opening Question

Ask the opening question: *How does technology help us learn?* Allow students to think about how they have learned something through technology and then to share their ideas.

A TRACK 10 TB p. 216 **Listen to an online video tutorial. What information does the tutorial give?**

- Ask students what a video tutorial does (shows how to do something) and discuss whether students have ever watched one. What was it about?
- Direct students to the question and have them guess what the tutorial video is about. Write their ideas on the board. Play the audio and check their guesses. Ask the question again and discuss.
- Ask *Why does Meg watch the video?* Play the audio again for students to check. Elicit ideas. (She wants to register for a website and she needs to do this safely.) Ask further comprehension questions (see **ETB**).
- Ask students if they have ever registered for a website and, if so, what information they had to include.

Answer

It tells you how you can register for a website safely.

B TRACK 11 TB p. 216 **Look at the pictures and definitions in A and write. Then listen and check.**

- Point out the example answer for number 1, *register*. Refer students to the vocabulary box in B and have them match the words and phrases to the pictures and definitions in A. Encourage students to make guesses if they are unsure.
- Play the audio for students to check their answers. Then play it again to practice the pronunciation, pausing after each word or phrase for them to repeat.

Answers

1 *register* 2 online privacy 3 online safety 4 create a profile 5 personal information 6 devices 7 secure 8 username 9 password 10 uppercase letters 11 lowercase letters 12 special characters

TRACK A TB p. 216 **Visualization**

The TTL has a visualization audio track for this vocabulary set. (See TB p. 21.)

C Read and complete the online safety rules.

- Have students quickly read the text. Ask what the purpose of the text is (to advise how to use the internet safely).
- Ask students how to check that a website is secure (the address starts with *https* and there is a padlock symbol). Have them complete the rules with words from B. Check answers.

Answers

1 *secure* 2 register 3 privacy 4 create a profile 5 username 6 password 7 lowercase 8 special characters 9 device 10 personal information

D TRACK 12 TB p. 216 **Now listen to Pablo and Mari presenting a podcast. What's the podcast about?**

- Ask students if they've ever listened to a podcast. If so, discuss what types they've listened to.
- Listening for gist: have students listen to Pablo and Mari presenting a podcast. Ask the question and play the audio. Have students discuss answers in pairs, then as a class.

Answer

It's about the benefits of technology for learning.

E Listen again. Write *True*, *False*, or *Doesn't Say*.

- Listening for details: have students look at the sentences to see how many things they remember. Play the audio for them to complete their answers.
- Put students in pairs and have them compare answers. Ask them to correct any false sentences orally. Check answers. Discuss whether students enjoy using technology to learn.

Answers

1 *True* 2 False (you need think carefully about which websites to ignore) 3 True 4 False (special interests, like music) 5 Doesn't Say

Discussion Questions

- Draw students' attention to the discussion questions: *How is technology a part of your everyday life? What are the benefits and dangers of posting online?* Have students discuss the questions in pairs or small groups (see **ETB**). Encourage them to recognize that technology is part of daily life, but that they need to ensure they are safe online.
- Return to the opening question: *How does technology help us learn?* Review the ideas discussed at the beginning of the lesson and encourage students to share any new ideas. Focus on the concept of technology as a tool and discuss how beneficial it can be when used safely.

Cool Down

Have students think about internet safety. Write the following prompts on the board: *You should …*; *You shouldn't …* What advice can they offer to others to improve their online safety? Have them share their ideas.

Next lesson: Ask students to bring a photo from home.

Practice Student's App: Vocabulary Practice; Listening Practice

Lesson 4 Walkthrough Explore Language

This grammar lesson presents and practices the second target structure using a simplified inductive approach. Differentiation ideas to support or challenge students are given in the **ETB** wherever it would be useful. See also TB p. 24 for some general ideas for differentiated learning. Further written practice is also available through Grammar Printouts in the Resource Bank.

Grammar Tip

After every grammar analysis table, there is a tip with additional information. These are divided into three categories:

Watch Out: highlights common errors

Remember: aspects of language students have seen before, e.g. contractions

Look: additional features students should be aware of, e.g. spelling patterns

A Contextualized Presentation

A gist question focuses students on the story and further comprehension questions are provided in the **ETB**.

B Grammar Analysis Table

The grammar table is reproduced in the TTL, allowing for this to be completed as a heads-up class activity.

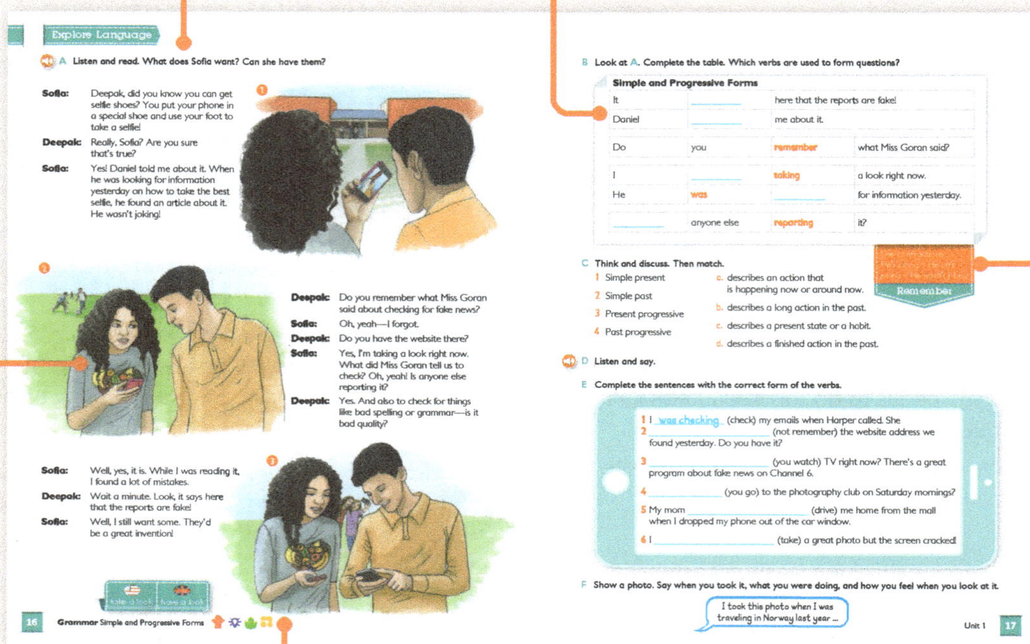

Explore Language

A Listen and read. What does Sofia want? Can she have them?

Sofia: Deepak, did you know you can get selfie shoes? You put your phone in a special shoe and use your foot to take a selfie!

Deepak: Really, Sofia? Are you sure that's true?

Sofia: Yes! Daniel told me about it. When he was looking for information yesterday on how to take the best selfie, he found an article about it. He wasn't joking!

Deepak: Do you remember what Miss Goran said about checking for fake news?

Sofia: Oh, yeah—I forgot.

Deepak: Do you have the website there?

Sofia: Yes, I'm taking a look right now. What did Miss Goran tell us to check? Oh, yeah! Is anyone else reporting it?

Deepak: Yes. And also to check for things like bad spelling or grammar—is it bad quality?

Sofia: Well, yes, it is. While I was reading it, I found a lot of mistakes.

Deepak: Wait a minute. Look, it says here that the reports are fake!

Sofia: Well, I still want some. They'd be a great invention!

16 **Grammar** Simple and Progressive Forms

B Look at A. Complete the table. Which verbs are used to form questions?

Simple and Progressive Forms

It	_____	here that the reports are fake!	
Daniel	_____	me about it.	
Do	you	remember	what Miss Goran said?
I	_____	taking	a look right now.
He	was	_____	for information yesterday.
_____	anyone else	reporting	it?

Remember

C Think and discuss. Then match.

1 Simple present
2 Simple past
3 Present progressive
4 Past progressive

a. describes an action that is happening now or around now.
b. describes a long action in the past.
c. describes a present state or a habit.
d. describes a finished action in the past.

D Listen and say.

E Complete the sentences with the correct form of the verbs.

1 I was checking (check) my emails when Harper called. She
2 _____ (not remember) the website address we found yesterday. Do you have it?
3 _____ (you watch) TV right now? There's a great program about fake news on Channel 6.
4 _____ (you go) to the photography club on Saturday mornings?
5 My mom _____ (drive) me home from the mall when I dropped my phone out of the car window.
6 I _____ (take) a great photo but the screen cracked!

F Show a photo. Say when you took it, what you were doing, and how you feel when you look at it.

I took this photo when I was traveling in Norway last year ...

Unit 1 17

Characters

One of the characters in this scene will appear in the next unit, in a new setting with a new group of friends.

Competency Icons

Competency icons indicate the areas covered in each lesson (see TB p. 19). The teaching notes tell you which activities address which competencies.

Explore Language

Lesson Objectives

- to review simple and progressive forms
- to describe a photo and feelings about it

Materials
Audio Tracks 13 and 14; students' photos, print or digital (F); a photo (F)

Warm Up

Ask students if they read articles in newspapers or online. Ask *What kinds of articles do you read? How else do you keep yourself informed? Do you talk with your friends about the news?*

A TRACK 13 TB p. 216 **Listen and read. What does Sofia want? Can she have them?**

- Have students look at the pictures on p. 16 and say who they can see (*Sofia* and *Deepak*). Ask them to predict what they are talking about and why they are smiling at the end.
- Play the audio. Have students follow the dialogue in their books and check to see if their predictions were correct.
- Then ask the questions and elicit the answers.

Answers
She wants a pair of selfie shoes. She can't have them because the news is fake.

International English

Ask students to look at the phrases and notice which word changes (the verb *take* changes to *have*). Explain that there are similar phrases for everyday activities, e.g. take or have a bath / a shower / a rest / a break / a holiday or vacation.

B Look at A. Complete the table. Which verbs are used to form questions?

- Have students complete the table. Tell them that all the sentences are in the dialogue in A and that they need to write the verbs. Have them work individually and then compare in pairs.
- Display the table and check answers as a class. Ask students if each sentence refers to the present or the past. Elicit the name of the verb form and how each one is made. Ask *Which verbs are used to form questions?* Elicit answers and discuss which verbs we use with the simple present (*do, does*), simple past (*did*), present progressive (*am, is, are*), and past progressive (*was, were*).
- Draw students' attention to the Grammar tip *Remember.* Elicit that *he's* is a contraction of *he is*, not *he was*. Remind students we only use the contraction in the present, not the past.

Answers
says; told; 'm; looking; Is
The verbs *do* and *be* are used to form questions.

Practice **Resource Bank:** Grammar Printout
Student's App: Grammar Practice

C Think and discuss. Then match.

- Have students match the verb forms to the explanations of when we use each. Do the first as an example (c) and elicit example sentences, e.g. *I live in (Spain).*
- Ask students to match the rest of the forms and explanations. Have them compare answers in pairs. Check answers. Then ask students to give an example sentence using each form. If you feel students need more guidance, the **ETB** provides a differentiation activity.

Answers
1 c 2 d 3 a 4 b

D TRACK 14 TB p. 216 **Listen and say.**

- Play the audio and have students repeat each example chorally. (See TB p. 23, Making Language Drills Fun.)

E Complete the sentences with the correct form of the verbs.

- This activity provides controlled practice of the simple and progressive forms. Read the example and elicit *was checking* is past progressive. Ask *Why do we use past progressive here?* (It describes a long action in the past that was interrupted by another event.) Ask *What words helped you decide which form to use?* ("when Harper called")
- Give students time to complete the sentences individually. Ask students to compare in pairs.
- To check answers, invite students to read a sentence aloud. Alternatively, project them on the board. Elicit what clues helped students decide which form to use.

Answers
1 *was checking* 2 doesn't remember 3 Are you watching 4 Do you go 5 was driving 6 took

F Show a photo. Say when you took it, what you were doing, and how you feel when you look at it.

- For this freer oral practice, show students a photo of yours and demonstrate a short description of it, using *when, what,* and *how.* Encourage students to ask you further questions.
- Put students in pairs or small groups. Ask them to take turns showing and talking about their photo. While students are listening, ask them to make notes of key words and ask at least one question.
- When they finish, put students in different pairs or groups to talk about what they saw and heard. Which photo sounds the most interesting?

Cool Down

Play *Disappearing Sentences* (see TB p. 25). Use sentences with simple and progressive forms. You can use sentences from E on p. 17 or write your own.

Lesson 5 Walkthrough Write About It

This first productive skills lesson is dedicated to writing, which now occupies a double page. In Levels 5 and 6, the lessons explore different genres of text, linked to those in the **Literacy Book**, and take students through the different stages of Process Writing.

The left-hand page presents the genre and highlights the structure, key features, and aspects of language. The right-hand page scaffolds students to produce their own writing, through carefully staged activities focusing on each step of Process Writing cumulatively: Units 1 and 2 look at brainstorming; Units 3–5 work on brainstorming and planning; Units 6–8 explore brainstorming, planning, and drafting & revising; Units 9 and 10 bring it all together to finish with editing and publishing.

A Contextualized Writing Mechanics

A model text continues the topic of the unit and a gist question ensures students are engaged with the text as readers, before becoming writers.

Further comprehension questions are provided in the **ETB**.

D Brainstorming

In every unit, students are encouraged to brainstorm ideas as the first step to writing. A variety of examples are given on the page to encourage students to be flexible and choose the right technique for the final product.

Process Writing

The pencils icon in Units 1, 3, 6, and 9, refer students to a page at the back of the book exploring a Process Writing stage. These can be done before the activities in the unit to give them a better understanding of why each stage is important and useful.

B Text Analysis

Students are guided to analyze the structure and textual features for the text type.

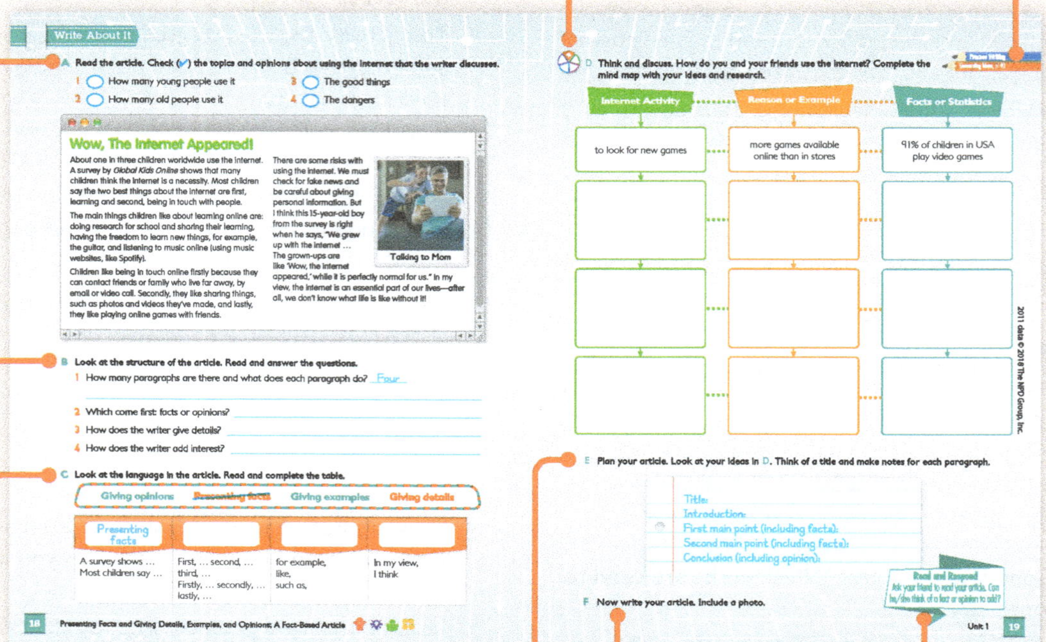

Write About It

A Read the article. Check (✓) the topics and opinions about using the internet that the writer discusses.

1 ◯ How many young people use it
2 ◯ How many old people use it
3 ◯ The good things
4 ◯ The dangers

Wow, The Internet Appeared!

About one in three children worldwide use the internet. A survey by *Global Kids Online* shows that many children think the internet is a necessity. Most children say the two best things about the internet are first, learning and second, being in touch with people.

The main things children like about learning online are: doing research for school and sharing their learning, having the freedom to learn new things, for example, the guitar, and listening to music online (using music websites, like Spotify).

Children like being in touch online firstly because they can contact friends or family who live far away, by email or video call. Secondly, they like sharing things, such as photos and videos they've made, and lastly, they like playing online games with friends.

There are some risks with using the internet. We must check for fake news and be careful about giving personal information. But I think this 15-year-old boy from the survey is right when he says, "We grew up with the internet … The grown-ups are like 'Wow, the internet appeared,' while it is perfectly normal for us." In my view, the internet is an essential part of our lives—after all, we don't know what life is like without it!

Talking to Mom

B Look at the structure of the article. Read and answer the questions.

1 How many paragraphs are there and what does each paragraph do? Four
2 Which come first: facts or opinions?
3 How does the writer give details?
4 How does the writer add interest?

C Look at the language in the article. Read and complete the table.

Giving opinions ~~Presenting facts~~ Giving examples Giving details

Presenting facts			
A survey shows … Most children say …	First, … second, … third, … Firstly, … secondly, … lastly, …	for example, like, such as,	In my view, I think

18 Presenting Facts and Giving Details, Examples, and Opinions; A Fact-Based Article

D Think and discuss. How do you and your friends use the internet? Complete the mind map with your ideas and research.

Internet Activity	Reason or Example	Facts or Statistics
to look for new games	more games available online than in stores	91% of children in USA play video games

2011 data © 2018 The NPD Group, Inc.

E Plan your article. Look at your ideas in D. Think of a title and make notes for each paragraph.

Title:
Introduction:
First main point (including facts):
Second main point (including facts):
Conclusion (including opinion):

Read and Respond
Ask your friend to read your article. Can he/she think of a fact or opinion to add?

F Now write your article. Include a photo.

Unit 1 19

E Planning

Every unit includes a planning stage, which is more scaffolded in the earlier units, drawing on the ideas gathered in Activity D.

Read and Respond

Students are invited to share their work with a friend, who will offer an opinion or some advice. This encourages students to write with a reader in mind, and to get into the habit of editing and making improvements to their work.

C Language Analysis

This activity focuses students on language used in the model text that they may find useful in their own writing.

Where relevant, a *callout* provides additional insights into the features or language in the model text

F (& G) Production: Writing Task

The final writing task can be done in notebooks. *Support* printouts are available in the Resource Bank for those students who need it.

For some more light-hearted writing practice, there is also a Writing Game for each unit in the Resource Bank.

Write About It

Lesson Objectives

- to plan and write a fact-based article
- to present facts and give details, examples, and opinions
- to learn to build sentences and paragraphs
- to learn to generate ideas to help your writing (Process Writing Step 1)

Materials
Support writing printouts from the Resource Bank (F)

Warm Up

Ask *When was the internet invented?* and elicit ideas. If students don't know, allow them to do a quick search to find out. (The internet was developed over a long time, but Tim Berners-Lee invented the World Wide Web in 1990.)

A Read the article. Check (✔) the topics and opinions about using the internet that the writer discusses.

- This lesson corresponds with the informational text in the Unit 1 nonfiction reading in the **Literacy Book**. Introduce students to the concept of a fact-based article. Ask where we usually find articles (newspapers, magazines, blogs, and websites) and elicit topics of articles students have read recently. Ask *Why do people write articles?* (to give facts and opinions)
- Have students look at the article title and the photo. Elicit ideas what it is about, then ask them to skim and find out.
- Have students look at the four options and check the facts they remember. Then have them read the article again to check their answers. Ask *Is the writer for or against the internet? How do we know?* See the **ETB** for further comprehension questions.

Answers
1; 3; 4

B Look at the structure of the article. Read and answer the questions.

- Look at the first question and discuss what the first paragraph does (it introduces the topic of the article). Then give students time to answer the rest of the questions. Allow them to work individually or in pairs. Check answers as a class.

Answers
1 *Four*; 1: introduction; 2: first main point (including facts); 3: second main point (including facts); 4: conclusion (including opinion) 2 facts 3 statistics and examples 4 a title taken from a quotation in the article; a photo

C Look at the language in the article. Read and complete the table.

- Look at the prompts in column 1 and highlight how they present the facts in the article.
- Have students complete the other headings by finding the prompts and noticing how they are used. Check answers as a class.

Answers
Presenting facts; Giving details; Giving opinions

- Ask students to turn to p. 140 to review ideas about **Process Writing Step 1: Generating Ideas** (see TB p. 211 for teaching notes). Students will need to do this step before they do D.

D Think and discuss. How do you and your friends use the internet? Complete the mind map with your ideas and research.

- This lesson practices the first stage of process writing: generating ideas. Tell students they are going to write about how and why they use the internet.
- Have students look at the question and the example answers. Ask them to do a Round Robin (see TB p. 20) to generate more ideas. Remind students of **Process Writing Step 1**. Tell them not to worry about facts or statistics for now.
- Have students write down the strongest ideas. Then ask them to find facts or statistics for each of their ideas by searching online.

Answers
Students' own answers

E Plan your article. Look at your ideas in D. Think of a title and make notes for each paragraph.

- This activity gets students to put into practice the brainstorming skills from **Process Writing Step 1** and the notes they made to plan their fact-based article.
- Have students plan their fact-based opinion article, using their ideas from D. Highlight the paragraph headings and refer students to the model in A for examples.
- Allow time for students to plan their article in note form. Encourage students to select information from D—they don't have to use everything.

F Now write your article. Include a photo.

- Have students write a draft of their articles in their notebooks, referring to their plan in E. They should read their drafts and make any corrections or improvements.
- Have students write their final versions neatly on paper. Alternatively, hand out the Support printouts.
- Have pairs read each other's article. Ask them to suggest at least one fact or opinion their friend could add.

Cool Down

Have students place their articles face up, then walk around and skim at least three. Ask them to look for the most interesting article with the most persuasive conclusion. Discuss their choices as a class.

Practice **Resource Bank:** Writing Game, *The Best Online* **Student's App:** Writing Practice

Lesson 6 Walkthrough Take the Stage / Talk About It

The second productive skills lesson is dedicated to speaking and functional language, and at this level is set on a single page. There are five *Take the Stage* lessons focusing on presentation skills, and five *Talk About It* lessons focusing on conversation skills. Each lesson starts with a video showing a child/children presenting or having a conversation, which helps to bring the language alive. If it isn't possible to watch the video during class time, encourage students to watch it at home beforehand (see The Flipped Classroom Approach TB p. 15).

A Video Showcase

The video sets the context for the lesson, showing students what they are working toward. It provides a natural context for the functional language as well as an opportunity to recycle some of the vocabulary and structures from the unit. A gist question gives them an initial reason to watch, and further comprehension questions are in the **ETB**.

Watch

The *Watch* callout encourages students to use all the clues available in the video to help figure out what makes the presentation/ conversation successful.

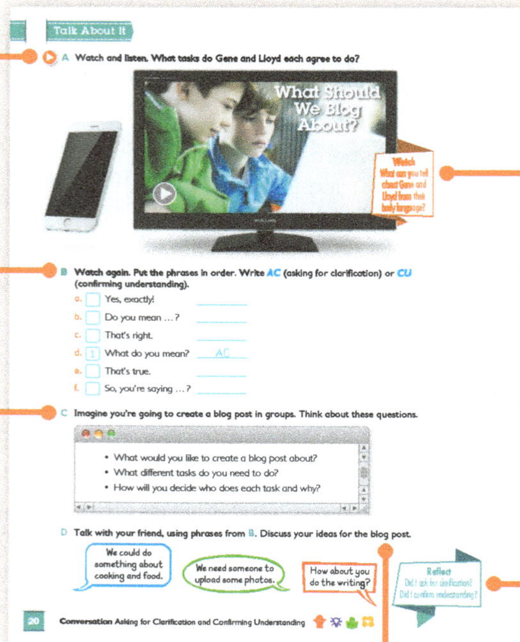

B Functional Language

Students work with the functional language from the video, which they can use in their own presentations/ conversations.

Reflect

As with the writing lessons, students are invited to give constructive feedback to their peers with the *Reflect* question. This analysis also helps them reflect on their own contributions and performance.

C Planning

Students are encouraged to brainstorm ideas and plan what they want to keep for the presentations.

For the conversations, students are encouraged to be spontaneous in Levels 5 and 6, so while some brainstorming and preparation activities are given, students are not expected to write a full dialogue.

D Production

Students have their conversations in pairs/ groups, or give their presentations to a group or the class using the language from Activity B. They should build on their notes and use the opportunity to pull together everything they have learned.

Talk About It

Lesson Objectives

- to prepare and have a conversation about a blog post
- to learn to ask for clarification and confirm understanding

Materials
Video

Warm Up

Give a riddle for the word *blog*, e.g. *Anyone can have one of these. It's online. It's a space to share your thoughts, opinions, and experiences. It can be about any topic. It's like an online diary.* Encourage students to shout out the answer. Then discuss what blogs students follow and what they like about them, or show them a blog you follow and talk about it.

A TB p. 239 **Watch and listen. What tasks do Gene and Lloyd each agree to do?**

- Tell students they are going to watch a video of a conversation between Gene and Lloyd about their blog. Have students guess what the two boys are going to blog about. Tell students to listen for the answer and watch the body language in the video.
- With books closed, play the video for students to check to see if they guessed correctly (they're going to blog about school lunches).
- Ask the comprehension question *What tasks do Gene and Lloyd each agree to do?* Have students remember what they heard. Play the video again and then check the answers. Ask further comprehension questions, e.g. *What are they going to ask Linda to do?* (search for information online and in the library).

Answers
Lloyd: make the lunch on video
Gene: write the blog post

B Watch again. Put the phrases in order. Write *AC* (asking for clarification) or *CU* (confirming understanding).

- Tell students that the phrases in this activity are all useful expressions when we are having a conversation. Have them read the phrases and look at the example number. Don't focus on *AC* or *CU* yet.
- Play the video again and have students order the phrases as they hear them. Play the video again and have students raise their hands when they hear a phrase. Pause the video and elicit the phrase and number.
- Point to the example *AC*. Ask *If we ask for clarification, what's the problem?* (We don't understand what someone said.) *If we want to confirm understanding, what do we do?* (We ask the other person if they've understood.) Give students time to go through each phrase and decide if it's asking for clarification or confirming understanding. Check answers as a class.
- Have students practice saying the suggestions and responses in a drill, encouraging them to use intonation to convey meaning.

Answers
1 d 2 a 3 f 4 c 5 b 6 e
Asking for clarification: Do you mean …?; *What do you mean?*; So, you're saying …?
Confirming understanding: Yes, exactly!; That's right.; That's true.

C Imagine you're going to create a blog post in groups. Think about these questions.

- Tell students they are going to discuss possible ideas for their own blog post to prepare for the conversation in D. Give students time to read and think about the questions individually and ask them to make simple notes.

Answers
Students' own answers

D Talk with your friend, using phrases from B. Discuss your ideas for the blog post.

- Project the phrases from B on the board using the TTL. Then demonstrate the example exchange with a confident student. Use the expressions from B to ask students for clarification and to confirm understanding.
- Have students discuss their ideas for the blog post in pairs. Remind them to use the phrases from B, to take turns, and to listen when their partner is speaking. Then ask pairs to join up with another pair to a have a new conversation and share ideas.
- Have students analyze their own performance and then check if their friend agrees.

Cool Down

Have students work in pairs or small groups and brainstorm ideas for a blog post. Ask them to make a note of their best ideas. Elicit ideas on the board and take a class vote on the best idea.

Practice **Student's App:** Speaking Skills Practice; Speaking Video

Lesson 7 Walkthrough Think It Over

The final lesson in the **Language Book** encourages students to reflect on what they have learned and what they need to work on. In Levels 5 and 6, students see different graphic organizers based on key strategies of Assessment for Learning: students reflect on their starting point, what they have learned, and what they need to learn or the next steps they can take to continue learning. By taking an active role in their learning, students can discover what works for them and their responses can help you, the teacher, to adapt future lessons to suit their needs or recommend targeted practice.

Graphic Organizers

There are five different graphic organizers: *3-2-1; Looking Back; My Planning Sheet; My Favorite Mistakes*; and *Monthly Goal Reflection*.

For each one, it's important that the students take time to reflect and respond for themselves on their progress or what they struggled with, rather than doing this as a class or group activity. Full sentences aren't necessary; the focus should be on the reflection and planning for ongoing learning.

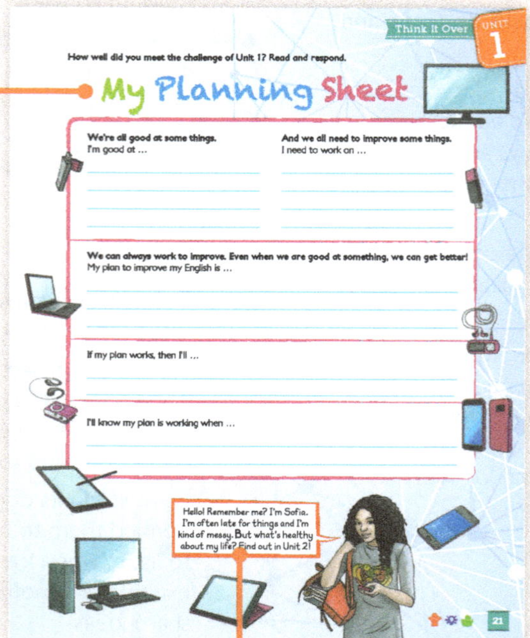
Think It Over

UNIT 1

How well did you meet the challenge of Unit 1? Read and respond.

My Planning Sheet

We're all good at some things.
I'm good at ...

And we all need to improve some things.
I need to work on ...

We can always work to improve. Even when we are good at something, we can get better!
My plan to improve my English is ...

If my plan works, then I'll ...

I'll know my plan is working when ...

Hello! Remember me? I'm Sofia. I'm often late for things and I'm kind of messy. But what's healthy about my life? Find out in Unit 2!

21

Looking Forward

At the end of every unit is a teaser question linking one of the characters with the next unit. At the start of the next unit in the **Language Book**, students can find this character in the picture dictionary scene and try to answer the question.

Put It Together

After Units 2, 4, 6, 8, and 10 there is a game that brings together the language and vocabulary of the two previous units. By setting the language in new contexts and adding in a fun and sometimes competitive element, students will want to play them again and again.

Think It Over

Lesson Objectives

- to review what has been learned in the unit
- to reflect on the unit and their own progress
- to think about learning strategies and how to continue learning at home

Warm Up

Review the unit with a quiz. Put students in pairs or small groups. Explain that you are going to ask questions and they must write down their answers. Allow them a minute to look through the unit. Then ask the following questions:

1 *What's Sofia doing in the big picture on pages 10 and 11?* (reading or sending a message)
2 *How many posters are there in the computer lab?* (three)
3 *Who's reading about Ghana on page 12?* (Daniel)
4 *Who's talking to Daniel about Ghana on page 12?* (Deepak)
5 *What time does the boy who wrote the blog post about Ghana wake up?* (4:30)
6 *What letters should a safe website start with?* (https)
7 *Sofia read a fake news story. What was it about?* (selfie shoes)
8 *What tip does Deepak give Sofia about spotting fake news?* (check for bad spelling or grammar)
9 *Gene and Lloyd are talking about a blog on page 20. What's the blog going to be about?* (school lunches)
10 *Who are they going to ask for help?* (Maria and Linda)

Go through the answers with the class.

How well did you meet the challenge of Unit 1? Read and respond.

My Planning Sheet

- Give students time to think about and discuss activities in the unit before they complete each section of the graphic organizer. Tell students they are going to review what they learned in the unit and what they need to improve at. Then they will make a plan outlining what they will do next in order to continue learning.
- Let them know that it's important that they think about themselves and not worry about what other people think or say, as different students will remember or enjoy different things. Tell them that it's OK if they found something difficult that their friend found easy—maybe their friend struggled with something they found easy. Explain that reflecting on what they've learned and what they enjoyed or found difficult can help them think about what to focus on next time or what they need to practice more or do again. It can help them learn about themselves.
- As a class, brainstorm a list or mind map of activities students have done and things they have learned. They can look back through the unit to help them. It is important that students lead this brainstorming session and that the ideas generated are things they remember rather than the things you want them to remember.
- Refer students to the graphic organizer on p. 21 and give an example for each prompt, e.g. *We're all good at some things. I'm good at asking for clarification. I need to work on my grammar because I make mistakes with simple and progressive forms.* Have students talk in pairs about the different sections. Encourage them to focus particularly on the second and third sections and to discuss what they can do to learn more about or how they can practice the areas they have problems with. Remind students about the online materials including the **Student's App**, but also encourage them to think of other ways they can practice English. Write some prompts on the board to support their conversation, e.g. *I'm going to …; I plan to …; I can try to …*
- When you feel they have enough ideas, have students work individually to complete the organizer. Remind them that they should write their own responses about themselves. Monitor and help as necessary. Look at what students are writing so you can tailor your classes and any additional practice to their needs.
- If you feel it is appropriate for your class, have students share their ideas with a friend. Encourage them to think together of how they can put their plans into practice. They can use phrases from the Talk About It lesson to clarify ideas and confirm understanding.
- Discuss the last two sections with the class before you have students write about them. Ask *How will you know if your plan works?* Elicit that students will be able to do some of the things they wrote about in the second section, which they need to improve on, without looking in their books. Ask students what they will do if their plan works. Encourage students to think of other areas they would like to practice. Remind them again about the **Student's App** and online materials. Then have students fill out the final two sections in the graphic organizer.

Looking Forward

Draw students' attention to the character at the bottom of the page. Have students say who she is and what they remember about her. (Sofia appears in Lesson 1, p. 10, and Lesson 4, p. 16. She wanted selfie shoes after reading and believing a fake news story.) Have students look at the speech bubble and make predictions about Sofia's lifestyle in Unit 2. Tell students they will find out the answer in Lesson 1 of the next unit.

Practice
Resource Bank: Unit Test
Student's App: Vocabulary and Grammar Review

Lesson 1 Walkthrough Get Ready to Read

There are two sections to this lesson: Section 1 is a Visible Thinking Routine (VTR) and Section 2 has pre-reading activities, which also preview the reading skill that will be explored in more detail in Lesson 4. The sections can be done in one lesson or spread over two lessons, e.g. allowing you to devote more time to the VTR and to do the pre-reading activities immediately before the reading text. In this lesson, there is no Cool Down activity suggested, but the **Enhanced Teacher's eBook (ETB)** has plenty of additional extension ideas if you choose to end the lesson after the pre-reading activities.

Warm Up activities are designed to generate interest in the topic and activate schema, thereby helping students make connections between their own experiences and the unit topic and readings. These activities are purposely not focused on vocabulary to give the **Literacy Book** a distinct first language (L1) feel.

In the **ETB**, there is also a **Two-Minute Review** that helps students make connections between the units.

A, B, C (& D) Visible Thinking Routine

The first three (or four) activities take students through the Visible Thinking Routine using the striking opening image to foster thoughtful and constructive discussion. Six different routines are used in Level 6, building on those seen in lower levels. The teaching notes give clear instructions for how to set them up and encourage participation without leading students to specific answers, including example conversations and prompts. See TB p. 19 for details on each VTR.

Unit Topic

The unit title is the same in the **Language Book** and the **Literacy Book**, with the topic explored in different ways across the two books.

Competency Icons

Competency icons indicate the areas covered in each lesson (see TB p. 19). The teaching notes tell you which activities address which competency.

Transition

A question linking the VTR discussion with the pre-reading activities is provided in the teaching notes. This could also be used as a Warm Up activity if you decide to do the pre-reading and reading on different days.

D, E (& F) Critical Thinking & Skill Preview

The pre-reading activities aim to prepare and motivate students for the reading text: fiction or nonfiction. The first activity focuses on critical thinking and discussion, and the second gives a preview of the reading skill that will be fully explored with the second text.

Literacy

Get Ready to Read

Lesson Objectives

- to activate prior knowledge about communication
- to guide inquiry and deepen understanding through a Think, Pair, Share Visible Thinking Routine (VTR)
- to preview the reading skill of understanding chronology

Materials
VTR printout from the Resource Bank (A, B, C)

Warm Up

Do a guided visualization (see TB p. 21) before students discuss the picture. Say *You're at a party. Where is it? Who are the guests? What are they doing? What can you hear/smell?* Encourage students to share their ideas with the class.

Think, Pair, Share

A Look at the picture. What is happening? Think about it.

- This VTR encourages students to explore the image of communication and the factors that influence this. Start by asking students *What do you see?* and give them up to a minute to look at the picture and think silently. Provide vocabulary where necessary.
- Have students brainstorm what they can see in the picture. Encourage them to use adjectives such as colors, shapes, and feelings, as well as nouns and verbs.
- Ask students to think silently about what is happening in the picture and why there are words on the page. Tell them to cross their arms when they have thought of some ideas. You could use the Think, Pair, Share printout.

B Discuss with your partner.

- Divide the class into pairs and have students share their ideas about the picture. Encourage them to discuss any questions they might have and to think of possible answers together. Write some prompts on the board to help them with their discussions, e.g. *Why do you think that?*; *I agree / don't agree because …*; *I think that too!*; *I don't think so because …*; *I like that idea!* Monitor and support students as they discuss their ideas.

C Share your ideas with the class.

- Ask pairs to decide which two ideas they would like to share with the class and think about how they will explain them.
- Invite pairs to share their ideas about the picture with the class. Encourage students to use *we*, as they are talking on behalf of their partner, too. When you ask a student a question, encourage other students to say if they agree or disagree. Allow the class to lead the discussion.
- Keep a record of students' ideas from the VTR to revisit in the Think Together lesson.

Here's an example of this part of the routine.

Teacher: What do you think is happening here?
Student A: We think they're friends planning a party.
Teacher: Why do you think that?
Student B: Because they're smiling and thinking about party food and who they'll invite.
Student C: We disagree. We think they're talking about a party they went to.
Teacher: That's interesting. So they are remembering something they did in the past?
Student D: Yes, that's why the word "experience" is there. They're talking about an experience they had.
Student E: No, I think they're talking about an experience they want to have. They're dreaming about the perfect party!
Student F: Yes, they want a good experience, good location, and noise at their party!

Transition

Ask *How are the friends communicating in the picture? Are they communicating face-to-face or online? Are they using body language to communicate, too? Would they do something differently if they were texting or talking on the phone?*

D Think and write. What different ways do we communicate with each other? Make a list.

- Ask students to think about how they communicate with their friends, family, and teachers. Brainstorm a few ideas on the board.
- Have students write their own list. Then have them compare their list with others in groups.

Suggested Answers
writing, speaking, drawing, sign language, body language / gestures, email, text messages, instant messaging, blogs, video calls

E Read and sequence the events.

- This activity previews the skill of understanding chronology. Tell students they are going to order the events of a story. Have them read the sentences to get an idea of the plot. Then have them work with a partner to order the events by noticing the time sequencers. Check answers as a class.
- Discuss what the story is about and what they think might happen to Helen and her parents.

Answers
4; 1; 3; 2

Now read **Urgent Message**

Lesson 2 Walkthrough Reading 1

The reading lessons develop literacy in English and aim to foster a love of reading, encouraging students to become lifelong readers and learners. Specific language is sometimes slightly above level because reasearch shows that with the right support, this sort of challenge significantly improves overall reading skills.

Text Type

Every unit has one fictional and one nonfictional text, spread over 10 pages. Texts are laid out to emulate first language (L1) / ESL materials, allowing students to draw on all the relevant contextual clues to support their understanding. Nonfictional texts provide an opportunity for students to learn new concepts and broaden their view of the world. With a realistic look and feel based on websites, articles and nonfiction books, these types of texts often appeal to reluctant readers.

International English

Regular *International English* features highlight differences between American and British English, helping raise awareness of different Englishes around the world. Audio for these words is available on the Tap & Teach Lessons (TTL).

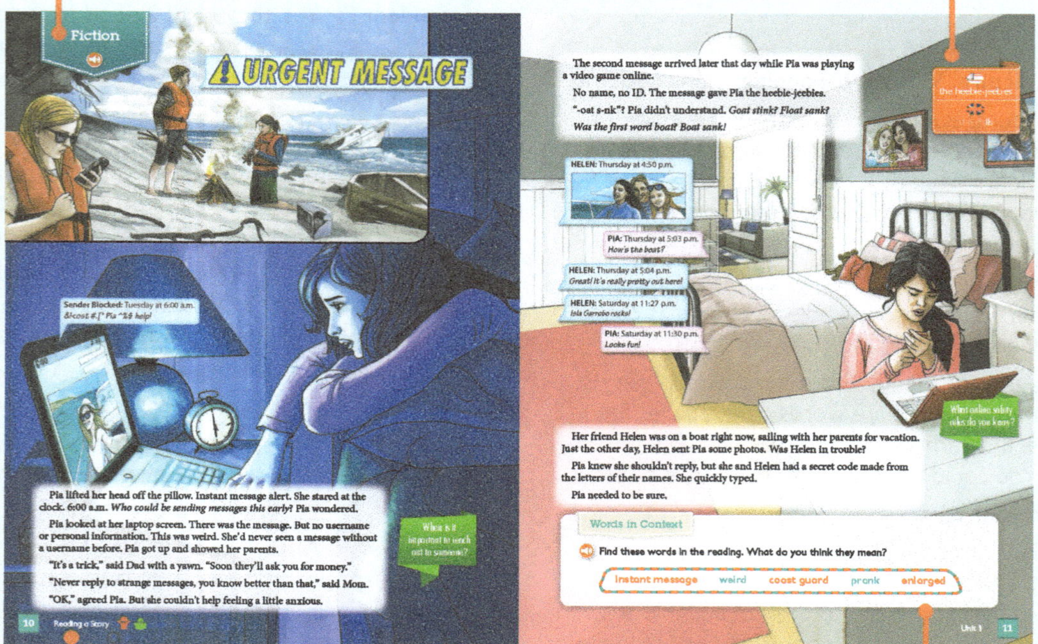

Genre

The footer tells you the genre of text, highlighting the wide variety of text types.

Words in Context

See the Walkthrough notes for lesson 5, TB p. 56.

Three-Stage Reading Approach

The teaching notes are broken into three stages, allowing students to read and work with the text on different levels and with different criteria (see TB p. 13). The main comprehension activities are in the next lesson.

First Reading: focuses on engagement and understanding the main idea. You can use prediction questions to stimulate curiosity and play the audio, with sound effects and character voices, to help set the scene and motivate students to want to understand the details.

Second Reading: encourages students to read more critically, using the embedded comments/questions as a guide. *Text Focus* comments embedded in blue in the texts highlight features of the genre so that students can recognize these traits in other similar texts.

Third Reading: takes students beyond the text to respond in different ways, e.g. perform a role-play, summarize it, or think about the characters' feelings.

Fiction: *Urgent Message—Story*

Lesson Objectives

- to read a story about an urgent message
- to make a personal connection to the reading

Materials
Audio Tracks 3 and 4; slips of paper (Cool Down)

Warm Up

Write the title on the board, leaving blanks for the vowels: *_rg_nt M_ss_g_*. Have pairs race to find the missing vowels. Ask *Have you ever received an urgent message? What was it?*

TRACK 3 TB p. 229 Reading Approach

First Reading: Engage with the Text

- Use the Story Player on the TTL to show the story, without the sound. Ask students to notice the title, text, and characters and to make predictions about the story.
- Play the audio and have students follow along.
- Pause the audio at the end of p. 11 for students to predict if the message was from Helen.
- Ensure students have read the whole story before looking at the Words in Context.

TRACK 4 TB p. 229 Words in Context

- Give students time to find and highlight each word.
- Have them identify the parts of speech, and elicit how they know (by looking at the structure of the sentences and at the form of the words themselves).
- Write these strategies on the board for students to use with the words: *pictures, synonyms, surrounding words and sentences, separate parts of word, world knowledge, word families*. Have students discuss the words in pairs.
- Remind students that different words will require different combinations of strategies to figure them out. Some key words appear more than once in the story, so students should read all the instances to help them.

instant message (p. 10, noun) The next sentences show the time and that it is early. Strategies to use: pictures, surrounding words and sentences, separate parts of word, world knowledge of the internet

weird (p. 10, adjective) A later sentence contains a synonym, *strange*. The sentence before says *But no username or personal information*. Strategies to use: surrounding sentences, world knowledge of the information messages usually contain, synonyms

coast guard (p. 12 / p. 15, noun) The sentences on p. 12 and 15 show this is someone or something you *contact* for help when it is *urgent*. Strategies to use: pictures, surrounding words and sentences, separate parts of word

prank (p. 13, noun) A previous paragraph (p. 12) has a synonym, *joke*. Strategy to use: synonyms

enlarged (p. 14, verb) This has the word *large* in it. The end of the sentence explains the result of the action (*looked closely at the details*). Strategies to use: word families, surrounding words and sentences, world knowledge of viewing images on a device

- Check each word in turn to elicit the meaning and how they know. Play the audio to practice the pronunciation.

Practice **Student's App:** Story Player

International English

Elicit what *the heebie-jeebies* (American English) and *the chills* (British English) mean. Ask *Is it a pleasant feeling?* (no) *How does it make us feel?* (uncomfortable, scared) Mime feeling a shiver down your spine to make this clearer. Ask *Which phrase will you use?* Tell students they can use British or American English, but they must be consistent.

Second Reading: Analyze the Text and Features

- Play the audio or have students read the story again to consolidate their understanding.
- Ask questions to check comprehension, e.g. *Who is sending the weird messages?* (Helen) See **ETB** for more questions.
- Discuss the questions in the green boxes. Then look at the text focus.
  - **Critical Thinking** (p. 10): *When is it important to reach out to someone?* Ask students who Pia reaches out to (her parents). Discuss how they respond.
  - **Personalization** (p. 11): *What online safety rules do you know?* Ask students to scan the story and find advice for online safety. Brainstorm more rules with the class.
  - **Critical Thinking** (p. 15): *What would you do to communicate if you were stuck on an island?* Have groups think of three possible ways of communicating. Elicit ideas on the board. Ask students to discuss which ways are the most effective and which are the least.
  - **Text Focus** (p. 13): *Who is the protagonist, or main character, in this story?* (Pia)

Third Reading: Interact with the Text

- Tell students they are going to do an interview role-play in groups of three (the interviewer, Pia, and Helen). They are going to ask and answer questions after being reunited.
- Give time for the interviewer to think of questions to ask and for "Pia" and "Helen" to revise the story. They can use facts from the story but also improvise. Then have students carry out their interview.

Cool Down

Give each student a slip of paper as an exit pass. Have them write a sentence describing what they liked about the story. They should give you the paper as they leave the classroom.

Lesson 3 Walkthrough Explore the Reading

This lesson is dedicated to detailed comprehension, analysis, and discussion of the text on the previous pages.

A Reading Comprehension

The first activity provides heads-down comprehension questions and students are often directed to write full sentences or provide evidence from the text for their answers.

Students should be encouraged to use strategies they have learned, such as scanning for key words or using pictures or headings, rather than re-reading the whole text.

B/C Post-Reading Discussion & SEL Competency

Fictional texts contain a social and emotional message which is explored in this lesson, often through discussion and reflection. The teaching notes provide ideas and further questions to help develop this discussion. (See TB p. 17)

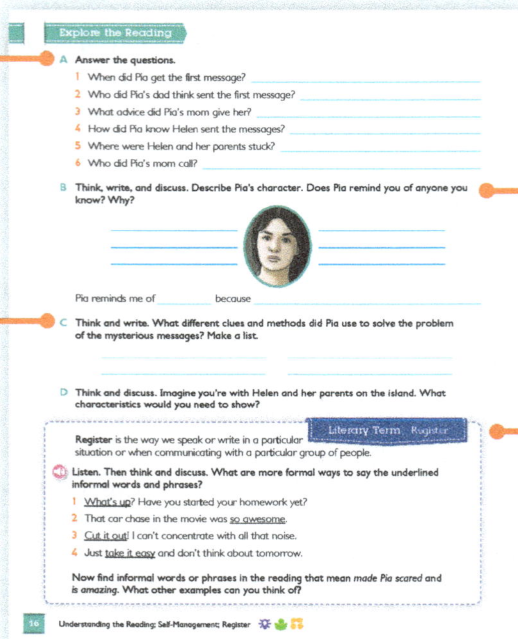

Explore the Reading

A Answer the questions.

1 When did Pia get the first message?
2 Who did Pia's dad think sent the first message?
3 What advice did Pia's mom give her?
4 How did Pia know Helen sent the messages?
5 Where were Helen and her parents stuck?
6 Who did Pia's mom call?

B Think, write, and discuss. Describe Pia's character. Does Pia remind you of anyone you know? Why?

Pia reminds me of ______ because ______

C Think and write. What different clues and methods did Pia use to solve the problem of the mysterious messages? Make a list.

D Think and discuss. Imagine you're with Helen and her parents on the island. What characteristics would you need to show?

Literary Term Register

Register is the way we speak or write in a particular situation or when communicating with a particular group of people.

Listen. Then think and discuss. What are more formal ways to say the underlined informal words and phrases?

1 What's up? Have you started your homework yet?
2 That car chase in the movie was so awesome.
3 Cut it out! I can't concentrate with all that noise.
4 Just take it easy and don't think about tomorrow.

Now find informal words or phrases in the reading that mean *made Pia scared* and *is amazing*. What other examples can you think of?

16 Understanding the Reading: Self-Management; Register

B/C Text Analysis

Further analysis of the text encourages critical thinking, critical literacy, and often includes opportunities for personalization.

Literary Terms

Building on the work on phonics and spelling in earlier levels, literacy is further developed through the section Literary Terms, looking at devices and structures writers use to convey their ideas. Having an awareness of these terms can help students analyze and understand a text. This section appears in one of the readings only. (See TB p. 13)

A **Cool Down** activity in the teaching notes helps bring the lesson to a close, often with a game, summarizing activity, or collaborative task.

Explore the Reading

Lesson Objectives

- to understand and analyze *Urgent Message* through reading comprehension activities
- to explore the SEL competency of self-management by displaying grit, determination, and perseverance
- to make a personal connection to the reading

Materials
Audio Track 5

Warm Up

Write the 5 Ws and 1 H on the board: *Who, What, Why, When, Where, How.* Write an example question: *Who are the characters in Urgent Message?* and elicit the answer. Then have pairs form questions about *Urgent Message* with the other question words. Have a class quiz.

A Answer the questions.

- Have students read the questions once and check they understand them. Then give them time to scan the story for the answers.
- Put students in pairs or small groups to compare their answers. Check answers as a class.

Answers
1 on Tuesday at 6.00 a.m. 2 someone who was playing a trick 3 never reply to strange messages 4 She sent a message in their secret code and Helen replied with the correct response. 5 Isla Violin (between Isla Garrobo and Isla Punta Zacate) 6 the coast guard.

B Think, write, and discuss. Describe Pia's character. Does Pia remind you of anyone you know? Why?

- Elicit an adjective to describe Pia and why the word describes her. Then ask the questions and elicit answers.
- Have students brainstorm more adjectives in pairs or small groups. Discuss their ideas as a class, encouraging them to give reasons.

Suggested Answers
Pia is determined/perservering/resourceful/intelligent/logical/reliable/loyal/thoughtful/clever/practical
Pia reminds me of … because … [Students' own answers]

C Think and write. What different clues and methods did Pia use to solve the problem of the mysterious messages? Make a list.

- Encourage students to think what actions Pia took to solve the problem of the mysterious messages. Ask *What different clues did she use? What were her methods?* Give them time to look through the story and make notes.
- Put students in small groups to compare their answers. Then have a Group Time discussion (see TB p. 21) on how effective Pia's methods were. Encourage them to think about what they would have done differently.

Suggested Answers
Pia used the following clues: incomplete messages, Helen's previous messages and photos, their secret code, online maps and information
She used the following methods: logical thinking, problem-solving, investigation, experimentation, math

D Think and discuss. Imagine you're with Helen and her parents on the island. What characteristics would you need to show?

- Students are going to connect the reading to their own lives. This activity encourages students to explore the SEL competency of self-management: displaying grit, determination, and perseverance.
- Do a guided visualization (see TB p. 21) to stimulate ideas for the discussion. Say *You're on Isla Violin with Helen and her parents. What are Helen and her parents doing? How are they feeling? How do you feel?* Then ask *What characteristics would you need to show if you were on that island?* Elicit examples, e.g. *I'd have to show patience. I'd have to be positive.*
- Have students discuss the characteristics in pairs. Monitor and provide language help when needed. Make a note of good ideas to share with the class.

Literary Term: Register

TRACK 5 TB p. 229 **Listen. Then think and discuss. What are more formal ways to say the underlined informal words and phrases?**

- Draw students' attention to the sentences. Play the audio once and ask if they would use the underlined words with someone they didn't know well. Elicit that they wouldn't because they're informal. Have them think about similar words and situations when they would use different phrases when speaking in L1.
- Put students in groups to think of more formal ways to say each phrase. Elicit ideas and write them on the board.

Now find informal words or phrases in the reading that mean *made Pia scared* and *is amazing*. What other examples can you think of?

- Have students scan the reading to find the informal words and phrases. Then ask students to compare answers in pairs. Check answers as a class.

Suggested Answers
1 How are you? / How are you doing? 2 very exciting
3 Please stop it! 4 relax / calm down
From the reading: made Pia scared = gave Pia the heebie-jeebies; is amazing = rocks

Cool Down

Have students work in pairs to write a newspaper headline for the story. Remind them that headlines include key information only and are in present forms. Give an example: *Firefighter saves dog from burning shed.* Invite students to share their headlines.

Practice **Resource Bank:** Literary Term Printout
Student's App: Reading Practice; Literary Term Practice

Lesson 4 Walkthrough Get Ready to Read

This lesson sets up the second reading, with focus on a reading skill and pre-reading activities to activate schema and create interest in the text.

A/B Reading Skill Focus

Using an inductive approach and building on skills they have learned in earlier levels, the first activity provides an opportunity for students to work with the reading skill in a short context. Sometimes drawing on texts read previously, students will actively notice what they have done, before reading the description in the *Skills Box*. Having students use the skill without thinking too much will encourage them to draw on reading skills from L1. At this level, reading skills include: understanding chronology; analyzing and evaluating; understanding author's word choice; making inferences; recognizing genres; understanding denotation and connotation; identifying text and graphic features; recognizing story structure; identifying internal and external conflict; and summarizing readings.

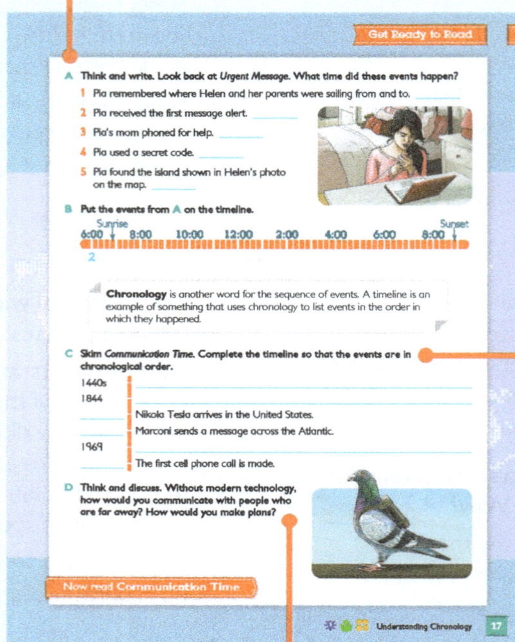
Get Ready to Read

A Think and write. Look back at *Urgent Message*. What time did these events happen?

1 Pia remembered where Helen and her parents were sailing from and to. ______
2 Pia received the first message alert. ______
3 Pia's mom phoned for help. ______
4 Pia used a secret code. ______
5 Pia found the island shown in Helen's photo on the map. ______

B Put the events from A on the timeline.

Sunrise 6:00 8:00 10:00 12:00 2:00 4:00 6:00 8:00 Sunset
2

Chronology is another word for the sequence of events. A timeline is an example of something that uses chronology to list events in the order in which they happened.

C Skim *Communication Time*. Complete the timeline so that the events are in chronological order.

1440s ______
1844 ______
______ Nikola Tesla arrives in the United States.
______ Marconi sends a message across the Atlantic.
1969 ______
______ The first cell phone call is made.

D Think and discuss. Without modern technology, how would you communicate with people who are far away? How would you make plans?

Now read Communication Time

Understanding Chronology 17

B/C Reading Skill Practice

In this activity, students put into practice the reading skill from Activity A. This is often related to the next reading. In this way, they work with the skill more consciously and their interest is piqued about the text to come.

C/D Pre-Reading Discussion

A discussion question activates schema for the next reading, often encouraging personal reflection, or for students to express an opinion before having it challenged by the text.

Get Ready to Read

Lesson Objectives

- to activate prior knowledge about the history of communication
- to practice the reading skill of understanding chronology
- to review the reading skill of skimming

Warm Up

Write *Inventors* on the board. Have students work in groups to brainstorm as many inventors as they can in two minutes. Discuss as a class, encouraging them to say what they know about the inventors and their inventions.

A Think and write. Look back at *Urgent Message*. What time did these events happen?

- This lesson practices the skill of understanding chronology, which students previewed on page 9.
- Before students do the activity, ask them to spend 30 seconds thinking about the story *Urgent Message*. Ask them to visualize the main events in the order that they happened.
- Draw students' attention to the events and ask them to find out what time each one took place. Do the first one as the example to make sure students understand they need to check the time on the messages and the laptop. Check answers as a class.

Answers
1 6:30 p.m. 2 6:00 a.m. 3 6:40 p.m. 4 3:25 p.m. 5 6:40 p.m.

B Put the events from A on the timeline.

- Project the timeline on the board if you're using the TTL. Point to the example and explain that it refers to the first message Pia received.
- Have students add the rest of the events on the timeline. Check answers by asking students what happened next and at what time.
- Then have students read the information in the skills box. Discuss why it's important to understand chronology. Point out that a writer doesn't always present the events in a linear (chronological) way. The plot can move backwards and forwards in time. In *Urgent Message*, the writer does this with Pia's and Helen's messages. Discuss why the writer does this. (so that the clues are revealed slowly; so that we follow Pia's train of thought and solve the problem with her; to keep us interested). Point out that informational texts, such as *Communication Time*, usually present events in chronological order.

C Skim *Communication Time*. Complete the timeline so that the events are in chronological order.

- Ask the students to look at the pictures in *Communication Time* and predict what the reading is about.
- Draw their attention to the timeline in C. Ask *What are the differences between the two timelines on this page?* (one is horizontal and the other is vertical; one has times and the other has years) Have students skim the text to complete the missing information.
- To check answers, have students read out a year and the corresponding event. Alternatively, project the answers on the board if you're using the TTL.

Answers
1440s The printing press is invented. 1844 The first message is sent along telegraph wires by Samuel Morse using his code. 1884 Nikola Tesla arrives in the United States. 1901 Marconi sends a message across the Atlantic. 1969 Scientists create a way of sending messages from one computer to another. 1973 The first cell phone call is made.

D Think and discuss. Without modern technology, how would you communicate with people who are far away? How would you make plans?

- Draw students' attention to the questions. Establish what modern technology refers to (phones, cell phones, internet, computers, etc.) and elicit an example answer to the questions.
- Have students brainstorm more ideas in groups using the Option Explosion routine (see TB p. 21). Encourage them to think about what they know about how people lived in the past and to use their imagination. Monitor and provide language help when needed.
- Then bring the class together and have students share their ideas.

Suggested Answers
Communicate: send letters by post; ask people travelling to that place to deliver a letter; Morse code; send telegraphs; use homing pigeons; fire and smoke signals
Make plans: make plans a long time in advance by writing letters or discussing them with people face-to-face; let other people know by word of mouth; use a diary or calendar to write dates down so as not to forget

Cool Down

Have students draw a timeline for "yesterday" or a special day they have had recently. Ask them to include at least four events and the rough time when each one happened. Prompt them to include *sunrise* and *sunset* as in the timeline in B. They should add key words or small drawings for each event. In groups, they take turns to show their timeline for their friends to guess and say what happened.

Now read **Communication Time**

Lesson 5 Walkthrough Reading 2

The second reading lesson follows the same structure as the first, and will be a fictional or nonfictional text depending on the first text. As before, multiple exposure and work with the text, including audio and visual support, helps develop strong literacy skills leading towards autonomy in reading.

Both the fictional and nonfictional texts can also be accessed through the Story Player in the TTL and the **Student's App** on **Navio** (see TB p. 14).

Photos and Illustrations

Nonfictional texts make use of photos or realistic illustrations wherever appropriate and are graphically dynamic, providing opportunities to develop skills in identifying hierarchy and reading paths.

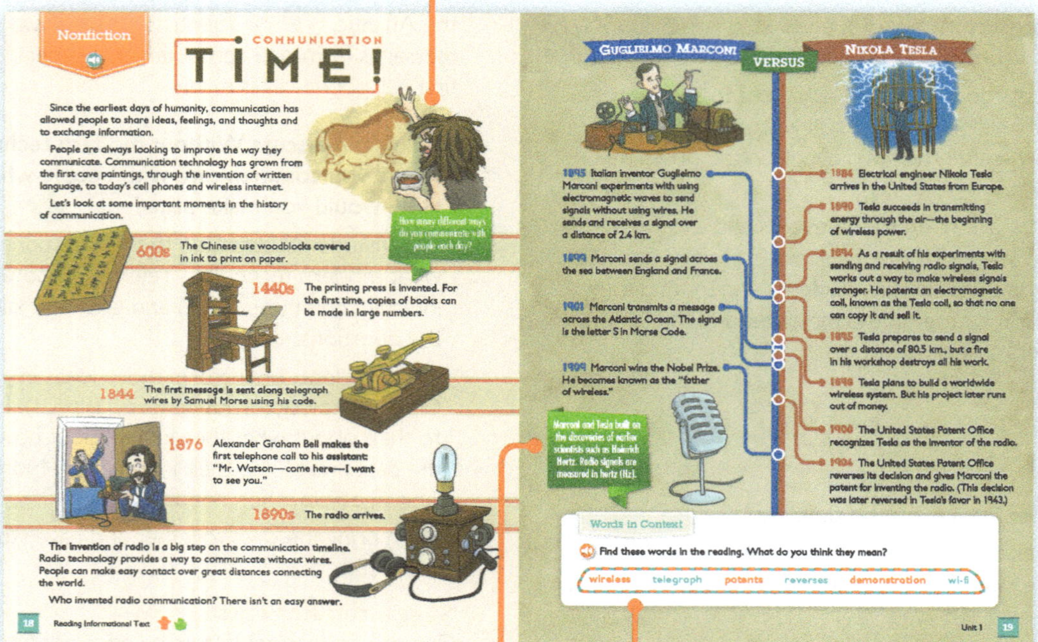

Text and Feature Analysis

Every text, both fictional and nonfictional, has several comments/questions in colored boxes to help guide students to take a critical approach to reading. These are dealt with in turn in the Second Reading stage of the lesson, and the teaching notes provide further ideas to prompt discussion on the different themes such as a Language Focus, Personalization, and Making Connections (e.g. CLIL/SEL).

Words in Context

This activity focuses on building strategies to deal with unknown words in a text, which is an important skill for a competent reader. These are not words to be learned or pre-taught. In Levels 5 and 6, the teaching notes encourage students to experiment actively with different strategies and to recognize that different texts/words will need different strategies. Each word is recorded in isolation on the audio.

Nonfiction: *Communication Time*—Informational Text

Lesson Objectives

- to read an informational text about the history of communication
- to make a personal connection to the reading

Materials
Audio Tracks 6 and 7; online photos of prehistoric cave paintings (Warm Up)

Warm Up

Show students pictures of cave paintings. Discuss what they know about them. Ask *How old are they?* (prehistoric) *How did people draw them?* (using natural paints, carving the stone) *Is this a form of communication?* (yes)

TRACK 6 TB p. 229 Reading Approach

First Reading: Read and Engage

- Have students look quickly at pp. 18-21 and notice when the timeline starts (600s) and ends (2040, the future). Have them point to where they are now on the timeline.
- Play the audio once and have students listen and follow in their books. Then ask students to share what facts they already knew and what facts surprised them.
- Have students look at the Words in Context.

TRACK 7 TB p. 230 Words in Context

- Play the audio to familiarize students with the words and practice the pronunciation.
- Brainstorm strategies with the class and write on the board including but not limited to: *pictures; prefixes/suffixes; word families; surrounding words and sentences; world knowledge; the result or the trigger of an action verb; L1 cognates; remembering other contexts*
- Divide the class into pairs. Assign two words to each pair. Have students find and discuss their words.
- Have pairs get together with two other pairs (groups of six, so all the words are covered) to explain their words to each other, saying which strategies they used.

wireless (p. 18, adjective) There are two explanations: *without wires* (p. 18) and *without using wires* (p. 19). The suffix *less* means *without*. Strategies to use: prefixes/suffixes; surrounding sentences

telegraph (p. 18, noun) There is a picture of one. The prefix *tele* means *distant*. Strategies to use: pictures; world knowledge of Morse code; prefixes/suffixes

patents (p. 19. verb) The last part of the sentence says *so no one can copy and sell it*. Strategies to use: surrounding sentences; the result or the trigger of an action verb

reverses (p. 19, verb) The sentences explain that first Tesla is decided as the inventor of the radio, then Marconi, then Tesla again. Students may already know *reverse* to mean *go backwards*. Strategies to use: surrounding sentences; remembering other contexts

demonstration (p. 20, noun) The previous sentence gives an example: *John Logie Baird sends a picture wirelessly.* Strategies to use: word families; surrounding sentences

wi-fi (p. 20, noun) The previous sentence gives an explanation: *wireless computer network*. Strategies to use: surrounding words; possible L1 cognate

- Bring the class together to discuss which strategies worked or didn't work.

Second Reading: Analyze the Text and Features

- Have students read the text silently. Allow them to jump from date to date, reading the information in any order. Ask students to decide which date in the timeline is the most important and why. Have students share their ideas.
- Ask questions to check comprehension: *Why was the radio an important invention?* (it allowed people to communicate over great distances) *Why isn't it easy to decide who invented the radio?* (because both Marconi and Tesla worked hard on this invention). There are more questions in the **ETB.**
- Discuss the questions in the green boxes as a class.
  - **Personalization** (p. 18): *How many different ways do you communicate with people each day?* Elicit the different ways that students communicated with others the day before. Ask students how they prefer to communicate with their friends and with their family? Why?
  - **Fact** (p. 19): Read the fact and check what students know about radio waves.
  - **Fact** (p. 20): Read the fact and discuss what students know about the Titanic and how it sank.
  - **Personalization** (p. 21): *How has communication technology changed for you in the past five years?* Ask students what technology they use to communicate with others. Then, ask what they used five years ago. What are the similarities and differences? Alternatively, have them write a paragraph on this for homework.

Third Reading: Interact with the Text

- Have students work in pairs to choose an era from the text and compare the communication tools people had then to tools that are available today. Encourage students to use a Venn diagram to make notes.
- Have pairs compare notes in groups. Prompt them to discuss the pros and cons of each era. Elicit ideas.

Cool Down

Put students in pairs or small groups and ask them to make a prediction about future communication technology. Allow students to be creative and accept all ideas. Invite them to present their ideas to the class.

Practice Student's App: Story Player

Lesson 6 Walkthrough Explore the Reading

This lesson follows the same structure as Lesson 3, with comprehension, analysis, and discussion activities related to the second reading.

A Reading Comprehension

The heads-down comprehension questions include many activities similar to tasks students might see in an exam. The variety of tasks ensures students are engaged and challenged throughout the course.

Explore the Reading

A Read and write *Fact* or *Opinion*.

1 Marconi's inventions were the best. Opinion
2 John Logie Baird's demonstration of television was in 1926. ______
3 Tesla was the world's greatest inventor. ______
4 Television is more fun than radio. ______
5 The first signal across the Atlantic was sent in 1901. ______
6 In 1973, the first cell phone call was made. ______
7 Radio is the world's most useful invention. ______

B Complete the graphic organizer with the main idea and details from *Communication Time*.

C Think and write. Use the graphic organizer in B. Write a paragraph explaining what the reading is about.

D Think and discuss. Has communication technology made our lives better? Why or why not?

22 Understanding the Reading: Science Link

B/C Text Analysis & Practice

Further practice of the reading skill is provided, where appropriate, and often students are asked for their opinion or a personal response, which encourages them to engage more deeply with the text, whether fictional or nonfictional.

C/D Post-Reading Discussion & CLIL Focus

The nonfictional texts are used as a springboard for a cross-curricular link, giving students the opportunity to pull together knowledge from across their learning journey. This helps to bring the language alive in a real-world context. The **ETB** has more ideas for exploiting this link. (See TB p. 18)

Explore the Reading

Lesson Objectives

- to understand and analyze *Communication Time* through reading comprehension activities
- to practice identifying facts and opinions
- to review the reading skill of identifying main idea and details
- to learn through CLIL (science): exploring the impacts of communication technology
- to make a personal connection to the text

Materials
Audio Track 6 (optional, WU)

Warm Up

Review the reading by playing *What's the Next Word* (see TB p. 27). You can either play the audio or do this orally, selecting sentences from the reading.

A Read and write *Fact* or *Opinion*.

- Tell students they are going to identify facts and opinions. Read the example with the class and elicit why it is an opinion.
- Then ask them to read the sentences and decide if they contain a fact or an opinion.
- Check answers by reading out the sentence and ask students to raise their arms in the air for *Fact*. If it's an *Opinion*, have them put their hands on their head.

Answers
1 Opinion 2 Fact 3 Opinion 4 Opinion 5 Fact
6 Fact 7 Opinion

B Complete the graphic organizer with the main idea and details from *Communication Time*.

- Ask students to think what the main idea of the *Communication Time* is. To guide them, ask *Why did the writer write the text? What was the main idea he wanted to share?* Accept different answers.
- Then elicit an example of a detail. Give students time to look back through the text and choose four details they would like to add to the graphic organizer. They can do this individually or in pairs.
- To check answers, have students compare their details in pairs or small groups. Monitor and check.

Suggested Answers
Main Idea: People are always looking to improve the way they communicate
Details: Communication technology has gotten faster over time. / Technology started with paper in the 600s and went to the internet in the 1970s. / Different inventors developed new technologies. / More and more people are using social media

Practice **Student's App:** Reading Practice

C Think and write. Use the graphic organizer in B. Write a paragraph explaining what the reading is about.

- Tell students they are going to write a few sentences to explain what the reading is about. Ask them to imagine they are writing the paragraph for someone who hasn't read the text.
- Use one of the students' graphic organizers in B to demonstrate how they can combine the information in a paragraph. You can do this orally. Say *Communication Time is about … One of the most important moments in the history of communication was … Another important invention was …*
- Give students time to write their paragraphs. Monitor and provide language help when needed.
- When students finish, ask them to exchange paragraphs with a friend and compare them.

D Think and discuss. Has communication technology made our lives better? Why or why not?

- Students are going to use their critical thinking skills to discuss whether communication technology has made our lives better. This draws on the CLIL science area of the impact of communication technology.
- Draw students' attention to the questions. Set a time limit for them to discuss the questions using a Round Robin routine (see TB p. 20). Encourage them to think about their own experiences as well as how people from other backgrounds and of different ages might feel. Prompt them to think about areas such as agriculture, medicine, education, entertainment.
- When the time is up, ask groups to reach a conclusion: is life better or worse with the communication technology we have? Take a class vote and elicit reasons from individual students.

Cool Down

Play a memory game. Ask students to spend a few seconds going over the important events and dates in *Communication Time!* Then put them in pairs and ask them to write two questions related to these facts. Explain they are going to test another pair. When they are ready, group pairs of students. They take turns asking their questions and answering them with closed books. If they finish quickly, they can continue making up questions orally.

Lesson 7 Walkthrough Think Together

This last lesson in the **Literacy Book** brings the unit full circle, uniting the two readings and the overarching theme to further develop critical literacy.

Key Concept Question

The lesson stems from the Key Concept Question that brings together the concepts explored in the reading texts. As students work through the activities, they will be considering the question; it is not necessary to answer it at the start.

A Text Comparison

The first activity is a text-to-text comparison, reviewing and comparing what they read in each.

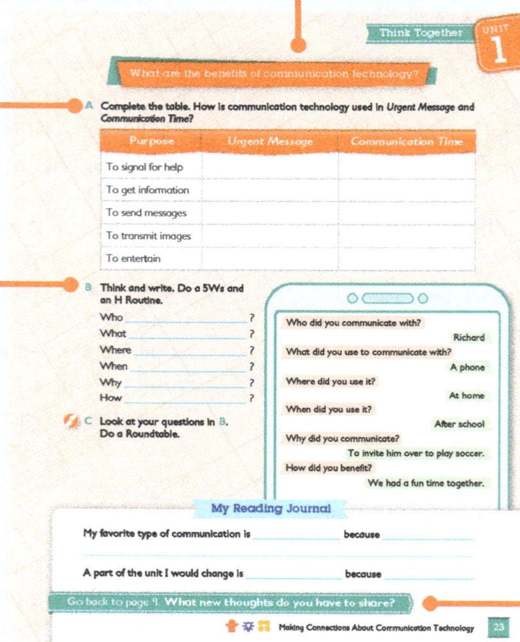

Think Together UNIT 1

What are the benefits of communication technology?

A Complete the table. How is communication technology used in *Urgent Message* and *Communication Time*?

Purpose	*Urgent Message*	*Communication Time*
To signal for help		
To get information		
To send messages		
To transmit images		
To entertain		

B Think and write. Do a 5Ws and an H Routine.

Who ______?
What ______?
Where ______?
When ______?
Why ______?
How ______?

C Look at your questions in B. Do a Roundtable.

My Reading Journal

My favorite type of communication is ______ because ______

A part of the unit I would change is ______ because ______

Go back to page 9. What new thoughts do you have to share?

Making Connections About Communication Technology 23

B/C Speaking Routine

These activities are designed to promote discussion with a text-to-world outlook, helping students compare, contrast, and draw conclusions for the key concept question. A cooperative learning routine helps ensure all students participate and creates an opportunity for purposeful communication and collaboration. (See TB p. 20)

My Reading Journal

In the Reading Journal, students give a personalized response to the readings and reflect on the unit as a whole. Through this self-reflection, students are empowered to guide their learning and motivated to participate actively in the process.

Finally, students are directed to return to the image at the start of the unit and revisit the VTR with new ideas and ways of thinking. This allows students to revise opinions and ideas and also serves to show students how much they have learned.

Think Together

Lesson Objectives

- to make connections between the readings
- to explore the key concept: What are the benefits of communication technology?
- to reflect on the unit and provide personal thoughts and opinions

Warm Up

Have students look back at the different types of communication in *Communication Time*. Ask how else Pia and Helen could have communicated. Have students discuss in groups and elicit ideas. You could also brainstorm a telegram Helen could have sent, e.g. *Help. Stop. On Isla Violin. Stop. With mom and dad. Stop.*

A Complete the table. How is communication technology used in *Urgent Message* and *Communication Time*?

- With books closed, write the question on the board. Have students recap how communication technology was used in *Urgent Message*. Then do the same with *Communication Time*. Brainstorm ideas as a class and write their suggestions on the board. Let students open their books to find more examples if necessary.
- Students can complete the table on their own or in pairs.

Suggested Answers

Urgent Message: Helen uses her phone to ask Pia for help; Mom calls the coast guard on her phone; Pia uses the internet to get sailing information/use a map; Helen sent Pia messages; Helen sent Pia photos; Pia plays a game on the internet.

Communication Time: Radio was used to save lives on the *Titanic*; The radio, television, and the internet are used for sharing news and information; Marconi sent a message across the Atlantic; Bell called his assistant; People use social media websites to communicate with each other; Television and the internet are used to send images; The radio, television, and the internet are used for entertainment.

B Think and write. Do a 5Ws and an H routine.

- Students are going to do a 5Ws and an H routine about when they last communicated with someone. Ask students to think about who they communicated with, how and why.
- Draw students attention to the six example questions on the right. Tell students to use these to help them write their own questions.

C Look at your questions in B. Do a Roundtable.

- Students are going to make connections to the key concept in the unit: *What are the benefits of communication technology?* by discussing their questions in B through a Roundtable routine (see TB p. 20).
- Give students three minutes to ask each other questions and share their experiences. Encourage them to ask follow-up questions if appropriate. They could create a mind map for each experience, writing the student's name in a circle in the middle and the main events/facts around it.

My Reading Journal

My favorite type of communication is … because …
A part of the unit I would change is … because …

This task encourages students to review and remember what they learned. Tell the class about your favorite type of communication and why; for example, *My favorite type of communication is the cell phone because you can talk to friends anywhere.* Then tell the class about one part of the unit you would change and why. Give students time to look through the unit and complete the sentences with their ideas. This encourages them to personalize what they have learned. Have them compare in pairs before eliciting a few examples with the class.

Example Answers

My favorite type of communication is (the radio) because (people can communicate with songs and music.)
A part of the unit I would change is (the end of *Urgent Message*) because (I would like to know what Pia and Helen said when they saw each other again. I would make the story longer.)

Go back to page 9. What new thoughts do you have to share?

This question encourages students to be creative and add new thoughts about the VTR picture on pp. 8 and 9.

Have students look back at the VTR picture on pp. 8–9. If you are using the TTL, project the image onto the board. Elicit what they had discussed in the Get Ready to Read lesson on p. 9 (use your notes to remind them). Ask them how they think the picture connects to the two readings in the unit and elicit any new thoughts that they have. Draw their attention to the words in the image: *experience, language, location, emotion, culture, noise.* Discuss how these words relate to the topic of communication.

Cool Down

Have students work in groups to write three quiz questions about the unit. The questions can be about the two readings, the VTR picture, or the Literary section. Students can choose to write true or false questions, multiple-choice questions, or challenge questions (e.g., Name five communication devices). Then they get together with another group and quiz each other.

Practice **Resource Bank:** Unit Test
Student's App: Key Concept Practice

UNIT 2

Time for a Change

Unit Overview

Themes

The importance of having a healthy lifestyle

Eating habits and how they affect our lives

Synopsis

In this unit, students will explore what a healthy lifestyle entails. They will learn about healthy habits and how to make positive changes in their day-to-day routines. They will discuss eating habits and how a balanced diet can have a positive impact on our performance in school and sports, and on our overall mood. Students will write a diary entry and plan and prepare a presentation about young people and adults leading stressful lives.

Language Book

Vocabulary

argue, be late, healthy diet, junk food, messy, polite, punctual, rude, sleep late, work out

Pronunciation: Sentence Stress: Weak Forms

p. 64

Explore Language

Present Perfect

p. 65

Global Citizenship

How do eating habits affect our lives?

convenience food, high in fiber, high in salt and sugar, in season, local produce, packaging, processed food, red meat, saturated fat, white meat, whole grains

p. 66

Explore Language

Present Perfect Progressive

p. 67

Write About It

A Diary Entry

Connecting Diary Entries; Using Informal and Emotive Language

p. 68

Take the Stage

Presentation: Supporting an Argument and Being Persuasive

p. 69

Think It Over

Review and Reflection: My Favorite Mistakes

p. 70

Think Together
Why is it important to have good lifestyle habits?
p. 77

Visible Thinking
Step Inside
p. 71

Nonfiction
Informational Text: *Why Do We Sleep?*
Words in Context: *hormones, process, clear away, weakens, caffeine, power nap*
p. 75

Literacy Book

Fiction
Diary: *My Stay at Camp Karma*
Words in Context: *glued to, fingernails, dreading, meditation, forced to*
p. 72

Reading Skill
Analyzing and Evaluating
p. 74

Literary Term
Dropped Subjects
p. 73

Language and Literacy Connections

The connecting theme for Unit 2 is well-being and healthy habits.

	Language	Literacy
Vocabulary	**Set 1:** lifestyle and habits **Set 2:** healthy food	**Fiction:** arguing, rude **Nonfiction:** healthy diet, junk food, work out regularly
Grammar	**Present Perfect** Have you ever been in one? Has technology really changed the way we communicate? We've just seen someone being pretty rude, haven't we? **Present Perfect Progressive** He's been helping me. I've been running a lot with my friend.	**Fiction** We have lost the ability to communicate. I've been spending too much time glued to screens. **Nonfiction** Scientists have developed several theories for why we sleep. Technology has made it harder for us to sleep.
Skills	**Pronunciation:** sentence stress: weak forms **Process Writing:** generating ideas	**Reading:** analyzing and evaluating **Literary Term:** dropped subjects
International English	messy/untidy; we've gotten better / we've got better	

Vocabulary

Lesson Objectives

- to learn vocabulary for lifestyle and habits: ***argue, be late, healthy diet, junk food, messy, polite, punctual, rude, sleep late, work out***
- to read a poem about doing better in life
- to recognize and practice sentence stress: weak forms

Materials
Audio Tracks 15 to 19; Video

Warm Up

Brainstorm what the class rules are. Write students' suggestions on the board to refer back to later.

A TRACK 15 TB p. 216 **Listen. What are the rules for the sports club?**

- Have students explore the picture. Ask them how they think each person is feeling.
- Have students listen to Ben and Cathy. Ask the question and elicit answers. If needed, play the audio again to check.
- Ask students to find Sofia and remind them about her teaser question at the end of Unit 1. Ask *What do you think is healthy about Sofia's life?* (she's in a sports club).

Answers
You need to be on time; you need to work out often; you need to have a healthy diet.

B TRACK 16 TB p. 217 **Find and number the words in A. Then listen and check.**

- Have students look at the list of words. Point out the example (1) and have students find who's late in the picture. Have students work in pairs to find the other words in the picture and to write the numbers in their books.
- Play the audio for students to check their answers.

Answers
1 *be late* 2 sleep late 3 punctual 4 healthy diet
5 work out 6 junk food 7 polite 8 messy
9 argue 10 rude

C TRACK 17 TB p. 217 **Close your eyes. Listen, visualize, and say.**

- Prepare students for the visualization (see TB p. 21).
- Play the audio for students to visualize the ideas.
- Have students compare their ideas in groups. Then ask them to share their ideas with the class.

D Look and write. Then put the good habits in order of importance for you (1 = most important).

- This activity helps students to contextualize the vocabulary. Elicit what an action plan is. Tell them to read the *New good habits* column first to help them complete the bad habits column with words from A. Check answers.
- Students now personalize the good habits by ranking them from 1 (most important) to 6 (least important). Have them work individually and then compare answers in pairs.

Answers
a *junk food*; healthy diet b rude; polite c sleep late; work out d argue e be late; punctual f messy
Numbering of Action Plan: Students' own answers

E TRACK 18 TB p. 217 **Listen and write. Then watch and say.**

- Point to the title *You Can Do Better.* Ask students to think what it means (you should improve your bad habits). Play the audio or video, allowing students to listen and enjoy the poem.
- Have students look at the poem and complete the blanks. Remind them that all the words can be found in A. Play the audio and have students check.
- Play the audio or video again and have students join in with the poem. Encourage them to copy the rhythm and pronunciation.

Answers
1 *sleeping late* 2 rude 3 junk food 4 argue
5 work out 6 healthy diet 7 punctual 8 polite

F TRACK 19 TB p. 217 **Pronunciation. Listen and say. Copy the weak forms. Find other examples in the poem.**

- Play the audio. Have students listen and notice the weak forms. Draw attention to the pronunciation of the schwa /ə/ and point out this is because the word isn't stressed.
- Remind students that these words may have different vowels, but the weak form is always pronounced /ə/. Play the video or audio again for students to listen for more weak forms. Check answers as a class.
- Have students work in pairs to find other sentences in the poem with a weak form. Elicit answers and write them on the board. Drill the weak forms.

Answers
a in: my room's <u>a</u> mess …; don't be <u>a</u> fool; So I have <u>a</u> plan …; have <u>a</u> healthy diet; I <u>a</u>gree
o in: t<u>o</u> wave my …
e in: work out oft<u>e</u>n

International English

Point out the two words in the box. Ask students if they know them both and which they prefer to use. Ask if they know the opposites (*neat/tidy*).

Cool Down

Play the *Yes/No Game* (see TB p. 27). For this version, students make statements using the keywords from the lesson, e.g. *My bedroom's messy.*

Practice Student's App: Vocabulary Practice; Spoken Word Video

Explore Language

Lesson Objectives

- to learn how to use the present perfect
- to practice vocabulary for lifestyle and habits

Materials
Audio Tracks 20 and 21

Warm Up

Write on the board *Technology has made us ruder.* Elicit students' opinions and reasons. Write them on the board.

A TRACK 20 TB p. 217 **Listen and read. Do Ziad and Isabella agree?**

- This is activity is a presentation of the grammar in context. Tell students that they are going to listen to Ziad and Isabella discussing the question from the Warm Up. Play the audio and have students follow along in their books.
- Ask the question and have students look at the dialogue again and find the answer. Check with the class. Then ask further comprehension questions (see **ETB**).

Answer
Ziad and Isabella don't agree. Ziad believes technology is making people rude, whereas Isabella thinks it has made people better at communicating.

International English

Point out the American English and British English participles *gotten* and *got*. Ask *Which verb is it?* (get) Encourage students to say which version they prefer to use and remind them to use the form consistently.

B **Look at A. Complete the table. What kinds of words come before the past participle?**

- Display the table using the TTL. Look at the first sentence together. Ask students to look at the dialogue in A to find the missing word (ever). Ask students to complete the table with the missing words. Remind them to refer back to the story if necessary. Students can work individually or in pairs.
- Check answers as a class. Review how to form the present perfect by conjugating the verb *have* on the board and eliciting the past participles from the table. Ask students to give example sentences and write these on the board. Then ask students to look at the table. Ask *What kinds of words come before the past participle?* and elicit the answer. If you feel that students need more guidance, the **ETB** provides a differentiation activity.

Answers
ever; Has; changed; just; seen; haven't; 's; already
Adverbs like *ever, just,* and *already* come before the past participle.

Practice **Resource Bank:** Grammar Printout
Student's App: Grammar Practice

- Refer students to the Grammar tip *Remember.* Check students understand the difference between *been* and *gone* by eliciting examples.

C **Think and discuss. Then choose.**

- Ask students to look at the first sentence in the table in B. Ask *Is Ziad asking Diego about something he has done in the past, present, or future?* Elicit that he wants to know if taking part in a debate is something Diego has experienced in the past. Refer students to the statement and elicit the answer.
- Have students work in pairs to discuss the remaining sentences and answer options. Check answers.

Answers
1 present perfect 2 unfinished 3 when

D TRACK 21 TB p. 217 **Listen and say.**

- Tell students they're going to practice saying sentences with the present perfect to help with pronunciation in fluent speech so that the language starts to feel natural. Play the audio and have students repeat each example chorally. (See TB p. 23, Making Language Drills Fun.)

E **Complete with the present perfect.**

- This activity provides controlled practice of the verb forms and adverbs. Read the example and remind students of the position of *ever, just,* and *already.*
- Have students complete the sentences and compare their answers in pairs.
- To check answers, invite students to read a sentence aloud. Elicit why *been* is the correct answer in question 4 and not *gone.* (It's a question about their life experiences.)

Answers
1 *'ve ever run* 2 Has; ever been 3 Have; changed 4 Have; ever been 5 has already finished 6 has just asked 7 Has; stopped 8 have not told

F **Ask and answer questions 1–4 in E. Then ask three new questions. Use time expressions in your answers.**

- This activity provides freer practice of the verb forms. Have two students read the example exchange. Explain that we often answer initially with the present perfect and then give more specific details about when, who, how, and so on with the simple past.
- Put students in pairs to ask and answer questions 1–4 in E. Monitor and check they are using the correct verb forms and time expressions.
- Give students time to think of their own questions and then put them in different pairs. Elicit anything interesting students found out.

Cool Down

Play *Stand Up, Sit Down* (see TB p. 26). Ask *Have you ever ...?* questions, e.g. *Have you ever eaten a very spicy pepper?* Prompt seated students to ask a follow-up question to those standing, e.g. *What did you do after eating the spicy pepper?*

Global Citizenship

Lesson Objectives

- to learn vocabulary related to healthy food: *convenience food, high in fiber, high in salt and sugar, in season, local produce, packaging, processed food, red meat, saturated fat, white meat, whole grains*
- to explore how eating habits affect our lives
- to practice listening for gist and details

Materials

Audio Tracks 22 to 24; Audio Track B

Opening Question

Ask the opening question: *How do eating habits affect our lives?* Have students brainstorm ideas using a Round Robin routine (see TB p. 20). Elicit ideas from different groups and write them on the board.

A TRACK 22 TB p. 217 **Listen to Victor talk to his dad. What changes is Victor's dad making to their meals?**

- Tell students Victor and his dad are discussing their eating habits. Have them guess what they're going to change.
- Play the audio and have students check their guesses.
- Ask the question and nominate students to answer. Elicit the disadvantage of making these changes. (They take longer to prepare.) Ask students if they eat these meals.

Answer

He's making healthier meals, including whole grains, fresh vegetables, and meat from the farmers' market.

B TRACK 23 TB p. 217 **Look at the pictures and definitions in A and write. Then listen and check.**

- Refer students to the vocabulary box in B and have them match the words and phrases to the pictures and the definitions in A. Encourage students to guess if necessary.
- Play the audio for students to check answers. Then play it again to practice the pronunciation, pausing after each word or phrase for them to repeat.

Answers

1 *in season* 2 saturated fat 3 convenience food
4 local produce 5 red meat 6 white meat
7 packaging 8 whole grains 9 high in salt and sugar
10 high in fiber 11 processed food

TRACK B TB p. 217 **Visualization**

The TTL has a visualization audio track for this vocabulary set. (See TB p. 21.)

C Read and complete. Then check (✔) the sentences that are true for you.

- Read the first sentence and elicit the missing phrase. Ask which students agree with this statement and explain that they should check the circle.
- Have students complete the sentences and then check answers with a friend before they do the second part of the task.
- Have students work individually to decide which sentences are true for them before comparing with a friend. Encourage them to explain their answers and say whether they think the habits are good or not.

Answers

1 *whole grains*; high fiber 2 produce 3 in season
4 convenience; packaging; high; salt; sugar 5 processed
6 white meat; red meat 7 saturated fat

D TRACK 24 TB p. 217 **Now listen to the fitness instructor. Why is she talking about diet?**

- Tell students they're going to listen to a fitness instructor. Elicit what a fitness instructor does (helps people stay fit).
- Listening for gist: ask *Why is she talking about diet?* and play the audio. Check the answer. Ask students who else has been learning about a healthy diet. Elicit that Victor from A has learned about healthy diets in school.

Answer

because it can help you achieve your goals in school and sports

E Listen again. Write *True*, *False*, or *Doesn't Say*.

- Listening for details: have students read the sentences before they listen again. Allow them to discuss in pairs any sentences they think they know the answer to.
- Play the audio and have students answer. Check with the class. Ask if any of the fitness instructor's advice is new or surprising.

Answers

1 *Doesn't Say* 2 False 3 True 4 Doesn't Say
5 False 6 True 7 True 8 Doesn't Say

Discussion Questions

- Draw students' attention to the discussion questions: *Why is it important for everyone to have a varied diet? How do you think our eating habits will change in the future?* Have students discuss the questions in pairs or small groups (see **ETB**). Encourage students to recognize that it is important to have a healthy and varied diet, but that it is never too late to change your eating habits.
- Return to the opening question to ask again *How do eating habits affect our lives?* Revisit any ideas discussed at the beginning of the lesson. Encourage students to share any new ideas.

Cool Down

Have students write about one of their eating habits on a piece of paper, e.g. *I usually eat toast for breakfast.* Collect the pieces of paper and have students sit in groups. Distribute a few sentences to each group. Students read the sentence and brainstorm advice to give.

Practice **Student's App:** Vocabulary Practice; Listening Practice

Explore Language

Lesson Objectives

- to learn how to use the present perfect progressive
- to practice vocabulary related to healthy food

Materials
Audio Tracks 25 and 26

Warm Up

Write *Mental health is …* on the board. Put students in pairs and give them one minute to finish the sentence in as many different ways as they can.

A TRACK 25 TB p. 217 **Listen and read. Are Samuel and Uncle Matias talking about food for physical health, for mental health, or for both?**

- Tell students they are going to listen to Samuel talking to his uncle, the coach from Lesson 1. Ask what type of food they think Uncle Matias will mention. Play the audio and have students follow the dialogue in their books.
- Ask the question *Are Samuel and Uncle Matias talking about food for physical health, for mental health, or for both?* Discuss as a class. Play the audio again for students to check. Ask more comprehension questions (see **ETB**).

Answer
They're talking about food for both physical and mental health.

B **Look at A. Complete the table. Where does *not* come in a negative statement?**

- Display the table using the TTL. Tell students that the words they need to complete the table are all in the dialogue in A. Have them complete the table individually or in pairs.
- Ask students which three words make up the verb form (*has/have* + *been* + verb *–ing*). Write it on the board and elicit the name. Then ask the question *Where does "not" come in a negative sentence?* Elicit the answer.
- Draw students' attention to the Grammar tip *Watch Out.* Elicit why the second sentence is wrong (*been* is missing). Elicit an example of the present perfect and the present perfect progressive and how each one is formed. Check understanding that both forms link the past to the present.

Answers
has; been; haven't; eating; have; been; Have; been; sleeping; haven't
It comes after *have* and before the past participle *been*.

C **Think and discuss. Then choose.**

- Ask students to read the statements on usage and refer to the table in B. Look at the first sentence in B. Elicit whether he (Samuel's friend) was helping in the past. Ask students if they think he will continue to help in the present and future.
- Have students work in pairs to discuss the statements. Refer them to the dialogue in A for examples. Then check answers. Draw timelines on the board as a visual aid.

Answers
1 present perfect progressive 2 duration of the activity

D TRACK 26 TB p. 218 **Listen and say.**

- Tell students they're going to practice saying sentences with the present perfect progressive to help with pronunciation in fluent speech and to consolidate what they've learned. Play the audio and have students repeat each example chorally. (See TB p. 23, Making Language Drills Fun.)

E **Complete with the present perfect progressive. Then write a cause or effect for each sentence.**

- This activity provides controlled practice of the present perfect progressive. Ask students to complete the first part individually. Check answers.
- Then put students in pairs to discuss possible causes and effects for each sentence. Read the example and elicit whether *I'm feeling very hot!* is a cause or effect (effect). Monitor and provide language help.
- To check answers, invite students to read a cause or effect for a sentence. The other students identify whether it's a cause or effect.

Answers
(Suggested causes/effects in parentheses)
1 *'ve been cooking (I'm feeling very hot!)* 2 've been going (You must be tired.) 3 haven't been swimming (They slept late.) 4 's been eating (He'll be in great shape for his next game.) 5 haven't been sleeping (I've been drinking too much soda.) 6 been doing? (I've been studying all night.) 7 hasn't been drinking (She must be really thirsty.) 8 've been going to bed (We used to feel very sleepy before.)

F **Play *True or False*. Write and say four sentences about you.**

- Students write four sentences individually. They can be true, false, or a mix. Monitor and provide language help if needed.
- For this freer oral practice, students read their sentences in pairs or small groups. Have two students read the examples on the page and check they understand the activity. Then have students play in groups. Have students count the number of times they guess true or false correctly to see who knows their friend best.

Cool Down

Have each student give you a present perfect progressive sentence about an activity they have been doing as an exit pass.

Practice **Resource Bank:** Grammar Printout
Student's App: Grammar Practice

Write About It

Lesson Objectives

- to plan and write a diary entry
- to make connections between diary entries
- to learn to use informal and emotive language

Materials
Support Writing printouts from the Resource Bank (F)

Warm Up

Write on the board *Dear Diary, …* Ask students to copy it in their notebooks and write a sentence to complete the prompt. Have students compare in pairs. Invite students to share with the class.

A Read the diary entries. What's Luca's problem and his solution?

- This lesson corresponds with the diary in the Unit 2 fiction reading in the **Literacy Book**. Tell students they are going to read a diary. Have them look at the pictures on the diary entry and make predictions about Luca's lifestyle.
- Ask *What's Luca's problem and his solution?* Have students skim the diary entries and discuss answers in pairs. Check answers. Ask more comprehension questions (see **ETB**).

Answers
He feels sick, out of shape, and tired. He sets himself some goals so he can improve.

B Look at the structure of the diary entries. Read and answer.

- Tell students they're going to look at the structure of the diary entries. First, have them compare the two longer entries to find similarities and differences. Elicit ideas.
- Put students in pairs to answer the questions. Check and discuss answers as a class.

Answers
1 The diary is chronological and shows what Luca is thinking and doing each day. 2 1 c; 2 a; 3 b; 4 d
3 to make his points clear, easy to read/check 4 They indicate when a diary entry starts and ends; they show the writer has started a new topic.

C Look at the language in the diary entries. Read and respond.

- Students are now going to focus on the language and register used in diary entries by finding examples.
- Read the example of informal language and elicit an example feeling. Have students find more examples of informal language and feelings in the diary entries. Point out that this can include more than just word usage and sentence structure (e.g. styling and punctuation). Check answers.

Answers
1 *Ugh!*, Hmm, using caps ("SO …"; "YES!"), using exclamation marks ("Bye for now!" "Thanks guys!"), using underlining, beginning sentence with "And" 2 I felt so sick, I've been feeling really tired, feel better, hard, how bad I was feeling, fun, very excited

D Think and discuss ideas for activities to achieve a better lifestyle. Use one of the Generating Ideas techniques.

- In this lesson, students decide which Generating Ideas technique they want to use. They can refer back to the lesson on p. 140. Encourage them to choose the technique they think will work best. Guide them, but try not to tell them what to do—it's important that they learn which techniques work better for them.
- Ask *What activities help you achieve a better lifestyle?* Elicit some answers to help students get started.
- Have them brainstorm ideas individually using their chosen technique. Then have them compare in pairs and generate more ideas.

Answers
Students' own answers

E Plan your diary entry. Choose one of your ideas in D. Make notes for each question.

- Tell students they are going to plan their own diary entry. Have them revise their ideas in D and choose one they would like to write about. Ask them to tell their partner and explain why.
- Read the questions and elicit a brief answer from one or two students. Then allow enough time for students to plan their diary entry in note form. Ask fast finishers to help other students who might need more support.

F Now write a diary entry about your plan.

- Have students write a draft of their diary entry, referring to their notes in E. They should read their drafts and make any corrections or improvements.
- Have students write their final versions neatly on paper or on the Support printout.
- Have pairs read each other's diary entry. Ask them to add a comment at the end to encourage their partner. Elicit examples: *You can do it! / Don't give up! / Go for it!* Then have them read their own entry again and think about how they feel about their plans.

Cool Down

Write on the board *How do you want to improve yourself?* Demonstrate an exchange with a student, prompting him/her to ask you *What about you?* after they've answered. Have students mingle and find out about their classmates' goals. Afterwards, invite them to share goals they found most interesting.

Practice **Resource Bank:** Writing Game, *Diary Consequences*
Student's App: Writing Practice

Take the Stage

Lesson Objectives

- to give a presentation about whether life is stressful for young people and adults
- to support an argument and be persuasive

Materials
Video

Warm Up

Ask students to mime being stressed (e.g. face tense and clenching their fists) and then relaxed (e.g. sitting back in their chair with arms hanging down). Call out different situations and activities, e.g. *Go for a walk. / Clean your bedroom. / Take a test. / Play computer games.* Prompt students to mime how each phrase makes them feel. You could also invite students to call out phrases.

A TB p. 239 **Watch and listen. Do you agree with Linda or Veronica?**

- Tell students they are going to watch a video of Linda and Veronica presenting their opinion on the question *Is life more stressful for young people or adults?* Point to the picture and have students predict what the two girls are going to say. Tell students to listen for their opinions and arguments.
- With books closed, play the video for students to watch, listen, and decide which of the two speakers they agree with.
- Ask the question *Do you agree with Linda or Veronica?* If necessary, play the video again and then allow some time for students to think about their answer and reasons why. Ask students to compare their answer with a partner and then elicit answers from the class.

Answer
Students' own answers

B Watch again. Put the information in the order it comes in both speeches.

- Tell students they are going to focus on how the girls structure their speeches. Have them read the information and look at the example number. Encourage them to remember the order from the first viewing of the video.
- Play the video again and have students order the information. Have students compare their answers in pairs before checking with the class.
- Play the video once more and ask students to notice what language they use for each part of their speech. Encourage them to make notes. Elicit language on the board and leave it there for students to refer to during their debate. (The subject I'm talking about: *I'm X and I'm going to agree with* / What I believe: *I'm speaking against the statement that …; I think that …; So I strongly agree/disagree with the statement.*)

Answers
1 b 2 d 3 a 4 e 5 c

C What do you think? Which argument do you want to support? Think and plan.

- Students are going to discuss arguments for and against to plan for their presentation in D.
- Put students in small groups, depending on whether they are for or against the statement, to brainstorm their ideas. Monitor and provide language help if needed. Then ask students to write down the strongest arguments individually.

Answers
Students' own answers

D Practice with your friends. Then share with the class. Take notes and give feedback.

- Tell students they are going to present their opinion in pairs or small groups with students with the opposing opinion. Encourage them to think of ways they can improve their arguments. You could write a checklist on the board, e.g. *Vocabulary, Grammar, Pronunciation, Ideas/ Arguments, Speed, Movement.*
- Pair students according to whether they have prepared an argument for or against the statement. Then invite volunteer students to present their sides of the debate in class. As students hear their classmates' presentations, have them make notes using the question prompts. Put students in groups to share their feedback. Monitor and provide your own, too, if appropriate.
- Have students analyze their own performance, thinking about whether they gave clear reasons and were persuasive.

Cool Down

Ask students to think of three reasons why life is fun for both young people and adults. Have them discuss in pairs or groups and then elicit the top three reasons.

Practice **Student's App:** Speaking Skills Practice; Speaking Video

Think It Over

Lesson Objectives

- to review what has been learned in the unit
- to reflect on the unit and their own progress
- to think about learning strategies and how to continue learning at home

Materials

Packs of sticky notes

Warm Up

Ask students what the unit theme was (healthy lifestyle and eating habits) and write it on the board. Brainstorm any words or phrases students can think of that relate to the topic and write them on the board. Encourage students to think about what habits have a positive effect on our bodies and minds.

How well did you meet the challenge of Unit 2? Read and respond.

My Favorite Mistakes

- Tell students they are going to think about what they learned during the unit and how they can improve. Point out that making mistakes is a natural part of learning and it can actually help you improve. Tell students that they are going to think about the mistakes they made in the unit, as well as what they have learned. Let them know that it's important that they don't worry about what other people think or say, as different students will have made different mistakes. Point out that everyone can find some way of improving, even if they think they didn't make any mistakes!
- Have students work in groups to think about the activities they did during the unit. Give each group a pack of sticky notes and have them write an idea on each one. Encourage students to think about the different things they studied or remember from the unit, e.g. present perfect progressive, how eating habits affect lives, writing a diary entry, being persuasive. Then have students stick their notes onto a board or a poster and display them on the wall. Have groups go around the classroom and look at each other's sticky note board.
- Draw students' attention to the graphic organizer. Refer students to the different sections: *Two mistakes I made in this unit that helped my learning are …; Two things (knowledge) I learned about lifestyles are …; Two things (experience and skills) I learned to say or do in English are …* Have students talk in pairs about the different sections. Encourage them to focus particularly on the first section and to discuss how they are going to avoid making these mistakes in the future and when they will use their experience and skills again.
- Ask students what they would like to work on to improve. Refer students to the final section in the graphic organizer, *One thing I want to work on next month is …*, and the notes below it. Have students think about their ideas and then discuss them with a friend.
- When you feel they have enough ideas, have students work individually to complete the organizer. Remind them that they should write their own responses about themselves. Monitor and help as necessary. Look at what students are writing so you can tailor your classes and any additional practice to their needs.
- Ask if anyone has the same goals as their friend. Point out that goals should be personal and each student should choose those they think they would benefit from most. Remind students that everyone learns differently, so they will all have different answers.

Looking Forward

Draw students' attention to the character at the bottom of the page. Have students say who he is and what they remember about him. (His name's Matias García and he's a coach. He's Samuel's uncle and he appears in Lesson 1, p. 22, and Lesson 4, p. 28. He gives Samuel advice about his mental and physical health.) Have students look at the speech bubble and make predictions about what kind of play he and his daughter are going to see. Tell students they will find out the answer in Lesson 1 of the next unit.

Put It Together

To further review and recycle the language in Units 1 and 2, play the game, *Know It, Win It*, on pp. 34–35. See TB p. 206 for teaching notes.

Practice **Resource Bank:** Unit Test
Student's App: Vocabulary and Grammar Review

Get Ready to Read

Lesson Objectives

- to activate prior knowledge about healthy lifestyles
- to guide inquiry and deepen understanding through a Step Inside VTR
- to preview the reading skill of analyzing and evaluating

Materials
VTR printout from the Resource Bank (A, B, C)

Warm Up

Write the unit title on the board: *Time for a Change*. Elicit that we use this phrase when there's a situation that needs to change and improve. Ask students to work in pairs to discuss a situation in their life that had to change.

Step Inside

A Look at the picture. Choose a person or a thing. What can they see?

- This VTR encourages students to explore different perspectives as they step inside a person or object that they can see and imagine their point of view. Start by asking students what they can see in the picture of people doing tai chi. Provide vocabulary where necessary.
- Ask students to imagine they are one of the people or things in the photo. Give them time to choose.
- Ask *What can you see* (from that person/thing's viewpoint)? Encourage students to really put themselves into their person/thing's shoes and look around, at the surroundings and the other people. Ask *What can you see in front of you? To the left/right? And if you turn around?*
- Students can discuss their ideas in pairs and then as a class.

B What do you think they believe?

- Tell students to keep thinking about their chosen person/ thing and to think about what he/she/it believes. Check understanding that *believe* means to have an opinion about something. Tell them that if they chose a thing instead of a person, they will need to be very imaginative about it!
- Say *I chose the young man's sneakers. I think the man's sneakers believe they're too good for tai chi and should be running. What does your person or thing believe?*
- Give students time to think about the person or thing they have chosen and their thoughts and opinions. Have students discuss their ideas in pairs and then as a class.

Here's an example of this part of the routine.

Teacher: Who or what are you, Student A?
Student A: I'm this woman who's doing tai chi. I think she believes tai chi helps her stay healthy.
Teacher: Why does she think that?
Student A: Because she feels good after she's done it.
Student B: Yes. I also think she believes that it's nice to do exercise with other people.

C What do you think they care about?

- Say *I care about my health, so I go running*. Then ask students *If you care about something, is that thing important to you or not?* (yes)
- Ask students to think about what is important to the people or things in the picture. Give students time to think and then discuss in pairs. Elicit ideas. Remember to keep a record of their ideas for use in the Think Together lesson.

Here's an example of this part of the routine.

Teacher: Student B, you chose the flower bed. What do you think it cares about?
Student B: I think it cares about the sun and the rain.
Teacher: Why do you say that?
Student B: It needs them to grow. It also cares about flowers and people.
Student C: I disagree. I think it's afraid of people because they step on it.
Teacher: That's interesting.

Transition

Ask *Do you think the people doing tai chi care about their diet? What kind of food do they eat? How often do they exercise?*

D Think and discuss. How healthy is your diet? How often do you exercise?

- This activity helps students make personal connections to the theme. Have students discuss the questions as a Think, Pair, Share routine (see TB p. 20).

Answers
Students' own answers

E Think and predict. Then write. Look at the pictures from *My Stay at Camp Karma*. What do you think happens at Camp Karma?

- This activity previews the skill of analyzing and evaluating by looking at a picture from the reading.
- Point to the pictures and explain that they both appear in the same passage. Write the title on the board: *My Stay at Camp Karma*. Elicit if students think it's fiction or nonfiction and why, but don't give them the answer.
- Have students think of one or two predictions on their own and then share ideas in pairs.
- Students write down two or more predictions that they agree with. Elicit ideas from the class.

Answers
Students' own answers

Now read **My Stay at Camp Karma**

Fiction: *My Stay at Camp Karma—Diary*

Lesson Objectives

- to read a diary about a stay at a camp
- to explore the SEL competency of responsible decision-making through becoming self-reflective and self-evaluative
- to make a personal connection to the reading

Materials
Audio Tracks 8 and 9

Warm Up

With books closed, hold up or project the photo of Cathy on p. 26. Elicit what the girl is doing and what this tells students about her stay at Camp Karma. Ask students if their predictions from the previous lesson have changed. Have students discuss briefly in pairs and elicit ideas from the class.

TRACK 8 TB p. 230 Reading Approach

First Reading: Engage with the Text

- Ask students to look at pp. 26–27. Ask them what features they can see (photo and illustrations, dates/headings). Elicit the genre (fictional diary). Ask prediction questions to generate interest, including the one in the blue box on p. 26 after they have read to the end of the page: *How do you think the family might change in their time at Camp Karma?* Elicit bad habits Cathy, Billy, and her parents have. Prompt students to brainstorm other bad habits they might have and how they might change at Camp Karma. Elicit ideas.
- Read the rest of the entries and elicit if Cathy's stay had a happy ending (yes). Then look at the Words in Context.

TRACK 9 TB p. 230 Words in Context

- Play the audio to familiarize students with the words and practice the pronunciation.
- Brainstorm strategies on the board for students to use: *pictures, separate parts of word, surrounding words and sentences, positive/negative, knowledge of similar words.*
- Put students in pairs to find and discuss each word in the text. Remind them that different words will require different combinations of strategies to figure them out.

glued to (p. 26, phrase) Students may already know *glue*. *Spending too much time* and *lost the ability to communicate* show it has a negative meaning. Strategies to use: surrounding words and sentences; positive/negative; knowledge of similar words

fingernails (p. 26, noun) The word *finger* is a part of the body, and the surrounding sentences show that biting them is a negative activity when you are stressed. Strategies to use: separate parts of word; positive/negative; surrounding words and sentences

dreading (p. 26, noun) The words *stressed* and *Aaargh* show it is something negative. Strategies to use: positive/negative; surrounding words and sentences; pictures

meditation (p. 29, noun) Later sentences show what it involves (*closed our eyes; concentrated on our breathing*), as well as the positive outcome (*felt … happy and calm*). Strategies to use: surrounding words and sentences; positive/negative; pictures

forced to (p. 29, verb) Later sentences show it is something they only did because they didn't have anything else to do, implying a negative meaning. Strategies to use: surrounding words and sentences; positive/negative

- Have students change partners and discuss which strategies they used and which worked best.

Second Reading: Analyze the Text and Features

- Play the audio or have students read the story again to consolidate their understanding. Ask some questions to check comprehension: *How did Cathy feel about the idea of spending a week at Camp Karma?* (She hated it.) *How did she feel at the end?* (She loved it.)
- Discuss the questions in the blue boxes. Then look at the text focus.
  - **Language in Context** (p. 28): *What do you think "Poof went our plan!" means?* Ask students to scan the story and find the phrase. Ask *Who said it?* (Cathy) *What was their plan?* (to buy candy at the store) *Did they make it?* (no) *Why not?* (They bumped into their parents.) Elicit what kind of image the sound *poof* creates (something that disappears in a puff of smoke).
  - **Personalization** (p. 31): *Have you ever been persuaded to do something you didn't want to do and ended up enjoying it?* Ask students to think and then discuss in pairs.
  - **Text Focus** (p. 30): Read the text focus and discuss the question. Ask students to give you examples of character arcs from other stories they know.

Third Reading: Interact with the Text

- Tell students they are going to explain what happened at Camp Karma in groups of three. In the groups, have each student choose two different days each.
- Give them time to study the events and Cathy's feelings for those days. Then they take turns explaining to their group what happened in their own words. Monitor and provide language help if needed.
- Project each diary entry on the board using the TTL. Invite volunteer students to describe the events of that day to the class.

Cool Down

Have students think what they would like the most or the least about Camp Karma. Ask them to discuss in pairs and give reasons. Elicit ideas from volunteers.

Practice **Student's App:** Story Player

Explore the Reading

Lesson Objectives

- to understand and analyze *My Stay at Camp Karma* through reading comprehension activities
- to review the SEL competency of responsible decision-making through becoming self-reflective and self-evaluative
- to make a personal connection to the reading

Materials
Audio Track 10

Warm Up

Invite students to act out one of the actions/activities that Cathy mentioned in her diary entries. Prompt the rest of the class to guess and call it out.

A Answer the questions. Use evidence from the reading to support your answer.

- Ask students to read the questions once and check they understand them. Then give students time to scan the diary entries for the answers individually.
- Put students in pairs or small groups to compare their answers. To check answers, choose students to answer a question and refer to the corresponding evidence in the reading.

Answers
1 She wanted the family to make some lifestyle changes (Dad needed more exercise / the kids were spending too much time looking at screens and were becoming uncommunicative / Mom was having difficulty sleeping and was feeling stressed). 2 At first she didn't like it (she was disappointed that there were no sugary cereals), but by the end she liked it (she asked for the green smoothie recipes). 3 She had to run in the morning (she wanted to go to the store) and exercise in the sand (she wanted to sunbathe). 4 She felt (unexpectedly) happy and calm after meditation. Everyone enjoyed a happy family lunch (they hadn't done that for a long time). She (actually) enjoyed talking to the other kids and had a fun evening. 5 It was their last day (she was enjoying the vacation and had to do many things for the last time and say goodbye to new friends). 6 They are all much happier and get along better. (Dad now enjoys running, Cathy has stopped biting her fingernails, Billy likes green vegetables, and Mom is smiling a lot.)

B Think and write. Imagine the week at Camp Karma from Mom's perspective. Write a diary entry for Mom for Friday, July 2.

- Elicit from students what happened at Camp Karma on July 2. Then ask *What did Cathy's mom do on that day? What did she think and feel?* Elicit one or two ideas.
- Have students brainstorm more ideas in pairs or small groups. Then give them time to write a short diary entry for Cathy's mom.

C Think and discuss. Why are vacations good for you? Why is it good to change your routine?

- Students are going to connect the reading to the SEL competency of responsible decision-making: becoming self-reflective and self-evaluative. They will think about how the family benefitted from the vacation and how their routine changed.
- Ask the questions *Why are vacations good for you? Why is it good to change your routine?* Give students some time to think about at least two reasons for each question. Consider using a cooperative learning routine like Rally Robin or Think, Pair, Share (see TB p. 20).

Literary Term: Dropped Subjects

TRACK 10 TB p. 230 **Listen. Circle the dropped subjects.**

- Ask students to read the paragraph. Elicit an example of a subject (e.g. *he*). Explain to students that they will hear the paragraph but some of the subjects will be left out.
- Play the audio and have them circle the dropped subjects. Check answers by reading the paragraph in the book and having students raise their hand when you say a dropped subject.

Now find more sentences with dropped subjects in the reading.

- Then have students scan the reading to find more sentences with dropped subjects.
- Ask students to compare answers in pairs, then check answers as a class.

Answers
He said he couldn't get to sleep last night. **We** went to school as usual but **we** got stuck in traffic. **I** was late for **my** first class and my teacher gave me an unhappy look. **She** never asked why I was late. **I** can't wait for this day to be over.
Dropped subjects in the reading: "in the car on the way to Camp Karma" (p. 26); "survived the first night in our yurt," "Getting ready for a *gentle* 15 km. hike" (p. 27); "Ached all over this morning," "Set off early for the store," "Had to join the Early Birds," "went to the beach" (p. 28); "felt unexpectedly happy and calm," "Actually had a good time" (p. 29); "Too busy having a wonderful day" (p. 30); "felt kind of sad," "had our last yoga class" (p. 31)

Cool Down

Play *Stand Up, Sit Down* (see TB p. 26) with sentences from the reading. For true sentences, have students stand and do a meditation gesture (e.g. join palms in front of their chest, or open arms out with thumb and middle finger touching). Encourage students to correct the false sentences.

Practice **Resource Bank:** Literary Term Printout
Student's App: Reading Practice; Literary Term Practice

Get Ready to Read

Lesson Objectives

- to activate prior knowledge about sleep and sleep patterns
- to practice the reading skill of analyzing and evaluating a text

Warm Up

Do a *Find Someone Who* about sleep (see TB p. 26). Write these questions on the board: *What time did you go to bed last night? How many hours did you sleep? When do you usually feel sleepy?* Then ask *Where did Cathy sleep at Camp Karma? How did her sleep change there?* (She slept in a yurt. She went to bed earlier and woke up earlier.)

A Think and write. Look back at *My Stay at Camp Karma* and answer the questions.

- This lesson practices the skill of analyzing and evaluating a text, which students previewed on p. 25. This first activity gets students to use the skill before considering how it can shape the way they think about what they've read.
- Have students look back at the diary entries and then write their answers. Don't discuss their answers yet.

Suggested Answers

1 Students' own answers 2 a family vacation to a health camp / fitness retreat 3 fiction 4 for enjoyment / to amuse us / to inform us about healthy living / to persuade us that healthy living can improve our lives 5 The story is written like a diary, so the narrator feels real / the narrator is funny / there are lots of pictures, like in a scrapbook, which help illustrate what the camp was like.

B Think and discuss. Look at your answers in A. Think about the information. What's your opinion of *My Stay at Camp Karma* now? Has the opinion you gave in A changed?

- Have students read the information in the skills box. Discuss why it's important to analyze and evaluate a text (because we need to question what we read and reach our own conclusions). Elicit what kinds of questions they can ask to help them analyze and evaluate, e.g. How do you know? Why do you think that? What evidence is there?
- Give students some time to think again about *My Stay at Camp Karma*. In pairs, have students think of two more analysis questions they could ask for each of the questions in A, e.g. *Is the author trying to persuade or inform? Is there any information that isn't included? Why did the author use this genre?*
- Have students discuss the questions and say whether their opinion has changed and why. Elicit ideas about how and why analyzing and evaluating in more detail may have affected their original answers in A.

C Read. Then analyze and evaluate the reading. Answer the questions.

- Tell students they are going to practice their analyzing and evaluating skills again with a short text. Ask them to read the paragraph and think about the questions.
- Put them in pairs to share their ideas. Then check answers as a class, eliciting reasons for their opinions. Discuss that often we may agree with some of the author's opinions and disagree with or be unsure about others.

Answers

1 It's about what time school starts. 2 nonfiction
3 To persuade the reader that it would be better if school started later. The author achieves this by giving research-based reasons and sharing an experience everyone can relate to by arguing that the change in time would improve everyone's lives, not just those of the students' 4 Students' own answers

D Think and discuss. Read the headings in *Why Do We Sleep?* Do you know the answers to the questions already?

- Students are going to have a discussion that will prepare them for exploring the key concept question *Why is it important to have good lifestyle habits?* later in the unit.
- Display the reading. Have students read the questions in the headings and think whether they know what the answers will be.
- Then quickly read each question heading and have students raise their hands if they think they know the answer.

Answers

Students' own answers

Cool Down

Write on the board *School should start at … and finish at …* In small groups, students decide what times to choose to complete the sentence. Prompt them to think of reasons why. Invite students to share their group's ideas.

Now read **Why Do We Sleep?**

Nonfiction: *Why Do We Sleep?*—Informational Text

Lesson Objectives

- to read an informational text about sleep and sleep patterns
- to make a personal connection to the reading

Materials
Audio Tracks 11 and 12

Warm Up

Draw a mind map on the board. In the circle, write *Why do we sleep?* and draw lines for four ideas with the prompt *to …* Have students discuss in small groups four reasons why we sleep. Elicit ideas and write them on the mind map. Leave it on the board to refer to after the second reading of the text.

TRACK 11 TB p. 230 Reading Approach

First Reading: Engage with the Text

- Display the reading or use the Story Player to show the questions and to reactivate schema. Have students recall some of the answers they predicted from the previous lesson.
- Play the audio once and have students follow along in their books. Give them time to think about what they read and then ask students to share what questions they answered correctly.
- Have students look at the Words in Context.

TRACK 12 TB p. 231 Words in Context

- Brainstorm strategies on the board for students to use with the words: *pictures, synonyms, surrounding words and sentences, positive/negative, separate parts of word, L1 cognates, word families.*
- Divide the class into groups. Assign each group either the three nouns or the three verbs. Have each group find and discuss their words.
- Have students work with a student from another group to explain their words to each other, saying which strategies they used.

hormones (p. 34, noun) An explanation is given directly after it. Strategies to use: surrounding words and sentences; possible L1 cognates

process (p. 34, verb) The surrounding sentences show it is something that happens when we sleep. The picture gives further clues. Strategies to use: pictures; surrounding words and sentences

clear away (p. 34, verb) The sentence says it happens to things we *don't need to remember.* The picture gives further clues. Strategies to use: pictures; surrounding words and sentences

weakens (p. 35, verb) This is the verb form of the adjective *weak.* Later in the sentence, *can't fight illness* and *become sick* show it has a negative meaning. Strategies to use: surrounding words and sentences; positive/negative; word families

caffeine (p. 36, noun) There are examples of things containing caffeine (soda, coffee, tea). The sentence states it is something you shouldn't have before bed. Strategies to use: surrounding words and sentences; possible L1 cognates

power nap (p. 37, noun) A synonym is given: *daytime nap.* It can *help boost energy,* showing a positive meaning. Strategies to use: surrounding words and sentences; positiee/negative; synonyms; separate parts of word

- Bring the class together to discuss which strategies worked or didn't work. Play the audio to practice the pronunciation.

Second Reading: Analyze the Text and Features

- Have students read the text silently. To keep them focused as they read, ask them to note down three interesting facts that they didn't know.
- To check comprehension, draw students' attention to the mind map on the board. Have them check which of their ideas are mentioned in the text. Elicit any new facts students learned and add them to the mind map. See the **ETB** for more comprehension questions.
- Discuss the questions in the blue boxes.
  - **Making Connections** (p. 34): *Do you have trouble sleeping on your first night in a new place? Why do you think that might be?* Have students discuss in pairs. Then invite students to share their answers.
  - **Personalization** (p. 35): *What's the last dream you can remember? Why do you think you had this dream?* Give students time to think and make notes. Then have them share their dreams in small groups or with the class.
  - **Making Connections** (p. 37): *Do you sleep well at night? Why do you think that is?* Even if students sleep well, ask them to think of at least three factors that affect sleep. Refer them to the list of factors that affect our sleep on p. 36. Have discuss in pairs and then as a class.

Third Reading: Interact with the Text

- Have students read the text again and underline at least three facts that are true for themselves. Give an example for you: *When I'm too tired, I can't remember new words.*
- Have students compare their ideas in pairs or small groups. Then invite students to share a fact with the class.

Cool Down

To promote critical thinking, put students in pairs and have them choose the most important piece of advice from the text. Explain it should be something everyone should know about. Elicit ideas from pairs.

Practice **Student's App:** Story Player

Explore the Reading

Lesson Objectives

- **to understand and analyze *Why Do We Sleep?* through reading comprehension activities**
- **to practice the reading skill of analyzing and evaluating a text**
- **to learn through CLIL (science): exploring the impacts of sleep on our health**
- **to make a personal connection to the reading**

Warm Up

With books closed, put students in pairs. Have them remember the six tips/factors that affect our sleep from p. 36. Ask *What six things should you do to sleep well?* Set this up as a race and invite the first pair to share their ideas. Prompt other students to correct or add to the information.

A Underline the part of each sentence that is false. Rewrite that part to make it true.

- Ask questions to help students recall the text, e.g. *Who needs to sleep?* (birds and mammals) *What happens to your immune system if you don't sleep?* (It is weakened.) *How much sleep do children need?* (8–10 hours)
- Give students time to read through the sentences. Point out that they should scan the text to find the relevant information.
- Have students do the task individually and then compare answers in pairs. Check answers as a class.

Answers

1 We spend about <u>half</u> of our lives asleep.; *a third*
2 <u>Most</u> mammals and birds sleep.; All 3 While we sleep, our bodies <u>use lots of</u> energy.; rebuild and replace
4 Our brains <u>do nothing</u> while we sleep.; recover from the day, store information, and process experiences and memories 5 <u>There are clear</u> reasons why we dream.; Nobody really knows 6 Looking at screens <u>might help us sleep</u>.; can keep us awake

B Answer the questions.

- Ask students to look at the questions and think about their answers individually and write them down. Encourage them to look back at the text if necessary.
- Have students compare answers in pairs. Check answers as a class.

Answers

1 It's about what happens to our bodies while we sleep.
2 nonfiction 3 To teach us about sleep. The author achieves this by explaining different theories about what happens to our bodies when we sleep. 4 Students' own answers

C Complete the table. Look back at *Why Do We Sleep?*. What are the pros of getting enough sleep and the cons of not getting enough sleep?

- Read the question and tell students they must combine information from different parts of the text to complete the table.
- Have them work in pairs and scan the text for pros and cons that are mentioned.
- To check answers, have students share a pro or a con. Project the answers and have students add any ideas they missed.

Answers

Pros of getting enough sleep: your body rebuilds and replaces energy; muscles grow and are repaired; hormones are produced; we process experiences and memories from the day; unnecessary information is cleared away
Cons of not getting enough sleep: we get confused, stressed; our brain becomes inactive; we forget things and can't concentrate; we can't follow directions well; our immune system gets suppressed, so we get sick

D Think and discuss. Think about people who have unusual sleep patterns. Who are they? How do they get enough sleep?

- Students are going to use their critical thinking skills to discuss the CLIL health science topic of unusual sleep patterns and how they affect health.
- Write *unusual sleep patterns* on the board and elicit what these could be (going to bed late; sleeping during the day; staying awake at night; waking up in the middle of the night; getting very little sleep, etc.).
- Ask *Who has unusual sleeping patterns? How do they get enough sleep?* Have students do a Think, Pair, Share routine (see TB p. 20) to generate ideas.
- Put pairs of students together to compare their ideas. Then invite students to share ideas.

Suggested Answers

People who work at night, police officers, emergency room workers, pilots, people traveling across time zones, parents of babies
They get enough sleep by sleeping during the day, working specific shifts, sleeping at work, or sleeping at the same time as their babies.

Cool Down

Put students in pairs to do a role-play. One of them has problems sleeping or sleeps very few hours. The other student gives advice. Have students practice and then invite one or two pairs to perform for the class.

Practice **Student's App:** Reading Practice

Think Together

Lesson Objectives

- to make connections between the readings
- to explore the key concept: Why is it important to have good lifestyle habits?
- to reflect on the unit and provide personal thoughts and opinions

Warm Up

Have students look at the two readings and choose their favorite picture from each reading. Ask them to compare in pairs and give reasons why they like each picture.

A Think and write. Complete the table. Look back at *My Stay at Camp Karma* and *Why Do We Sleep?* What do the readings say about these subjects?

- Before students complete the table, put them in pairs to discuss what they remember about each reading and what each one taught them about healthy lifestyle habits.
- Students can complete the table on their own or in pairs. Monitor and provide language help if needed.
- Project answers onto the board using the TTL.

Answers

My Stay at Camp Karma
Sleep: Cathy's mom feels stressed because she isn't getting enough sleep. / Cathy's mom thinks the family will sleep better in a yurt away from technology.
Food / diet: green vegetables, fruit and fish are good for you, sugar is bad for you
Exercise: Exercising in the sand is hard. Yoga, running, hiking, swimming are all good for you.
Happiness: They feel happier after meditating. / Everyone is happier after a week of exercise and healthy food.
Why Do We Sleep?
Sleep: We feel tired and stressed if we don't get enough sleep. / We sleep better when it's cool, dark, and quiet.
Food / diet: You might not sleep so well after eating junk food.
Exercise: We should do regular exercise but not just before bed.
Happiness: When we sleep enough, we are happier.

B Think and discuss. What can you change in your own life to be healthier? Do a Three-Step Interview.

- Students are going to do a Three-Step Interview routine (see TB p. 20) to discuss what changes they can make to their own lifestyle in order to be healthier.
- In Step 3, students share what they have learned about their friend with the class. With large classes, students can share their ideas in groups. Ask students the key concept question: *Why is it important to have good lifestyle habits?* Recap ideas from the whole class.

Practice **Resource Bank:** Unit Test
Student's App: Key Concept Practice

Suggested Answers

Go to bed and get up at the same time every day.
Stop looking at a screen before bed.
Try meditating for 10 minutes every day.
Eat more green vegetables and fish.
Make sure you get 8–10 hours of sleep.
Exercise regularly.
Don't eat sugar.

C Think and write. What steps could you take to make the changes from B?

- Students are going to come up with an action plan and make connections to the key concept question at the top of the page: *Why is it important to have good lifestyle habits?*
- Give students time to think about steps they can take to make the changes they discussed in B. Elicit an example from one or two students.
- Students write their ideas individually. Then they share in small groups and ask their partners for any more ideas to add.

My Reading Journal

What's the most important information you learned in this unit?

What are some good habits you already have? How did you learn them?

These questions encourage students to personalize what they have learned in the unit and relate this to their own life.

Give students time to look through the unit and answer the questions with their ideas. Have them share ideas in pairs before eliciting a few examples with the class.

Example Answers

The most important information is that (if you don't sleep enough, you get sick more easily).
I (go to sleep at the same time every day). I learned this (from my parents).

Go back to page 25. Do the routine again.

Have students look back at the VTR picture on p. 25 and elicit what they discussed in the Get Ready to Read lesson on p. 25 (use your notes to remind them). Discuss how the picture connects to the two readings in the unit. Focus on how the people doing tai chi felt before taking it up and after trying it. Ask if they think doing it helps them sleep better.

Then guide students to do the Step Inside VTR again. How have the people's perspectives in the picture changed after everything students learned?

Cool Down

Play *Test the Teacher* (see TB p. 26) with information from the two readings.

UNIT 3

Dream Big

Unit Overview

Themes

The importance of having dreams and ambitions

The importance of persevering to succeed

Synopsis

In this unit, students will discuss their dreams and ambitions. They will learn about the importance of perseverance in order to achieve their goals in life. They will discuss how children can make a positive impact and help solve the world's problems. Students will plan and write a cause-and-effect article. They will also have a discussion to gather ideas about celebrating Universal Children's Day.

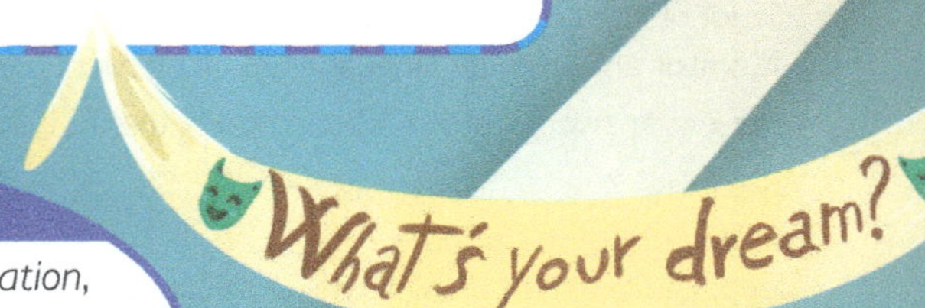

Language Book

Vocabulary

ambition, confidence, determination, happiness, health, pride, success, wealth

Pronunciation: Connected Speech: Consonant-Vowel Linking

p. 80

Explore Language

Second Conditional

p. 81

Global Citizenship

How can children help solve the world's problems?

be the hero, do things for fun, experience failure, fear of the unknown, find joy in, fresh start, notice the small things, nurture friendship

p. 82

Explore Language

Wish + Past Forms

p. 83

Write About It

A Cause-and-Effect Article

Describing Causes and Effects, and Suggesting Solutions; Positive and Negative Adjectives

p. 84

Talk About It

Conversation: Asking for Ideas and Summarizing Points

p. 85

Think It Over

Review and Reflection: Monthly Goal Reflection

p. 86

Literacy Book

Think Together
Why is it important to have dreams?
p. 93

Visible Thinking
3–2–1 Bridge
p. 87

Fiction
Poem: *Dreams*
Words in Context: *stop-motion movie, gulps, tuning out, twitch, hay*
p. 91

Nonfiction
Creative Nonfiction: *Communities Making Dreams Come True*
Words in Context: *cash flow, nonprofit, tiller, campaign, went viral, walks of life*
p. 88

Reading Skill
Understanding Author's Word Choice
p. 90

Literary Term
Prefix
p. 89

Language and Literacy Connections

The connecting theme for Unit 3 is dreams and ambitions, and persevering to succeed.

	Language	Literacy
Vocabulary	**Set 1:** dreams and ambitions **Set 2:** persevering to succeed	**Nonfiction:** make a fresh start **Fiction:** ambition, determination, just for fun
Grammar	**Second Conditional** If you could be anyone, who would you be? She would be a gymnast if she could choose. ***Wish* + Past Forms** I wish I didn't find math so hard. My cousin wishes she was better at photography. Do you wish you were a great athlete?	**Nonfiction** If they didn't meet their goal, they would delay their plan. **Fiction** Isabel wishes she could feel the string break. He wishes he had a rabbit.
Skills	**Pronunciation:** connected speech: consonant-vowel linking **Process Writing:** planning	**Reading:** understanding author's word choice **Literary Term:** prefix
International English	soccer uniform / football kit	ready, set, go! / ready, steady, go!; sled/sledge; grades/marks

Vocabulary

Lesson Objectives

- to learn vocabulary for dreams and ambitions: *ambition, confidence, determination, happiness, health, pride, success, wealth*
- to read a poem about following your dreams
- to notice and practice linking consonant-vowel sounds

Materials
Audio Tracks 27 to 31; Video

Warm Up

Write the unit title on the board: *Dream Big*. Elicit some examples of big dreams. Then have students close their eyes and dream big. After a few minutes, ask them to draw a picture of their dream. Finally have students discuss their drawings and dreams in small groups.

A TRACK 27 TB p. 218 **Listen. What's different about this theater experience?**

- Have students look at the picture in their books and find Coach García and his daughter Camila. Explain that they are going to hear them talking to an actor.
- Ask the question and elicit some predictions. Then play the audio. Have students listen and check. Elicit the answer.
- Then ask the teaser question from the end of Unit 2 *What kind of play do you think we'll see?* If necessary, play the audio again and elicit opinions (students' own answers).

Answer
You enter a room and you can become a different person as part of the experience.

B TRACK 28 TB p. 218 **Find and number the words in A. Then listen and check.**

- Ask students to call out the words in the list they already know. Then have them work in pairs to number the words. Point out that the picture on each door represents one of the words. Then play the audio for students to listen and check their answers.

Answers
1 *ambition* 2 health 3 success 4 happiness
5 pride 6 determination 7 confidence 8 wealth

C TRACK 29 TB p. 218 **Close your eyes. Listen, visualize, and say.**

- Prepare students for the visualization (see TB p. 21).
- Play the audio, allowing students to visualize the ideas as they listen.
- Have students choose one of the situations from the visualization and share their ideas in pairs. Then put students in different pairs to explain what they found out about their partner.

D **Put the words in order of importance for you (1 = most important).**

- Students are going to rank the vocabulary. This encourages critical thinking and the development of important life skills and values.
- Point to the list and explain there are no correct answers. Students must think about what's important to them and decide their ranking. Let them have some thinking time to decide the order. Elicit which is the most and least important concept from students around the class.

Answers
Students' own answers

E TRACK 30 TB p. 218 **Listen and write. Then watch and say.**

- Have students look at the poem and unscramble the letters to complete each blank with words from A. Play the audio and have students check their answers.
- Play the audio or video again and have students join in with the poem. Encourage students to copy the rhythm and pronunciation.
- Have students read the poem silently. Then, in pairs, take turns reading a line each. They can swap turns and repeat.

Answers
1 *ambition* 2 determination 3 success 4 happiness
5 wealth 6 pride 7 health

F TRACK 31 TB p. 218 **Pronunciation. Listen and say. Copy the linking. Find other examples in the poem.**

- This task raises students' awareness of consonant-vowel linking by noticing phrases in the poem.
- Play the audio once. Have students listen and notice what happens to *have a* and *full of*. Point to the line that joins the end of the first word to the beginning of the next one. Elicit that the /v/ "runs into" /ə/ in *have a* /hævə/ and the /l/ runs into /ə/ in *full of* /fʊləv/. Ask students whether *a* and *of* have a full form or weak form (weak).
- Play the audio again for students to repeat. Then ask them to find more phrases with linking in the poem. Elicit answers and write them on the board. Drill the phrases.
- Put students in pairs. They take turns saying a phrase from the board. Their partner must listen and confirm he/she can hear the linking.

Answers
dream of; of ambition; have a lot; I'm ambitious, right up; love and; strong, I'll; of energy

Cool Down

Write on the board *I dream of …* Ask students to choose one of the words from A to complete the sentence in their head. Then have them mingle and say their sentence. Their goal is to find other people with the same dream and form a group. Prompt students or groups to call out their sentence.

Practice **Student's App:** Vocabulary Practice; Spoken Word Video

Explore Language

Lesson Objectives

- to learn how to use the second conditional
- to practice vocabulary for dreams and ambitions

Materials

Audio Tracks 32 and 33; small ball or crumpled-up paper (CD)

Warm Up

Have students imagine they're at *Life Is a Theater*. Ask them to think which room they want to enter and why. Say *Imagine you're inside the room. What do you think happens? How do you feel?* Put students in pairs to share ideas.

A TRACK 32 TB p. 218 **Listen and read. Which doors do Elise and Ji-su choose? Why?**

- Display the picture and point out Elise and Ji-su. Have students find Ji-su in the picture on p. 36. Tell students they are going to listen to the two friends talking in the theater. Elicit ideas on what they are talking about. Play the audio and have students listen and check their answers.
- Ask the questions *Which doors do Elise and Ji-su choose? Why?* Have students find the answers and check by looking at the dialogue again. Elicit from students what other doors Elise and Ji-su consider ("Success" and maybe "Determination"). Ask students which of the three doors discussed they would choose. Ask further questions to check comprehension (see **ETB**).

Answers

They both choose the "Pride" door because they want to experience how amazing achievements would make them feel / because they want the pride of going to the Olympics and maybe winning a medal.

B **Look at A. Complete the table. How many times does *would* appear in each sentence?**

- Tell students to scan the dialogue in A and complete the table with the missing words. Have them compare answers in pairs.
- Display the table using the TTL and check answers. Elicit that *would* appears once in each sentence. Then ask *How many clauses are there in each sentence?* (two) *What follows "would"?* (a verb in base form) *What word does the other clause start with?* (if) *What verb form do we use in the "if" clause?* (simple past) *Does the "if" clause come first or second?* (both) *What punctuation do we use if "if" appears at the beginning?* (a comma)
- Elicit and write the structure on the board: *if* + simple past → *would/wouldn't* + verb base form.

Answers

be; would; If; would; be; had; would; could

Would appears once in each sentence.

Practice **Resource Bank:** Grammar Printout
Student's App: Grammar Practice

- Refer students to the Grammar tip *Remember*. Point out that *'d* is *would* in second conditional sentences, not *had*.

C **Think and discuss. Then choose.**

- Ask students to look at the table in B and discuss the statement and answer options in pairs. Then check the answer. Ask questions to check understanding: *Can Ji-su be anyone?* (No, she can only be herself.) *Is she famous?* (No, she isn't.) If you feel that students need more guidance, the **ETB** provides a differentiation activity.

Answer

1 unreal or impossible

D TRACK 33 TB p. 218 **Listen and say.**

- Tell students they're going to practice saying sentences with the second conditional to help with pronunciation in fluent speech and so that they begin to internalize the structure. Play the audio and have students repeat each example chorally. (See TB p. 23, Making Language Drills Fun.)

E **Read and complete the paragraph.**

- This activity provides controlled practice of the grammar. Prompt students to read the paragraph and notice all the instances of *if*. Elicit what verb form is used in the *if* clause (simple past).
- Have students complete the paragraph individually before comparing their answers in pairs. Remind students to use contractions where possible.
- Check answers as a class, confirming the spelling by writing or projecting them on the board.

Answers

1 *had* 2 *'d go* 3 won 4 would/be 5 were
6 wouldn't spend 7 wouldn't leave 8 became
9 would move 10 could

F **Think and discuss. Complete the questions. Then ask and answer.**

- Students now personalize the language by completing the questions with their own ideas. Brainstorm some ideas as a class. Monitor and check they are using the correct verb forms.
- Put students in pairs to ask and answer their questions. Monitor and make sure they are answering with full sentences. Invite students to say something interesting they found out about their partner.

Cool Down

Ask students to stand in a big circle. Ask a question with the second conditional and answer it, e.g. *What animal would you be if you could choose? I'd be a cat.* Then throw a ball to a student and elicit a reply: *I'd be a(n) …* Students continue throwing the ball around until everyone has replied. To make this more challenging/fun, set a fast pace and ask students not to repeat a reply. Continue with more questions.

Global Citizenship

Lesson Objectives

- to learn vocabulary related to perseverance: *be the hero, do things for fun, experience failure, fear of the unknown, find joy in, fresh start, notice the small things, nurture friendship*
- to explore how children can help solve the world's problems
- to practice listening for gist and details

Materials

Audio Tracks 34 to 36; Audio Track C

Opening Question

Ask the opening question: *How can children help solve the world's problems?* Elicit examples of world problems and brainstorm ideas of how children can help solve them.

A TRACK 34 TB p. 218 **Listen to Kamala interviewing three of her teachers. How can adults learn from children?**

- Explain that Kamala is doing a school project. Have students predict what the school project is about. Play the audio for students to check.
- Write the teachers' names on the board and ask the question *How can adults learn from children?*
- Play the audio again for students to listen, answer, and check. Ask what else adults can learn from children.

Answers

See every day as a fresh start. Move on quickly after failure. (Mrs. Taylor) / Be the hero of your own story. It's important to spend time on friendships. (Mr. Addison) / Be creative. Remember the importance of doing things for fun, and noticing the small things. (Ms. Asal)

B TRACK 35 TB p. 218 **Look at the pictures in A and write. Then listen and check.**

- Have students match the words and phrases to the pictures in A.
- Play the audio for students to check answers. Then play it again to practice the pronunciation, pausing after each word or phrase for them to repeat.

Answers

1 *fresh start* 2 experience failure 3 fear of the unknown
4 notice the small things 5 nurture friendship
6 do things for fun 7 find joy in 8 be the hero

TRACK C TB p. 219 **Visualization**

The TTL has a visualization audio track for this vocabulary set. (See TB p. 21.)

C **Read and complete. Then ask and answer.**

- Point out that the example contains the first and last word in the phrase on either side of the blank.
- Have students complete the questions. Check answers by nominating students to read a question aloud.
- Do the second part of the activity as a Think, Pair, Share routine (see TB p. 20).

Answers

1 *joy* 2 fresh 3 fear 4 nurture 5 fun 6 notice
7 experience 8 hero

D TRACK 36 TB p. 219 **Now listen to Feliks. How successful were the children in the soccer tournament?**

- Have students look at the photo and describe it.
- Listening for gist: ask the question and play the audio. Students discuss the answer in pairs. Check as a class.

Answer

They got to the semifinals, but they didn't win.

E **Listen again. Answer the questions.**

- Listening for details: have students read the questions and answer any they remember.
- Play the audio and have students write their answers. Check answers as a class. Discuss their opinion of what the children did. Are they surprised by what they achieved?

International English

Point out the American English and British English noun phrases *soccer uniform* and *football kit*. Ask *What do you wear as a soccer uniform or football kit?* (shirt, shorts, shin pads, etc.)

Answers

1 *Because they had no space in their village, where all the buildings are over water.* 2 They made fun of it (and thought it wouldn't work). 3 pretty small, not very flat, and open to the water 4 Because they loved having a community soccer team. 5 They are really proud.

Discussion Questions

- Draw students' attention to the discussion questions: *What could you do in your community that would benefit young people? What skills do children need to become positive members of the community?* Have students discuss the questions in pairs or small groups (see **ETB**). Encourage students to recognize that children can make a difference in both their local community and the world, and that there are skills they can develop to help them do this.
- Ask the opening question to ask again. Encourage students to add any new ideas. Focus on the concept of children being the world's best hope for the future and how important it is to listen to them and protect them.

Cool Down

Play a variation of *Snowballs* (see TB p. 26). Elicit a problem in the world like famine, war, or pollution. Students should write down suggestions for fixing the problem.

Practice **Student's App:** Vocabulary Practice; Listening Practice

Explore Language

Lesson Objectives

- to learn how to use *wish* and past forms
- to discuss things you would like to change

Materials
Audio Tracks 37 and 38

Warm Up

Tell students they can make three wishes. Allow them to use *I want …* to say what they wish for. Let them discuss their ideas in pairs and then share answers as a class. See what the class's most popular wish is.

A TRACK 37 TB p. 219 **Listen and read. How does Juan feel about joining the softball club?**

- Display the picture using the TTL. Elicit what clubs the students can see. Ask whether there are similar clubs in their school.
- Tell students they are going to listen to the children talk about the softball club. Point to Juan (the boy with the baseball cap) and ask *Do you think he's going to join the club?* Elicit answers and play the audio for students to check.
- Ask the question *How does Juan feel about joining the softball club?* Invite students to discuss the question in pairs before you elicit the answer from the class. Ask further comprehension questions (see **ETB**).

Answer
He isn't sure, because he says he is not very good.

B Look at A. Complete the table. What kinds of words come after *wish*?

- Have students scan the dialogue in A and find the missing words in the table individually or in pairs.
- Display the table using the TTL and check answers as a class. Ask the question *What kinds of words come after "wish"?* and elicit answers.
- Then ask *What form do we use for "wish"?* (simple present) *What form do we use for the verb after "wish"?* (simple past) Draw students' attention to the Grammar tip *Watch Out.*

Answers
didn't; wasn't; play; would; wishes; was; Do; wish
Subject pronouns and nouns come after *wish*.

C Think and discuss. Then choose.

- Ask students to read the sentences and refer to the examples in the table in B. Have them work in pairs to discuss and decide on the correct usage.
- Check answers as a class and discuss further. Elicit that although we use the simple past, the wish refers to a present or future situation. Point out that in the dialogue example in A, Juan can actually change things if he practices more! (See **ETB**.)

Answers
1 unlikely 2 unlikely 3 irritation

D TRACK 38 TB p. 219 **Listen and say.**

- Tell students they're going to practice saying sentences with *wish* to help with pronunciation in fluent speech and to consolidate what they've learned. Play the audio and have students repeat each example chorally. (See TB p. 23, Making Language Drills Fun.)

E Find and correct the errors.

- Read the wrong version of the example and have students read the correct question.
- Give students time to correct the rest of the items individually. Then put students in pairs to compare their answers. Check answers by projecting them on the board.

Answers
1 ~~*wished*~~ *wish*; ~~*live*~~ *lived* 2 ~~wishes~~ wish; ~~can~~ could
3 ~~be~~ were 4 ~~have~~ had 5 ~~wish~~ wishes; ~~they'll~~ they'd
6 ~~wish~~ wishes; ~~won't~~ wouldn't

F Write three things you wish you could change. Then discuss with a friend.

- This activity gives students freer practice of the language with a personal response to local or global problems. Invite two students to read the exchange. Ask the first student to answer the question asked by the second student if possible.
- Students write their three wishes individually. Monitor and provide language help if needed.
- In pairs, students take turns saying their wish and asking a follow-up question. Encourage them to continue the conversation if they are interested in the topic.

Cool Down

Put students in pairs. Choose who they want to be: the children at the Art Club or at the Soccer Club stand. Give them a few minutes to act out a dialogue similar to the one in A between Max and Juan. Tell them they must each say at least one wish sentence. Elicit from pairs what wish sentences they said.

Practice **Resource Bank:** Grammar Printout
Student's App: Grammar Practice

Write About It

Lesson Objectives

- to plan and write a cause-and-effect article
- to describe causes and effects
- to learn to use positive and negative adjectives
- to learn to plan effectively to help your writing (Process Writing Step 2)

Materials

Support Writing printouts from the Resource Bank (F)

Warm Up

Play *Shark* (see TB p. 26) with *electricity*. When students find the word, write this prompt on the board: *If we didn't have electricity, we wouldn't be able to …* Give students a minute to think of ideas in pairs. Then elicit ideas and write them on the board.

A Read the article. What problems does the lack of electricity cause?

- This lesson corresponds with the Unit 3 nonfiction reading in the **Literacy Book**. Tell students they are going to read an article about parts of the world that don't have electricity. Draw their attention to the first question heading: *What's the problem?* Have them read the first paragraph. Then have them make predictions about the second question heading in pairs: *What does that mean for children?*
- After they've brainstormed a few ideas, have them read the second paragraph and check. Follow the same procedure for the two remaining paragraphs.
- Then ask the question *What problems does the lack of electricity cause?* Nominate students to answer. Check whether these ideas were mentioned in the Warm Up.

Answer

It's difficult to study after dark, and communication is limited.

B Look at the structure of the article. Read and respond.

- Tell students they're going to look at the cause and effect structure in the article. Review *cause* and *effect*. Students should remember these terms from Level 5.
- Draw students' attention to the questions. Put students in pairs to answer the questions, referring to the article as needed. Check answers as a class.

Answers

1 Students' own answers 2 The headings make the article more organized, easier to read, and engaging.
3 1 b; 2 d; 3 c; 4 a

C Look at the language in the article. Complete the Venn Diagram.

- Students are going to analyze the language from the article. In pairs, have students look at the words in the box and decide if they are positive, negative, or neutral. Discuss answers as a class.
- Read the Reflect tip. As an extension, elicit two more positive and two more negative words that the writer could have used in the article.

Suggested Answers

Positive: *solution*, reliable, inexpensive
Middle (Neutral): effects
Negative: limited, unreliable, difficult, problem

D Think and discuss problems in your local area or region. Complete the mind map.

- In this lesson, the focus is on the planning stage of the writing process. Tell students they are going to write a cause-and-effect article about a problem in their area or region. Put them in small groups to brainstorm ideas and complete the mind map.
- Elicit problems and write them on the board.

Answers

Students' own answers

- Ask students to turn to p. 141 to learn about **Process Writing Step 2: Planning** (see TB p. 212). Students will need to do this step before they do E.

E Plan your article. Choose one of your ideas in D. Make notes.

- Tell students they are going to plan their cause-and-effect article. Have them revise their ideas in D and choose a problem they would like to write about. Ask them to tell their partner and explain why.
- Allow enough time for students to think of the three effects and the solution(s) to the problem. Monitor as they complete the flow chart plan and provide language help if necessary.
- Put students in pairs to explain the effects and solution(s). Encourage students to give more ideas to their partner.

F Now write your article.

- Have students write a draft of their article in their notebooks, referring to their notes in E. They should read their drafts and make any corrections or improvements.
- Have students write their final versions neatly on paper. Alternatively, hand out the Support printouts.
- Ask students to read a friend's article and identify the cause, effects, and solutions to the problem.

Cool Down

Play a *Chain Game* (see TB p. 25) to practice causes and effect. Start with the sentence *There was a big storm, so we didn't have electricity all day.*

Practice **Resource Bank:** Writing Game, *What's the Problem?*
Student's App: Writing Practice

Talk About It

Lesson Objectives

- to prepare and have a conversation about Universal Children's Day
- to practice asking for ideas and summarizing points

Materials
Video

Warm Up

Write *The Best Day of the Year* on the board. Have students discuss which day of the year they think is the best and why. Now, write *International Day of Happiness* and *Universal Children's Day*. Have them discuss what each day is about and whether they have celebrated these days in the past. If not, ask how they would like to celebrate them.

A TB p. 239 **Watch and listen. What ideas are discussed for International Day of Happiness?**

- Tell students they are going to watch a video of three children (Lloyd, Maria, and Linda) discussing ideas for how to celebrate the International Day of Happiness. Have students predict what ideas the children are going to discuss.
- With books closed, play the video for students to watch, listen, and make notes of the ideas discussed. Check their predictions.
- Ask the comprehension question *What ideas are discussed for International Day of Happiness?* If necessary, play the video again and then allow some time for students to discuss answers in pairs. Elicit answers.

Answers
send messages, photos, and cards; give presents like pictures and cakes

B Watch again and number the phrases. Then write *AI* (asking for ideas) or *SU* (summarizing points to ensure understanding).

- Tell students they are going to focus on how Maria guides the discussion. Point out she asks for Lloyd and Linda's ideas before summarizing them.
- Play the video again and first have students order the phrases. Have them compare their answers in pairs. Then have students decide the function of each phrase individually or in pairs. Check answers.

Answers
1 b 2 d 3 c 4 f 5 e 6 a 7 g
Asking for ideas: b; d; f
Summarizing points to ensure understanding: a; c; e; g

C Imagine your school is celebrating Universal Children's Day. What ideas do you have?

- Put students in pairs to discuss one or two ideas for Universal Children's Day. After they've had time to discuss ideas, have them make notes individually. Monitor and provide language help if needed.

Answers
Students' own answers

D Talk with your friends using phrases from B. Choose the best three ideas.

- Tell students they are going to have a discussion in groups about Universal Children's Day. Tell them they are going to use their ideas from C as well as the ideas in D.
- Draw their attention to the ideas in D. Ask them if these ideas are the same as any they thought of. Put students in pairs to brainstorm ideas for "other." What other different ways of celebrating the day did they think of in C? Elicit ideas.
- Put students in small groups of three or four. Ask them to decide who is going to lead the discussion, just like Maria did. Remind them to use phrases from B and their preferred ideas.
- Allow time for students to have their discussions and decide on the best three ideas. You could write phrases on the board for students to reach conclusions, e.g. *So, let's decide on the three best ideas. / Do you think this idea is a really good one? / I think we should choose (inviting people). It's a very good idea.*
- Invite students who lead the discussion to share the ideas with the class.
- Have students reflect on their performance and think about whether everyone contributed ideas. Ask them to share ideas in their groups.

Cool Down

Ask students to make their own *International Day of* ... Have them brainstorm ideas in pairs or groups. Ask them to name their day and explain what it celebrates. They should also suggest a few ideas for celebrations. Invite students to present their ideas to the class.

Practice **Student's App:** Speaking Skills Practice; Speaking Video

Think It Over

Lesson Objectives

- to review what has been learned in the unit
- to reflect on the unit and their own progress
- to think about learning strategies and how to continue learning at home

Warm Up

Ask students what the unit theme was (dreams and ambitions; persevering to succeed). Write on the board *I wish I could … My biggest ambition is to … If I want to succeed, I need to …* Give students a minute to think about their own ideas to complete the prompts. Have them compare ideas in small groups. Elicit ideas from each group.

How well did you meet the challenge of Unit 3? Read and respond.

Monthly Goal Reflection

- Tell students they are going to review what they learned in the unit and also think about their own learning and whether they have reached their goals from Unit 3. This time students are also going to evaluate how hard they worked and think about whether they need to do more in order to progress in their learning.
- Review what students have done in the unit with an Inside-Outside Circle routine (TB p. 21). Have students on the outside of the circle start by remembering something they did. Students can have their books with them and show their partner the page they are referring to if necessary. The student on the inside of the circle then says something different that they did. On the signal, students rotate and try to think of something new. Encourage students to remember information they learned, as well as activities they did. After a few minutes, stop the routine and move on to the next stage.
- Draw students' attention to the heading *Monthly Goal Reflection*. Have students look back at the end of Unit 2 and remember what their goal was. Ask students if they think they have worked hard to reach their goal and whether they feel they have succeeded. Have them think about what they have done in order to achieve their goal and discuss with a partner.
- Allow students to work individually to fill out the first two parts of the organizer. Remind them that they should write their own responses about themselves. Monitor and help as necessary. Look at what students are writing so you can tailor your classes and any additional practice to their needs.
- Ask students what they would like to work on and improve in the future. Refer students to the final section in the graphic organizer. Tell students to think about whether they still need to work more to achieve their goal or, if they have succeeded, whether they will choose a different one. Have them look back through the unit and evaluate their learning in each lesson. Then have them write their ideas about their plans for their next goals. They can then share their ideas with a friend.
- Ask if anyone has the same goals as their friend. Point out that goals should be personal and each student should choose those they think they would benefit from most.

Looking Forward

Draw students' attention to the character at the bottom of the page. Have students say who he is and what they remember about him. (Max likes softball, photography, and astronomy. He appears in Lesson 1, p. 36, and Lesson 4, p. 42. He's responsible for recruiting new players for the softball club together with Nella, and he encourages Juan to join.) Have students look at the speech bubble and discuss what ball lightning is. Tell students they will find out the answer in Lesson 1 of the next unit.

Practice **Resource Bank:** Unit Test
Student's App: Vocabulary and Grammar Review

Literacy

Get Ready to Read

Lesson Objectives

- to activate prior knowledge about dreams
- to guide inquiry and deepen understanding through a 3–2–1 Bridge VTR
- to preview the reading skill of understanding author's word choice

Materials
VTR printout from the Resource Bank (A, B, C, D)

Warm Up

With books closed, have students guess the two animals in the opening image (cat and lion) by telling them riddles: *We both walk quietly. We both have beautiful eyes. I'm much bigger. I live in Africa,* and so on. When students find the two animals, see if they can guess what the image is. Project the image using the TTL for students to check ideas.

3–2–1 Bridge

A Look at the picture. Write three thoughts or ideas you have.

- This VTR encourages students to analyze and interpret the meaning behind the image of a cat and a lion. Start by having students look at the picture while reading the quote. Then say *I think the cat wants to be as tall as the lion. What do you think?*
- Give students some time to brainstorm ideas individually. Encourage them to think about the wider topic of dreams, not just about the picture. They can make notes in their notebooks.
- Put students in small groups to compare ideas and decide on the three best to write down. You could use the 3-2-1 Bridge printout.

B Write two questions you have.

- Put students in pairs to discuss questions they have about the picture. Give an example first: *I wonder if my dreams are going to come true.*
- Prompt students to write down two of the questions they discussed. Encourage them again to think about the wider topic.

C Write a metaphor.

- Invite a student to read the metaphor. In pairs, students discuss a few metaphors and then decide on the best one. They can also think of a simile or any kind of analogy. Monitor and provide language help if needed.

D Share your ideas with the class.

- Start from A and work down to B and C. Each time, invite students to share ideas with the class. Keep a record of students' ideas from the VTR to revisit in the Think Together lesson.

Here's an example of this part of the routine.

Teacher: What thoughts or ideas did you have?
Student A: We think the cat is afraid of lions because it looks a bit scared.
Student B: We think the opposite, —that the cat thinks it's as brave as the lion.
Teacher: OK, good. What questions did you have, Student C?
Student C: We asked why it's important to dream.
Student D: And how to make our dreams come true.
Teacher: OK, Thank you. Who would like to share their metaphor?
Student E: Dreams are like ice. They're hard, but they can melt.
Student F: Dreaming is breathing. You can't live without dreams.

Transition

Ask *What does the cat dream of?* (being a lion; being bigger) *What if a person was standing—what would the shadow be? What would your dream shadow look like?*

E Think and discuss. Dreams don't only happen when we sleep. A dream is also something that we hope for or want to achieve. What dreams do you have?

- Read the question and write the synonyms on the board: *Dream–Hope–Wish–Goal.* Check again what *daydreaming* is.
- Have students daydream for a few seconds and then discuss their dreams in pairs.
- Have some students share their dreams with the class.

Answers
Students' own answers

F Think and write. Look at the headings in *Communities Making Dreams Come True*. What do you think the reading is about?

- This activity previews the skill of understanding author's word choice by making predictions from the title and headings of the reading.
- Look at the headings and elicit the important words the author chose to use, e.g. *communities, dreams, problems.*
- Have students predict what the reading is about in pairs. Encourage them to share any knowledge they already have about microloans or crowdfunding.
- Invite students to share their ideas with the class.

Answers
Students' own answers

Now read **Communities Making Dreams Come True**

Nonfiction: *Communities Making Dreams Come True—Creative Nonfiction*

Lesson Objectives

- to read a text about microloans and crowdfunding
- to make a personal connection to the reading

Materials
Audio Tracks 13 and 14

Warm Up

With books closed, write the title in scrambled order on the board, e.g. *Come Dreams Communities True Making.* Have students to reorder the words correctly. Then discuss the students' predictions from the previous lesson.

TRACK 13 TB p. 231 Reading Approach

First Reading: Engage with the Text

- Ask students to look at the headings and pictures and predict what dreams or projects they will read about.
- Have students read the text silently to check their predictions.
- Elicit the main idea of the text (achieving dreams through crowdfunding). Then look at the Words in Context.

TRACK 14 TB p. 231 Words in Context

- Give students a few minutes to find and highlight each word. Have them identify the kind of word it is.
- Write these strategies on the board for students to use with the words: *surrounding words and sentences, positive/negative, understanding main ideas, separate parts of word, pictures, L1 cognates.*
- Have students work in pairs to discuss the words. Then check as a class and discuss the strategies they used.
- Finally, play the audio to practice the pronunciation.

cash flow (p. 42, noun) *Problems* show it's a negative thing. The main idea is about Rupa needing to borrow money. Strategies to use: understanding main ideas; positive/negative; separate parts of word

nonprofit (p. 43, adjective) This describes an organization. The word can be broken down: *non* + *profit*. Strategies to use: surrounding words and sentences; separate parts of word

tiller (p. 43, noun): The article *a* shows it is a noun, and, *harvest* is mentioned, so it is something that helps with this. The pictures above illustrate this sequence. Strategies to use: surrounding words and sentences; pictures

campaign (p. 45 / p. 47, noun) The sentences on p. 47 show it can be crowdfunded and can reach a goal. The sentence on p. 45 shows that people contribute money to it. Strategy to use: surrounding words and sentences

went viral (p. 45, verb phrase) *Thousands of people saw* shows that something that *goes viral* is seen by many people. Strategies to use: surrounding words and sentences; possible L1 cognates

walks of life (p. 47, noun phrase) *People from* shows it is something that people belong to. The whole article gives examples of different kinds of people in different situations. Strategies to use: surrounding words and sentences; understanding main ideas

Second Reading: Analyze the Text and Features

- Play the audio and have students read along. Invite students to explain *microloan* and *crowdfunding*. See the **ETB** for more comprehension questions.
- Discuss the questions in the green boxes.
  - **Critical Thinking** (p. 42): *Is it easy for people to achieve their dreams? Why or why not?* Elicit opinions and reasons. Discuss the problems from the passage, e.g. lack of money and tools, as well as other obstacles that might prevent a dream from coming true.
  - **Language in Context** (p. 43): *What do you think "didn't give up" means?* Have students scan the passage to find the verb. Elicit whether Rupa was successful in getting a loan (no). Ask *Did that stop her?* (no)
  - **Language in Context** (p. 45): *What do you think "be onto a winner" means?* Have students find the phrase and read the conditions before it, i.e. *if Jorani drew the characters and backgrounds*, and *if Leap wrote the game for cell phones and tablets.* Elicit what *a winner* refers to (the app game) and if it would be successful (yes).
  - **Fun Fact** (p. 46): *In 2014, crowdfunding raised $16 billion for different projects. One year later, this amount more than doubled to $34 billion!* Tell students that one of the most successful crowdfunding campaigns was for a smartwatch. Let them guess how much was raised. ($20,338,986).
  - **Personalization** (p. 47): *What type of business would you start if you had the funding?* Give students some time to think and discuss in pairs before sharing as a class.

Third Reading: Interact with the Text

- Have students read again and choose the campaign they prefer. Have them compare choices and reasons in pairs.
- Put students into small groups according to the story they chose. Tell them they are going to represent Rupa, Noam, Jorani, Leap, or LeVar and try to convince a banker to give them a loan. Give them time to prepare a short speech.
- Invite students to give their speeches. If there is time, ask three students to sit at the front of the class as bankers and decide which campaign to give the loan to.

Cool Down

Play *Correct the Teacher* (see TB p. 25) with the sentences from the reading.

Practice **Student's App:** Story Player

Explore the Reading

Lesson Objectives

- to understand and analyze *Communities Making Dreams Come True* through reading comprehension activities
- to learn through CLIL (social studies): communities
- to make a personal connection to the reading

Warm Up

Ask students to look at *Communities Making Dreams Come True* again and write one question about the reading. When students are ready, put them in groups to ask and answer their questions with books closed. Monitor and provide language help if necessary.

A Answer the questions.

- Ask students to read the questions once and check they understand them. Then give students time to scan the text for the answers. Allow them to work in pairs if they prefer.
- Put students in pairs or small groups to compare their answers. To check answers, choose students to answer a question and point out the part of the text where they found the answer.

Answers
1 They don't have anything valuable to offer as a guarantee. 2 a loan of a small amount of money to someone who finds it difficult to get a bank loan 3 where a large group of people give money to help a particular project or dream become a reality 4 mostly over the internet 5 a copy of the game once it was complete 6 just one day

B Think, discuss, and write. Do you think the title fits the article? Why or why not? Write a different title for the article.

- Elicit the title and write it on the board. Ask the question *Do you think the title fits the article?* Students discuss their ideas in small groups.
- Prompt students to think of a different title. Monitor and help if necessary.
- Elicit different titles and write them on the board.

Answers
Students' own answers

C Think and discuss. After getting a microloan or donation, what else will someone need to do to make their dream or project a reality? What are ways communities are improved by these dreams and projects?

- Students are going to connect the reading with their own understanding of the power of communities. This draws on the CLIL social studies focus of exploring how people work together as a community.
- Have students work in pairs to brainstorm some steps people need to take after getting the microloan or donation. Invite students to list some ideas. Write them on the board and discuss the order these steps need to happen.
- Ask students to brainstorm ways in which communities can be improved by these initiatives. Have a class discussion.

Example Answers
Step 1: Stay focused on the project and work hard.
Step 2: Give information about how the project progresses to people who have supported you.
Step 3: Prepare for promoting your product or service and selling it to others.
Step 4: Pay off loans or give rewards to people who have supported the campaign.

Literary Term: Prefix

Think, read, and write. What do you think the prefixes *micro–*, *inter–*, and *un–* mean?

- With books closed, write the three prefixes on the board: *micro–*, *inter–*, *un–*. Put students in pairs and have them brainstorm a word for each prefix. Elicit ideas and write them on the board.
- Have students work in pairs to read the sentences and discuss the meaning of each prefix.
- Elicit answers.

Now find more words with the prefixes *micro–*, *inter–*, and *un–* in the reading.

- Have students scan the reading to find more words with the prefixes.
- Ask students to compare answers in pairs. Then check answers as a class.

Answers
1 *Micro–* means "very small."
2 *Inter–* means "between."
3 *Un–* means "not."
Words with the prefixes *micro–*, *inter–*, and *un–* in the reading: microloans, internet, unfortunately.

Cool Down

Have students choose a person from the reading and imagine in pairs what he/she is doing now. What projects is he/she working on? Elicit ideas from students.

Practice Resource Bank: Literary Term Printout
Student's App: Reading Practice; Literary Term Practice

Get Ready to Read

Lesson Objectives

- **to activate prior knowledge about dreams**
- **to practice the reading skill of understanding author's word choice**
- **to review the reading skill of scanning**

Warm Up

Help students think of words they associate with other words by playing *Word Tennis* (see TB p. 27). Put students in pairs and give them each the same word to start with: *silent*. Have students carry on exchanging words in pairs for a minute or two. At the end of the time limit, tell students to stop. Ask each pair to say what word they finished with and compare them.

A Read and write. Read the poem. Look at the underlined words. What different words or phrases might the author have used?

- This lesson practices the skill of understanding author's word choice, which students previewed on p. 41. Have students look at the poem in their book or project it with the TTL. Read it aloud with feeling to support the meaning.
- Draw students' attention to the underlined words and ask the question *What different words or phrases might the author have used?* Elicit or remind students that words that have the same meaning are called *synonyms* and words with opposite meanings are called *antonyms*.
- Have a race to get students to think of as many synonyms and antonyms as possible for each word (tell them they can use phrases as well). Give students one minute per word. Then elicit ideas on the board.
- Have students read the skills box. Discuss why it's important to notice what words the author chose. Point out that specific words reveal the author's opinions, feelings, and attitude. If it's a story, they may also give clues about the characters' personality, their attitude, and what's going to happen next in the story. In nonfictional texts, the author chooses words to make a point, show their opinion, persuade the reader, show cause and effect, and so on.

Suggested Answers
1 quiet, without sound, noiseless, noisy, loud 2 level, flat, shiny, rough, bumpy 3 welcoming, saying hello to, saluting, hiding from, turning away from

B Look at the underlined words or phrases. Rewrite them using more interesting words or phrases.

- Have students read the sentences and replace the underlined words. Encourage them to read the sentence again with the new word to make sure that the new word fits in the context even if the meaning has changed.
- Have students compare their ideas in pairs and add new words if they wish to.
- Elicit ideas and discuss whether the meaning changes with different options.

Example Answers
1 replied / shouted / cried 2 felt poorly / was feeling sick / had a terrible pain / was on top of the world 3 beautiful gown / stunning dress / shiny spacesuit 4 were beautiful / had amazing colors / looked majestic / were noisy 5 brand new / shiny / in perfect condition / broken / rusty 6 zoomed / slowly chugged / rattled

C Think and discuss. How can someone work towards these dreams?

- Elicit a few examples for the first sentence. Write prompts on the board: … *they have to / they must / they should / it's important that they / it's a good idea to* …
- Have students discuss the sentences in pairs or small groups. Encourage them to think of as many ideas as they can for each sentence.
- Invite different students to share ideas for each sentence.

Suggested Answers
1 train really hard, practice taking free kicks and penalties, practice teamwork with the other players 2 find out what skills and qualifications a firefighter needs, work toward those goals, get fit, speak to a firefighter and ask for advice 3 see if they can find it secondhand or in a library, save up money for it, ask a friend who also wants to read it to go halves on it

Cool Down

Have students write a sentence with a minimum of eight words, including an adjective. Tell them to leave a blank for the adjective. They can do this in pairs. Collect the sentences and read them aloud or write them on the board. Have students guess what the missing adjective is in each sentence and discuss why the "author(s)" chose that adjective.

Now read **Dreams**

Fiction: *Dreams—Poem*

Lesson Objectives

- to read a poem about dreams
- to make a personal connection to the reading

Materials
Audio Tracks 15 and 16

Warm Up

Ask *What do children dream of?* Put students in groups and have them brainstorm four ideas. Elicit and write them on the board. Have students vote on the most common dream.

TRACK 15 TB p. 231 Reading Approach

First Reading: Engage with the Text

- Display the pictures on p. 50 for 30 seconds, then ask students what they remember about the pictures and the title. Ask *What dreams do you think you will read about?*
- Play the audio and have students read along. Stop before the stanzas on pp. 52–53. Have students look at the pictures and explain what the dreams are.
- Read the whole poem before looking at the Words in Context. Elicit whether students' suggestions in the Warm Up were mentioned.

TRACK 16 TB p. 232 Words in Context

- Give students a few minutes to find and highlight each word and identify the kind of word.
- Write these strategies on the board for students to use with the words: *surrounding words and sentences, separate parts of word, world knowledge, pictures, word families.*
- Tell students there is one strategy they can't use: they may or may not use all the strategies to figure out the words, but there is one strategy that can't be used at all.
- Have students work in pairs to discuss the words. Remind students that different words will require different combinations of strategies to figure them out.

stop-motion movie (p. 50, noun) This can be broken down: *stop + motion + movie*. A later sentence explains the process: *Move, click, move, click. The process takes forever* shows it takes a long time to make. Strategies to use: surrounding words and sentences; separate parts of word

gulps (p. 51, verb) The sentence shows this is something you do with water in your mouth. Strategy to use: surrounding words and sentences

tuning out (p. 51, verb) Earlier in the sentence it says *really noisy*, which shows that this is something you can do if you want to tune out. Strategy to use: surrounding words and sentences

twitch (p. 53, verb) This is used with *noses*; it shows it's an action rabbits' noses do. Strategies to use: surrounding words and sentences; world knowledge of rabbits

hay (p. 53, noun) The sentence says this is used to fill a rabbit's pen. Strategies to use: surrounding words and sentences; pictures; world knowledge of rabbits' habitats

- Go through each word in turn to elicit the meaning and how they know. Ask students which strategy on the board can't be used and why (word families). Play the audio to practice the pronunciation.

Practice **Student's App:** Story Player

International English

Highlight the different phrases on p. 51: *Ready, set, go!* and *Ready, steady, go!* Elicit the equivalent phrase in students' L1. Discuss which phrases on pp. 51-52 students prefer to use.

Second Reading: Analyze the Text and Features

- Have students close their books. Read the poem to them, using gesture and your voice to show emotion. Encourage students to watch and listen to you.
- Have students open their books. Ask some questions to check comprehension: *What's Faisal's dream?* (to make a stop-motion movie) *Who has to train hard to make their dream come true?* (Isabel) *What's Lilly's dream?* (to see/touch snow) See the **ETB** for more questions.
- Discuss the questions in the orange boxes. Then look at the text focus.
  - **Critical Thinking** (p. 50): *What kinds of things do people wish for?* Have students brainstorm a few ideas. They can refer to the poem and use their own ideas. Elicit ideas and discuss these questions: *Do people wish for material things only? Do they wish they had certain abilities and skills, and do they wish for situations?*
  - **Making Connections** (p. 53): *How do you feel when you accomplish something you've dreamed about achieving?* Have students think about something they achieved recently and discuss the question in pairs.
  - **Text Focus** (p. 52): *This poem is an example of free verse. Does it rhyme? What else do you notice about it?* Elicit that it doesn't rhyme and also that there's no set rhythm or structure. Have students notice which line is repeated at the end of each stanza.

Third Reading: Interact with the Text

- Put students in pairs and have them choose a section each that they would like to read aloud, e.g. the stanzas for Faisal or the stanzas for Isabel. When they are ready, students read the stanzas together, taking turns reading a line.
- Invite different pairs to read together a stanza for the class.

Cool Down

Write theses lines from the poem on the board: *Every dream needs a dreamer with special dream eyes.* Underline *special dream eyes*. Have students work in pairs to replace the underlined phrase. Give an example: *... with a big hopeful heart.* Allow students to be creative and accept all ideas.

Explore the Reading

Lesson Objectives

- to understand and analyze *Dreams* through reading comprehension activities
- to practice the reading skill of understanding author's word choice
- to explore the SEL competency of self-management through exhibiting positive motivation, hope, and optimism
- to make a personal connection to the reading

Materials
Pieces of paper (WU)

Warm Up

Write the names of the children from the poem (Faisal, Isabel, Sofia, Lilly, Seth) on pieces of paper and display them around the classroom. Say sentences from the poem in first person, e.g. *I wish I could feel it, just once.* (Lilly) *I want to shoot it on my phone.* (Faisal) After each sentence, students point to the corresponding name. Elicit what you are referring to each time, e.g. *it* is snow for Lilly; *it* is the stop-motion movie for Faisal.

A Read and choose the answer.

- Ask students *Wh–* questions to help them remember the reading, e.g. *What does Isabel want to win? Who's dream won't come true for a long time?*
- Prompt students to read the sentences first and check what they remember. Have them discuss answers in pairs without referring to the stanzas yet.
- Encourage students to scan the stanzas to find the correct answer and make their final decision. Check answers as a class.

Answers
1 b 2 d 3 c 4 b 5 a 6 c

B Think, underline, and write. Underline the verbs in each sentence. Write a synonym for the verb.

- Students are going to practice the reading skill of word choice by replacing verbs the author chose with synonyms.
- Do an example with the class. Elicit the verb in the first sentence (grasping). Have students discuss the meaning and think of possible synonyms in pairs. Bring the class together to share ideas.
- Have students work in pairs to do the other sentences. Allow them to use a dictionary or a thesaurus if they wish to.
- To check answers, read a sentence and elicit as many verbs as possible. Write them on the board and discuss any suggestions that don't work in the context.

Suggested Answers
1 grasping: grabbing, gripping 2 slip: slide, glide 3 shapes: makes, models, sculpts 4 gulps: swallows, drinks 5 feels like: wants to; tuning out: shutting out, ignoring 6 zooms: zips, races, whooshes

C Read and write. Look at the first two stanzas of *Dreams*. What are some words and phrases the author uses to describe the ways dreams move and sound?

- This activity provides further practice of thinking about word choice. Have students look at the first two stanzas on p. 50. Give them time to find the movements and sounds and notice the words and phrases used.
- Have students compare answers with a partner before checking as a class.

Answers
Move: grasping; slip; falling; spinning; floating
Sound: like notes from a guitar; the ringing of the bell; the whoosh of a roller coaster

D Think, discuss, and write. What advice would you give someone who is struggling to achieve their dream? What important characteristics do you need to achieve a realistic dream?

- Students are going to use their critical thinking skills and the SEL competency of exhibiting positive motivation, hope, and optimism to discuss how to achieve a dream.
- Draw students' attention to the questions. Ask them to spend a minute brainstorming advice for the first question in pairs. Encourage students to refer back to the poem. Invite students to share ideas with the class.
- Put students in different pairs to discuss what characteristics a person needs to achieve a realistic dream. Give an example if necessary: *You need to be optimistic.* Invite students to share ideas with the class. Encourage other students to agree or disagree with ideas they hear.
- Then have students work in pairs and think of one piece of advice for Isabel, Sofia, and Lilly.

Cool Down

Have students decide on a dream they have. Then ask them to role-play a conversation in pairs. They take turns sharing their dreams and giving each other advice. Do an example with a student to demonstrate.

Practice **Student's App:** Reading Practice

Think Together

Lesson Objectives

- to make connections between the readings
- to explore the key concept: Why is it important to have dreams?
- to reflect on the unit and provide personal thoughts and opinions

Warm Up

Have students look back at the two readings and discuss in pairs which one they prefer and why. Prompt them to think of three reasons. Elicit ideas from students.

A Complete the table. Look back at *Communities Making Dreams Come True* and *Dreams*. What are their dreams? How do they work toward their dreams?

- Draw students' attention to the table and elicit which reading each person is from.
- Give students time to complete the table on their own or in pairs. Then check answers as a class.
- Ask which dream they prefer and which way of achieving it they think was the best.

Answers

Rupa: Grow her business.; Gets a microloan, buys a tiller, hires two employees, pays back her loan.
Jorani and Leap: Design, make, and launch a new app game.; Plan out the game. Draw up a business plan. Organize a crowdfunding campaign to raise money. Make and release the game.
Faisal: Make his own stop-motion movie.; Makes the scene and the hero. Takes lots of pictures.
Isabel: Win a race.; Practices after school.

B Choose a dream you have. Why is it important to you? How can you achieve it? Do a Three-Step Interview.

- This routine (see TB p. 20) personalizes the topic of dreams. Ask the questions and give an example. Prompt students to ask you follow-up questions.
- Give students time to think of a dream and have them write it down with some ideas to achieve it before they conduct the interviews.
- After the interviews, ask if anyone had the same dreams and if their ways of achieving it were the same or different.

C Look back at *Dreams*. Use your ideas in B to write two new stanzas about yourself.

- Project two of the stanzas from the poem on the board and demonstrate adapting them so they are true for you and your dream. Then draw students' attention to the two headings: *Your Dream* and *What You'll Do* on p. 55.
- Have students write their two stanzas, referring to *Dreams* for guidance on sentence length, word choice, and so on.
- Have students read their stanzas in small groups.

Practice Resource Bank: Unit Test
Student's App: Key Concept Practice

- Ask the key concept question: *Why is it important to have dreams?* Have students reflect on what they learned and why having their dreams is important to them.

My Reading Journal

One thing I will remember from this unit is …

Who do you know who might find the information in this unit useful? Why?

These questions encourage students to personalize what they have learned and to make connections to others.

Give students time to look through the unit and complete the reading journal with their ideas. Have them compare in pairs before eliciting a few examples with the class.

Example Answers

One thing I will remember from this unit is you have to be optimistic to make your dreams come true.
I think my brother might find the information useful because his dream is to become a fashion designer.

Go back to page 41. Do the routine again. How do your new and old responses connect?

Have students look back at the VTR picture on p. 41 and elicit what they discussed in that lesson. Ask how they think the picture connects to the two readings in the unit. Ask *Is the cat's dream of becoming a lion realistic?* Discuss the importance of dreaming big.

Have students do the 3–2–1 Bridge VTR again and compare their old responses to the new ones. Elicit how they connect.

Here's an example of this part of the routine.

Teacher: So how did your responses change?
Student A: I thought the cat was afraid of the lion, but now I agree the cat dreams of being a lion. We can dream of something impossible.
Teacher: Good. And what about your questions?
Student B: First, we asked why it's important to dream. Now we know it's because it makes you happy. Now we wonder how to help people who don't dream.
Teacher: Great question. And a new metaphor?
Student C: Dreams are life. You can't live without dreams.
Teacher: So how do your ideas connect?
Student D: Well, the connection is dreams. Before I thought it was enough to just dream, but now I think we should all have big dreams.

Cool Down

Play a *Chain Game* (see TB p. 25). Prompt with *To make your dreams come true, you need to (be) …* Demonstrate with a few students and then have students play in teams.

UNIT 4

How's That Possible?

Unit Overview

Themes

The importance of exploring things we don't understand

Environmental science and fascinating mysteries

Synopsis

In this unit, students will discuss solved and unsolved mysteries related to natural places, as well as legends. They will study various theories behind each mystery, and they will be encouraged to form their own. They will read about two case studies and learn from the scientific investigations and conclusions. They will read a story and write the beginning of their own story. They will discuss the importance of exploring what we don't understand, and they will give a presentation about a natural place and its mysteries.

Language Book

Vocabulary

evidence, fact, have a feeling, make up, optical illusion, play a trick, puzzle, see things

Pronunciation: Connected Speech: Elision, Dropping the *t*

p. 96

Explore Language

Modals of Deduction: Past Forms

p. 97

Global Citizenship

Why is it important to explore things we don't understand?

ancient monument, archaeologist, clue, expert, legend, prehistoric times, solve, theory

p. 98

Explore Language

Modals of Obligation: Past Forms

p. 99

Write About It

A Story Beginning

Paragraph Building: including and omitting information

Word Study: Review: time phrases and adjectives about feelings and reactions

p. 100

Take the Stage

Presentation: asking questions and pausing for effect

p. 101

Think It Over

Review and Reflection: 3–2–1

p. 102

Think Together

Why are mysteries so fascinating?

p. 109

Visible Thinking

The Explanation Game

p. 103

Fiction

Fantasy: *An Enlightening Journey*

Words in Context: *hovered, firefly, swamp, glowing, swirling, hurling*

p. 107

Literacy Book

Nonfiction

Informational Text: *The Sci-Files*

Words in Context: *geological, GPS trackers, uniform, termites, colony, ecologists, aerial*

p. 104

Reading Skill

Making Inferences

p. 106

Literary Term

Personification

p. 108

Language and Literacy Connections

The connecting theme for Unit 4 is natural mysteries and their possible explanations.

	Language	Literacy
Vocabulary	**Set 1:** facts, mysteries, and illusions **Set 2:** historical discoveries	**Nonfiction:** evidence, puzzled, solve **Fiction:** clue, expert, optical illusion
Grammar	**Modals of Deduction: Past Forms** They must have put the shoes by the camera. They may/might have put two photographs together. They can't have spent very long on that one! Could they have done it with a computer? **Modals of Obligation: Past Forms** We had to get pretty close. We didn't have to stay late at school. You should have taken some photos. You shouldn't have gotten too near.	**Nonfiction** It could have been a trick. Someone might have moved the rocks. **Fiction** I can't have imagined them. All this must have been made by insects.
Skills	**Pronunciation:** connected speech: elision, dropping the *t* **Process Writing:** planning	**Reading:** making inferences **Literary Term:** personification
International English		forest/wood

Vocabulary

Lesson Objectives

- to learn vocabulary for facts, mysteries, and illusions: *evidence, fact, have a feeling, make up, optical illusion, play a trick, puzzle, see things*
- to read a poem about a friend
- to recognize and practice elision, dropping the *t*

Materials
Audio Tracks 39 to 43; Video

Warm Up

Have students look at the picture on pp. 48–49 for 30 seconds. Then they close their books and describe as many details as they can in pairs. Elicit ideas. If students haven't mentioned the club, ask *What kind of club was it?* (a photography club)

A TRACK 39 TB p. 219 **Listen. What mystery are Sachin and his friends discussing?**

- Describe Sachin (the boy in the blue T-shirt and white shorts) and have students find him in the picture. Elicit what students think he and his friends are talking about.
- Play the audio. Students listen and check their guesses.
- Have students find Max from Unit 2 and elicit his teaser question from the end of Unit 3: *Do you know what ball lightning is?* Play the audio again and elicit answers. (Also known as fireball, it's a ball with a strange light around it seen in the sky during a thunderstorm. There's no specific explanation for it.)

Answer
They are discussing ball lightning and whether it's real.

B TRACK 40 TB p. 219 **Find and number the words in A. Then listen and check.**

- Have students work in pairs to number the words and phrases. Play the audio for them to listen and check. Elicit the answers.

Answers
1 *evidence* 2 make up 3 play a trick
4 optical illusion 5 fact 6 see things 7 puzzle
8 have a feeling

C TRACK 41 TB p. 219 **Close your eyes. Listen, visualize, and say.**

- Prepare students for the visualization (see TB p. 21).
- Play the audio, allowing students to visualize the ideas as they listen. Check if they have any problems repeating the words.
- Have students choose one of the situations from the visualization and write a few sentences about it. Put students in pairs to exchange sentences and ask a follow-up question.

D **Look and write.**

- Students are going to create collocations using words from A and the verbs in the box. This helps consolidate the target vocabulary. Give students a minute to create the collocations. Then check answers.

Answers
1 *puzzle* 2 evidence 3 optical illusion 4 fact
5 feeling 6 up 7 things 8 trick

E TRACK 42 TB p. 219 **Listen and write. Then watch and say.**

- Have students read the poem quickly. Elicit what it is about (a boy who likes mysteries and playing tricks).
- Have students look at the verses and guess what words are missing. Remind them all the words can be found in A. Play the audio and have students check their answers.
- Play the audio or video again and have students join in with the poem. Encourage students to copy the rhythm and pronunciation.
- Have students read the poem silently to themselves. Then have them work in pairs, taking turns to read a line each. They can replace *Oscar* with a friend's name if they wish.

Answers
1 *tricks* 2 optical illusion 3 feeling 4 facts 5 made
6 seeing things 7 puzzle

F TRACK 43 TB p. 219 **Pronunciation. Listen and say. Copy the linking. Find other examples of linking in the poem.**

- This task raises students' awareness of elision and, in particular, of the dropped *t*, which is a feature of spoken English.
- Play the audio once. Have students listen and notice what happens to the *t* sound in the phrases. Elicit whether they can hear it. Point to the line that joins the /t/ to the first letter of the next word, as well as the parentheses. Invite students to explain what these symbols mean (the /t/ runs into the next consonant and disappears).
- Have them find more phrases with the elided /t/ in the poem. Elicit answers and write them on the board. Drill the phrases.
- Put students in pairs to take turns saying phrases from the board. Partners listen and confirm they can't hear the /t/.

Answers
bu(t)‿then we see; he's jus(t)‿made them up;
grea(t)‿big puzzle

Cool Down

Write the rhyming words from the poem on the board in random order. Divide students into two groups. Prompt a student from one group to call out a word from the board. The other group must call out the rhyming word in unison on the count of three. Then the groups swap roles.

Practice **Student's App:** Vocabulary Practice; Spoken Word Video

Explore Language

Lesson Objectives

- to learn how to use modals of deduction: past forms
- to practice vocabulary for facts, mysteries, and illusions

Materials

Audio Tracks 44 and 45; photo of an optical illusion (WU, CD); pictures from magazines or a collage of online pictures (F)

Warm Up

Show a photo of an optical illusion (e.g. someone pushing the Tower of Pisa). Have students discuss what's weird about the photo and prompt them to give an explanation. Elicit ideas.

A TRACK 44 TB p. 219 **Listen and read. What do all the photos have in common?**

- With books closed, ask students to listen to Max and two friends talk about three photos. Ask the question and play the audio. Have students discuss the answer in pairs.
- Have students open their books and look at the pictures on p. 50. Invite students to explain why each photo is strange. Ask further comprehension questions (see **ETB**).

Answer

They contain optical illusions of some kind.

B Look at A. Complete the table. How many verbs are in this structure?

- Display the table using the TTL. Tell students that the words they need to complete the table are in the dialogue in A. Have them complete the table individually and then compare answers in pairs. Check answers as a class.
- Ask the noticing question *How many verbs are in this structure?* Elicit how many and what the verbs are.
- Write the structure on the board: *must/may/might/can't/could* + *have* + past participle. Ask *Can you use "has" instead of "have" here?* (no)

Answers

put; might; can't; have; Could; done

Two verbs are used: the modal verb, e.g. *must*, and the auxiliary *have* (students may say three if they include the past participle).

- Refer students to the Grammar tip *Watch Out*. Read the first sentence with the contraction *must've* so that students notice it's easy to confuse *'ve* with *of*. Point out that even if it sounds similar, their knowledge of the structure will help them visualize the verb *have/'ve* whenever they hear it.

C Think and discuss. Then choose and write.

- Point to the arrow and explain the meaning from left to right. Ask students to refer back to the table in B to complete the answers.

- Elicit answers, then ask *What do we use if we're very sure something is true? What do we use if we're quite sure something is true? What do we use if something is possibly true? What do we use if we're sure that something isn't true?*
- Point out that the positive form of *can* is never used for deduction. It is always used for permission.

Answers

1 deduction
2 must have; *may have*; might have; can't have

D TRACK 45 TB p. 220 **Listen and say.**

- Tell students they're going to practice saying sentences with past modals of deduction to help with pronunciation in fluent speech and so that they begin to internalize the structure. Play the audio and have students repeat each example chorally. (See TB p. 23, Making Language Drills Fun.)

E Complete the dialogue with the correct form of the verbs.

- This activity provides controlled practice of past forms of modals of deduction. Invite two students to read the first exchange. Elicit the context of the dialogue. Then have students read the dialogue once for meaning. Then they complete the sentences individually.
- Before checking answers, ask students to compare in pairs and discuss any differing answers. Remind students that there may be more than one answer.

Answers

1 *Could*; *have left* 2 might not have lost
3 must have gone 4 can't have taken
5 must/may have been 6 might/could have done

F Think and discuss. Look at some pictures in this book or in magazines. What deductions can you make?

- This activity provides freer practice of past forms of modals of deduction. Ask two students to read the example exchange and elicit which photo on p. 40 it refers to. Accept all answers.
- Project the photos you found or hand them out if you printed them. Alternatively, choose another picture from the **Language Book** or **Literacy Book** and project it. Have students think of one or more deductions on their own.
- Put students in pairs to compare their ideas. Encourage them to agree or disagree with each other.
- Have students choose one more picture each and repeat the procedure.

Cool Down

Use the photo of an optical illusion you showed students in the Warm Up Project it on the board or display it so students can see. Have them review their original ideas and make new deductions. Elicit ideas.

Practice **Resource Bank:** Grammar Printout
Student's App: Grammar Practice

Global Citizenship

Lesson Objectives

- to learn vocabulary related to historical discoveries: *ancient monument, archaeologist, clue, expert, legend, prehistoric times, solve, theory*
- to discuss the importance of exploring things we don't understand
- to practice listening for gist and details

Materials
Audio Tracks 46 to 48; Audio Track D

Opening Question

Ask the opening question: *Why is it important to explore things we don't understand?* Have students think when they've explored things they didn't understand. Encourage them to use vocabulary from Lesson 1. Invite students to share their ideas with the class.

A TRACK 46 TB p. 220 **Listen to Fairuza and Theo watch a TV documentary about Stonehenge. Why is Stonehenge a mystery?**

- Tell students they are going to listen to Fairuza and Theo watching a TV documentary about Stonehenge. Elicit what students know about Stonehenge. Play the audio and have students check their ideas.
- Ask the question and have students discuss in pairs. Play the audio again for students to check their answers. See the **ETB** for more comprehension questions.
- Ask students if they know of more sites like Stonehenge. What can they tell the class?

Answers
Nobody knows what Stonehenge was for or how it was built. / Nobody is sure why the stones were put there. There are a lot of theories but no facts.

B TRACK 47 TB p. 220 **Look at the pictures and definition in A and write. Then listen and check.**

- Refer to the vocabulary box in B and have students match the words and phrases to the pictures and definition in A.
- Play the audio for students to check their answers. Then play it again to practice the pronunciation, pausing after each word or phrase for them to repeat.

Answers
1 *prehistoric times* 2 archaeologist 3 legend 4 expert 5 solve 6 clue 7 theory 8 ancient monument

TRACK D TB p. 220 **Visualization**
The TTL has a visualization audio track for this vocabulary set. (See TB p. 21)

C **Read. Write the words for the underlined part of the sentences.**

- Read the first sentence and the example. Then have students replace the underlined phrases with the words and phrases from B. Check answers as a class.

Answers
1 *ancient monument* 2 theory 3 solve 4 prehistoric times 5 legend 6 archaeologist 7 expert 8 clue

D TRACK 48 TB p. 220 **Now listen to Fairuza's classmate Yasin. Which site is his presentation about? Do experts know all the facts about this place?**

- Discuss what students can see in the photo and where they think it is.
- Listening for gist: tell students they're going to listen to Fairuza's classmate Yasin give a presentation about another site. Ask the questions and play the audio. Elicit answers.

Answers
He is talking about an underwater city in Japan. Experts do not know all the facts.

E **Listen again. Read and choose.**

- Listening for details: have students read the sentences and consider the options before they listen again.
- Play the audio and have students choose the correct answer. Check answers as a class. Ask students to say whether they think it was made by humans or the ocean.

Answers
1 *ancient history* 2 thousands 3 large 4 disagree 5 pyramid 6 a natural disaster

Discussion Questions

- Draw students' attention to the discussion questions: *What mysteries surround different historical sites in your country? What problems are causing damage to the world's cultural sites? Are there any solutions?* Have students do some research on their own and then discuss the questions in pairs or small groups (see **ETB**). Encourage students to recognize that it is important to explore historical sites in order to understand the past, and that we have a responsibility to protect such places from damage.
- Return to the opening question to ask again *Why is it important to explore things we don't understand?* and ask students to share any new ideas. Focus on the concept of understanding the past, as well as our ancestors' values, dreams, and fears. Take a class vote on the question *Do you think all mysteries have a logical explanation?*

Cool Down

Do a visualization. Say *You're inside your time machine, thinking about which ancient civilization and site to visit.* (pause) *You've decided. Type the year or century and travel back in time.* (pause) *You've arrived. What do you see? Who do you meet? What do you talk about?* Have pairs to share their visualizations.

Practice **Student's App:** Vocabulary Practice; Listening Practice

Explore Language

Lesson Objectives

- to learn how to use modals of obligation: past forms
- to practice vocabulary related to historical discoveries

Materials
Audio Tracks 49 and 50

Warm Up

Ask *Which two creatures did Yasin mention in his introduction?* (the Loch Ness Monster and Bigfoot) Elicit what students know about Bigfoot.

A TRACK 49 TB p. 220 **Listen and read. What do you think the children see in the park?**

- With books closed, project the first picture from p. 54 on the board. Have two students read the dialogue, then ask the question *What do you think the children see in the park?* Put students in pairs to discuss ideas and elicit a few from the class.
- Play the audio and have students follow along in their books. Prompt students to discuss their ideas again. Elicit and accept all answers, but check whether students can see the toy panda in the last picture. Ask more comprehension questions (see **ETB**).

Suggested Answer
someone carrying a very large toy (panda) bear

B **Look at A. Complete the table. What's the opposite of *had to*?**

- Have students scan the dialogue in A individually to find the missing words in the table. This will help students focus on the structure of the past forms of modals of obligation.
- Write or project the table onto the board. Check answers as a class and ask the noticing question *What's the opposite of "had to"?* Elicit the answer and then draw students' attention to the Grammar tip *Watch Out*. Explain that we use *had to* instead of *must* to talk about obligation in the past.
- Draw students' attention to the last row with *should/shouldn't have*. Elicit the structure they saw in Lesson 2: modal verb + *have* + past participle.

Answers
had; have; stay; should; have; have; gotten
The opposite of *had to* is *didn't have to*.

C **Think and discuss. Then choose.**

- Ask students to read the sentences on usage and refer to the table in B. Have them think about meaning individually and then discuss in pairs.
- To check answers, read the sentences aloud. Clarify that *had to* has a meaning of obligation in the past, whereas *didn't have to* means "it wasn't necessary, but it's OK if you did it."

Answers
1 was; wasn't 2 past

D TRACK 50 TB p. 220 **Listen and say.**

- Tell students they're going to practice saying sentences with past modals of obligation to help with pronunciation in fluent speech and so that they begin to internalize the structure. Play the audio and have students repeat each example chorally. (See TB p. 23, Making Language Drills Fun.)

E **Complete the email with the correct form of the verbs.**

- This activity provides controlled practice of the past forms of modals of obligation. Ask students to skim the email. Ask *What is it about?* Elicit the answer and then have students complete the email with the correct modal verbs in the past form.
- Put students in pairs to compare their answers. Check answers by projecting them on the board.

Answers
1 *had to choose* 2 didn't have to do 3 had to find
4 shouldn't have chosen 5 should have taken

F **Think of a project you had to do for school. What did/didn't you have to do? Make notes and then talk with a friend. Give each other advice.**

- For this free oral practice of the past forms of modals of obligation, explain to students that they are going to talk in pairs about a school project and what they had to or didn't have to do to complete it. While they listen to their partner, students should be encouraged to interrupt and give opinions or advice.
- Have students look at the notes and the example exchange. Read the example exchange with a student and elicit example responses for the other two items in the notes.
- Give students enough time to think about their school project individually. Tell students they can also discuss other projects or work they had to do recently.
- In pairs, students take turns explaining their project and giving their partner opinions or advice.

Cool Down

Ask students to think of a past situation or past decision they had to make. Then put them in small groups to share their situations or decisions. Ask students to give advice with *should/shouldn't have*.

Practice **Resource Bank:** Grammar Printout
Student's App: Grammar Practice

Write About It

Lesson Objectives

- to plan and write a story beginning
- to include and omit information
- to learn to use time phrases and adjectives

Materials
Support Writing printouts from the Resource Bank (F)

Warm Up

Put students in groups to share what they know about Russia. To set this up as a game, have the groups compete by trying to note down as much as possible. Elicit as a class.

A Read the beginning of a story. What do we learn about the Russian Guide?

- This lesson corresponds with the fantasy story in Unit 4 of the **Literacy Book**. Draw students' attention to the title of the story and the picture. Elicit what they think it is about. Ask them to read the beginning of the story and check their guesses. Ask the question *What do we learn about the Russian Guide?* Discuss as a class.

Answer
He was the same age as the children and was tall with blond hair. He knew a lot about Russia.

B Look at the structure of the beginning of the story. Check (✔) the information you need to include. Say why.

- Tell students they're going to look at the content and structure of the beginning of a story. Have them read the information in B.
- Have students refer to the story and check the information that is included. Elicit the answers.

Answers
1; 3; 4; 5; 7; 8; Note: not usually 2 or 6 because this will be part of the main story
Suggested answers: We include 1, 3, 4, 5, 7 and 8 as it helps set the scene (by telling us details such as where the story is set and who is in the story). It also creates interest in the reader. We don't include 2 and 6 because these details appear later in the story (2 in the conclusion; 6 in the main body).

C Look at the language in the beginning of the story. Read and answer.

- Elicit examples of time phrases (yesterday, etc.) and adjectives of feelings and reactions (happy, etc.).
- Have students find time phrases and adjectives of feelings and reactions in the story. Check answers as a class. Ask students to discuss in pairs why these words and phrases are important. Elicit ideas.

Answers
1 Time phrases: when, *last year,* in the winter, the first morning, Then, Suddenly, that morning; because it's important to know when something is happening and in what order 2 Feelings: strange, bored, sad; Reactions: amazing, unexpected, surprised, absorbed, fascinating; because the combination of adjectives helps the reader have a better understanding of the characters' personality, behavior, and attitude

D Think and discuss. Choose a vacation, cultural visit, or weekend outing for your story. Brainstorm some ideas using one of the Generating Ideas techniques.

- This lesson focuses on another way of planning before you write. Review the different ways of generating ideas students discussed in **Process Writing Step 1: Generating Ideas** on p. 140.
- Tell students that they are going to plan and write the beginning of a story about a vacation, cultural visit, or weekend. Draw the students' attention to the table and tell them to think about these categories. You can project the table using the TTL.
- Give students enough time to think about the categories. Students can compare their ideas with a friend. Monitor and provide language help.

Answers
Students' own answers

E Plan the beginning of your story. Look at your ideas in D. Make notes. Then order the events.

- Have students plan the beginning of their story using the sticky-note planning technique. If they wish, they can review **Planning Techniques** on p. 141.
- Have them revise their ideas in D and make notes in the boxes. Point out that it is important to use time phrases and adjectives of feeling and reaction. Then they order the events.

F Now write the beginning of your story.

- Have students write a draft of their story beginning, referring to their notes in E. They should read their drafts and make any corrections or improvements.
- Have students write their final versions neatly on paper. Alternatively, hand out the Support printouts.
- Ask students to work with a partner and read their story. Encourage them to think about what might happen next.

Cool Down

Ask students to imagine they are Talia or the narrator of the story in A. Say they are sightseeing in Moscow and suddenly they see the mysterious boy again. What do they do? How does the boy react? Students discuss ideas in small groups.

Practice **Resource Bank:** Writing Game, *The Editor*
Student's App: Writing Practice

Take the Stage

Lesson Objectives

- to give a presentation about a place of cultural interest
- to ask questions and pause for effect

Materials
Video

Warm Up

Give a riddle for the word *statue*. Say *I look like you, and people like you like to look at me. I live indoors, but I have friends who live outdoors. I don't have bones or muscles, but I have arms, legs, a head, and a body. I wish I could move, but I can't. What am I?* Have students guess the secret word in pairs and raise their hand when they think they have it. Elicit the answer and ask students to name any famous statues they know or have seen.

A TB p. 239 **Watch and listen. What would you most like to know about the statues?**

- Draw students' attention to the pictures or project them on the board using the TTL. Explain that they are going to watch a video of two children (Maria and Lloyd) giving a presentation about these statues. Ask the question *What would you most like to know about the statues?* Students discuss the question in pairs and make notes. Elicit ideas and write them on the board.
- With books closed, play the video for students to watch and listen. Are any of the students' ideas answered in the video?

Answers
Students' own answers

B Watch again. Read and respond. Then discuss.

- Tell students they are going to focus on what Maria and Lloyd do during the presentation and why. Draw their attention to the prompts and questions in B.
- Play the video again and have students check what they hear and answer the questions. Ask them to compare answers in pairs before you check with the class.

Answers
1 a; b; d 2 The first speaker uses questions to engage the audience. 3 She uses pauses to give the audience time to think and for dramatic effect. 4 The second speaker doesn't ask questions because he is giving the audience background information (about the topic).

C Think of a cultural place you would like to talk about. Think and plan. Then write notes for your presentation.

- Put students in pairs to discuss possible places. These can be places they have visited or places they would like to go. Alternatively, ask students to discuss the places that were mentioned in the Global Citizenship lesson.
- Once they have decided on a place they want to talk about, have them write brief notes for their presentation using the information in the table to help them. They can do this individually or in pairs. Monitor and provide language help if needed.

D Practice with your friends. Then share with the class. Take notes and give feedback.

- Tell students they are going to give their presentations in small groups, using their notes from C. Remind students of the presentation skills discussed in B and write them on the board (*speak clearly, use gestures, ask questions, explain facts clearly, pause at the right moment*).
- Put students in pairs or small groups to give their presentations. Tell them that while they listen to the presentations, they need to note whether the speaker is using the presentation skills. Monitor and make sure students are taking notes while they are listening.
- Have students give feedback in their groups. Monitor and provide feedback of your own.
- Invite students to give their presentation to the class.
- At the end, have students analyze their own performance.

Cool Down

Put students into groups of three or four and play *60 Seconds* (see TB p. 25). They can mention anything they have learned about any of the places discussed in the lesson.

Practice **Student's App:** Speaking Skills Practice; Speaking Video

Think It Over

Lesson Objectives

- to review what has been learned in the unit
- to reflect on the unit and their own progress
- to think about learning strategies and how to continue learning at home

Warm Up

Ask students what the unit theme was (mysteries and historical discoveries) and write it in the middle of the board. Brainstorm any words or phrases students can think of that relate to the topic and write them on the board. Encourage students to think about how historical discoveries can tell us about how people lived in the past.

How well did you meet the challenge of Unit 4? Read and respond.

3–2–1

- Tell students they are going to review what they learned in the unit and think about their own learning.
- Have students work in small groups to brainstorm different categories related to the unit and make mind maps of what they learned, e.g. words, grammar, things I learned about mysteries, things I learned about historical discoveries, give a presentation, facts, interesting ideas, things I'd like to discover. They can also include ideas from the **Literacy Book**. Then have students display their mind maps on the wall. Have groups go around the classroom and look at each other's maps.
- Refer students to the graphic organizer in the book and the prompt sentences: *3 things I learned in this unit; 2 "Ah-ha!" moments I had; 1 big question I still have.* Draw their attention to the explanation of an "Ah-ha!" moment and elicit an example to check they understand. Have students talk in pairs about the different sections. Encourage them to focus particularly on the second and third sections. Explain that the big question can be related to facts, mysteries, illusions, or any other topic that was discussed in the unit.
- When you feel they have enough ideas, have students work individually to fill out the organizer. Remind them that they should write their own responses about themselves. Monitor and help as necessary. Look at what students are writing so you can tailor your classes and any additional practice to their needs.
- If you feel it is appropriate for your class, have students share their ideas with a friend. Encourage them to think together of how they can find the answer to the big questions they have. They can take guesses as to what the answers are as well.

Looking Forward

Draw students' attention to the character at the bottom of the page. Have students say who she is and what they remember about her. (Mrs. Lewis enjoys photography. She appears in the photography club in Lesson 1, p. 48, and Lesson 4, p. 54. She listens to Inez and Kayla's adventure and advises them.) Have students look at the speech bubble and guess what subject she teaches. Tell students they will find out the answer in Lesson 1 of the next unit.

Put It Together

To further review and recycle the language in Units 3 and 4, play the game, *Chatter Boxes*, on pp. 60–61. See TB p. 207 for teaching notes.

Practice **Resource Bank:** Unit Test
Student's App: Vocabulary and Grammar Review

Literacy

Get Ready to Read

Lesson Objectives

- to activate prior knowledge about mysteries
- to guide inquiry and deepen understanding through an Explanation Game VTR
- to preview the reading skill of making inferences

Materials
VTR printout from the Resource Bank (A, B, C, D); a map of the world (WU)

Warm Up

Ask students to look at the image (or project it with the TTL). Have them discuss in pairs where the image was taken. Elicit ideas and explain it's a lake in Siberia called Lake Baikal. Give students a minute to discuss what they know about Siberia. If possible, let them find it on a map. Elicit ideas.

Explanation Game

A Look at the picture. Choose a thing. What is it?

- This VTR encourages students to identify interesting features in an object and explore the reasons why it is this way, through observation, questioning, and hypothesis. Start by asking students what they can see in the picture of the lake. Provide vocabulary where necessary.
- Say *I think that cloud in the sky looks interesting.* Tell students to choose something in the picture that they think is interesting or would like to know more about. Have students look at the picture and choose an object in pairs.

B What do you notice about it? Tell your partner.

- Say *I notice that the cloud is yellow. What do you notice about it?* Elicit ideas and write them on the board. Then say *What do you notice about your object?*
- Give students time to think about the interesting things they notice about the object they have chosen and share their ideas in pairs. Encourage students to write their ideas in their notebooks. Monitor and provide language help.

Here's an example of this part of the routine.
Student A: This piece of ice is very clean.
Student B: Yes, it's transparent.
Student A: And it's thick. It must be very cold, too.
Teacher: What about the shape?
Student B: Oh, it looks like a triangle.

C Why do you think it is that way?

- Ask *Why do you think the cloud is yellow?* and elicit ideas.
- Have students think about what they noticed about their object and take turns in pairs to ask *Why do you think it is that way?* Encourage them to ask *What makes you say that?*
- Students should make a mind map or other visual representation of their ideas.

D What are some other reasons it might be that way? Share with the class.

- Tell students that they are going to share their ideas with the class. They need to say (a) what the object is, (b) what they noticed about it, (c) why they think it is this way, and (d) their reasons for thinking this.
- Have students share their ideas. Encourage the class to think of and add ideas about the explanations and reasons.

Here's an example of this part of the routine.
Teacher: What did you discuss?
Student A: We chose the ice. It's very thick.
Student B: We think that's because the temperature is very cold. But we aren't sure why it's so sharp. What do other people think?
Student C: Maybe there was a lot of rain and it broke.
Student D: Hmm, no. If it rained, the ice would melt.
Teacher: Does anyone have a different idea?
Student E: Well, what if the ice broke because of wind?
Student B: But how strong does it have to be to break ice that's so thick?

Transition

Ask students *Are there any more natural mysteries related to snow or ice? What do you know about them?* Have students discuss in small groups and elicit ideas.

E Think and write. What real-world mysteries have you heard about? Make a list.

- Write *Real-world mysteries* on the board and elicit this refers to natural phenomena that are strange, similar to the ice in Lake Baikal.
- Have students discuss ideas in pairs and make a list. Then invite students to share ideas with the class.

Answers
Students' own answers

F Think, predict, and discuss. Look at the headings and pictures on the next page. What do you think the reading is about? Why do you think it's called *The Sci-Files?*

- This activity previews the skill of making inferences. Have students look at the headings and the pictures on p. 58. Have them discuss their ideas in pairs.
- Invite students to share their ideas. Ask *Why did the author choose this title?* Elicit *science* from *sci* and the film/literary genre *science fiction.*

Answers
Students' own answers

Now read **The Sci-Files**

Nonfiction: *The Sci-Files—* Informational Text

Lesson Objectives

- to read a text about natural mysteries
- to make a personal connection to the reading

Materials

Audio Tracks 17 and 18; time-lapse video

Warm Up

Elicit what a *case study* is (a scientific study of a case/ phenomenon). Ask students to look at the headings and pictures and discuss in pairs, then as a class, which case study they think will be the most interesting and why.

TRACK 17 TB p. 232 Reading Approach

First Reading: Engage with the Text

- Have students read only *The mystery* and *Possible theories* sections for each case study. Then ask the question in the red box on p. 58: *What do you think the explanation might be for the two mysteries?* Put students in pairs or groups to discuss. Elicit their ideas and write them on the board.
- Have students read the rest of the texts to find out. Elicit the explanations for the two mysteries and check to see if anyone was correct. Then look at the Words in Context.

TRACK 18 TB p. 232 Words in Context

- Brainstorm strategies on the board for students to use: *surrounding words and sentences, prefixes/suffixes, L1 cognates, pictures, knowledge of similar words.*
- Divide the class into groups of six (three pairs). Have each pair in each group find and discuss two words.
- Have students work back in their group of six to explain their words, saying which strategies they used.

geological (p. 58, adjective) Students may know other words with the prefix *geo–* (e.g. *geography*). The following sentence mentions rocks and mud. Strategies to use: prefixes/suffixes; surrounding words and sentences; possible L1 cognates

GPS trackers (p. 59, noun) *Nobody ever saw the rocks moving* is the problem, and GPS trackers are a solution. The sentence says *to record any movement*. Strategies to use: surrounding words and sentences, possible L1 cognates

uniform (p. 60, adjective) Students may know the noun *uniform* (identical clothes worn for school/work). *Uniform in size* shows it relates to the size of the circles. Strategies to use: knowledge of similar words; pictures; surrounding words and sentences

termites (p. 60 / p. 61, noun) It's used with *nests, look for food, eating the plants' roots,* which show it's an animal. Another sentence mentions *animals*. Strategies to use: surrounding words and sentences; pictures

colony (p. 61, noun) *If they meet another colony* and *termite colonies* show it has to do with a group of termites. Strategy to use: surrounding words and sentences

ecologists (p. 61, noun) A definition is given after the word. Strategies to use: surrounding words and sentences, prefixes/suffixes, possible L1 cognates

aerial (p. 61, adjective) This describes a way of taking a photo. The pictures show where the camera is. Strategies to use: surrounding words and sentences; pictures; knowledge of similar words with *aer* (e.g. *aerodynamic*).

- Discuss as a class which strategies worked or didn't work. Play the audio to practice pronunciation.

International English

Elicit which word is American English (*forest*), which word is British English (*wood*), and which students have encountered more often. Ask if they know any forests/woods nearby.

Second Reading: Analyze the Text and Features

- Play the audio while students follow along in their books.
- Ask questions to check comprehension: *How did the rocks move?* (because of the wind and ice) *What caused the small and big fairy circles?* (termites searching for food and plants searching for water) See the **ETB** for more questions.
- Discuss the questions in the red boxes and the text focus.
  - **Fun Fact** (p. 59): *It can take more than 50,000 photos to make a time-lapse video of only 76 seconds.* Show students an online time-lapse video, e.g. a person growing up. Elicit how it is made.
  - **Language in Context** (p. 61): *"They couldn't see the forest for the trees." What do you think this means?* Have students read the whole paragraph again. Elicit ideas and whether there's a similar expression in the students' L1 (When someone is too absorbed in the details of a problem and they fail to see the situation as a whole).
  - **Text Focus** (p. 60): *Are these case studies primary sources (where the information came from) or secondary sources (a description of the primary sources)?* Elicit examples of primary sources (e.g. school announcement) and secondary sources (e.g. a student's comment on the announcement). Elicit the answer (secondary sources) and what the primary source would be (the scientists' papers or articles explaining the research and results).

Third Reading: Interact with the Text

- Divide the class into two teams. Each team reads one case study and then works together to write quiz questions. Then they take turns quizzing the other team.

Cool Down

Play *Correct the Teacher* (see TB p. 25) with the sentences from the reading.

Practice **Student's App:** Story Player

Explore the Reading

Lesson Objectives

- to understand and analyze *The Sci-Files* through reading comprehension activities
- to learn through CLIL (science): environmental science
- to make a personal connection to the reading

Warm Up

Put students in pairs and have them recall the names of the case studies. Invite volunteer students to write the names on the board: *Sliding Rocks* and *Fairy Circles*. Call out random facts about the two case studies. After each fact, have students do a sliding movement for "sliding rocks" or a circle with their arms for "fairy circles" to indicate which case study each fact refers to.

A Think and write. Complete the table.

- Ask students to read the questions once and check they understand them. Then give them time to scan the text and complete the table. Put students in pairs to compare their answers. Project the answers if using the TTL. Alternatively, copy the table onto the board and invite students to come to the front of the class and complete it.

Answers

Sliding Rocks
1 Death Valley National Park, California
2 Somebody moved the rocks. / Wind blew them.
3 No evidence of trucks or footprints; / Many of the rocks are very heavy.
4 GPS trackers, (time-lapse) photography

Fairy Circles
1 Namib Desert
2 Termites nests caused them. / Dying plants poisoned the soil. / Plants competing for water caused them.
3 They were uniform in size; / No evidence of poison; / Hasn't been proven with tests.
4 computer software, aerial photos

B Write *True* or *False*. Then discuss. What makes you say that?

- Ask students to read the sentences and discuss in pairs whether they are true or false based on what they remember. Then ask them to check their answers in the text. Check the answers as a class. Encourage students to justify their answers.

Answers

1 True ("Years can pass without a drop of rain falling here.") 2 False ("It was going to be a long experiment taking up to 10 years. But only two years later, … was solved!") 3 False ("At night, the temperature drops suddenly.") 4 False ("They are known as fairy circles and have puzzled the local Himba people for generations.") 5 True ("These roots take water from the soil further away, causing the plants there to die.") 6 False ("The software predicted regular patterns … of the plants competing for water … The aerial photos confirmed the predictions of the software … between the large circles.")

C Scientists use the Scientific Method to answer a question or solve a mystery. Choose a mystery from E on page 57. Complete the diagram with the different stages.

- Students are going to look at the reading through a scientific lens. This draws on the CLIL environmental science focus.
- Draw students' attention to the categories in the diagram. Do an example with the sliding rocks. Then have students choose a mystery from their answers to E on p. 57 and complete the diagram individually or in pairs. Allow plenty of time for them to research their ideas. Monitor and provide language help if needed. If they aren't able to test their hypotheses, have them draw a conclusion based on the success of their research, i.e. was it a good question to ask? If they learn through their research that the mystery has already been solved, they can include that information.
- Invite students to present their notes in small groups or to the class.

Example Answers

Ask a question: Why does sand in some deserts make noises?
Research the topic: In some deserts like in China and Chile, sand makes "music" or whistling sounds. It's called singing sand.
Write a hypothesis: Sand grains move down the dunes and create sounds.
Test the hypothesis: French scientists studied and recorded the singing sand in Morocco and Oman. They recreated the avalanches in a lab and studied the size of the sand grains.
Make conclusions: Sand grains collide with each other as they roll down a dune and create sounds. The sounds are melodic when the sand grains are the same size.

Cool Down

Have students choose which place they would like to visit: Death Valley National Park or the Namib Desert. Allow them to revise what they learned about each place from the reading and decide. Ask them to think what they'd need to take with them. Have students compare ideas in pairs and then elicit some ideas from the class.

Practice Student's App: Reading Practice

Get Ready to Read

Lesson Objectives

- to activate prior knowledge about journeys
- to practice the reading skill of making inferences
- to review the reading skill of scanning

Materials
Sticky notes (CD)

Warm Up

Write the story title on the board: *An Enlightening Journey*. Drill *enlightening* chorally. Ask students what the word means (something that helps you better understand something). Then ask them to find a noun in enlightening (*light*). Explain that this noun may give us a clue as to what the story is about. In groups, have them discuss what they think the story is about. Elicit answers and write them on the board.

A Read and make inferences from the reading to answer the questions. Support your answers with evidence from the reading.

- This lesson practices the skill of making inferences, which students previewed on p. 57. Draw the students' attention to the skills box and read it aloud to review the skill of making inferences. Elicit a synonym of *inferences* (*guesses*). Discuss what students need to use to make inferences (textual evidence, their own knowledge and experience). Point out that with stories they can also look at the illustrations for visual clues.
- Have students read the paragraph and ask *Who was the first European to discover Easter Island?* (Jacob Roggeveen) Elicit other facts they know about Easter Island.
- Then read the first question and example answer. Point out how, in the text, *Instead* replaces the idea of *He didn't find the place he was searching for, but Easter Island.* Give them time to answer the questions individually or in pairs, using evidence from the reading. Elicit answers.

Answers
1 *No, he didn't. He found Easter Island, not Terra Australis.* 2 No, it wasn't. He was looking for a continent but found a small island. 3 No, he wasn't. He was the first European, but other people were already living on the island. 4 Possibly because there were also only a few trees, or the 15,000 people that lived there a century earlier could have hunted them all, which is why they needed to start fishing and hunting seabirds.

B Read and write. Read the introduction to *An Enlightening Journey*. What evidence can you find to support the sentences below?

- Ask students to read the introduction once to check if any of their ideas in the Warm Up were correct.
- Then have them read the sentences and find the evidence to support them in the introduction. Have them compare answers in pairs, then check as a class.
- Have students discuss in pairs who the characters could be and where they might be. Elicit ideas.

Answers
1 "It was hot and the sun was already high in the sky" 2 "A perfect day to take Nora and Josh on another adventure" 3 "I haven't decided yet"

C Think and discuss. Look at the pictures in *An Enlightening Journey* and think about the title. What mysterious things do you think happen on the journey?

- Have students look at the pictures in the story and think about the title (if necessary review their ideas from the Warm up). Put students in pairs to brainstorm mysterious things the characters encounter on their journey. You can vary the activity by using a cooperative learning routine such as a Round Robin (see TB p. 20).
- Elicit ideas by writing them on the board. You could take a photo of these notes and project them to activate schema before students read the story.

Answers
Students' own answers

Cool Down

Have students write a sentence on a sticky note predicting what they think will happen in the story. Put the sentences on the wall and direct students to the predictions when they have read the story for the first time. Were any correct?

Now read **An Enlightening Journey**

Fiction: *An Enlightening Journey—Fantasy*

Lesson Objectives

- to read a story about an enlightening journey
- to make a personal connection to the reading

Materials
Audio Tracks 19 and 20

Warm Up

Have students look through the story pictures again and choose one they like. Ask them to compare pictures in pairs and give one reason why they like it.

TRACK 19 TB p. 232 Reading Approach

First Reading: Engage with the Text

- Elicit from the class what they remember about the introduction on p. 63. Then ask them to discuss in pairs what they think is going to happen in the story. Play the audio and have students read along as they listen. Pause before the last scene on p. 67. Invite students to say what's going to happen next. Discuss as a class.
- Play the rest of the story and check if students' guesses were correct. Ask if their sentences from the Cool Down in the previous lesson were correct. Then look at the Words in Context.

TRACK 20 TB p. 233 Words in Context

- Give students a few minutes to find and highlight each word. Have them identify the kind of word. Remind them it may appear more than once.
- Write these strategies on the board for students to use with the words: *surrounding words and sentences, pictures, separate parts of word, positive/negative, world knowledge.*
- Have students work in pairs to discuss the words.

hovered (p. 66, verb) This is used with *a single light*. *In front of* shows that it has to do with the position and movement of the light. Strategies to use: surrounding words and sentences; pictures

firefly (p. 66, noun) This can be broken down: *fire* + *fly*. Surrounding sentences tell us it has a tail and there are lots of them. Strategies to use: separate parts of word; pictures; surrounding words and sentences

swamp (p. 66 / p. 67, noun) *It smells bad* shows it's a negative thing. The sentence before that refers to the ground as *softer* and *wetter*. Strategies to use: positive/ negative; surrounding words and sentences

glowing (p. 66, adjective) In the previous sentence are the words *follow the lights*. Strategy to use: surrounding words and sentences

swirling (p. 66, adjective) It describes a *dark shape*. On p. 67, the dark shape is explained as a tornado. Strategies to use: surrounding words and sentences; pictures; world knowledge of the movement tornados make

hurling (p. 67, verb) The subject of the verb is the tornado, and the objects are branches and rocks, so it is an action a tornado does with these. *In anger* shows the way it does this. Strategy to use: surrounding words and sentences

- Go through each word in turn to elicit the meaning and how they know. Play the audio to practice the pronunciation.

Second Reading: Analyze the Text and Features

- Ask students to read the story on their own and choose their favorite scene or event. Ask them to compare ideas in pairs. Invite students to share ideas.
- Ask some questions to check comprehension: *Does the story have a sad or happy ending?* (happy) *Where and why do the characters hide?* (They hide in a cave because there's a storm/tornado.) See the **ETB** for more questions.
- Discuss the questions in the red boxes.
  - **Making Connections** (p. 64): *What were you afraid of when you were young?* Give students time to think and then compare answers in pairs. Discuss ideas as a class.
  - **Fun Fact** (p. 65): *Some plants, animals, and bacteria can create their own light, called "bioluminescence."* Ask if students have seen bioluminescence before, and where.
  - **Fun Fact** (p. 66): *Fireflies light up their tails to attract other fireflies.* Have students say whether they have ever seen a firefly. Ask *Can you think of any more reasons why fireflies light up their tails?* Have them discuss in pairs and elicit ideas.
  - **Making Connections** (p. 69): *What are you still afraid of? Have you ever had to face your fear?* Explain *face your fear* if necessary (to confront something you are afraid of). If students haven't had to face a fear, prompt them to imagine they did and say how they would react or how they would make the experience less unpleasant. Write a prompt on the board: *If I had to (touch a spider), I would …* Elicit ideas.

Third Reading: Interact with the Text

- Put students in groups of four. Ask them to choose their favorite page and act out the scenes. One of the students is the narrator. If one of the characters doesn't speak in the scenes, ask students to think of a line or two he/she can say.
- Invite groups to act out their scenes for the class.

Cool Down

Put students in pairs or small groups to think about the message of the story. Then ask them to write a short description. Elicit ideas as a class.

Practice **Student's App:** Story Player

Explore the Reading

Lesson Objectives

- to understand and analyze *An Enlightening Journey* through reading comprehension activities
- to practice making inferences
- to explore the SEL competency of relationship skills through preventing interpersonal conflict, but managing to resolve it when it does occur
- to make a personal connection to the reading

Warm Up

Elicit the story title and ask why the author chose it and what it refers to. Students discuss in pairs and then with the class.

Suggested Answer

The journey is enlightening for the characters in many ways. The literal meaning is that it's a journey lit by bioluminescent plankton, lightning, and fireflies. They learn about natural phenomena, but they also get to know themselves and each other a bit better. They learn what they are afraid of and how to respond to their fears.

A Read and answer the questions. Write evidence from the reading to show how you found your answer.

- This activity gives students more practice of inferences. Ask them to read the questions first and find the relevant part of the story. Have them discuss answers in pairs before they write. Then elicit answers.

Answers

1 He was scared of the dark.; "I have bad dreams when it's dark." 2 He hoped to find a town.; "That must be a town." "Where's the town?" "I saw lights." 3 Fireflies lit the path to the cave.; "It's a firefly." "There are lots of them." "I think we should follow the lights"; "the glowing path"
4 He faced his fear and fought the thing he was scared of in his dreams.; "I'm not scared of the dark anymore."

B Think and discuss. What do you think really happened? Give a scientific explanation for these mysterious things from the story.

- Read the sentences and have students race to find which scene they're in.
- In pairs, have students use their own knowledge and clues from the text to think of their scientific explanations. Have them share ideas as a class.

Suggested Answers

1 There was bioluminescence / plants and animals like plankton that light up in the water. 2 He probably saw lights from the fireflies. 3 The tornado was rustling the leaves behind them. 4 The tornado was pulling trees out of the ground. 5 There were lots of fireflies in the cave making it light. 6 The branch was caught in the tornado.

C Think and discuss. How did the children stop each other from getting upset? Now think of a time you've had a problem. What did you do?

- Students are going to explore the SEL competency of preventing interpersonal conflict, but managing to resolve it when it does occur. In pairs, have students find the scenes and lines that show the characters upset. For example, Josh looks upset in the first picture.
- Have students discuss the question *How did the children stop each other from getting upset?* Elicit answers before students discuss the questions about themselves. Invite students to share their experiences.

Suggested Answers

Eddy told Nora getting lost was all part of the adventure to make her feel more positive. / Nora told Josh that there's nothing to worry about so that he would feel better. / Eddy asked Nora and Josh to focus on the fireflies so they would forget about the swamp. / Eddy carried Josh to make him feel safer. / Nora told Josh he was very brave, and this probably helped him go to sleep.

Literary Term: Personification

Underline the objects that are personified.

- Read the information about personification and have students find the personified object in each sentence. Allow them to work in pairs.
- Elicit answers and discuss what human characteristics or feelings are given to each object.

Now find more examples of personification in the reading.

- Have students scan the story to find more personified objects, animals, or ideas. Ask students to compare answers in pairs, then check answers as a class.

Answers

1 moon 2 leaves 3 the sea 4 plants
Examples of personification in the reading: "the sparkling waves dance along the beach" (p. 65); "The dark shape followed them, pulling trees out of the ground as it chased them through the swamp" (p. 67)

Cool Down

Have students look through the story and think of one more object, animal, or idea they would personify. Prompt them with an example: *The trees could be arms moving in the wind.* Have students share ideas in pairs, then with the class.

Practice **Resource Bank:** Literary Term Printout
Student's App: Reading Practice; Literary Term Practice

Think Together

Lesson Objectives

- to make connections between the readings
- to explore the key concept: Why are mysteries so fascinating?
- to reflect on the unit and provide personal thoughts and opinions

Warm Up

Ask students to look at the photos and pictures in Unit 4 and have them choose the place they would like to visit the most. Ask them to think about what they would see, how they would feel, and what they would do there. Have students compare ideas in pairs before sharing with the class.

A Complete the table. What are the explanations for the mysteries in *The Sci-Files* and *An Enlightening Journey*?

- Draw students' attention to the table in the book or, if you are using the TTL, project it onto the board. Explain that the first two mysteries are from *The Sci-Files* and the last four are from *An Enlightening Journey*.
- Do the first as an example. Elicit what students know about the fairy circles and complete the explanation if this has been elicited. If not, allow students to find the answer in their books. Then give students time to complete the table on their own or in pairs. Monitor and provide language help if needed.
- Check answers or project them onto the board.

Answers

fairy circles: termites and plants competing for water
sliding rocks: melting ice and wind
fire in the sea: bioluminescence
hovering light: firefly
swirling dark shape: tornado
strings of lights: insects

B Look at A. What do all the explanations have in common?

- Ask students to think about what the explanations in A have in common. Put them in pairs to discuss ideas before they write the answer. Then invite students to share their answer with the class.

Suggested Answer

They are all things that happen naturally

C Which mysteries in nature fascinate you? Do an Inside-Outside Circle.

- Students are going to do an Inside-Outside Circle cooperative learning routine (see TB p. 21) to personalize the topic of natural mysteries.
- First, give students time to think about one or more natural mysteries that fascinate them. Allow them to do a quick search on the internet if possible. You can also refer students back to the list they made in E on p. 57.
- Have students discuss their ideas with an Inside-Outside Circle. Then elicit ideas as a class and write them on the board.

D Think and write. Choose questions from C. How are you going to find out the answers? Make a list.

- Put students in pairs and ask them to look at their questions in C again. Ask *How are you going to find out the answers?* Refer them back to *The Sci-Files* and how the scientists solved the mysteries.
- Have students discuss their ideas in pairs and make notes. Monitor and provide help if needed.
- Then put students in small groups to share their ideas. Invite different students to share with the class.

My Reading Journal

What stories do you know about mysteries?

Which of the mysteries from this unit did you find most fascinating? Why?

These questions encourage students to personalize what they have learned in the unit.

Give students time to look through the unit and complete the reading journal with their ideas. Have them compare in pairs before eliciting a few examples with the class.

Example Answers

I know about the mystery of (the Great Pyramid of Giza. We still don't know how the ancient Egyptians built it.)
I think (the tornado) is the most fascinating mystery because (it's very powerful).

Choose an object from the unit. Then play the Explanation Game.

Have students look back at the VTR picture on pp. 56–57. If you are using the TTL, project the image onto the board. Elicit what students discussed in the Get Ready to Read lesson on p. 57 (use your notes to remind them). Discuss how the picture connects to the two readings in the unit.

Have students choose another object from either *The Sci-Files* or *An Enlightening Journey* and do the Explanation Game VTR again.

Cool Down

Play *Disappearing Sentences* (see TB p. 25) with sentences from the two readings. Invite students to choose a sentence and write it on the board.

Practice **Resource Bank:** Unit Test
Student's App: Key Concept Practice

UNIT 5

What Is Art?

Unit Overview

Themes

Analyzing art to understand different cultures and our past

The importance of expressing ourselves through art

Synopsis

In this unit, students will describe paintings and discuss elements and features of different kinds of art. They will hear about the Statue of Liberty and discuss works of art that represent their country. They will read mini sagas and write their own mini saga based on a painting. They will also prepare a welcome speech for a school event.

Language Book

Vocabulary
abstract shapes, complex, doodles, dots, lines, playful, powerful, serious, simple, squiggles
Pronunciation: Sentence Stress: Content Words
p. 112

Explore Language
Past Perfect and Past Perfect Progressive
p. 113

Global Citizenship
What can art tell us about different countries and periods of time?
contrast, creativity, depict, iconic, large-scale, masterpiece, style, symbolize
p. 114

Explore Language
Narrative Tenses
p. 115

Write About It
A Mini Saga
Linking the Beginning, Middle, and End of a Story; Using Descriptive Language
p. 116

Take the Stage
Presentation: Organizing and Summarizing Points
p. 117

Think It Over
Review and Reflection: Looking Back
p. 118

Think Together
What would our world be like without art?
p. 125

Visible Thinking
See, Think, Wonder
p. 119

Literacy Book

Fiction
Folk Tale: *The Boy Who Drew Cats*

Words in Context: *swarms, scurrying, rakes, beasts, fled*
p. 123

Nonfiction
Creative Nonfiction: *Cave Painting*

Words in Context: *charcoal, recreate, stylus, tablet, smudge, strokes, slider*
p. 120

Reading Skill
Recognizing Genres
p. 122

Literary Term
Synonym
p. 124

Language and Literacy Connections

The connecting theme for Unit 5 is art and how it helps us understand the past and other cultures.

	Language	Literacy
Vocabulary	**Set 1:** describing paintings **Set 2:** artistic elements and features	**Nonfiction:** confused, upset, worried, positive **Nonfiction:** lines, powerful, squiggles **Fiction:** playful, style
Grammar	**Past Perfect and Past Perfect Progressive** I'd read about a lot of artists. I'd already been thinking about different ways of painting. **Narrative Tenses** In the past, artists painted self-portraits. I was thinking about how things are now.	**Nonfiction** She had painted many of her animals in black or charcoal. Dark smoke rose to the roof of the cave. **Fiction** Snow had been falling for weeks on end. There above them, an army of giant cats was staring down at them.
Skills	**Pronunciation:** sentence stress: content words **Process Writing:** planning	**Reading:** recognizing genres **Literary Term:** synonym
International English	leaned/leant	

Vocabulary

Lesson Objectives

- to learn vocabulary for describing paintings: *abstract shapes, complex, doodles, dots, lines, playful, powerful, serious, simple, squiggles*
- to read a poem inspired by the artwork of Wassily Kandinsky
- to recognize and practice sentence stress: content words

Materials
Audio Tracks 51 to 55; Video

Warm Up

Ask a few students up to the front and secretly tell them they are at an art gallery. Have them walk around the class pretending they are at an exhibition. Invite the rest of the class to guess what they are doing. Elicit the answer and write *Art gallery* and *Exhibition* on the board.

A TRACK 51 TB p. 220 **Listen. Which two paintings does Tyler like? Why?**

- Display the picture using the TTL and ask students if they recognize any of the paintings or styles. Explain that they are going to listen to some students and their teacher talking about the paintings.
- Ask the questions and play the audio. Have students listen and discuss their answers in pairs. Then check as a class.
- Have students identify the teacher. (She's Mrs. Lewis from Unit 4.) Ask the teaser question from the end of Unit 4: *What do you think she teaches her students? How can you tell?* Elicit ideas. (She's probably an art teacher because she knows about paintings.)

Answers
He likes the one with the family and the cat (number 7) and the one of the colorful shapes (number 8).

B TRACK 52 TB p. 220 **Find and number the words in A. Then listen and check.**

- Ask students to look at the vocabulary list and say how many adjectives (six) and nouns (five) there are. Have them work in pairs to number the words. Play the audio for them to listen and check.
- Call out a number for students to say the word or phrase.

Answers
1 *doodles* 2 dots 3 squiggles 4 powerful
5 complex 6 playful 7 serious 8 simple
9 abstract shapes 10 lines

C TRACK 53 TB p. 220 **Close your eyes. Listen, visualize, and say.**

- Prepare students for the visualization (see TB p. 21).
- Play the audio, allowing students to visualize the ideas as they listen.
- Have students choose one of the situations from the visualization and make a quick drawing of the description. Then put students in pairs to talk about their pictures, answering the question from the audio.

D Look and write.

- Draw students' attention to the prompts and elicit what each one refers to (the first one refers to nouns, and the second one refers to adjectives). Give students a minute to copy the words from A in the correct category. Point out that there is no correct order. Check answers as a class.

Answers
1 Things you can see in a painting: *dots* 2 lines
3 doodles 4 squiggles 5 abstract shapes
6 Ways of describing a painting: serious 7 playful
8 powerful 9 complex 10 simple

E TRACK 54 TB p. 221 **Listen and write. Then watch and say.**

- Point to the poem title *The More I Look* and elicit which artist inspired the author (Kandinsky). Explain he was a Russian artist who lived between 1866 and 1944.
- Have students read the poem and guess the missing words. Remind them all the words can be found in A. Play the audio and have students check their answers.
- Play the audio again and have students join in. Encourage students to copy the rhythm and pronunciation.
- Have students read the poem silently. Then in pairs they take turns reading a line each. They can replace the verbs after *the more* if they wish to.

Answers
1 dots 2 abstract 3 squiggles 4 simple
5 powerful 6 Doodles 7 lines 8 playful

F TRACK 55 TB p. 221 **Pronunciation. Listen and say. Copy the sentence stress. Think of other sentences like these.**

- This task practices sentence stress, which almost always falls on content words in English. Play the audio once. Have students listen and notice which words are stressed. Elicit whether they are important words. (Yes, because they are content words.)
- Play the audio again for students to repeat. Encourage them to clap along with the rhythm.
- Elicit the meaning of *the more* + clause, *the more* + clause (the more something happens, the more another thing happens). Give an example: *The more I exercise, the healthier I get.* Ask students to think of similar sentences.
- Put students in small groups to share their sentences. Monitor and make sure they are stressing the content words. Elicit their sentences.

Cool Down

Ask students to look at the paintings in the picture again. Have them choose one they like and one they dislike and say why. Put students in small groups to compare ideas.

Practice **Student's App:** Vocabulary Practice; Spoken Word Video

Explore Language

Lesson Objectives

- to learn how to use the past perfect and the past perfect progressive
- to describe different situations and how you got into them

Materials
Audio Tracks 56 and 57; online photos of Patrick Commecy's murals (CD)

Warm Up

Ask *Which capital city is known as "the capital of art"?* Put students in small groups to discuss. Elicit ideas from groups and reasons why they think so. Then confirm the answer (Paris). Elicit what students know about Paris.

A TRACK 56 TB p. 221 **Listen and read. How did Kofi's paintings change when he came back from Paris?**

- Tell students they are going to listen to Mrs. Lewis and her son Kofi talk about his paintings. Ask the question *How did Kofi's paintings change when he came back from Paris?* Play the audio for students to listen and discuss the answer in pairs. Check the answer. Ask more comprehension questions (see **ETB**).
- Invite students to say whether they like Kofi's painting. Encourage them to say why or why not.

Answer
He decided to make his paintings bigger.

B Look at A. Complete the table. What's the difference between the simple and progressive forms?

- Tell students to look at the first two sentences in the table and think of the first word that's missing. Have them scan the dialogue in A and complete the rest of the table.
- Display the table on the board and check answers. Ask the noticing question *What's the difference between the simple and progressive forms?* Elicit answers.

Answers
'd; read; 'd; seen; 'd; thinking; Had
The simple form is *had* + past participle, whereas the progressive form is *had* + been + verb *–ing*.

- Refer students to the Grammar tip *Watch Out*. Drill the contraction *I'd been thinking*. Encourage students to check their writing for missing contractions.

C Think and discuss. Then choose.

- Ask students to look at the table in B and think about the sentences and answer options individually. Then they discuss in pairs.
- Elicit answers. Ask which past verb form is used for the action that happens after the past perfect action. Prompt students to find an example sentence in A and elicit the answer (simple past). Elicit the time word that helps them understand the order of events (before). If you feel that students need more guidance, the **ETB** provides further support.

Answers
1 before 2 past perfect 3 past perfect progressive

D TRACK 57 TB p. 221 **Listen and say.**

- Tell students they're going to practice saying sentences with the structures to help with pronunciation in fluent speech and so that they begin to internalize them. Play the audio and have students repeat each example chorally. Point out the weak form of *been* **/bɪn/** in the fourth sentence. (See TB p. 23, Making Language Drills Fun.)

E Write full sentences using the correct form of the underlined verbs.

- This activity provides controlled practice of the grammar. Draw students' attention to the sentences and have them identify the time words (*before*, *until*, and *when*). Elicit the verb form that follows these words (simple past).
- Have students complete the sentences and compare in pairs. Remind them to use contractions where possible.
- To check answers, invite students to read a sentence aloud.

Answers
1 *Before I started adding doodles, I hadn't realized drawing was so fun.* 2 He'd / He had never wanted to go to an art gallery before his uncle took him. 3 I hadn't heard of Commecy until my mother told me about him. 4 She'd / She had been drawing for years before she started painting as well. 5 They had been looking at paintings for hours when they realized the gallery was about to close.

F Imagine you're in these situations. How did you get into them? Talk to your friend.

- This activity provides freer practice of the verb forms. Read the first situation and example to the class. Elicit ideas as to how you had gotten into that situation, e.g. *I'd been painting my tree house and I hadn't seen a ball behind me. I tripped and the paint went all over the place.*
- Give students time to think about each situation and what events preceded them. Then put them in pairs to compare ideas. Invite students to share ideas with the class.

Cool Down

Show students murals created by Patrick Commecy. Encourage them to comment. Then put them in small groups to think of a building in their area that they would like to decorate with a big mural. Ask them to decide what images they would include in the mural. Share ideas as a class.

Practice **Resource Bank:** Grammar Printout
Student's App: Grammar Practice

Global Citizenship

Lesson Objectives

- to learn vocabulary related to artistic elements and features: *contrast, creativity, depict, iconic, large-scale, masterpiece, style, symbolize*
- to discuss art as a tool for understanding cultures and the past
- to practice listening for gist and details

Materials

Audio Tracks 58 to 60; Audio Track E

Opening Question

Ask the question: *What can art tell us about different countries and periods of time?* Look at the paintings on pp. 62–63 and discuss what can be learned from them, e.g. *What does painting 7 tell us about Colombia and life in the past there?*

A TRACK 58 TB p. 221 **Listen to Eugene ask Felicity about the Statue of Liberty. Do they think the Statue of Liberty is a work of art?**

- Draw students' attention to the picture of the Statue of Liberty and discuss what they know in pairs. Elicit ideas.
- Explain that they are going to listen to two friends talking about the statue. Ask the question and have students guess and explain why.
- Play the audio and have students listen and check. Elicit the answer and discuss whether students agree with Felicity or Eugene. Ask more comprehension questions (see **ETB**).

Answer

Felicity thinks it is art, but Eugene doesn't.

B TRACK 59 TB p. 221 **Look at the pictures and definitions in A and write. Then listen and check.**

- Refer students to the vocabulary box in B and have them match the words and phrases to the pictures and definitions in A. Allow them to work in pairs and discuss.
- Play the audio for students to check answers. Then play it again to practice the pronunciation, pausing after each word or phrase for them to repeat.

Answers

1 *symbolize* 2 masterpiece 3 large-scale 4 contrast
5 style 6 creativity 7 iconic 8 depict

TRACK E TB p. 221 **Visualization**

The TTL has an optional visualization audio track for this vocabulary set. (See TB p. 21.)

C Read and complete. Then ask and answer.

- Have students complete the questions. Check as a class.
- Have students discuss the questions in pairs. Encourage them to have a conversation and ask follow-up questions. They could also refer to the paintings on pp. 62–63.
- Invite students to share some ideas with the class.

Answers

1 *masterpiece* 2 depict 3 iconic 4 style
5 symbolizes 6 large-scale 7 contrast 8 creativity

D TRACK 60 TB p. 221 **Now listen to Bo, the art gallery guide. How were kites used in the past?**

- Draw students' attention to the pictures. Elicit what they can see and what they think the kites represent. Have them guess what country they are from.
- Listening for gist: tell students they're going to listen to a guide in an art gallery talk about kites. Ask the question and elicit ideas.
- Play the audio. Students discuss answers in pairs before checking with the class.

Answer

They were used as children's toys and even by scientists.

E Listen again. Answer the questions.

- Listening for details: have students read the questions and discuss in pairs.
- Play the audio and give students time to write their answers. Check and discuss whether kite-flying is popular in the students' country.

Answers

1 *Because his parents and grandparents used to play with kites.* 2 about 2,500 years ago 3 that a farmer tied his hat to a piece of string to stop it blowing away
4 Kite-flying was popular in China, Korea, and India.
5 in the 16th century 6 large kite festivals in China
7 They're amazing, but the simple ones are his favorite.

Discussion Questions

- Draw students' attention to the discussion questions: *What objects do you think best represent your country? In what ways does art benefit individuals and communities?* Have students discuss each question in pairs or small groups (see **ETB**). Encourage students to recognize that art has a number of different functions: it can tell us something about a particular country or time, but it can also benefit people, either those who make the art or those who experience it.
- Return to the opening question to ask again *What can art tell us about different countries and periods of time?* Review the ideas discussed at the beginning of the lesson and then encourage students to add new ideas. Focus on iconic works of art in their country and the concept of art as a source of cultural, historical, and political information.

Cool Down

Have students draw new versions of the Statue of Liberty, e.g. in modern clothes, with a new feature to symbolize something, e.g. a broken phone symbolizing breaking free from social media. Students explain their drawings in pairs.

Practice **Student's App:** Vocabulary Practice; Listening Practice

Explore Language

Lesson Objectives

- to learn how to use narrative tenses
- to play a chain game to tell an anecdote

Materials
Audio Tracks 61 and 62
Before the lesson: Think of an anecdote with as many details as possible (CD).

Warm Up

Draw a frame on the board. Elicit what a self-portrait is. Explain that you are going to ask students to help you to draw your self-portrait. Ask questions like *What is my hair like? Is my nose small or big?* When the self-portrait is finished, have students evaluate it.

A TRACK 61 TB p. 221 **Listen and read. Describe Aaliyah's self-portrait.**

- Tell students they are going to listen to a description of a special self-portrait. Have students discuss why it is special.
- Play the audio and have students check their answers (it's a selfie taken with a cell phone). Play the audio again and have students think how they would describe Aaliyah's self-portrait.
- Students compare their ideas in pairs. Invite students to share with the class.

Suggested Answer
It's a selfie showing her playing chess. It's playful and bright.

B Look at A. Complete the table. How many verbs does each narrative tense have?

- Display the table using the TTL and elicit the meaning of *narrative* (for telling a story). Have students scan the dialogue in A and find the missing words in the table.
- Check answers and ask the noticing question *How many verbs does each narrative tense have?* Elicit answers and draw students' attention to the Grammar tip *Look*. Elicit an example sentence from the dialogue with more than one narrative tense.

Answers
was; thinking; 'd/had; decided; been; thinking
Simple past: 1 (or 2 in negatives/questions (with *did*); past progressive: 2; past perfect simple: 2; past perfect progressive: 3

C Think and discuss. Then choose.

- Ask students to read the sentences and refer to the table in B. Have them think about the sentences individually and then decide in pairs.
- Check answers as a class. Elicit that we often use the past progressive to set the background of the story and we use other past forms to describe the events that take place.

Practice **Resource Bank:** Grammar Printout
Student's App: Grammar Practice

Answers
1 past 2 stories and personal anecdotes 3 sequence

D TRACK 62 TB p. 222 **Listen and say.**

- Tell students they're going to practice the structures orally to help with pronunciation in fluent speech and to consolidate what they've learned. Play the audio and have students repeat each example chorally. (See TB p. 23, Making Language Drills Fun.)

E Read the anecdote and choose. Then underline the time phrases and connecting words.

- Elicit what an anecdote is (a funny story/incident). Look at the picture and elicit ideas of what the anecdote could be about. Have students read the text and check.
- Give students time to choose the correct forms. Prompt them to think about meaning, the order of events, and duration. Put students in pairs to compare answers. Check answers by projecting them on the board.
- Ask students to underline the time phrases and connecting words. Elicit answers and discuss which narrative tense each phrase or word usually goes with.

Answers
1 *saw* 2 decided 3 was setting up 4 was leaning 5 'd forgotten 6 hadn't been planning
Time phrases and connecting words: While, While (past progressive), when (simple past), so (simple past), As (past progressive), Before that (past perfect or past perfect progressive)

International English

Elicit which form is American English and which is British English. Highlight the spelling difference and demonstrate the pronunciation. Elicit other similar pairs of simple past verbs, e.g. *learned-learnt, burned-burnt*. Point out that the *–ed* spelling is accepted in both American and British English.

F Play a chain game. Think of a situation to start the game. Then say what happened next.

- This activity is freer practice of narrative tenses. Students are going to play a *Chain Game* (see TB p. 25) to tell a story. Ask two students to read the example. Then ask a third student to repeat and add his/her own idea.
- First, ask students to think of a situation individually. Put them in groups and have students take turns repeating the previous situations/events before adding their own idea. Students can decide when to end the story and start again with a new situation.
- Invite students to share a story from their group.

Cool Down

Explain that you are going to tell a story and students can interrupt with questions. Tell your story using gestures and intonation, pausing for students to come up with questions.

Write About It

Lesson Objectives

- to plan and write a mini saga
- to link the beginning, middle, and end of a story
- to learn to use descriptive language

Materials

A selection of paintings (D); Support Writing printouts from the Resource Bank (F)

Warm Up

Put students in pairs to do a picture dictation. One student (with book open) describes the picture on p. 70 and their partner (with book closed) draws it. When they are ready, put students in groups to compare their pictures. Then project the picture from p. 70 on the board.

A Look at the picture. What kind of story does it make you think of? Read. Which of the three mini sagas is most like your idea?

- Ask *What kind of story does the picture make you think of?* Give students a few seconds to think before comparing ideas in pairs. Invite students to share ideas with the class.
- Ask students to read the texts and decide which is most like their idea. Have students discuss their ideas in pairs.
- Explain that these texts are mini sagas. Ask a student to read the information in the green box. Discuss what could be challenging about this type of text (the word limit).

Answers

Students' own answers

B Look at the structure of the mini sagas. Read and answer.

- Tell students they're going to look at the content and structure of the mini sagas. Have students read the questions and discuss them in pairs. Check as a class.
- You can connect this activity to the Unit 5 fiction reading in the **Literacy Book**, which is also structured with a clearly linked beginning, middle, and end.

Answers

1 a the end; b the beginning; c the middle 2 builds tension and climax and ties the story together cohesively
3 … something incredible … → … useless things … → … change his life …

C Look at the language in the mini sagas. Copy and complete the table.

- Look at the examples and discuss any questions. Then ask students to complete the table with language from the mini sagas.
- Check answers. Then read the statement in the orange box and ask students to say if they agree or disagree. Ask which mini saga they enjoyed more and why.

Answers

A: calm sea / stormy; exciting / terrified; on my birthday / finally
B: *blue fishing boat / hundreds of silver fish / just one; think about dinner / hungry / couldn't believe my eyes; all night*
C: torn nets / one shoe; had a feeling / incredible / amazingly; as usual / so far / would change his life

D Think and discuss. Choose a painting you like for a mini saga. Brainstorm lots of ideas for each of the headings using a Generating Ideas technique.

- In this lesson, students decide which Generating Ideas and Planning techniques they want to use. They can refer back to the lessons on pp. 140-141. Encourage them to choose the technique they think will work best. Guide them, but try not to tell them what to do—it's important that they learn which techniques work better for them.
- Tell students they are going to write their own mini saga based on a painting. Hand out or display the paintings you brought, or ask students to search for a painting they like. Alternatively, they can choose a painting from pp. 62-63.
- When students have chosen their painting, draw their attention to the headings. Using their chosen brainstorming technique, have them make notes individually.
- If possible, put students with the same painting in groups to compare and add ideas to their brainstorm. If students have different paintings, they can still discuss and add more ideas to their friend's brainstorm.

E Plan your mini saga. Use some of your ideas in D and one of the Planning techniques.

- Have students plan their mini sagas individually using their chosen technique and their ideas in D. Remind them that they don't have to use all of their ideas from D.
- Once they have finished, you could ask if they felt they chose the right Generating Ideas and Planning techniques for them and the task and why they think that.

F Now write your mini saga in 50 words. Give your mini saga a title.

- Have students write their mini saga and a title. Remind them to use a variety of narrative tenses. They should read their drafts and make any corrections or improvements.
- Have students write their final versions neatly on paper. Alternatively, hand out the Support printouts.
- Put students into pairs to read their partner's mini saga and identify the beginning, middle, and end.

Cool Down

Ask students to set their mini sagas on their desk face-up so that other students can read them. Prompt students to walk around the class, notice the titles, and read the mini sagas. Have students sit down again and invite students to say which stories they enjoyed and why.

Practice Resource Bank: Writing Game, *Rhyming Picture Poem*
Student's App: Writing Practice

Take the Stage

Lesson Objectives

- to give a welcome speech for a school event
- to organize and summarize points

Materials
Video

Warm Up

Ask students to imagine they are going to prepare an art exhibition at their school. Put them in small groups to brainstorm possible titles for the exhibition. Elicit ideas and write them on the board. Take a class vote on the best title.

A TB p. 239 **Watch and listen. What are the points Gene wants to emphasize in his speech?**

- Explain that students are going to watch a video of a boy (Gene) giving a welcome speech for a school art exhibition.
- With books closed, play the video for students to watch, listen, and make notes of the information given in the speech.
- Ask the question *What are the points Gene wants to emphasize in his speech?* Students compare their notes and ideas. Check answers. Ask if students have ever listened to a welcome speech. If so, where was it? Who gave it?

Answers
the variety of artworks, that students have been thinking about the question "What is art?", and that there are two competition winners in the show

B Watch again. Put the phrases in the order you hear them.

- Tell students they are going to focus on the phrases Gene uses in his welcome speech. Have students look at the phrases and guess the order.
- Play the video again and have students check their guesses and put the phrases in the correct order if necessary. Ask them to compare answers in pairs before you check with the class.

Answers
1 b 2 d 3 c 4 g 5 f 6 a 7 e

C You're going to make the welcome speech for an event at your school. Think and plan.

- Explain that students are going to prepare a welcome speech for an event at their school. Put them in pairs to discuss possible events their school could hold. Monitor and provide language help if needed.
- Ask students to make notes under the headings in C individually. Encourage them to think of Gene's example in the video and how he made it interesting for the audience. Remind them they can use the phrases in B.

D Practice with your friends. Then share with the class. Take notes and give feedback.

- Have students practice giving their welcome speech on their own. Prompt them to use phrases from B and to look up from their notes.
- Put students in pairs or small groups and ask them to take turns giving their speech. Encourage them to give each other feedback.
- Invite some students to give their welcome speech to the class. Have the "audience" make notes while they listen and then give feedback.
- Have students analyze their performance and encourage them to think about whether they summarized the points of their speech.

Cool Down

Ask students to look through Unit 5 and find a painting, photo, or picture they would recommend including in the "Be Brave, Be Creative!" exhibition. Ask them to choose one and think of reasons why they think it should be included. (If they can't choose between two, allow them to recommend two options.) Have students compare ideas in pairs, giving reasons to support their recommendations. You could also put students in small groups to negotiate and choose one item for the exhibition.

Practice **Student's App:** Speaking Skills Practice; Speaking Video

Think It Over

Lesson Objectives

- to review what has been learned in the unit
- to reflect on the unit and their own progress
- to think about learning strategies and how to continue learning at home

Materials
Large sheets of paper

Warm Up

Ask students to look through Unit 5 and write a question related to any of the topics or language they studied. Have students compare their questions in small groups.

How well did you meet the challenge of Unit 5? Read and respond.

Looking Back

- Tell students they are going to review what they learned in the unit and also think about their own learning. *Looking Back* encourages students to remember enjoyable moments in the unit and in the course. By sharing ideas with friends, they will remember more activities and things they learned, and they may also be encouraged to go back and review things they had forgotten.
- Have students do a Chalk Talk routine (see TB p. 20) to recap as many things that they have done during the unit as possible. Elicit categories from the class (e.g. words, grammar, things I learned about paintings and art, things I learned about art in my country, write a mini saga, give a welcome speech, interesting ideas, art in my life) and write each one in the middle of a large sheet of paper. Give students a couple of minutes to do each stage of the Chalk Talk routine.
- When students have finished adding ideas to the Chalk Talk posters, have them stick the posters on the wall for reference. Then refer students to the graphic organizer in the book and the prompt sentences: *My favorite activity was …; One thing I learned is …; I'll never forget when …; The funniest moment this month was when …* Have students talk in pairs about the different sections. Remind students to give reasons for their answers by explaining why they have chosen these things. Ask students what they particularly remember from the unit. Making connections between the material, activities, and personal emotions can help students remember what they have learned. Encourage them to focus particularly on the last section and elicit some funny moments students had this month.
- When you feel they have enough ideas, have students work individually to fill out the organizer. Remind them that they should write their own responses about themselves. Monitor and help as necessary. Look at what students are writing so you can tailor your classes and any additional practice to their needs.
- If you feel it is appropriate for your class, have students share their ideas with a friend. Encourage them to think together of how they can improve or practice the thing they struggled with and to give each other advice.

Looking Forward

Draw students' attention to the character at the bottom of the page. Have students say who she is and what they remember about her. (Aaliyah likes painting and chess. She appears in the art gallery in Lesson 1, p. 62, and Lesson 4, p. 68. She talks to Hugo about using her selfie for the Art Club portrait competition.) Ask the question *What games does she play?* Tell students they will find out the answer in Lesson 1 of the next unit.

Practice **Resource Bank:** Unit Test; Mid-year Test
Student's App: Vocabulary and Grammar Review

Literacy

Get Ready to Read

Lesson Objectives

- to activate prior knowledge about art and painting
- to guide inquiry and deepen understanding through a See, Think, Wonder VTR
- to preview the reading skill of recognizing genres

Materials
VTR printout from the Resource Bank (A, B, C)

Warm Up

Draw an outline of an elephant on the board. Put students in small groups and have them brainstorm facts about elephants. Elicit ideas and write them inside the outline.

See, Think, Wonder

A Look at the picture. What do you see?

- This VTR encourages students to make predictions, observations, and interpretations about the image of an elephant inside a house. Start by asking students *What do you see?* and give students up to a minute to look at the picture and think silently.
- Guide students to focus answers on what's visible, not how they interpret it. Let them share more in pairs or small groups. Then bring the groups together for a discussion.
- Keep a record of students' ideas from the VTR to revisit in the Think Together lesson.

Here's an example of this part of the routine.
Teacher: What do you see?
Student A: I see an elephant inside a room.
Teacher: What else do you see?
Student B: I see a white fence and grass, but it isn't real.
Teacher: What about the elephant? What is it doing?
Student C: It's standing there. It looks a bit sad.

B What do you think?

- Ask students *What do you think about the picture?* Give them one minute to think silently about the picture and then share their ideas in pairs before sharing as a class. Encourage students to discuss together, not only with you.

Here's an example of this part of the routine.
Teacher: What do you think?
Student A: I think it's a type of art. Maybe in a museum.
Student B: I think it looks real, but it's only a painting or photo. You can't put elephants in museums.
Student D: I think the elephant is real. Maybe the artist wants to say something about wild animals.
Teacher: Can you explain?
Student D: He's saying wild animals don't have enough space. People are destroying their habitats.

C What do you wonder?

- Say *I wonder why the elephant is in a room.* Then ask *What do you wonder? What questions do you have?* Give students one minute to look at the picture and think.
- Have students discuss their ideas in groups or as a class.

Here's an example of this part of the routine.
Teacher: What do you wonder?
Student A: I wonder how the elephant is feeling because I don't think it likes to be inside a room.
Student B: And I wonder how they put the elephant in this room.
Student C: I wonder who the artist is. I think he or she is very talented.
Student D: I wonder what they are going to do with the elephant. Are they going to let it free?

Transition

Ask students whether they have seen other works of art with animals. Encourage them to say what kind of art they are talking about, e.g. a painting, a sculpture, live art, digital art.

D Think, brainstorm, and discuss. What is art? What different kinds of art do you know?

- Draw students' attention to the title of the unit. Ask *What is art? What different kinds of art do you know?* Write *Art is …* on the board.
- Give students one minute to think of ideas on their own. Then put them in small groups to compare ideas. Have them share ideas with the class.

Answers
Students' own answers

E Skim *Cave Painting*. Think and discuss. Then write. What do you notice about the reading? What type of text is it? Why do you think that?

- This activity previews the skill of recognizing genres. Ask them to skim *Cave Painting*. Encourage them to notice the language used and to think about the type of text it is.
- Have students discuss ideas in pairs and write their answers. Then invite different students to share ideas with the class.

Suggested Answers
Type of text: informational
Why: It is nonfiction / has pictures of real people and things / talks about the past / doesn't have characters that speak or have names / has captions under the photos.

Now read **Cave Painting**

Nonfiction: *Cave Painting—* Creative Nonfiction

Lesson Objectives

- to read a text about art in different eras
- to make a personal connection to the reading

Materials

Audio Tracks 21 and 22

Warm Up

Look at the first picture of the cave artist. Ask when this person might have lived (in the Upper Paleolithic or Late Stone Age, between 50,000 and 10,000 years ago). Elicit what students know about this time in history.

TRACK 21 TB p. 233 Reading Approach

First Reading: Engage with the Text

- Project the first spread of the reading on the board to activate schema. Ask students to focus on the pictures of the cave painting and the computer artist, and decide which way of painting seems more difficult and why.
- Play the audio and have students read along. Then look at the Words in Context.

TRACK 22 TB p. 233 Words in Context

- Brainstorm strategies on the board for students to use with the words: *surrounding words and sentences, prefixes/suffixes, separate parts of word, pictures, synonyms, knowledge of similar words.*
- Divide the class into groups. Assign groups either nouns relating to art tools (*charcoal, stylus, tablet, slider*) or words relating to art techniques (*recreate, smudge, strokes*). Have groups find and discuss their words.
- Have students work with a student from another group to explain their words to each other, saying which strategies they used.

charcoal (p. 74 / p. 75 / p. 76, noun) A later sentence shows it is something used to draw and sketch with. *Black or charcoal* (p. 76) shows it is a similar color to black. Strategies to use: surrounding words and sentences; pictures

recreate (p. 74, verb) The prefix *re–* means "again." The word can be broken down: *re* + *create*. Strategies to use: prefixes/suffixes; separate parts of word

stylus (p. 75, noun) This is preceded by the words *The artist moves*. There is an explanation: *The stylus acts and feels just like a pencil.* Strategies to use: surrounding words and sentences; pictures

tablet (p. 74 / p. 75, noun) On p. 74 this is used with the word *drawing*. On p. 75, it says that a stylus moves over its surface. Strategies to use: surrounding words and sentences; pictures

smudge (p. 75, adjective) This is used with the word *effect*. Later there is a loose synonym, *messy*. Strategies to use: synonyms; surrounding words and sentences

strokes (p. 75, noun) The word before is *stylus*, so it's something a stylus does. Strategies to use: surrounding words and sentences; pictures

slider (p. 76, noun) Students may know *slide*. It is used with the word *tools*, and there is a description of what it does: *mix red, green, and blue*. Strategies to use: knowledge of similar words; surrounding words and sentences

- Bring the class together and discuss which strategies worked or didn't work. Play the audio to practice the pronunciation.

Second Reading: Analyze the Text and Features

- Ask students to read the text again on their own to consolidate understanding. Ask them to find one similarity and one difference between the artists.
- Check the answer. Then ask *What is the digital artist painting?* (the same horse as the cave artist) See the **ETB** for more comprehension questions.
- Discuss the questions in the blue boxes.
  - **Critical Thinking** (p. 74): *Why do you think early humans used caves for their paintings?* Have students brainstorm ideas in pairs, then share with the class. (Caves were probably safe places for early humans to paint. There were no wild animals around. Caves were also a safe place for the paintings, as they were protected there.)
  - **Language in Context** (p. 75): *Does the word "filter" here mean an object that removes solids from liquid; or a digital effect that changes the way the image looks?* Have students decide in pairs and elicit the answer (a digital effect that changes the way the image looks).
  - **Fun Fact** (p. 76): *Iron oxides are chemical compounds, or mixtures of chemicals. They can be used to make paints.* Explain that iron oxides contain iron and oxygen. Have students think where the artist might have found these iron oxides (e.g. in minerals).
  - **Discussion** (p. 77): *What other art forms do you know?* Have students brainstorm ideas in pairs or small groups and refer to their ideas in D on p. 73. Then invite students to share and make a list on the board.

Third Reading: Interact with the Text

- In pairs, have one student read and make notes of the procedure of cave painting while the other reads and makes notes of the procedure of digital painting. Then have students explain their procedures to their partner.

Cool Down

Have students draw an outline of their hand and write six interesting words or phrases from the text inside the outline. Students compare and explain their choices in pairs.

Practice **Student's App:** Story Player

Explore the Reading

Lesson Objectives

- to understand and analyze *Cave Painting* through reading comprehension activities
- to learn through CLIL (arts and humanities): art history
- to make a personal connection to the reading

Warm Up

Do a Total Physical Response activity to review the creative process for the cave painting. Have students stand up and do actions or gestures as you call out the steps.

The cave artist drew simple lines with a piece of charcoal. / She took a thicker piece of charcoal and sketched the neck and the mane of the horse. / She smudged the lines with her finger to create shadows. / Then she mixed her powdered red clay with some water. / She added some more powder. / She took her brush and started painting. / She filled a hollow bone with red paint. / She put her hand on the wall and blew into the bone.

A Think and write. Choose the word or phrase that matches the definition.

- Ask students to read the words, phrases, and definitions once. Have them write the words or phrases they are sure of. Encourage them to look back at the text and read the whole sentence for the words or phrases they are unsure of.
- Have students compare their answers in pairs. Then check answers as a class.

Answers

1 charcoal 2 monitor 3 flint 4 stylus 5 oil lamp
6 file 7 horse-hair brush 8 slider

B Compare and contrast the cave painting and today's digital art. Complete the Venn diagram.

- Invite a student to explain how the Venn diagram works. Then elicit an example for each of the sections and write them on the board.
- Have students discuss ideas in pairs referring to the text. Check answers as a class.

Suggested Answers

Cave Painting: done with a brush and natural tools; in a cave/specific place; in the dark / smoke / difficult conditions
Digital Art: done on a computer; can be done anywhere (on a computer); faster to create; can share instantly with people around the world
Both: artistic; colorful; take skill/talent; done by hand; signed by artist

C Think, discuss, and write. What do you notice about the way the author organized the reading? Why do you think they did that?

- Have students look at the text in pairs and discuss how it is organized and why. Monitor and prompt students with questions if necessary, e.g. *Which style of painting does the author describe first? Which style next? Why?*
- Have students share their ideas with the class.

Suggested Answers

The author organized the reading by first describing what the cave painter did, then describing what the digital artist did. The author did this so that the reader could compare and contrast their actions easily.

D Think and discuss. Why did people want to paint all those years ago? Why did they need art?

- Students are going to use their critical thinking skills to think about the function of art in prehistoric times (CLIL: art and humanities). Ask the questions and give students some time to think of ideas on their own before comparing ideas in pairs or small groups.
- Bring the class together to compare ideas and discuss.

Cool Down

Have students decide whether they'd like to make a cave painting or a digital painting. Encourage them to think about what they'd draw and make a simple sketch. Have students compare their ideas in small groups.

Practice **Student's App:** Reading Practice

Get Ready to Read

Lesson Objectives

- to activate prior knowledge about folk tales
- to practice the reading skill of recognizing genres
- to review the reading skill of skimming for gist

Warm Up

Write the following titles on the board: *An Enlightening Journey, Communities Making Dreams Come True, Urgent Message*, and *Communication Time!* Ask students what they remember about each of the texts. Elicit ideas.

A Read, think, and write. What genre are these readings? Why do you think that?

- To practice the reading skill of recognizing genres, ask students to read the two excerpts and think about the genre of each. Have them compare ideas and give reasons for their answers.
- Elicit answers and then read the information in the skills box about genres.

Answers

1 Genre: Fantasy
Why: The picture shows a strange light. The text has characters, dialogue, and the beginning of a mysterious adventure.
2 Genre: Informational text
Why: The text gives facts, figures, and dates and mentions a real-life person, a TV show, a website, and products.

B Label the features that are in *Urgent Message* with a *U*. Label the features that are in *Communication Time!* with a *C*. Then discuss which genre each reading is.

- Give students time to skim the Unit 1 readings to refresh their memories.
- Then draw their attention to B on p. 79. Ask students to match each of the features to one of the readings.
- Have students compare their answers in pairs and discuss what genre each reading is. Check answers, eliciting evidence for each feature.

Answers

1 U 2 C 3 C 4 U 5 U 6 C 7 U 8 C
Urgent Message is a fiction story. *Communication Time!* is a nonfiction timeline/informational text.

C Think and discuss. Skim *The Boy Who Drew Cats*. What genre is it? Why do you think that?

- Have students quickly skim the story and discuss in pairs what genre it is and why.
- Discuss their ideas, encouraging them to say what clues or language features helped them decide.

Answers

Genre: a story and, in particular, a folk tale
Why: It's fiction / it has illustrations, characters, dialogue, and action / it's a folk tale because it has a message and the character faces an impossible test.

D Think and discuss. Think of a story in the same genre as *The Boy Who Drew Cats*. Describe it briefly.

- Have students think about a folk tale that they know. Encourage them to think about stories they have read at school or at home, or stories they have heard from an older family member. Monitor and provide help if necessary.
- Invite students to share their story with the class. Ask students to say whether they like the story or not and why.

Answers

Students' own answers

Cool Down

Ask students to think about their favorite story and draw a picture to describe it. Have students place their drawings face-up on their desk and ask them to walk around the class, identifying the stories and the genres. Encourage them to say some things about each story, e.g. who the main characters are, what happens and whether they like it or not.

Now read **The Boy Who Drew Cats**

Fiction: *The Boy Who Drew Cats—* Folk Tale

Lesson Objectives

- to read a story about a boy and his passion for drawing
- to make a personal connection to the reading

Materials
Audio Tracks 23 and 24

Warm Up

Project the first spread onto the board and draw students' attention to the title and the pictures. Ask *What will happen to this boy in the story? What will he do?* Elicit ideas and write them on the board.

TRACK 23 TB p. 233 Reading Approach

First Reading: Engage with the Text

- Play the audio and have students read along as they listen. Pause at the end of p. 81 and encourage students to say whether they now have any different ideas from those in the Warm Up.
- Play the rest of the story and pause before the last scene. Ask *How do you think people's attitude changed toward Jun?* Elicit ideas and play the last scene. Then look at the Words in Context.

TRACK 24 TB p. 233 Words in Context

- Play the audio to familiarize students with the words and practice the pronunciation.
- Brainstorm strategies on the board for students to use with the words: *surrounding words and sentences, pictures, world knowledge, similes, synonyms.*
- Put students in pairs to find and discuss each word in the text. Remind them that different words will require different combinations of strategies to figure them out.

swarms (p. 82, noun) This describes the rats and how they come. Strategies to use: surrounding words and sentences; pictures

scurrying (p. 84, verb) This describes the rats and how they move *from place to place*. Strategies to use: world knowledge of rats and how they move; pictures

rakes (p. 84, noun) This is used in a simile to describe the rats' claws. Strategies to use: similes; world knowledge of things that make a similar movement to animals' claws

beasts (p. 85, noun) There is a synonym in the next sentence: *creatures*. The previous paragraph talks about cats. Strategies to use: surrounding words and sentences; synonyms

fled (p. 85, verb) This is used with *they* (the rats), showing it is a movement that the rats do. *As fast as they could* shows it is a quick movement. Strategies to use: surrounding words and sentences; pictures

Practice **Student's App:** Story Player

- Have pairs work with another pair to discuss the strategies they used and which worked best. Which strategies didn't help them figure out the meaning?

Second Reading: Analyze the Text and Features

- Ask students to read the story on their own and identify three main events. Ask them to compare ideas in pairs. Invite students to share ideas.
- Ask some questions to check comprehension: *What did Jun's family think of his drawing at first?* (They thought it was a waste of time.) *What did Jun's parents do to help him?* (They sent him to Hideaki to learn to write in the old style.) *How did Jun help his village?* (He drew cats that scared the rats.) See the **ETB** for more comprehension questions.
- Discuss the questions in the blue boxes. Then look at the text focus.
  - **Discussion** (p. 80): *How do people feel when they make art?* Elicit how Jun feels (very happy) and how other people feel when they make art. Have students discuss in pairs reasons why making art is a pleasant experience. Elicit ideas. (Making art reduces stress, distracts from worries, helps us relax, builds our confidence, helps us express our feelings, etc.) You may like to share and discuss Picasso's quote: "Art washes away from the soul the dust of everyday life."
  - **Making Connections** (p. 85): *Do you prefer to communicate by drawing, writing, or speaking?* Have students discuss in pairs the advantages and disadvantages of each form of communication. Then share their preferences. Elicit ideas.
  - **Text Focus** (p. 83): *Foreshadowing is when the author gives hints or clues to something that is going to happen later in the story.* Ask students to work in pairs and discuss the hints or clues the author gives in that scene. Elicit answers (… *weren't the only ones* refers to the fact that rats noticed the cats and is a hint that they will run away.)

Third Reading: Interact with the Text

- Ask students to think about Jun, especially his actions, behavior, and feelings. Give them a minute to think on their own and decide how they would describe him and what they admire about him. Then put students in pairs to share their ideas and write a short description of Jun.
- Invite students to share their descriptions.

Cool Down

Put students in pairs to think of another title that conveys the moral of the story. Monitor and provide help with questions if necessary. Elicit ideas from students.

Explore the Reading

Lesson Objectives

- to understand and analyze *The Boy Who Drew Cats* through reading comprehension activities
- to practice the reading skill of understanding author's word choice
- to explore the SEL competency of self-awareness: identify what triggers our own emotions
- to make a personal connection to the reading

Warm Up

Ask students to look through the story pictures on pp. 80–85 and choose one that they like. Have them brainstorm words and phrases to describe the picture and explain why they like it. Monitor and provide language help if needed. Have students discuss their picture in pairs. Invite some students to share ideas with the class.

A Read and choose the answer.

- Ask students to read the questions to see if they remember any of the answers. Then give them time to find the answers in the text and compare in pairs.
- Check answers by inviting students to read a sentence aloud. Encourage the other students to answer and give evidence from the text.

Answers
1 c 2 c 3 b 4 c 5 d

B Think and write. How does the author of *The Boy Who Drew Cats* describe these things?

- This activity provides further practice of understanding an author's word choice, which students looked at in Unit 3. Read the items and have students scan the text to find the expressions the author used to describe them. Allow students to work in pairs. Then check answers.

Suggested Answers
1 "like a tiger" 2 "like a snake" 3 "like a quilt"
4 "like daggers"

C Think and discuss. What activity makes you really happy? What makes you excited or scared? Why?

- Students are going to explore the SEL competency of identifying what triggers their emotions. Have them think about the questions on their own first and brainstorm activities that make them happy, excited, or scared. Then put students in pairs to compare ideas.
- Draw three columns on the board for *Happy, Excited*, and *Scared*. Elicit ideas from students and write them in the categories. Prompt students to draw conclusions, e.g. *Are the activities that make them happy physical or artistic? Are the activities that scare them sports or activities they do on their own?* You can also discuss activities that come up in more than one column, e.g. going on a roller coaster could belong to the *Excited* column for some students and in the *Scared* column for others. Discuss why this is so and the importance of respecting other people's feelings.

Literary Term: Synonym

Write the synonym for each underlined word.

- Read the information about synonyms and have students match the underlined words to their synonyms.
- Elicit answers.

Now find three pairs of synonyms in the reading.

- Have students scan the story to find three pairs of synonyms.
- Ask students to compare answers in pairs, then check answers as a class.

Answers
1 hilarious 2 pretend 3 minor 4 positive
Examples of words and their synonyms in the reading: little/small; enormous/huge; cold/frosty

Cool Down

Play *Change Places* (see TB p. 25) asking yes/no questions about the story. Some example questions you could use: *Did Takeshi and Aki have four sons and a daughter?* (no) *Does Jun/"obedient" mean doing what other people tell you to do?* (yes) *Is Jun's name suitable for Jun?* (no) *Did Jun have a pet cat of his own?* (no) *Did drawing make Jun feel free?* (yes)

Practice **Resource Bank:** Literary Term Printout
Student's App: Reading Practice; Literary Term Practice

Think Together

Lesson Objectives

- to make connections between the readings
- to explore the key concept: What would our world be like without art?
- to reflect on the unit and provide personal thoughts and opinions

Warm Up

Remind students of the unit title: *What Is Art?* Have them discuss their ideas again in pairs, thinking about the two readings in the unit. If necessary, prompt them with more questions, e.g. *Has art changed through time? Why do people make art? Who decides if something is art or not? Is it easy for everyone to understand or accept an artist's work?*

A Compare and contrast the artists from *Cave Painting* with Jun from *The Boy Who Drew Cats*. Complete the Venn diagram.

- Project the Venn diagram on the board and explain each section and where they overlap. Point out the sections that are common for the Cave Painter and the Digital Artist; the Digital Artist and Jun; Jun and the Cave Painter; and all three of them. Elicit an example for one or two of them, e.g. Cave Painter and Digital Artist both drew horses.
- Have students discuss their ideas in pairs and complete the diagram. Encourage them to infer from what is not said as well as what is clearly stated. Then have students share their ideas as a class.

Suggested Answers
Cave Painter: painted with natural materials
Cave Painter and Digital Artist: drew a horse; they're adults; they signed their work
Digital Artist: illustrates with a computer; creates her art indoors
Digital Artist and Jun: went to school
Jun: drew cats; he's a child; he saved his village with his drawings; he drew despite other people being against it
Jun and Cave Painter: sketched with coal; drew on walls
All three: creative; drew animals; they work on their own

B Read and think about the questions. Then discuss with your group. Do a Four Corners routine.

- Students are going to do a Four Corners routine (see TB p. 20) to use their critical thinking for art-related topics.
- Point out the four questions that you've put in the corners of the classroom. Tell students they can choose which question they want to discuss. Give students some time to think and decide. Have them make some notes individually. (Ensure there are at least two students for each question; if not, you may need to ask a student for their second choice.)
- Have students go to the relevant corner to discuss the question. Encourage students to use turn-taking phrases to ensure they listen and respond to each other's comments rather than just stating their opinion.

C Share your group discussion with the class.

- Invite students from each corner to share the group's ideas with the class. Encourage those who didn't discuss that question to add their thoughts and ideas.

My Reading Journal

One question I have after reading this unit is …

Who do you know that would enjoy this unit? Why?

Give students time to look through the unit and complete the reading journal with their ideas. Have them compare in pairs before eliciting a few examples with the class.

Example Answers
One question I have after reading this unit is (where I can see cave paintings).
I think (my friend Laura) would enjoy this unit because (she loves drawing and painting).

Go back to page 73. What new things do you see, think, or wonder?

Have students look back at the VTR picture on pp. 72–73. If you are using the TTL, project the image onto the board. Elicit what students discussed in the Get Ready to Read lesson on p. 73 (use your notes to remind them). Discuss how the picture connects to the two readings in the unit.

Have students look back at the VTR picture on pp. 72–73 and do the See, Think, Wonder VTR again.

Cool Down

Play *Disappearing Words* (see TB p. 25) with five important words from each reading.

Practice **Resource Bank:** Unit Test; Mid-year Test
Student's App: Key Concept Practice

UNIT 6

It's Your Turn

Unit Overview

Themes

The importance of play

Playing different types of games and learning through them

Synopsis

In this unit, students will explore different kinds of traditional and modern games, rules, and strategies. They will discuss how games can help children learn about other ways of life. They will look at game rules and write a for-and-against article. Students will have a conversation about games and practice negotiating and compromising.

Language Book

Vocabulary

board game, chance, land on, lose, miss a turn, pieces, players, strategy, throw the dice, win

Pronunciation: Intonation in Exclamations

p. 128

Explore Language

Indirect Questions

p. 129

Global Citizenship

How can games help you learn about other ways of life?

avatar, collaborate, collect points, gaming, graphics, instructions, level up, multiplayer, role-playing game, virtual

p. 130

Explore Language

Defining and Non-defining Relative Clauses

p. 131

Write About It

A For-and-Against Article

Introducing Ideas and Making Comparisons; Collocations

p. 132

Talk About It

Conversation: Negotiating and Compromising

p. 133

Think It Over

Review and Reflection: My Planning Sheet

p. 134

Literacy Book

Think Together
Why do people play games?
p. 141

Visible Thinking
Question Starts
p. 135

Fiction
Story: *The Game of Life*
Words in Context: *headset, tackled, bully, forum, opponent, tactics*
p. 139

Nonfiction
Informational Text: *The History of Board Games*
Words in Context: *grid, strategic thinking, pawns, gracefully, intricately*
p. 136

Reading Skill
Understanding Denotation and Connotation
p. 138

Literary Term
Antonym
p. 137

Language and Literacy Connections

The connecting theme for Unit 6 is the environment.

	Language	Literacy
Vocabulary	**Set 1:** playing traditional board games **Set 2:** playing video games	**Nonfiction:** board game, gaming, lose, piece, player, win **Fiction:** player, strategy, win
Grammar	**Indirect Questions** I wonder whether you know the two opposites of *lost*. I wonder if you can answer this one. I'm not sure what the two opposites of *right* are. Can you tell me what the opposites of *light* are? **Defining and Non-defining Relative Clauses** It must be someone who/that you all know. "He lives in the place where a lot of actors live." Put them in a hat, which you put in front of everyone.	**Nonfiction** We also learn more than just vocabulary and spelling when we play Scrabble, which requires us to be patient and wait our turn. Creative types enjoy playing Pictionary, in which teammates try to guess what image is being drawn. For people who don't like competition, there are cooperative games like Pandemic or Forbidden Island. **Fiction** Sometimes kids who are mean to others are having problems themselves. I wonder if you have any tips?
Skills	**Pronunciation:** intonation in exclamations **Process Writing:** introducing ideas and making comparisons	**Reading:** understanding denotation and connotation **Literary Term:** antonym
International English		goalie / goal keeper

Vocabulary

Lesson Objectives

- to learn vocabulary for playing traditional board games: *board game, chance, land on, lose, miss a turn, pieces, players, strategy, throw the dice, win*
- to read and say a poem about fun and games
- to recognize and practice intonation in exclamations

Materials
Audio Tracks 63 to 67; Video

Warm Up

Have students look at the picture on pp. 74–75. Elicit where the children are (at a games club) and the games there. Ask which other games students would like to see in the club.

A TRACK 63 TB p. 222 **Listen. Which game is Simon most interested in playing: chess, *Go*, or backgammon? Why?**

- This activity introduces the new vocabulary in context. Have students find Aaliyah in the picture or point her out (she's wearing overalls and an orange T-shirt). Point out that she is talking to Simon, who's at the games club for the first time. Ask the Unit 5 teaser question *What games does Aaliyah play?* (traditional board games like *Go*, chess, and backgammon) and have students guess which game Simon is interested in playing.
- Play the audio and have students listen for answers to both questions. Replay the audio if needed. Then ask further comprehension questions about the scene (see **ETB**).

Answers
Simon wants to play backgammon because it's a strategy game that has an element of chance.

B TRACK 64 TB p. 222 **Find and number the words in A. Then listen and check.**

- Ask students to work in pairs and say which words and phrases they already know. Then point out the example (1) and have students find the definition. Have students work in pairs to find the other words in the picture and to write the numbers in their books.
- Play the audio for students to check their answers.

Answers
1 *strategy* 2 miss a turn 3 players 4 pieces
5 board game 6 chance 7 throw the dice 8 lose
9 win 10 land on

C TRACK 65 TB p. 222 **Close your eyes. Listen, visualize, and say.**

- Prepare students for the visualization (see TB p. 21). This visualization is a scenario where students imagine they are playing a game.
- Play the audio, allowing students to visualize the ideas as they listen.
- Have students make notes about the board game they visualized and share them in pairs.

D Complete the crossword.

- Students are going to internalize the spelling of the new vocabulary by doing a crossword. Display the crossword using the TTL. Look at the example together. Point out that there's no space between *board* and *games*.
- Give students time to complete the crossword individually or in pairs. Check answers by projecting them on the board.

Answers
Across: 2 throw the dice 4 players 6 land on
7 strategy 9 miss a turn
Down: 1 *board games* 3 change 4 pieces 5 lose
8 win

E TRACK 66 TB p. 222 **Listen and write. Then watch and say.**

- Have students look at the title and guess words or phrases that might be in the poem. Then play the video or audio, allowing students to listen and enjoy the poem.
- Read the first line and elicit they need to order the letters to make the words in A. Have students complete the blanks, then play the audio to check answers.
- Play the audio or video again and have students read the poem silently, noticing the words that rhyme.
- Have students read the poem aloud in groups of three. They take turns reading a verse and read the last one together.

Answers
1 *chance* 2 land 3 turn 4 miss 5 dice 6 piece
7 lose

F TRACK 67 TB p. 222 **Pronunciation. Listen and say. Copy the intonation. Think of other phrases like these.**

- Draw students' attention to the phrases from the poem and play the audio once. Have students listen and notice the falling and rising intonation.
- Draw the falling and rising arrows on each side of the board. Read each phrase and have students point to the correct arrow. Ask *What does my voice do when I'm happy or excited?* (It goes up.) *And when I'm disappointed or annoyed?* (It goes down.)
- Have students work in pairs to think of other phrases with rising and falling intonations. They can look back through the book to help them. Elicit phrases on the board and drill them chorally.

Answers
Students' own answers

Cool Down

Put students in small groups to pretend they are playing a board game like *Catan* or *Forbidden Island*. They can use phrases from the lesson and make exclamations while acting out taking turns, throwing the dice, moving their piece, etc.

Practice **Student's App:** Vocabulary Practice; Spoken Word Video

Explore Language

Lesson Objectives

- to learn how to use indirect questions
- to role-play an interview with a famous person

Materials
Audio Tracks 68 and 69

Warm Up

Ask students to open their books to p. 74 and find Marge and Simon. Elicit what games they played (*Go* and backgammon). Explain that they are now doing an activity/playing a game on their own and have students guess the activities/games.

A TRACK 68 TB p. 222 **Listen and read. What activities are Simon and Marge doing?**

- This activity is a presentation of the grammar in context. Books closed, play the audio for students to check their guesses from the Warm Up, having students follow the dialogue in their books.
- Ask the question *What activities are Simon and Marge doing?* and elicit the answer.
- Ask *Who can't concentrate on an activity and why?* (Simon, because Marge is constantly asking him questions) Then ask further comprehension questions (see **ETB**). Elicit whether students have ever done a puzzle book and if they have played a word game.

Answer
He's doing a puzzle book, and she's playing a word game on her tablet.

B **Look at A. Complete the table. Is the word order after the *wh–* word like a statement or a question?**

- Display the table using the TTL. Tell students to scan the dialogue in A and complete the table with the missing words. Have them compare answers in pairs.
- Students should now have the skills and strategies to be able to discuss the grammar forms and notice patterns by themselves. When they have completed the table, discuss the word order, form, and patterns together, but let your class guide the discussion. If you feel that students need more guidance, use the notes in the **ETB**.

Answers
whether; if; what; are; tell; what
The word order after the *wh–* word is like / the same as in a statement.

- Refer students to the Grammar tip *Remember.* Remind them that they studied *I wonder* in Unit 1, p. 13. Check if they remember which is more formal—*if* or *whether*? (whether)

C **Think and discuss. Then choose.**

- This activity focuses on the usage of indirect questions. Have students refer back to the table in B and discuss the statement in pairs. Then check their answer and elicit how *Can you tell me* … can be even more polite (by using *Could* instead of *Can*).

Answer
1 False

D TRACK 69 TB p. 222 **Listen and say.**

- Tell students they're going to practice asking indirect questions to help with pronunciation in fluent speech and so that they begin to internalize the structure. Play the audio and have students repeat each example chorally. (See TB p. 23, Making Language Drills Fun.)

E **Read and write the indirect questions.**

- This activity provides controlled practice of indirect questions. Read the example direct and indirect question. Have students write the indirect questions individually and compare their answers in pairs. Point out again that we can form indirect questions with any *wh–* word, not only *what.* You could also point out that in number 3, the main verb shifts from the infinitive to the simple past.
- To check answers, invite students to read an indirect question aloud or display answers with the TTL.

Answers
1 *if you like playing card games* 2 which board game is the most popular? 3 when you last did a puzzle from a book? 4 whether/if you've ever played a board game online. 5 if/whether you'd like to invent a board game?

F **Interview your friend. Follow the instructions. Then ask and answer.**

- This activity provides freer oral practice of indirect questions. Have students read the instructions and the example exchange. Give students time to choose a famous person and think about the questions they are going to ask. Allow them to write their questions if they need to. Monitor and provide language help if needed.
- Put students in pairs. They take turns asking and answering questions. Encourage fast finishers to ask follow-up questions. Elicit what celebrity students interviewed and what they found out.

Cool Down

Ask students to think of a question they would like to know the answer to and write it down. Then ask them to change the question so it's indirect using *I wonder, I'm not sure,* or *Can you tell me.* Have students walk around the class asking different students their question. Set a time limit and have students share their findings in pairs and then with the class.

Practice **Resource Bank:** Grammar Printout
Student's App: Grammar Practice

Global Citizenship

Lesson Objectives

- to learn vocabulary for playing video games: *avatar, collaborate, collect points, gaming, graphics, instructions, level up, multiplayer, role-playing game, virtual*
- to explore how games can help us learn about other ways of life
- to practice listening for gist and details

Materials

Audio Tracks 70 to 72; Audio Track F

Opening Question

Ask the opening question: *How can games help you learn about other ways of life?* Do a Think, Pair, Share routine (see TB p. 20) to brainstorm ideas. Then invite students to share examples of games with the class.

A TRACK 70 TB p. 222 **Listen to Kendra help her brother Malik to choose an online game. Can you describe the game?**

- Tell students they are going to listen to Kendra and her brother Malik talking about choosing an online game. To activate schema, invite students to briefly mention any online games they have played and their opinion of them.
- Ask *Can you describe the game Malik chose?* and play the audio. Students discuss the answer in pairs before you elicit ideas from the class.
- Elicit why Malik is looking for a video game (to help with homework) and discuss whether students ever play games for homework or for educational reasons. Then ask further comprehension questions (see **ETB**).

Suggested Answer

The main focus of the game is that it's about building communities.

B TRACK 71 TB p. 222 **Look at the pictures and definitions in A and write. Then listen and check.**

- Look at the example together. Refer students to the vocabulary box in B and have them match the words and phrases to the pictures and definitions in A. Allow them to work in pairs and discuss their answers.
- Play the audio for students to check answers. Then play it again to practice the pronunciation, pausing after each word or phrase for them to repeat.

Answers

1 *avatar* 2 collect points 3 instructions 4 gaming
5 virtual 6 graphics 7 multiplayer 8 collaborate
9 level up 10 role-playing game

TRACK F TB p. 222 **Visualization**

The TTL has a visualization audio track for this vocabulary set. (See TB p. 21.)

C Read and complete.

- This activity provides contextualized controlled practice of the vocabulary. Ask students to read the sentences once and guess what type of word is missing.
- Have students complete the sentences in pairs. Then check answers.

Answers

1 *level up* 2 gaming 3 instructions 4 avatar
5 virtual 6 multiplayer 7 graphics 8 collaborate

D TRACK 72 TB p. 223 **Now listen to Mr. Suvlu, an Inupiat teacher from Alaska. What's special about this game?**

- Tell students they are going to listen to an Inupiat teacher talk about a video game. Explain that the Inupiat are native people who live in Alaska. Look at the photos and elicit how life for the Inupiat might be different from theirs.
- Listening for gist: ask *What's special about the game?* and play the audio. Students discuss the answer in pairs. Encourage students to make connections with the game in A.

Answer

It gives you cultural information about the Inupiat people and animals of Alaska.

E Listen again. Read and match the sentence halves.

- Listening for details: have students read the sentence halves and try to match them before they listen again.
- Play the audio and have students check their ideas. Check answers as a class. Discuss whether students think the game sounds interesting and if a similar game could work to teach people about their own community or culture.

Answers

1 *f* 2 d 3 a 4 c 5 b 6 e

Discussion Questions

- Draw students' attention to the discussion questions. Have students discuss each question in pairs or small groups (see **ETB**). Encourage students to recognize that playing games can teach us skills that can help us in all areas of our lives, and that in some games we can learn about and communicate with people in other parts of the world.
- Return to the opening question to ask again *How can games help you learn about other ways of life?* Review the ideas discussed at the beginning of the lesson and then encourage students to share any new ideas.

Cool Down

Put students into two large groups for a class debate. One group brainstorms the pros of playing video games, and the other group brainstorms the cons. When time is up, invite a student from the "pro" group to explain an advantage. Have a student from the "con" group reply, "Yes, but ..." and add a con. Continue until one group has run out of ideas.

Practice **Student's App:** Vocabulary Practice; Listening Practice

Explore Language

Lesson Objectives

- to learn how to use defining and non-defining relative clauses
- to practice vocabulary for playing video games

Materials
Audio Tracks 73 and 74

Warm Up

Write *The Name in the Hat* on the board. Explain that it is a team game and have students discuss ideas in pairs about how they think the game is played. Elicit ideas.

A TRACK 73 TB p. 223 **Listen and read. What does a team have to do to win *The Name in the Hat* game?**

- This activity is a presentation of the grammar in context. Tell students they are going to listen to Guan from Lesson 1 (the tall man in the blue shirt) explaining how *The Name in the Hat* is played.
- Play the audio. Have students follow along in their books and check their predictions from the Warm Up.
- Ask the question *What does a team have to do to win The Name in the Hat game?* Elicit the answer. Find out if students have played this game or a version of it and elicit the name. Then ask further comprehension questions (see **ETB**).

Answer
guess the most names correctly

B **Look at A. Complete the table. Which sentence has a comma before the relative pronoun?**

- Display the table using the TTL. Tell students to scan the instructions in A to find the missing words in the table. Have them work individually or in pairs.
- Students should now have the skills and strategies to be able to notice the grammar patterns by themselves using the examples. When they have completed the table, discuss the word order, form, and patterns together, but let your class guide the discussion. If you feel that students need more guidance, use the notes in the **ETB**.

Answers
whose; where; which
The last sentence (the non-defining relative clause) has a comma.

- Draw students' attention to the Grammar tip *Watch Out*. Point out that when the subject in the main clause and the relative clause is the same, we don't use it again in the relative clause.

C **Think and discuss. Then choose.**

- Ask students to read the statements on usage and refer to the table in B. Have students identify the subject and object in each sentence. Ask them what the relative pronouns refer to. Have students discuss the answers in pairs.
- Check answers as a class. Ask students if each example sentence has essential or extra information. Elicit that we use *that* in defining relative clauses only and point out that it sounds slightly more informal.

Answers
1 subject and/or object 2 non-defining 3 True

D TRACK 74 TB p. 223 **Listen and say.**

- Tell students they're going to practice saying sentences and questions with relative clauses to help with pronunciation in fluent speech and to consolidate what they've learned. Play the audio and have students repeat each example chorally. (See TB p. 23, Making Language Drills Fun.)

E **Complete the anecdote. Use a relative pronoun and one of the relative clauses in the box.**

- This activity provides controlled practice of relative clauses. Read the example and elicit what type of relative clause it is (defining) and who it refers to (Hannah).
- Give students time to choose an appropriate relative pronoun and clause for each sentence. Then have them compare answers in pairs and discuss who or what the information refers to.
- To check answers, ask students to read a sentence, explain the type of defining clause, and say who/what it refers to.

Answers
1 *who enjoyed playing games with her friends* (defining)
2 that/which she needed to dress up for (defining)
3 which was exciting (non-defining) 4 whose bedroom door was open (non-defining) 5 which was sitting on the bed. But it was only her sister playing a trick! (non-defining)

F **Read and complete the sentences about yourself. Then talk with a friend.**

- For this freer oral practice, students write sentences individually before reading them and responding in pairs. Have two students read the examples on the page and check they know they should ask a follow-up question.
- Have students write their sentences and then take turns saying a sentence for their partner to ask a follow-up question.

Cool Down

Divide the class into two teams to play *The Name in the Hat*. With larger classes, have students play in different groups of two teams. Monitor the game and encourage students to use relative clauses to describe the celebrities. Assign a student to keep a stopwatch and make a note of relative clauses.

Practice **Resource Bank:** Grammar Printout
Student's App: Grammar Practice

Write About It

Lesson Objectives

- to learn how to draft (Process Writing Step 3)
- to plan and write a for-and-against article
- to introduce ideas and make comparisons
- to learn how to use collocations

Materials

Support Writing printouts from the Resource Bank (G)

Warm Up

Write on the board *Old Games & New Games*. Elicit examples of games from Lesson 1 and which category each belongs in, writing them on the board. Then put students in small groups to brainstorm what's good and bad about old games and new games. Elicit ideas and make notes on the board.

A Read the article. Which type of games does the writer prefer? Why?

- This lesson corresponds with the Unit 6 nonfiction reading in the **Literacy Book**. Tell students they are going to read an article about new and old games. Have them read the article and check for any ideas from the Warm Up.
- Ask the questions and have students read the article again and discuss the answers in pairs. Then check as a class. Ask whether students are surprised by the answer and who they think wrote the article. Elicit ideas, and if necessary, point out that the writer is a parent (as shown in the web address). Ask more comprehension questions (see **ETB**).

Answer

traditional games because they're more fun, as you can spend quality time with your friends

B Look at the structure of the article. Check (✔) what information is included. Then put the information in order.

- Tell students they're going to look at the structure of the article. First, have them look at the list of information and work in pairs to discuss what information is included, referring back to the article. Check answers.
- Then have students put the information in order. Check answers as a class.

Answers

1 d 2 a 3 e 4 c 5 g (b and f not included)

C Look at the language in the article. Read and match the collocations.

- Have students read the collocations 1–5. Check if there are any words they don't understand.
- Give students time to scan the article for the collocations and match them to what they refer to. Have them compare answers in pairs before checking as a class.

Answers

1 e 2 b 3 a 4 c 5 d

D Think and discuss. Choose two kinds of games you've played. Complete the mind map with your ideas.

- This lesson introduces the idea of writing a draft before writing the final piece.
- Have students think of two games they have played. They can be any type of game, old or new. Have them compare ideas in pairs and discuss why each game is good.
- Quickly review the different ways of generating ideas that students learned in **Process Writing Step 1: Generating Ideas** on p. 140 and encourage students to choose one to use. Then have students complete the mind map individually.
- Have students compare notes in pairs. Then elicit ideas.

E Plan your article. Use your ideas in D and one of the Planning techniques. Make notes for each paragraph.

- Ask students to choose a suitable Planning technique from **Process Writing Step 2: Planning** on p. 141, and before they start, elicit what each paragraph should contain. (Paragraph 1: Introduction; Paragraph 2: Reasons why the first type of game is good; Paragraph 3: Reasons why the second type of game is good; Paragraph 4: Comparison and summarizing comment)
- Give students time to make notes for each paragraph. Encourage them to think of collocations they can use, as well as relative clauses. Provide language help if needed.
- Ask students to turn to p. 142 to learn about **Process Writing Step 3: Drafting** (see TB p. 213). Students will need to do this step before they do F.

F Write a first draft for your article. Read it and decide how you can improve it.

- Have students write a draft of their article in their notebooks, using the plan on the page and referring to their notes in E. They should read their draft and think of how they can improve it.

G Now write your article.

- Give students time to write their final versions neatly on paper or on the Support printout.
- In pairs, students take turns reading each other's article and thinking about which games their friend prefers.

Cool Down

Elicit video games students play and write them on the board. Have students discuss in small groups what they learn from each game and what some disadvantages might be. Then have them discuss whether they think they spend too much time playing video games. Invite students to share the ideas they discussed.

Practice **Resource Bank:** Writing Game, *How Good Is It?*
Student's App: Writing Practice

Talk About It

Lesson Objectives

- to have a conversation about games suitable for a vacation
- to negotiate and compromise

Materials
Video

Warm Up

Write a prompt on the board: *On a rainy day, I like to play …* Have students discuss ideas in small groups. Invite students to share ideas with the class.

A TB p. 240 **Watch and listen. What do Veronica and Linda decide to do?**

- Tell students they are going to watch a video of Veronica and Linda talking about games. The video provides a presentation of the functional language needed for negotiating and compromising.
- With books closed, play the video and have students listen for the types of game the girls suggest (board games, video games).
- Ask the comprehension question *What do Veronica and Linda decide to do?* If necessary, play the video again and then allow some time for students to discuss the answer in pairs. Elicit the answer from the class. Ask more comprehension questions (see **ETB**).

Answer
They decide to invent a new video game.

B Watch again. Check (✔) the phrases you hear. Write *APV* for phrases to suggest an alternative point of view and *D* for phrases to disagree.

- Tell students they are going to focus on the functional language the girls use to suggest alternative points of view and to disagree. Make sure that students know that an *alternative point of view* is a different opinion or idea. Have them read the phrases and the example.
- Play the video again and have students label the phrases. Have students compare their answers in pairs before checking with the class.
- Play the video once more and ask students to notice the intonation the girls use. Tell students to listen out for rising or falling intonation. Write some of the key phrases from the video on the board and have students draw arrows to show rising or falling intonation.

Answers
1; 2; 3; 4; 6
Suggest an alternative point of view: 1; 3; 4; 7; 8
Disagreeing: 2; 4; 5; 6

C Imagine you're going on vacation with a friend and you want to take some games. Think and make notes.

- Put students in pairs and explain that they are going to go on vacation with a friend. Have students first decide where they are going to go, e.g. the beach or the mountains. Then have students read the questions about which games to take.
- Give students time to think about their answers to the questions and make notes individually. Monitor and provide language help if needed. Planning will help students structure their conversations, but they will also need to be able to respond to their friend's ideas spontaneously. Remind students that they only need to write brief notes to prompt them during the conversation and not full sentences.

D Discuss with your friend using phrases from B. Do you agree?

- Tell students they are going to discuss the games they want to take with their partner. They should try to disagree with each other a few times and suggest alternative points of view using phrases from B.
- Give students a minute or so to have their conversations. Monitor and make sure they use the phrases in natural contexts, responding spontaneously to what their partner says. Then ask them to repeat and improve their discussion.
- Have students analyze their own performance and think about whether they listened and responded to their partner's points. Then they check to see whether their partner agrees.

Cool Down

Play *Versus* (see TB p. 26). For this version, call out a situation and two options, e.g. *You're having a party. Are you going to play a board game or a video game? / It's a sunny day. Are you going to go out or play an online game?* Students then turn to a friend and say what they are going to do.

Practice **Student's App:** Speaking Skills Practice; Speaking Video

Think It Over

Lesson Objectives

- to review what has been learned in the unit
- to reflect on the unit and their own progress
- to think about learning strategies and how to continue learning at home

Warm Up

Ask students to look through the unit and think about how their attitude toward board games and video games is different. Write prompts on the board: *Before, I thought that … Now, I think …* Have students complete the sentences with their ideas and compare in pairs. Invite students to share ideas with the class.

How well did you meet the challenge of Unit 6? Read and respond.

My Planning Sheet

- Give students time to think about and discuss activities in the unit before they complete each section of the graphic organizer. Tell students they are going to review what they've successfully learned and what they need to improve at. They will then make a plan outlining what they will do next in order to continue learning.
- Tell students to imagine they have to tell a new student what they have done during the unit. Have students work in pairs or small groups to come up with a list or mind map of activities they have done and things they have learned. They can look back through the unit to help them.
- Refer students to the graphic organizer and prompt sentences and give an example for each one, e.g. *We're all good at some things. I'm good at writing a for-and-against article. I need to work on my grammar because I make mistakes with indirect questions.* Have students talk in pairs about the different sections. Encourage them to focus particularly on the second and third sections and to discuss what they can do to learn more about or how they can practice the areas they have problems with. Remind students about the online materials including the Student's App, but also encourage them to think of other ways they can practice English. Write some prompts on the board to support their conversation, e.g. *I'm going to …; I plan to …; I can try to …*
- When you feel they have enough ideas, have students work individually to fill out the organizer. Remind them that they should write their own responses about themselves. Monitor and help as necessary. Look at what students are writing so you can tailor your classes and any additional practice to their needs.
- If you feel it is appropriate for your class, have students share their ideas with a friend. Encourage them to think together of how they can put their plans into practice. They can use phrases from the speaking lesson to clarify ideas and confirm understanding.
- Discuss the last two sections with the class before you have students write about them. Ask *How will you know if your plan works?* Elicit that students will be able to do some of the things they wrote about in the second section, which they need to improve on, without looking in their books. Ask students what they will do if their plan works. Encourage students to think of other areas they would like to practice. Remind them again about the Student's App and online materials. Then have students fill out the final two sections in the graphic organizer.

Looking Forward

Draw students' attention to the character at the bottom of the page. Have students say who he is and what they remember about him. (Guan appeared in the games club in Lesson 1, p. 74. He also explained how to play *The Name in the Hat* in Lesson 4, p. 80.) Have students look at the speech bubble and make predictions about what he designs. Tell students they will find out the answer in Lesson 1 of Unit 7.

Put It Together

To further review and recycle the language in Units 5 and 6, play the game, *Yesterday's Vacation Fun*, on pp. 86–87. See TB p. 208 for teaching notes.

Practice **Resource Bank:** Unit Test
Student's App: Vocabulary and Grammar Review

Literacy

Get Ready to Read

Lesson Objectives

- to activate prior knowledge about games
- to guide inquiry and deepen understanding through a Question Starts VTR
- to preview the reading skill of understanding denotation and connotation

Materials
VTR printout from the Resource Bank (A, B, C)

Warm Up

Ask students to think about how many hours a week they spend playing games. Explain it can be any kind of game. Have them compare answers in small groups, then as a class.

Question Starts

A Look at the picture. Then brainstorm questions. Write a list.

- This VTR encourages students to think of a variety of interesting questions that will help them explore their ideas about virtual reality and gaming. Start by having students look at the picture for one minute and say what they see. Provide vocabulary where necessary.
- Draw students' attention to the question words and elicit an example question students have about the picture.
- Have students brainstorm as many questions as they can individually at first. Then have them compare and combine their lists in pairs. You could divide the question words between the students so they focus on three each.

B Look at your list from A. Which questions seem most interesting? Discuss them with the class.

- Put students in groups of four. Ask them to share their ideas and choose the three most interesting questions. Encourage them to negotiate and explain why they think a question is more interesting than another.
- Discuss their choices as a class, encouraging students to listen to each other and perhaps suggest answers.

Here's an example of this part of the routine.

Teacher: What questions did you think were interesting?
Student A: Well, we weren't sure if the dog and slug are part of the game.
Student B: We also asked what game they're playing.
Teacher: What other interesting questions did you think of, Student C?
Student C: One of our questions is, where are they playing this game? The room looks strange.

C What new ideas or questions do you have now? Talk about your ideas with your partner.

- Now that students have heard some example questions, ask them to think of some more. Encourage them to think about virtual reality and video games more broadly. They shouldn't limit themselves to what they see in the picture.
- Bring the class back together to discuss further. Encourage students to ask as many questions as they want, to express their ideas, and to talk to each other, not just to you. Students can be as imaginative and creative as they like. Keep notes of ideas to revisit in the Think Together lesson.

Here's an example of this part of the routine.

Teacher: What new questions do you have?
Student A: Well, we'd like to know how many hours a week is OK to play video games?
Student B: I think it's OK to play for an hour every day.
Student C: I think that's too much. We should only play on the weekend.
Teacher: Any other new questions?
Student D: Are there benefits of playing video games?
Student E: Yes! You can learn a lot of things by playing video games, like history and geography.

Transition

Ask students what other games they think the people in the picture play. Discuss ideas as a class.

D Think and discuss. What games do you play?

- Ask students to make a list of the games they play. They can list any type, e.g. video games, outdoor games, etc.
- Have students share the games they play in groups. Encourage them to discuss why they like these games.
- Invite students to report the games they discussed.

Answers
Students' own answers

E Read and underline. Choose the words or phrases that you think make the paragraph sound more positive.

- This activity previews the skill of understanding denotation and connotation. Read the first line and point out both options are both grammatically correct. However, one of the two words sounds more positive. Elicit the answer (*rainy*). Explain that *stormy* implies worse weather.
- Have students read the rest of the paragraph on their own and choose the more positive options. Have them compare answers in pairs before checking as a class.

Answers
rainy; at home; relaxing; invite; friends; play; a simple; challenging; have fun

Now read **The History of Board Games**

Nonfiction: *The History of Board Games*—Informational text

Lesson Objectives

- to activate prior knowledge about board games
- to make a personal connection to the reading

Materials

Audio Tracks 25 and 26; pieces from board games (WU)

Warm Up

Bring in some parts and playing pieces from board games, or ask students to bring them in. If possible, include some from the games in the reading. These could include playing pieces, cards, play money, etc. Give students a few items in groups and have them say what game they think each one is from and how to play each game.

TRACK 25 TB p. 234 Reading Approach

First Reading: Engage with the Text

- Ask students to read the text once on their own and check to see if any of the games they discussed in the Warm Up are mentioned.
- Put them in pairs to discuss what information they found interesting. Invite students to share ideas with the class. Then look at the Words in Context.

TRACK 26 TB p. 234 Words in Context

- Give students a few minutes to find and highlight each word. Remind them it may appear more than once. Have them identify the kind of word.
- Write these strategies on the board for students to use with the words: *pictures, comparison, surrounding words, positive/negative, separate parts of word, word families, world knowledge.*
- Have students work in pairs to discuss the words. Remind them that different words will require different combinations of strategies to figure them out and that they should use all the instances of a word to help them.

grid (p. 90, noun) The sentence shows that a *grid* is a place where the game is played and that backgammon also has a grid. Strategies to use: surrounding words; pictures; world knowledge of board games

strategic thinking (p. 91, noun) The two sentences tell us that *strategic thinking* is a kind of skill needed in games such as *Go* and chess to *carefully plan each step.* Strategies to use: surrounding words; word families; separate parts of word

gracefully (p. 92, adverb) The sentence uses the adverb to describe the way in which someone may behave as they win or lose a game and states that this positive adverb is an important life skill. Strategies to use: positive/negative; world knowledge of feelings and behaviors associated with winning and losing

intricately (p. 93, adverb) The sentence compares two elements of modern games inspired by video games, both positive. The following words show that *intricately* means something has *wonderful details.* Strategies to use: comparison; surrounding words; positive/negative

- Go through the words as necessary to elicit the meaning and how they know. Play the audio to practice the pronunciation.

Second Reading: Analyze the Text and Features

- Play the audio and have students listen and follow in their books. Elicit what kind of text it is (informational).
- Ask some questions to check comprehension: *Is the text about old or new board games?* (both) *Is it about board games for two players or multiplayer board games?* (both) See the **ETB** for more comprehension questions.
- Discuss the questions in the orange boxes.
  - **Personalization** (p. 90): *Which of the board games in this reading do you know?* Put students in pairs to share ideas and experiences. Elicit ideas from students and whether they enjoyed playing the games.
  - **Fun Fact** (p. 91): *AlphaGo, a computer program, beat the three-time European Go champion Fan Hui in an amazing scientific breakthrough in 2016.* Have students discuss in pairs whether they think it's fair for someone to play a game against a computer. Elicit ideas and whether students have ever played video games against a computer. How did they feel about the experience?
  - **Personalization** (p. 93): *Do you prefer board games or video games? Why?* Ask students to raise their hand if they prefer board games to video games. Form two groups and have students discuss reasons for their preference in pairs or small groups. Then pair students up so they are discussing different opinions. Elicit ideas from volunteer students.

Third Reading: Interact with the Text

- Ask students to choose two of the board games from the reading and find differences and similarities. Have them discuss ideas in pairs. Monitor and provide language help if needed.
- Invite students to summarize their findings about the two games for the rest of the class.

Cool Down

Have students call out all the benefits mentioned in the text related to playing board games. Put students in pairs to think of one more benefit. Elicit ideas and add them to the list. Then have students decide in pairs which is the most important benefit and why. Compare answers.

Practice **Student's App:** Story Player

Explore the Reading

Lesson Objectives

- to understand and analyze *The History of Board Games* through reading comprehension activities
- to learn through CLIL (history): civilizations
- to make a personal connection to the reading

Warm Up

- Ask students to quickly reread *The History of Board Games*. Then, with books closed, invite volunteer students to the front to describe or mime one of the board games from the reading. The rest of the class has to guess the game.

A Read and choose the answers to complete each sentence.

- Ask students to read the questions once and see if they remember the information. If they aren't sure, encourage them to choose the option they think is most probably the correct answer. Have them discuss their answers in pairs.
- Then give students time to scan the reading to check their answers. Remind them to look for key words in the question and the text rather than reading the whole thing.
- Put students in pairs or small groups to compare their answers before checking as a class. Have students say where the evidence is in the text.

Answers
1 a; d 2 b; d 3 c 4 c 5 c

B Write *True* or *False*. Then discuss evidence from the reading.

- Have students read the statements first and check if they have any questions.
- Put students in pairs to discuss whether the statements are true or false. Then have them look for evidence in the reading that confirms their answers. Encourage them to underline key words in the sentences to help them identify the information they are looking for more easily.
- Check the answers as a class and encourage students to justify their answers.

Answers
1 True 2 False (It's hard to win because Go is challenging and it requires discipline and strategic thinking.) 3 False (Chess pieces have changed through time.) 4 False (They are very popular with most board game lovers.) 5 True 6 False (Cooperative games are ideal for people who don't like competition and don't care about winning.)

C Think and discuss. What are the traditional board games in your country? Compare and contrast them to the games in the reading.

- Students are going to compare traditional games they play with the games in the reading. This draws on the CLIL history focus of civilizations.
- Have students brainstorm ideas in small groups. If necessary, allow them to do quick research. Encourage them to focus on the CLIL history topic of civilizations by thinking about or researching how long ago the game was invented and who invented it.
- When students have thought of some board games, elicit them and write them on the board. Put students in pairs to choose a traditional board game and compare it to the games in the reading. Students can make notes in their notebooks. Monitor and provide language help if needed.
- Invite pairs of students to share their ideas in class. Encourage other students to add ideas.

Literary Term: Antonym

Underline the antonyms in each pair of sentences.

- Review what an antonym is and elicit a few examples from the class, e.g. *buy/sell*.
- Then have students look at the pairs of sentences and underline the antonyms in each pair. They can compare answers in pairs. Check answers.

Now find four pairs of antonyms in the reading.

- Have students scan the reading to find four pairs of antonyms.
- Ask students to compare answers in pairs, then check answers as a class.

Answers
1 borrowed; lend 2 expensive; cheap 3 dangerous; safe. 4 sick; healthy
Examples of antonyms in the reading: old/young; simple/challenging; traditional/modern; win/lose

Cool Down

Play *Draw It!* (see TB p. 25) with words from the reading, e.g. *ladder, bone, race, grid, knight, chariot*. You can also challenge them with more abstract vocabulary such as *lose, interactive, collaborate*, and *face-to-face*.

Practice **Resource Bank:** Literary Term Printout
Student's App: Reading Practice; Literary Term Practice

Get Ready to Read

Lesson Objectives

- to activate prior knowledge about video games
- to practice the reading skill of understanding denotation and connotation

Materials

Pieces of paper with the names of board games, one set of cards per group (WU)

Warm Up

Divide the class into small groups. Give each group a set of board games cards. Tell them to keep them facedown. One student picks up a card and the rest of the group asks yes/ no questions to guess the game. The games can be from the reading or other common board games they will know.

A Complete the table. Look back at *The History of Board Games*.

- This lesson practices the skill of understanding denotation and connotation, which students previewed on p. 89.
- Look at the example together. Explain that for each word they have to find a synonym in the paragraph listed in the second column. Then have them look for the other words individually.
- Have students compare answers in pairs and discuss whether the words used in the text make it read more positively or negatively. (positively)
- Have students read the skills box. Remind students also of the short text they read in E on p. 89 and point out that an author's choice of words in a text may depend on what meaning they're trying to convey.

Answers

Played: *enjoyed*; Getting away from: escaping; Give ideas for: inspired; Difficult or complicated: challenging; Players on the same team: teammates; Not competitive: cooperative; Kind and pleasant: friendly

B Read, think, and discuss. Look at the underlined words and phrases. Which have a similar meaning? Explain how each word or phrase has a positive or negative connotation.

- Have students skim the paragraph and say what it's about (a game called SuperSoccer). Then draw their attention to the underlined words and phrases. Have them work in pairs to find the words and phrases that have a similar meaning and write them in their notebooks, e.g. *interesting/ fascinating*.
- Have students look at each word and discuss whether it has a positive or negative connotation. Point out that some words may also be neutral. Monitor and provide help if needed. See **ETB** for suggestions.
- Check answers by having students raise their hands for *positive*, cross their arms for *negative*, or stay as they are for *neutral*.

Suggested Answers

Words with similar meanings:
interesting/fascinating; new/orignial; compete/play against; international/all over the world; favorite/ like most; players/competitors
Words with positive connotations:
interesting, fascinating, new, original, play against, all over ther world, favorite
Words with neutral connotations:
compete, international, like most, players
Words with negative connotations:
competitors

C Think and discuss. Have you ever played online multiplayer games? How did you feel about playing with others?

- Find out with a show of hands whether students have played online multiplayer games. If most of them have, put students in pairs to discuss how they felt about the experience. If not many have, put students in small groups with one student sharing their experience and the other students asking questions.
- Invite students to share the group's ideas with the rest of the class.

Answers

Students' own answers

Cool Down

Ask students what some of the players in SuperSoccer look like (wolves and robots). Put students in pairs to brainstorm other possible characters. Have students compare ideas in small groups before eliciting a few as a class. Tell them they will find out in the next lesson.

Now read **The Game of Life**

Fiction: *The Game of Life—Fantasy*

Lesson Objectives

- to read a story about a multiplayer video game
- to make a personal connection to the reading

Materials
Audio Tracks 27 and 28

Warm Up

Elicit what students remember about SuperSoccer from the text on p. 95. Explain that they are going to read a story related to SuperSoccer called *The Game of Life*. Have pairs predict what will happen.

TRACK 27 TB p. 234 Reading Approach

First Reading: Engage with the Text

- Ask students to look through the story pictures on the first spread to check their guesses from the Warm Up. Then play the audio and have students follow.
- Give them time to discuss their predictions in pairs and summarize the story. Elicit the main characters and a brief recap of the plot. Then look at the Words in Context.

TRACK 28 TB p. 234 Words in Context

- Brainstorm strategies on the board: *separate parts of word, surrounding words and sentences, pictures, world knowledge, positive/negative, whole story context.*
- Put students in pairs. Assign two words to each pair. Have them find and discuss their words. Remind them to look at the pictures before and after the words.
- Have pairs get together with two other pairs (groups of six) and explain their words to each other, saying which strategies they used. Then discuss as a class.
- Play the audio to familiarize students with the words and to practice the pronunciation.

headset (p. 97, noun) This can break down: *head* + *set*. *Then I can't hear the arguing* suggests it covers his ears, and there are pictures showing it. Strategies to use: separate parts of word; surrounding words and sentences; pictures

tackled (p. 98, verb) The context is soccer and the surrounding words show it's a typical action in the game between two players, but that time it was *hard*. The picture on p. 97 shows it. Strategies to use: pictures; surrounding words and sentences; world knowledge of soccer

bully (p. 98, noun) The surrounding sentences tell us it is a negative noun describing a person. In a later paragraph, it is defined: *kids who are mean to others*. Strategies to use: positive/negative; surrounding words and sentences

forum (p. 98, noun) The sentence and following pictures show it's a website where people ask and answer questions. Strategies to use: pictures; world knowledge of types of websites

opponent (p. 99, noun) The use of the pronoun *his* shows it is a person. The whole story context is about a team game and the surrounding words tell us this person isn't on the same team. Strategies to use: surrounding words and sentences; pictures; whole story context

tactics (p. 100, noun) *Amazing* shows a positive connotation. The speaker is the commentator, so it refers to moves in the game. Strategies to use: positive/negative; whole story context; world knowledge of competitive sports

Practice Student's App: Story Player

International English

Draw students' attention to the American English *goalie* and the British English *goal keeper*. Elicit which they have encountered more often and which they have used so far.

Second Reading: Analyze the Text and Features

- Play the audio again. Ask students to follow in their books silently and to think about who their favorite character is and why. Then have them compare ideas in pairs.
- Ask questions to check comprehension: *How does Tom change in the story?* (At first, he's frustrated and sad. At the end, he's happy and nicer to Will.) See the **ETB** for more.
- Look at the questions in the orange boxes and the text focus.
  - **Critical Thinking** (p. 96): *Why do you think some people are unkind to others?* Have students discuss ideas in pairs. Then invite students to share their answers.
  - **Language in Context** (p. 97): *What do you think Tom means by "stuff at home"?* Have students discuss ideas in pairs first. (It means "problems at home.")
  - **Language in Context** (p. 99): *Why do you think the trick is called "a rainbow kick"?* Have students read the description of the trick and discuss ideas in pairs. (The path of the ball in the air forms an arc like a rainbow.)
  - **Critical Thinking** (p. 101): *What lessons can you learn from video games?* Put students in small groups to brainstorm ideas. Elicit ideas from different groups.
  - **Text Focus** (p. 98): *Conflict in a story is a struggle between two opposing forces. In this story there are two types of conflict: external conflict and internal conflict.* Elicit the main conflict from the story. (Tom behaves badly toward Will. Will and Caitlin have an external conflict about helping Tom. The internal conflict is Will's dilemma between beating or helping Tom.)

Third Reading: Interact with the Text

- In pairs, have students act out the scenes on pp. 98–101 between Will and Caitlin, and Will and Tom.

Cool Down

Play *Correct the Teacher* (see TB p. 25) with events from the story.

Explore the Reading

Lesson Objectives

- to understand and analyze *The Game of Life* through reading comprehension activities
- to practice the reading skill of understanding denotation and connotation
- to explore the SEL competency of social awareness: respect others
- to make a personal connection to the reading

Warm Up

Play *Who Said It?* (see TB p. 27) with quotations from the story. Suggested sentences: *I barely touched you!* (Tom) *You seemed distracted out there.* (Tom's friend) *He tackled me really hard today at soccer practice.* (Will) *Sometimes kids who are mean to others are having problems themselves.* (Caitlin) *Want to kick a ball around after dinner … if you have time?* (Tom) *Actually that's a great idea! We can go together.* (Tom's mom) *Pleased to meet you, TacklerTom.* (Will)

A Answer the questions.

- Give students time to read the questions and discuss initial ideas in pairs.
- Then have them scan the text to find the relevant information and write their answers. Encourage students to write full sentences.
- If you're using the TTL, display the answers on the board. If not, have students share their answers orally.

Answers

1 He tackles him really hard when he doesn't have the ball / he calls him Wilfred. 2 because there are problems at home 3 He hears Tom saying he's been playing against their usernames. 4 Plan your strategy and visualize what you want to do before you play. 5 because he's feeling happier/more confident 6 because Will says the same words that Dribbler said: "Soccer starts in your head."

B Think, write, and discuss. Write whether the underlined words and phrases have positive (*P*) or negative (*N*) connotations. Discuss why.

- Review the meaning of *connotation* (an additional idea or emotion associated with a word). Then give students time to look at the words and phrases and think about their connotation. Have students look back at the story to see the phrases in context to help them.
- Have students compare answers in pairs. Then check answers as a class and elicit reasons why each word has a negative or positive connotation.

Answers

1 N; *Stuff* is a very vague word. It has a negative connotation because it refers to problems and it also implies that Tom doesn't want them to know the details of what is happening at home.
2 N; *Barely* is used to emphasize how small an amount is, so here it has a negative connotation, as Tom is minimizing how bad his tackle was.
3 N; *Just one* means "only" and is used in a negative way to show that Will is reluctant to play a game against Tom.
4 P; *Amazing tactics* implies that the speaker is impressed with the way Tom has played the game.

C Think and discuss. Other than Caitlin, who else could have recognized that Tom was unhappy? What could they have done about it?

- Have students discuss the questions in pairs. Encourage them to think not only the about people we see in the story but also the people who aren't shown but would be part of Tom's life.
- Have students compare ideas with another pair. Then invite students to share ideas.

Suggested Answers

Tom's parents could have recognized that he was unhappy, and they could have helped him by discussing their problems as a family. Tom's teachers could have recognized he was unhappy, too. They could have talked to his parents about his behavior and attitude.

D Think and discuss. Which of these statements do you agree with? Why?

- Students are going to explore the SEL competency of respecting others in the context of social media and online interaction.
- First, have students read the statements and check any unknown words. Then give them a few minutes to read each statement carefully and decide how they feel about them and why.
- Put students in small pairs or groups to discuss their answers. Then read a statement and invite students to stand up if they agree with it. Have students explain their answers, and encourage everyone to listen and respect each other's opinions. See the **ETB** for further discussion of the SEL competency.

Cool Down

Put students in pairs to do a role-play between Tom and Will. Explain that Tom is apologizing to Will for treating him badly and Will forgives Tom. The dialogue should end with the two friends arranging to do something together. Give students time to think about their dialogue and practice it in pairs. Invite volunteer students to act out their role-play in class.

Practice **Student's App:** Reading Practice

Think Together

Lesson Objectives

- to make connections between the readings
- to explore the key concept: Why do people play games?
- to reflect on the unit and provide personal thoughts and opinions

Warm Up

Have students work in pairs to look back at the two readings and think of one main similarity and difference in the texts. Elicit ideas from different students. (Similarities: Both texts are about playing games; they both include ideas about how games benefit players. Difference: The informational text is about board games, whereas the story is about video games.)

A Complete the table. What do *The History of Board Games* and *The Game of Life* say about these topics?

- Read the topics and check if students have any questions.
- Have students complete the table individually. Monitor and provide language help if needed.
- Display answers using the TTL. Alternatively, invite some students to share their answers.

Answers

The History of Board Games: games are an important form of social interaction now and in the past; the ancient Egyptians used games to escape from daily life; life skills like patience, how to win and lose, and how to think strategically; families and friends love getting together to play games / people enjoy the face-to-face interaction
The Game of Life: the characters interact through the video game and the real soccer game; Tom used games to help him when things were difficult at home; to plan ahead, to be patient, to practice, to do specific tricks like rainbow kicks; Will and Caitlin love playing SuperSoccer together; Tom feels happier about life when he plays well; he interacts with other players and wins some games

B Think and discuss. Look at A. Do *The History of Board Games* and *The Game of Life* have similar messages? Why do you think that?

- Give students time to look at their notes in A and think about what messages the two texts want to transmit.
- Have them discuss in pairs and encourage them to justify their opinions.
- Refer back to the key concept question for the unit: *Why do people play games?* Elicit answers based on the two readings. Then ask students if they can think of any other reasons not mentioned in the readings.

Suggested Answer

Yes, they have similar messages. I think that because they both explain/show how games can help people in life.

Practice Resource Bank: Unit Test
Student's App: Key Concept Practice

C What different types of games do you play? Do a Think, Pair, Share. Make a list.

- Students are going to do a Think, Pair, Share routine (see TB p. 20) to personalize the topic of games.
- Have students make a list of the different types of games they play on their own and with other people. Then have them compare and discuss with a partner.
- Invite students to share ideas with the class. Elicit whether the games they mention are cooperative (playing together to achieve something) or competitive (playing against someone else in order to win).

D Think and discuss. Do you prefer cooperative or competitive games? Why?

- Elicit some advantages and disadvantages of cooperative and competitive games on the board.
- Ask students to think about which they prefer and why. Have them compare preferences in pairs before you elicit ideas from volunteer students.

My Reading Journal

How did the readings in this unit make you think differently about games?

Can you recommend a game, a video about games, or a game strategy?

These questions encourage students to personalize what they have learned in the unit.

Give students time to look through the unit and answer the questions with their ideas. Have them share ideas in pairs before eliciting a few examples with the class.

Example Answers

I used to think (video games were a waste of time), but now I know that (I can learn useful life skills by playing).
I recommend (playing Pictionary because it makes you think about words in a creative way and it's really fun).

Go back to page 89. What new questions do you have?

Have students look back at the VTR picture on pp. 88–89. If you are using the TTL, project the image onto the board. Elicit what they discussed in the Get Ready to Read lesson on p. 95 (use your notes to remind them). Discuss how the picture connects to the two readings in the unit.

Then have them think about one or more new questions. Students compare ideas in small groups. Then invite students to share questions with the class.

Cool Down

Play *What Was the Last Word?* (see TB p. 27) using the audio from both readings.

UNIT 7

All About Ads

Unit Overview

Themes

How ads are designed and created

The impact ads have on customers

Synopsis

In this unit, students will learn about the world of advertising. They will think about marketing strategies, what ads sell, and how ads persuade the audience. They will discuss the advantages and disadvantages of advertising and write an opinion essay. Students will practice interviewing each other and talk about their qualities, skills, and experience.

Language Book

Vocabulary

advertisement, bargain, billboard, customer, discount, persuade, products, profit, quality, value

Pronunciation: Intonation

p. 144

Explore Language

Reported Speech: Statements and Commands

p. 145

Global Citizenship

What do advertisements sell, other than physical products?

brand, claims, false impression, image, promote, slogan, small print, target market

p. 146

Explore Language

Reported Speech: Questions

p. 147

Write About It

An Opinion Essay

Giving Reasons and Summarizing Ideas; Using Adjectives to Reinforce Opinions

p. 148

Talk About It

Conversation: Preparing for an Interview; Describing Qualities, Skills, and Experience

p. 149

Think It Over

Review and Reflection: Monthly Goal Reflection

p. 150

Literacy Book

Think Together
Does advertising influence the way we think?
p. 157

Visible Thinking
3–2–1 Bridge
p. 151

Nonfiction
Persuasive Text: *Ad Smart*
Words in Context: *service, product placement, spending power, catchy, cookie*
p. 155

Fiction
Science Fiction: *Commercial Break*
Words in Context: *lenses, popped up, lockers, squinted, distracting*
p. 152

Reading Skill
Identifying Text and Graphic Features
p. 154

Literary Term
Alliteration
p. 153

Language and Literacy Connections

The connecting theme for Unit 7 is advertising and how it affects us.

	Language	Literacy
Vocabulary	**Set 1:** advertising **Set 2:** branding in advertising	**Fiction:** advertisement, bargain, discount, persuade **Nonfiction:** billboard, promote
Grammar	**Reported Speech: Statements and Commands** They said (that) it would remove stains from your teeth. We thought (that) the puzzle should be easier. People told the presenter (that) they'd never used a better toothpaste. **Reported Speech: Questions** We asked (them) which product was top in the sports category. We questioned if/whether people remembered the advertising messages. We wanted to know if people knew how much money is spent on advertising.	**Fiction** Cassie's glasses told her that she should "book a flight now." Frank asked her how she would get her news and messages.
Skills	**Pronunciation:** intonation **Process Writing:** giving reasons and summarizing ideas	**Reading:** identifying text and graphic features **Literary Term:** alliteration
International English	donut/doughnut; advertisement/advert	garbage/rubbish; advertisement/advert

Vocabulary

Lesson Objectives

- to learn vocabulary for advertising: *advertisement, bargain, billboard, customer, discount, persuade, products, profit, quality, value*
- to read and say a poem about buying things
- to recognize and practice rising and falling intonation

Materials
Audio Tracks 75 to 79; Video

Warm Up

Ask *What ads did you see on TV yesterday? What ads have you seen or heard today?* If necessary, explain what *ad* means. Have students discuss ideas in groups and report back.

A TRACK 75 TB p. 223 **Listen. Why is advertising important?**

- This activity introduces the new vocabulary in context. Have students look at the picture on pp. 88–89 in pairs and speculate about what is happening.
- Have students find Guan (blue shirt and glasses). Ask the teaser question from the end of Unit 6: *What does Guan design?* (He designs ads.) Elicit ideas but don't confirm yet.
- Ask students to listen to Guan talking about advertising. Ask *Why is advertising important?* and elicit ideas.
- Play the audio and have students listen and check. Elicit the answer to both questions. Then ask further comprehension questions (see **ETB**) about the scene.

Suggested Answer
Advertising is important because it allows companies to persuade people to buy their products so that they can make a profit.

B TRACK 76 TB p. 223 **Find and number the words in A. Then listen and check.**

- Read the words out loud once and have students whisper after you. Point out the example (1) and have students find the discount in the picture. Have students work in pairs to find and number the other words in the picture.
- Play the audio for students to check their answers. Check pronunciation and drill the words or phrases if necessary.

Answers
1 *discount* 2 bargain 3 customer 4 persuade
5 products 6 quality 7 value 8 profit
9 advertisement 10 billboard

International English

Point out the different spellings for *donut* and *doughnut*. Then look at *advertisement* and *advert* and point out the change in stress patterns. Remind them also that in American English, we can say *ad*, but this isn't common in British English.

C TRACK 77 TB p. 223 **Close your eyes. Listen, visualize, and say.**

- Prepare students for the visualization (see TB p. 21).
- Play the audio, allowing students to visualize the ideas.
- Have students discuss a few of the questions in pairs.

D Look and write. Then put the sentences in order of importance for you (1 = most important).

- This ranking activity encourages critical thinking and self-awareness because students must think about what they value when buying. Read the example and ask students to complete the sentences individually. Check answers.
- Then ask students to number the sentences in order of importance to them, from 1 (most important) to 10 (least important). Have them discuss their choices and reasons.

Answers
products discount bargain value quality profit
customer advertisement persuade billboard
Students' own answers for ordering

E TRACK 78 TB p. 223 **Listen and write. Then watch and say.**

- Play the video or audio once with books closed, allowing students to listen and enjoy the poem.
- Have students open their books and recall the missing words in pairs. Play the audio again for students to check.
- Play the audio once more for students to join in, taking turns reading lines in pairs while copying the intonation.
- Then divide in the class into two groups to read lines aloud. Students can clap the rhythm as they say the words.

Answers
1 *Bargains*, bargains! 2 Products, products!
3 Discounts, discounts! 4 Profits, profits!
5 Billboards, billboards!

F TRACK 79 TB p. 223 **Pronunciation. Listen and say. Copy the intonation. Find three more sentences like these in the poem.**

- This task raises awareness of intonation to show surprise and encouragement (rising) and to finish a statement (falling). Play the audio and have students notice the intonation, using their hands to show the rising and falling.
- Play the audio again for students to notice which sentences are said with surprise or encouragement and which show the end of a statement, again miming with their hands.
- Have pairs practice the sentences with correct intonation.

Answers
Rising intonation: The ad—it's true!; We want them, yes!
Falling intonation: Buy for a friend!; More for you!; Come and buy.; We sell happiness!

Cool Down

Play *Disappearing Words* (see TB p. 25) with the vocabulary.

Practice **Student's App:** Vocabulary Practice; Spoken Word Video

Explore Language

Lesson Objectives

- **to learn how to use reported speech: statements and commands**
- **to practice vocabulary for advertising**

Materials
Audio Tracks 80 and 81

Warm Up

With books closed, ask what Guan talked about in the previous lesson (ads). Explain that next, Guan showed the students two TV ads for everyday products. Have students discuss in pairs what everyday products they see in TV ads.

A TRACK 80 TB p. 223 **Listen and read. What products do the girls describe?**

- This activity is a presentation of the grammar in context. Have students look at the pictures on p. 90 and play the audio. Have students follow the dialogue in their books and check if their ideas are mentioned.
- Ask the question and elicit the answer.
- Ask *Which product do you find more unusual? Why?* Students discuss ideas in pairs and then share with the class. Then ask further comprehension questions (see **ETB**).

Answer
a puzzle alarm clock and black toothpaste

B Look at A. Complete the table. How do the verbs change from direct speech to reported speech with *should*?

- Display the table using the TTL. Tell students to scan the dialogue in A in pairs and complete the table with the missing words.
- Students should now have the skills and strategies to be able to discuss the grammar forms and notice patterns by themselves. When they have completed the table, discuss the word order, form, and patterns together, but let your class guide the discussion. If you feel that students need more guidance, use the notes in the **ETB**.

Answers
would remove; thought; should; that; had; used
Verbs used with *should* don't change.

- Refer students to the Grammar tip *Look*. Elicit other examples of time and place expressions that change in reported speech, e.g. *tomorrow* → *the following/next day*, *today* → *that day*, *now* → *then*. Also, review how the personal pronouns and possessive adjectives change, e.g. *I* → *he/she*, *me* → *him/her*.

C Think and discuss. Then choose.

- This activity focuses on the usage of reported speech and reporting verbs. Have pairs refer to the table in B and discuss and complete the sentences. Check as a class.
- Write on the board *said me* and *told me*. Elicit which one is wrong (said me) and discuss whether this is a common error for your students. Point out that we never use an indirect object after *say*.

Answers
1 similar words 2 *tell*

D TRACK 81 TB p. 224 **Listen and say.**

- Tell students they're going to practice saying sentences with reported speech to help with pronunciation in fluent speech and so that they begin to internalize the structure. Play the audio and have students repeat each example chorally. (See TB p. 23, Making Language Drills Fun.)

E Read and write the reported speech statements.

- This activity provides controlled practice of reported statements and commands. Have students look at the sentences in pairs and identify the tense and the shift.
- Have students complete the statements individually and then compare them in pairs. To check answers, invite students to read pairs of statements and explain the shifts.

Answers
1 *she had decided not to eat any more junk food*
2 that his favorite advertisements were the ones for sportswear 3 he was interested in working in the advertising industry 4 we/they had to think more carefully about what we/they spend/spent our money on
5 to stop putting billboards in the town

F Do you agree or disagree with the sentences in E? Do a class survey. Report your results.

- This activity provides freer oral practice of reported speech. First, ask students to think about the idea in each sentence in E and whether they agree or disagree with it. Monitor and provide help if needed.
- Then ask students to choose one sentence they are interested in and form a question. Demonstrate with an example: *Do you think there shouldn't be any billboards in town?* Monitor and provide language help if needed.
- When students have their questions ready, have them mingle and complete the survey. Encourage students to give extended answers. They should also make note of any interesting details.
- Finish by asking students to sit down and count the results. Have them share their results in pairs and report interesting details. Invite students to share with the class.

Cool Down

Ask students to write down a command in direct speech. Give them two minutes to mingle, saying their command to as many students as possible. Then have them sit down in groups and write down the commands they heard, using reported speech. Groups take turns to reading aloud a reported command. Award a point for each correct one.

Practice **Resource Bank:** Grammar Printout
Student's App: Grammar Practice

Global Citizenship

Lesson Objectives

- **to learn vocabulary related to branding in advertising:** ***brand, claims, false impression, image, promote, slogan, small print, target market***
- **to explore what advertisements sell, other than physical products**
- **to practice listening for gist and details**

Materials
Audio Tracks 82 to 84; Audio Track G

Opening Question

Ask the opening question: *What do advertisements sell, other than physical products?* Write students' ideas on the board and ask them for example ads to help with brainstorming.

A TRACK 82 TB p. 224 **Listen to Naomi talk to her mom. What does she learn about advertising strategies?**

- Tell students they are going to listen to Naomi and her mom talking about advertising strategies. Discuss how the word *strategy* can be used for games (Unit 6) and for advertisements. Elicit any advertising strategies students may already be familiar with.
- Play the audio. Students listen and discuss the strategies mentioned in pairs.
- Ask the gist question *What does Naomi learn about advertising strategies?* and check the answer. Invite students to say whether they have seen any ads where software like Photoshop has been used and how they felt about it.
- Then ask *How does Naomi feel about these strategies, and what does she plan to do?* Play the audio again if necessary and elicit ideas. (She feels upset/angry, and she plans to write a post about it on the school blog.) Then ask further comprehension questions (see **ETB**).

Answer
She learns you can't believe everything you see in ads.

B TRACK 83 TB p. 224 **Look at the pictures and definition in A and write. Then listen and check.**

- Ask students to look at the words and point out or elicit any that are similar in their L1.
- Refer students to the vocabulary box in B and have them work in pairs to match the words and phrases to the pictures and definition in A and discuss their answers.
- Play the audio for students to check their answers.

Answers
1 *promote* 2 brand 3 slogan 4 claims 5 target market 6 image 7 small print 8 false impression

TRACK G TB p. 224 **Visualization**
The TTL includes an optional visualization audio track for this vocabulary set. (See TB p. 21.)

C **Read and complete the blog post.**

- This activity provides contextualized controlled practice of the vocabulary. Point to the title of the blog post and elicit what *it* refers to (advertisement).
- Have students complete the post on their own. Then check answers.

Answers
1 *brands* 2 image 3 promote 4 false impression 5 claims 6 target market 7 slogan 8 small print

D TRACK 84 TB p. 224 **Now listen to Gail's podcast. What problems and solutions does she mention?**

- Look at the photo and elicit what students can see. Play the audio for students to listen and make notes on the problems and solutions mentioned.
- Listening for gist: ask the question and have students discuss in pairs. Play the audio again and elicit answers.
- Ask students which problem they think is the most serious one and whether it's a problem that exists in their country.

Answers
The problems are people buying too much and creating too much waste. The solutions are recycling more, changing packaging, and reusing trash.

E **Listen again. Write *True*, *False*, or *Doesn't Say*.**

- Listening for details: have students read the sentences before they listen again. Allow them to discuss any sentences they think they know the answer to in pairs.
- Play the audio and have students write their answers. Have them compare in pairs and then check answers as a class. Encourage students to make connections with the conversation in A by asking them to think about what negative effects buying things we don't need can have.

Answers
1 *False* 2 True 3 True 4 Doesn't Say 5 True 6 Doesn't Say

Discussion Questions

- Draw students' attention to the discussion questions. Have students discuss each question in pairs or small groups (see **ETB**). Encourage students to recognize that we live in a consumer-driven society that can have negative effects on the planet and society and to suggest steps we can take to remedy these problems.
- Return to the opening question *What do advertisements sell, other than physical products?* Review the ideas discussed at the start of the lesson and encourage students to share any new ideas. Focus on the stereotypes and lifestyles projected in ads and the promises made to buyers.

Cool Down

Have students work in pairs to make a more truthful slogan for the running shoes on p. 92, then share ideas as a class.

Practice **Student's App:** Vocabulary Practice; Listening Practice

Explore Language

Lesson Objectives

- **to learn how to use reported speech: questions**
- **to practice vocabulary related to branding in advertising**

Materials
Audio Tracks 85 and 86

Warm Up

Brainstorm TV game shows with the class (including a TV quiz show). Ask students to discuss in small groups which TV game shows they enjoy watching and why. Elicit ideas.

A TRACK 85 TB p. 224 **Listen and read. What's the TV quiz about?**

- This activity is a presentation of the grammar in context. Tell students they are going to listen to Ludka from Lesson 2 take part in a TV quiz. Explain that they are going to hear the beginning of the show.
- Play the audio. Have students follow along in their books.
- Ask the gist question *What's the TV quiz about?* Invite students to discuss the question in pairs before you elicit the answer from the class. Then ask further comprehension questions (see **ETB**).

Answer
The TV quiz is about advertising.

B Look at A. Complete the table. Which words come after the reporting verb in *Yes/No* questions?

- Display the table using the TTL. Ask students to look at the blanks in pairs and see if they remember or can figure out the missing words. Then have them refer to the text in A and check/complete their answers.
- Students should now have the skills and strategies to notice and discuss the grammar patterns by themselves using the examples. When they have completed the table, discuss the word order, form, and patterns together, but let the class guide the discussion. If you feel students need more guidance, use the notes in the **ETB**.

Answers
which; was; if/whether; remembered; to know
Whether/if come after the reporting verb in *Yes/No* questions.

- Draw students' attention to the Grammar tip *Look*. Elicit that the object pronoun after *asked* can be omitted.

C Think and discuss. Then choose.

- Ask students to read the statements on usage and refer to the examples in the table in B. Have them choose the answer in pairs. Check the answer. Elicit when we use quotation marks (when we write the same words someone said) and point out that when we report what someone said we are using our own words.
- Discuss the contexts in which people usually report questions. Ask if it is more common to hear a reported question on the news or in an informal conversation between friends (on the news). Point out that some reporting verbs (e.g. *questioned*) are more formal than others (e.g. *asked*).

Answer
1 reported

D TRACK 86 TB p. 224 **Listen and say.**

- Tell students they're going to practice saying reported questions to help with pronunciation in fluent speech and to consolidate what they've learned. Play the audio and have students repeat each example chorally. (See TB p. 23, Making Language Drills Fun.)

E Read the questions a student asked Guan. Write reported questions.

- This activity helps students consolidate the word order of reported questions. Read the example and elicit the change in verb forms (simple present → simple past).
- Give students time to write the reported questions individually. Monitor and check if students are struggling. Make a note of the problems and address them as a whole class. Ask them to compare answers in pairs and then nominate students to read a reported question. If any corrections are needed, elicit them from other students.

Answers
1 *I asked him when he watched advertisements on TV.*
2 I wanted to know if/whether he preferred TV or billboard ads. 3 I wondered why there were so many advertisements nowadays. 4 I questioned if/whether the way products were promoted was going to change in the future. 5 I asked (him) how people could make sure the claims in advertisements were accurate.

F Ask and answer three questions about a product you use. Then write about the questions your friend asked and your answers.

- This activity provides freer practice of reported questions. First, have students think about a product they use and share with their partner. Then ask them to write three questions they would like to ask about their partner's product.
- Students take turns asking their questions and answering their partner's questions. Allow them to make notes if necessary.
- Put students in different pairs to report what questions they were asked and what answers they gave.

Cool Down

Play *Pass the Whisper!* (see TB p. 26). Students whisper a direct question down the line, and the student who says the question aloud must do so using reported speech.

Practice **Resource Bank:** Grammar Printout
Student's App: Grammar Practice

Write About It

Lesson Objectives

- to plan and write an opinion essay
- to give reasons and summarize ideas
- to learn how to use adjectives to reinforce opinion

Materials
Support Writing printouts from the Resource Bank (G)

Warm Up

Write on the board *Good Things About Advertising.* Ask students to brainstorm ideas in small groups. Elicit ideas and write them on the board. If necessary, prompt students with questions, e.g. *Are there any ads that advertise a good product or service? Are there ads for charities?*

A Read the essay. How does the writer feel about advertising?

- This lesson corresponds with the nonfiction reading in Unit 7 of the **Literacy Book.** Ask students to read the essay once to find out if the writer included any of their ideas from the Warm Up. Check answers.
- Ask the question *How does the writer feel about advertising?* Put students in pairs to discuss their answer and whether they agree or disagree with the author. Then check with the class. Ask more comprehension questions (see **ETB**).

Answer
The writer thinks advertising is a very good thing because it gives us choices by showing us what is out there.

B Look at the structure of the essay. Read and answer.

- Tell students they're going to look at the structure of the essay. First, ask them to read the questions and discuss their ideas in pairs.
- Ask students to write their answers. Check answers as a class. Point out that both the introduction and conclusion include the writer's opinion expressed with different words and ideas.

Answers
1 1 b; 2 ed 3 d; 4c a 2 It gives both—it says what advertisements do and the writer's opinion about this.
3 formal—no contractions; use of formal words e.g. *complain* vs. *moan*; *useful* vs. *good*; *compete* vs. *fight*
4 It repeats ideas/opinion but in new words.

C Look at the language in the essay. Read and respond.

- Students are now going to focus on the adjectives used in the opinion essay. Read the prompts and have students work in pairs to find adjectives and answer the questions. Check answers. In question 2, point out that using different adjectives and varied vocabulary in general makes the essay more interesting to read.

Answers
1 *great*; useful; new; different; latest; newest; best; lowest; wide; best; modern; creative; fabulous; powerful; interesting; funny; informative; brighter; good; boring
2 Only one – best 3 boring 4 great/good; newest/latest 5 Students' own answers

D Think and discuss. Brainstorm some disadvantages of advertising using one of the Generating Ideas techniques.

- In this lesson, students look at revising a draft once they've written it.
- Have students work in small groups and brainstorm disadvantages of advertising. They can either use the mind map to help them generate and record their ideas, or they can use another of the Generating Ideas techniques (see TB p. 211).
- Encourage students to look back through the unit and find ideas. Then invite them to share ideas with the class.

E Plan your essay called *Switch Off Advertising*. Use your ideas in D and one of the Planning techniques.

- Write the essay title on the board and elicit what *switch off* refers to in this context (stop advertising.)
- Tell students they are going to plan their own opinion essay. Have them choose some of their ideas in D and either complete the plan in E or use another suitable planning technique (see TB p. 212). Ask them to compare plans in pairs.

F Write a first draft of your essay. Then think about how you've organized the information and revise it.

- Have students write a draft of their essay in their notebooks, referring to their plan in E. Remind them to use a variety of adjectives and vocabulary, as well as a formal register. You can also remind them to use linkers to organize their paragraphs.
- Ask students to read their drafts and notice whether it's easy to follow and if their ideas flow well. Have them make improvements. Allow them to discuss this in pairs.

G Now write your essay.

- Have students write their final versions neatly on paper or on the Support printout.
- In pairs, ask students to read each other's essay and decide if they are persuaded by the arguments.

Cool Down

Write on the board *Disadvantages of Buying Stuff.* Put students in small groups and have them brainstorm as many ideas as they can in a minute. Elicit ideas on the board in a mind map. Then discuss the concept of downsizing (or decluttering) in which people reduce their belongings and only buy the essentials. Would students try this? Would they become happier?

Practice **Resource Bank:** Writing Game, *Buy Me!*
Student's App: Writing Practice

Talk About It

Lesson Objectives

- to practice interviewing and being interviewed
- to describe qualities, skills, and experience

Materials
Video

Warm Up

Write *Promote Yourself!* on the board. Have students brainstorm situations when they might need to promote themselves, i.e. talk about their skills, knowledge, or abilities. Give an example if necessary: *You need to promote yourself if you want to join a sports team. You can do that by demonstrating your abilities and showing how much you know about the sport.* Elicit ideas from students.

A TB p. 240 **Watch and listen. Do you think Maria is right for the job?**

- Tell students they are going to watch a video of Maria and Linda talking about a job. The video provides a presentation of the functional language needed for a job interview. Elicit what the job could be and explain it's as a student community leader. Discuss whether there are student community leaders at their school, what roles they have, what they have to do to become a leader, and so on.
- Have students guess whether Maria is right for the job and what qualities, skills, and experience she needs for it. With books closed, play the video for students to watch, listen, and check their guesses.
- Ask the comprehension question *Do you think Maria is right for the job?* If necessary, play the video again and then allow some time for students to discuss their answers and reasons in pairs. Check answers as a class. Ask more comprehension questions (see **ETB**).

Answer
Students' own answers (However, she does seem ideal for the job.)

B Watch again. Match the phrases. Then write *QS* (qualities and skills) or *E* (experience).

- Tell students they are going to focus on the functional language the girls use to talk about qualities, skills, and experience. Have them read the phrases first and see if they can match them.
- Play the video again and have students check their answers.
- Then ask students to work in pairs and decide whether the phrases refer to qualities and skills or experience. Check answers.

Answers
1 f 2 d 3 e 4 c 5 h 6 a 7 g 8 b
Qualities and skills: 1; 2; 3; 4; 5; 6
Experience: 7; 8

C Imagine you're going to be interviewed to be a student community leader. What skills, qualities, and experience do you have? Think and plan.

- Ask students to imagine they want to be a leader of their student community. Ask them to think why they would be strong candidates and to complete the table with their ideas.
- Have students compare answers with a partner and suggest more ideas if necessary.

Answers
Students' own answers

D Take turns to interview each other. Use phrases from B.

- Put students in new pairs and explain that they are going to take turns interviewing each other. Encourage them to use their ideas from C and phrases from B when they are being interviewed. Before their interviews, draw students' attention to the example exchange. What do students notice about the question? (It's indirect.) Encourage students to use indirect questions.
- Have students interview each other. Monitor and notice students' use of the phrases from B and indirect questions. Address any issues after the task.
- Put students in different pairs and have them discuss the main points of the interview and whether they would give the job to the candidate.
- Have students analyze their own performance, thinking about whether the language they used is positive and persuasive.

Cool Down

Ask students to think of two ways they could become a stronger candidate. Prompt them with a few questions: *Do you think you're organized enough? Do you need experience working with a team?* Have students think on their own and then discuss in small groups.

Practice **Student's App:** Speaking Skills Practice; Speaking Video

Think It Over

Lesson Objectives

- **to review what has been learned in the unit**
- **to reflect on the unit and their own progress**
- **to think about learning strategies and how to continue learning at home**

Warm Up

Ask *What was the most important thing you learned about advertising in this unit? How do you think advertising will change in the future?* Allow students some thinking time and then have them discuss ideas in small groups. Invite students to share with the class.

How well did you meet the challenge of Unit 7? Read and respond.

Monthly Goal Reflection

- Tell students they are going to review what they learned in the unit and also think about their own learning and whether they have reached their goals from Unit 7. This time students are also going to evaluate how hard they worked and think about whether they need to do more in order to progress in their learning.
- Review what students have done in the unit with an Inside-Outside Circle routine (TB p. 21). Have students on the outside of the circle start by remembering something they did. Students can have their books with them and show their partner the page they are referring to if necessary. The student on the inside of the circle then says something different that they did. On the signal, students rotate and try to think of something new. Encourage students to remember information they learned, as well as activities they did. After a few minutes, stop the routine and move on to the next stage.
- Draw students' attention to the heading *Monthly Goal Reflection*. Have students look back at the end of Unit 6 and remember what their goal was. Ask students if they think they have worked hard to reach their goal and whether they feel they have succeeded. Have them think about what they have done in order to achieve their goal and discuss with a partner.
- Allow students to work individually to fill in the first two parts of the organizer. Remind them that they should write their own responses about themselves. Monitor and help as necessary. Look at what students are writing so you can tailor your classes and any additional practice to their needs.
- Ask students what they would like to work on and improve in the future. Refer students to the final section in the graphic organizer. Tell students to think about whether they still need to work more to achieve their goal or, if they have succeeded, whether they will choose a different one. Have them look back through the unit and evaluate their learning in each lesson. Then have them write their ideas about their plans for their next goals. They can then share their ideas with a friend.
- Ask if anyone has the same goals as their friend. Point out that goals should be personal and each student should choose those they think they would benefit from most.

Looking Forward

Draw students' attention to the character at the bottom of the page. Have students say who she is and what they remember about her. (Ludka is one of the students who was at the China Global Advertising Agency in Shanghai, in Lesson 1, p. 88. She also appeared in Lesson 2, p. 90, where she talked about the advertisement for the alarm clock, and in Lesson 4, p. 94.) Have students look at the speech bubble and call out any beautiful designs they can think of that are in nature. Tell students they will find out the answer in Lesson 1 of the next unit.

Practice **Resource Bank:** Unit Test
Student's App: Vocabulary and Grammar Review

Get Ready to Read

Lesson Objectives

- to activate prior knowledge about advertising
- to guide inquiry and deepen understanding through a 3–2–1 VTR
- to preview the reading skill of identifying text and graphic features

Materials

VTR printout from the Resource Bank (A, B, C, D)

Warm Up

Find out how students feel about advertising before reading the story and information in this unit. It will be interesting to see if they change their mind at the end of the unit. Ask *Do you like advertisements?* Elicit reasons why and why not from various students.

3–2–1 Bridge

A Look at the picture. Write three thoughts or ideas you have.

- This VTR encourages students to think of a variety of interesting questions that will help them explore their ideas about advertising and shopping. They will do the first part here and complete the routine in the Think Together lesson. Make sure you keep a record of the ideas students share.
- Start by having students look at the picture in silence for a few seconds and let thoughts come and go. Prompt them to work alone to list three thoughts. If necessary, give an example thought to get them started, e.g. *I think the boy is worried about something.* Then ask them to compare ideas in pairs.

B Write two questions you have.

- Tell students to write two questions they have about the picture. If necessary, give an example first: *What is the boy thinking about?* Have students think of questions on their own, then compare with a partner.

C Write a metaphor.

- Ask pairs to write a metaphor related to the picture or the topic of the unit. Remind students that a metaphor uses direct comparison between two things in a creative way. Give them an example if necessary: *Advertisements are stories and fairy tales.*

D Share with the class.

- Invite students to share their thoughts, questions, and metaphors with the class. Encourage students to guide the discussion and respond to each other, not just to you. Keep a record of students' ideas from the VTR to revisit in the Think Together lesson.

Here's an example of this part of the routine.

Teacher: Who would like to share their thoughts?
Student A: I think the boy wanted to buy a real bike and he bought a toy. He made a mistake.
Student B: Not a mistake. Maybe the advertisement wasn't clear. Or he didn't understand it.
Student C: Yes, and he probably spent a lot of money. That's why he looks worried or angry.
Teacher: Any thoughts about what the boy will do?
Student D: I think he's going to return the toy and ask for his money back.
Teacher: So, what questions do you have?
Student E: Why do we buy so many things? Is it dangerous to shop online?
Teacher: Good. Anyone else?
Student B: How much money do advertisers make? How long does it take them to make an ad?
Teacher: Very interesting questions. Now, who would like to share their metaphor?
Student C: Shopping is a game.
Teacher: Why do you think that?
Student C: Because sometimes you win and you get what you were expecting. But sometimes you lose because the product isn't good.

Transition

Ask *Where did the boy in the photo see the advertisement?* (online, on a website) *Where else do you think he saw the same advertisement?* Elicit ideas.

E Think and write. Where do you see advertising? Make a list.

- Put students in small groups to brainstorm a list of places where they see advertising. You can set this as a race by giving them a time limit of one minute. Elicit ideas and find out who has the longest list.

Suggested Answers
online / the internet, on billboards, on TV, in the mail, in app games

F Think and discuss. Look at the pictures in *Commercial Break*. What kind of reading is it? How can you tell?

- This activity previews the skill of identifying text and graphic features. Ask students to look at the pictures in *Commercial Break* and discuss what kind of reading it is. Elicit ideas and reasons.

Now read **Commercial Break**

Fiction: *Commercial Break—* Science Fiction

Lesson Objectives

- to activate prior knowledge about ads in the future
- to make a personal connection to the reading

Materials

Audio Tracks 29 and 30; students' own sunglasses or a few old pairs (props for acting out the story)

Warm Up

Write the story title on the board. Point out that *advertisement* and *commercial* are synonyms. Have pairs discuss what they do and how they feel when there's a commercial break during a program they're watching.

TRACK 29 TB p. 234 Reading Approach

First Reading: Engage with the Text

- Have students look at the pictures and predict the main events in the story.
- Play the audio and have students follow along in their books to check their predictions.
- Pause the audio at the end of p. 109 and say *In the next scene, Cassie is in art class. What will change now that she isn't wearing her glasses?* Elicit ideas and play the rest of the audio. Then look at the Words in Context.

TRACK 30 TB p. 235 Words in Context

- Brainstorm strategies on the board for students to use: *surrounding words and sentences, pictures, world knowledge, contrasting ideas.*
- Have students work in pairs to discuss each word. Remind them that different words will require different combinations of strategies, and that they should read all the instances of the word to help them.

lenses (p. 106 / p. 107, noun) The surrounding sentences and context of the story show that this word is related to glasses. Strategies to use: surrounding words and sentences; pictures

popped up (p. 106, phrasal verb) The subject of the sentences are *advertisement* and *message*. Knowing how messages appear on a cell phone or computer will help. The adverb (*suddenly*) also gives us a clue. Strategies to use: surrounding words and sentences; world knowledge of seeing ads/messages on devices

lockers (p. 108, noun) The sentence shows that this is a place, and the picture confirms that. Strategies to use: surrounding words and sentences; pictures

squinted (p. 109, verb) The second part of the sentence explains why Cassie does this action. The following sentence shows that you use your eyes to do it. Strategy to use: surrounding words and sentences

distracting (p. 111, adjective) The sentence gives a definition (*get in the way*). Here the situation shows a contrasting idea to the beginning of the story where messages *pop up* constantly. Strategies to use: surrounding words and sentences; contrasting ideas

- Have students change partners and discuss which strategies they used and which worked best. Discuss as a class. Then play the audio to practice pronunciation.

International English

Point out the American English *garbage* and the British English *rubbish*. Elicit another synonym (*trash*). Then elicit the differences between *advertisement* and *advert*.

Second Reading: Analyze the Text and Features

- Play the audio again to consolidate students' understanding of the reading.
- Ask questions to check comprehension: *Is Cassie happier with or without her glasses? Why?* (without, them because messages/ads are distracting and she can see things that she normally would miss.) See the **ETB** for more questions.
- Discuss the questions in the orange boxes. Then look at the text focus.
  - **Critical Thinking** (p. 106): *How can you escape advertising?* Elicit where we see ads in real life, e.g. TV, billboards, newspapers, websites, social media, on public transportation. Have pairs discuss , then share as a class.
  - **Personalization** (p. 110): *Are there laws or organizations in your country to make sure advertising is fair?* Give students time to research this in class or at home. Elicit what students found out and if they think there should be more laws or stricter laws.
  - **Personalization** (p. 111): *How do you feel about advertising?* Ask students to think about this on their own first. Encourage them to note down their thoughts. Then have them compare answers and reasons in pairs.
  - **Text Focus** (p. 106): *Science fiction allows us to consider the potential consequences of our current technology choices.* Have students think of other science fiction stories, movies, or series that do this.

Third Reading: Interact with the Text

- Have students read and act out scenes from the story in groups of three or four. Encourage students to use actions and gesture as they read together. They can use sunglasses as Insta-Glasses if they have them. (See TB p. 23.)

Cool Down

Elicit how students at Cassie's school use technology in art and science class. Then let students work in groups to imagine how technology is used in other school subjects. Elicit ideas.

Practice **Student's App:** Story Player

Explore the Reading

Lesson Objectives

- to understand and analyze *Commercial Break* through reading comprehension activities
- to explore the SEL competency of responsible decision-making through discussing strategies used to resist peer pressure
- to make a personal connection to the reading

Materials
Audio Track 31

Warm Up

Elicit from students what Cassie shared with her friends using her Insta-Glasses (an advertisement about shoes). Ask students to think about an advertisement, a poster, a video, or something else they saw recently that they would share with their friends if they had Insta-Glasses. Put students in groups to share their ideas.

A Answer the questions.

- Have students work in pairs to discuss the questions based on memory.
- Then have students work individually to read the story and write their answers. Check answers as a class.

Answers
1 The message in the park trees that says "Love your park. Don't be lazy, grab your garbage." 2 Cassie shares the ad because she can get a 20% discount. 3 There are news headlines running down the side of the lenses. 4 She says that she has a headache. 5 Cassie misses the zoom feature in science class. 6 because it feels good to hold the brush in her hand and the colors seem so bright and alive

B Think and write. What are the pros and cons of wearing Insta-Glasses? Make a list.

- Copy the two headings onto the board. Have students do a Think, Pair, Share routine (see TB p. 20) to think of an example pro and con of wearing Insta-Glasses. Write some ideas on the board.
- Then ask students to work on their own and refer back to the reading to complete their lists. Have them compare lists in pairs before checking as a class.

Suggested Answers
Pros: can zoom in / look closely at images; can learn more about products and special offers can keep up with the news; can communicate and share information with friends instantly; can be creative
Cons: always see advertising—distracting; too much information—tiring; may replace hands-on activities like painting; can't see the beauty of nature; isolating/bad for real face-to-face communication

C Think and discuss. Would you go offline like Cassie, even if all your friends were online? Why or why not?

- Students are going to connect the reading to the SEL competency of responsible decision-making: discuss strategies used to resist peer pressure.
- Elicit how Cassie's friends reacted to her going offline and how she resisted peer pressure. (Frank and Eva said she'd miss out on loads of stuff; Eva said that using a painting app was the same as painting. / She didn't respond to Eva even though she didn't agree. She recognized the benefits of not wearing the glasses.) Then have students think about themselves and their friends.
- Have students discuss the questions in small groups. Remind them to respect each other's opinions and ideas, and not to be influenced by peer pressure during the discussion! Invite students to share their ideas with the class.

Literary Term: Alliteration

TRACK 31 TB p. 235 **Listen and say. Underline the letters or sounds that are the same.**

- Draw students' attention to the explanation of alliteration. Play the audio once and have students notice the sounds that are repeated. Ask them to underline them in pairs. Check answers.
- Play the audio again for students to repeat.

Now find more examples of alliteration in the reading and pictures.

- Have students scan the reading to find more examples of alliteration in the reading and pictures.
- Ask students to compare answers in pairs, then check answers as a class.

Answers
1 Peter Piper picked a pickled pepper. 2 Five fat flamingos flew fast. 3 Round the rocks the rascal ran. 4 I used to yearn for Europe in my youth.
In the reading: grab your garbage; Great. Grand. Go Shoes. Be happy with Heart; Buy Cute Kitty cat food; SuperSoccer

Cool Down

Have students work in pairs to write a slogan or silly sentence containing alliteration. They can then read their slogan or sentence to the class or write it on the board and have the other students practice it.

Practice **Resource Bank:** Literary Term Printout
Student's App: Reading Practice; Literary Term Practice

Get Ready to Read

Lesson Objectives

- to activate prior knowledge about ads for children
- to practice the reading skill of identifying text and graphic features

Warm Up

Ask students to open their books on p. 42 and quickly look through *Communities Making Dreams Come True* again. Ask *Who advertises or promotes their idea? How do they do it?* Elicit ideas. (Jorani and Leap promoted their video game on a crowdfunding site. LeVar Burton also advertised his project on Kickstarter.)

A Think and write. Look at the excerpt from *Communities Making Dreams Come True*. What text and graphic features can you see?

- This lesson practices the skill of identifying text and graphic features, which students previewed on p. 105. Ask students how they guessed what kind of reading *Commercial Break* was. Elicit that the reading had narrative pictures/illustrations, text, and direct speech.
- Brainstorm the different genres of texts students have read and write them as headings across the board (*Story, Diary, Informational Text/Article, Poem, Fantasy, Folk Tale, Instructional Text, Science Fiction, Essay*). Then have students think of different text features they know and write these in a column down the side of the board (*pictures, headings, captions, labels, speech bubbles*, etc.). Ask students whether each feature usually appears in each type of text and have volunteers come and add checkmarks and crosses to the table.
- Ask students to open their books on p. 113. First, ask them to read the information about text and graphic features. Then ask them to look at the excerpt in pairs and write their list of features.
- Check answers by displaying the excerpt with the TTL and inviting students to identify and point to a feature. Have students refer to the list of features in B if necessary.

Answers
1 heading 2 diagram/illustration 3 callout 4 text

B Check (✔) and write. Which of these text and graphic features can you find in *Ad Smart*? Write any other text and graphic features you can see.

- Ask students to first look through the list of features. Have students work in pairs to race to find the features in different units of their books, including the **Language Book**. If students have trouble identifying a feature, provide them with a page number on which to look. Have the first pair to finish use the TTL to display their answers. Discuss what authors use each feature for.
- Then have students look through *Ad Smart* individually and check the features they see. Ask them to compare answers in pairs. Then check answers.

Answers
Checked answers: Heading, Title, Caption, Photograph, Callouts, Illustration

C Think, discuss, and write. Is advertising aimed at children a good thing? Why or why not?

- As with the unit opening, this question gets students to share their opinions before reading the text so they can reassess them after learning more about the topic. First, brainstorm as a class some ads that students have seen that are aimed at children (cereal, toys, kids' snacks, soda, etc.). Discuss what students think about these ads.
- Then ask students to think about the question on their own and discuss their ideas in pairs or small groups using a Think, Pair, Share routine (see TB p. 20).
- Have them think about their opinion on their own once more and then write their answer, making sure they give reasons for their ideas.
- Check answers by having students raise their hands if they think advertising aimed at children is a good thing. Elicit reasons from both sides and allow students to answer *I don't know*, again justifying why they aren't sure.

Answers
Students' own answers

Cool Down

Write on the board *By reading Ad Smart, I'd like to find out …* Have students complete the prompt with a question they have. Monitor and provide language help if needed. Find out if their questions have been answered after they read the text the first time.

Now read **Ad Smart**

Nonfiction: *Ad Smart*—Persuasive Text

Lesson Objectives

- to read a persuasive text about advertising for children
- to make a personal connection to the reading

Materials
Audio Tracks 32 and 33

Warm Up

Look at the pictures on p. 114 or display them using the TTL. Have students discuss the question in pairs: *Three busy cities, three different countries, three different languages. What looks the same?* Elicit ideas and invite students to share experiences if they have been to a similar place.

TRACK 32 TB p. 235 Reading Approach

First Reading: Engage with the Text

- Ask students to estimate and write down how many ads they see on TV per day and year. Encourage them to guess if they aren't sure.
- Play the audio and have students follow along. Elicit how many ads an average child in the USA sees (45/day or 16,000/year). Have students compare that to their estimate and say whether they were close. Do they find the number surprising?
- Then look at the Words in Context.

TRACK 33 TB p. 235 Words in Context

- Give students a few minutes to find and highlight each word and identify the kind of word it is.
- Write these strategies on the board for students to use with the words: *surrounding words and sentences, pictures, contrasting ideas, separate parts of word, knowledge of similar words/L1 cognates, world knowledge.*
- Have students work in pairs to discuss the words. Tell them there is one strategy they can't use; they may not actually use all the strategies to figure out the words, but there is one strategy that can't be used at all.

service (p. 115 / p. 116, noun) The two sentences show that the word is something that is advertised and it is something we spend money on / is sold. It is contrasted with a physical *product*. Strategies to use: surrounding sentences; contrasting ideas; L1 cognates

product placement (p. 115, noun) The phrase can be broken down, and the following clause defines the word. Strategies to use: surrounding words and sentences; separate parts of word

spending power (p. 115, noun) The phrase can be broken down, and the previous sentence and following clause explain it. Strategies to use: surrounding words and sentences; separate parts of word

catchy (p. 116, adjective) The sentence provides a definition following the word. Strategy to use: surrounding words and sentences

cookie (p. 116, noun) The whole paragraph explains it. Strategies to use: L1 cognates; surrounding words and sentences; world knowledge of technology

- Go through each word to elicit the meaning and how they know. Ask students which strategy on the board can't be used and why (pictures). Play the audio to practice pronunciation.

Practice **Student's App:** Story Player

Second Reading: Analyze the Text and Features

- Have students read the text silently to consolidate understanding. Ask them to think about whether the writer is for or against advertising. (Neither: on pp. 115–116, the writer gives reasons against advertising, but on p. 117, the writer balances the article with a positive aspect of advertising and advice on how to be ad smart.)
- Invite students to discuss again their answers to C on p. 113 in pairs. Elicit whether their opinion has changed and how. See the **ETB** for comprehension questions.
- Discuss the questions in the orange boxes.
  - **Discussion** (p. 114): *What different kinds of advertising are there?* Have students make a list in pairs. Then elicit ideas on the board, e.g. TV commercials, print advertising, product placement, targeted advertising.
  - **Fun Fact** (p. 115): *153 = Number of hours of television an average person in the USA watches in a month.* Elicit whether students think this is too much. Then ask them to estimate in pairs how many hours they spend a month watching TV. Discuss answers.
  - **Personalization** (p. 116): *Which of these advertising techniques have you noticed?* Give students time to read through the techniques again and make notes of examples and real experiences they've had. Have students discuss ideas in pairs, then as a class.
  - **Critical Thinking** (p. 117): *Are you ad smart? Why or why not?* Ask students to think about and discuss their answers using a Think, Pair, Share routine (see TB p. 20). If students don't feel they are ad smart, ask them if they are now going to be more prepared.

Third Reading: Interact with the Text

- Have students read the text again and write down three questions about advertising for an interview.
- Put students in pairs. They act out the interview with one of them asking the questions and the other answering as the "ad expert."

Cool Down

Ask students to think about a person they know who is easily convinced by advertisements. What advice would they give them after reading this text? Have students discuss in pairs and then invite students to share with the class.

Explore the Reading

Lesson Objectives

- to understand and analyze *Ad Smart* through reading comprehension activities
- to practice the reading skill of identifying text and graphic features
- to learn through CLIL (social studies): communication
- to make a personal connection to the reading

Warm Up

Play *Disappearing Sentences* (see TB p. 25) using sentences or information from *Ad Smart*. This will help students remember key information and prepare for A.

A Write three questions about the reading to ask a partner. Trade and answer your partner's questions.

- Tell students they are going to write three questions about the reading to ask a partner. Give them time to skim the reading before they write their questions. Encourage students to write challenging questions that their partner will need to look back at the reading to answer. Monitor and provide language help if needed.
- Have students trade questions and write their answers. Invite students to share a question and answer for the class.

B Think and discuss. Why do some countries have rules about advertising aimed at children?

- This activity encourages students to analyze and evaluate what they've read. Elicit what rules the students read about in the text (rules in Sweden and Norway that ban advertising to children under the age of 12). Then ask the discussion question *Why do some countries have rules about advertising aimed at children?*
- Have students discuss ideas in pairs and then compare with another pair.

Suggested Answers

Children don't have enough experience in life to understand the advertisements and spot advertising tricks. Children may believe things in advertisements that aren't true. Also, advertisements may present stereotypes and unhealthy lifestyles that can have a negative effect on the children's future. Another reason for advertising rules is that advertisements can pressure parents into buying their children things they saw in advertisements.

C Think and discuss. Why did the author write *Ad Smart*? How does the author achieve that purpose?

- Have students think about the two questions individually; they can make notes if they want to. Remind them of the main reasons for writing (e.g. with the acronym PIE: to persuade, to inform, to entertain). Encourage them to refer to both the text and graphic features used by the author.
- Have them discuss with a partner to see if they agree. Then invite students to share with the class.

Suggested Answers

The author wrote *Ad Smart* to persuade people to be careful about interpreting the ads they see. The author has also used a number of different text and graphic features to highlight his/her point of view, e.g. the photo showing the child staring at the TV to illustrate the negative side of advertising, the photo of the theater to show the positive side of advertising, the callout about the number of hours watching TV, the list of advertising techniques and graphic examples of each one, headings that emphasize the author's view, etc.

D Think and write. What advertising techniques do you see in the ad?

- Look at the ad or display it on the board using the TTL. Have students refer to the advertising techniques on p. 116 and discuss in pairs which are used in the ad.
- Have students write their answers and check as a class by projecting them on the board.

Suggested Answers

Promotion: Download today and get a free level!
Association: Everything is OK with Octopus Knight!
Emotional appeal: Octopus Knight is protector of the kingdom! Be a hero and save the world!

E Think and write. Do you think advertisements are a necessary part of daily life? Why or why not?

- Students are going to explore the CLIL social studies focus of communication by first thinking about how advertisers use advertisements to communicate with the general public.
- Put students into pairs to brainstorm a list of ideas of how advertisements are used by advertisers to communicate with the general public. If students are struggling, encourage them to think about how advertisers use advertisements to inform us about the latest products, developments in research, claims about the benefits of products, and so on.
- Ask students to discuss in pairs if advertisements are necessary in our life and give reasons.
- Have students write their own answer including reasons. Invite a few students to read their answer to the class. Prompt other students to say if they agree or disagree and why.

Cool Down

Ask *Would you like to work in advertising? Why or why not?* Have students discuss the questions in small groups. Then do a class survey having students stand in two opposite sides of the class for yes and no. Elicit reasons from each side.

Practice **Student's App:** Reading Practice

Think Together

Lesson Objectives

- to make connections between the readings
- to explore the key concept: Does advertising influence the way we think?
- to reflect on the unit and provide personal thoughts and opinions

Warm Up

Ask *How would our lives be different if there were no advertisements?* Have small groups think of three ways our lives would change for the better or for the worse. Elicit ideas.

A Complete the table. List the advertising techniques in *Ad Smart* and examples of these advertising techniques in the pictures and text in *Commercial Break*.

- Display the table and elicit the advertising techniques from *Ad Smart*, completing the first column together as a class.
- Then have students scan the reading in pairs to find examples of each technique.
- Check answers as a class, having students come to the front to fill in the table or projecting the answers using the TTL.

Answers

Advertising Techniques in *Ad Smart*	Examples in *Commercial Break*
Repetition	*the ads the children see on the bus*
Slogans	Great. Grand. Go Shoes; Don't be lazy, grab your garbage!; Be happy with Heart.; Buy Cute Kitty cat food.
Promotion	Share this message with your friends for 20% off!
Targeted ads	Book a flight now; The latest Skate Duty album is on sale

B Think, discuss, and write. Your class is going to hold an event to raise money for charity. Do a Roundtable. Complete the table.

- Students are going to do a Roundtable routine (see TB p. 20) to brainstorm ideas for promoting a fundraising event at their school. This helps them make connections to the key concept in the unit: *Does advertising influence the way we think?*
- Decide as a class what cause to raise money for. Then have students choose a type of event in groups.
- Let students think about ads and techniques individually. Then have them share ideas in their groups following the Roundtable. Invite groups to present their ideas.

C Think and write. Look at B. Write an advertising slogan to persuade people to come to your event using one technique you discussed.

- Have the groups decide on their slogans. Point out that slogans need to be short and catchy. You can also remind them of the alliteration they studied in *Commercial Break*.
- Invite a student from each group to write their slogan on the board. Prompt students to discuss other groups' slogans and decide which event they would like to go to. Ask them to discuss what persuaded them. Elicit ideas.

My Reading Journal

Which of the text and graphic features did you find useful in the unit? Why?

Who do you think might learn something by reading this unit?

These questions encourage students to personalize what they've learned in the unit and relate it to their lives.

Give students time to look through the unit and answer the questions. Have them share in pairs, then as a class.

Example Answers

I found the (illustrations in *Commercial Break*) useful because (they helped me understand the story better). I think (my granddad) would learn a lot by reading this unit because (he thinks ads always tell the truth).

Go back to page 105. Do the routine again. How do your new and old responses connect?

Have students look back at the VTR picture on p. 105 and elicit what they discussed in the Get Ready to Read lesson (use your notes to remind them). Discuss how they think the picture connects to the two unit readings.

Have students do the 3–2–1 Bridge VTR again and compare their old responses to the new ones. Ask them to say how their old responses connect to the new ones.

Here's an example of this part of the routine.

Teacher: So, what new thoughts, questions, and metaphors do you have?

Student A: Well, before I thought the boy had made a mistake, but now I think the ad was a trick.

Student B: I have a new question: What new rules can we have to stop advertisers from lying?

Student A: My metaphor is Advertisements are tricks.

Teacher: Why do you think that?

Student A: Because they tell us things that aren't true.

Teacher: And how do your new answers relate to your old answers?

Student C: Now I know about advertisers' techniques. Before I wasn't aware of the tricks they play.

Cool Down

Play *Snowballs* (see TB p. 26). Have students write one thing they learned or enjoyed during the unit on their paper.

Practice **Resource Bank:** Unit Test
Student's App: Key Concept Practice

UNIT 8

What Are the Odds?

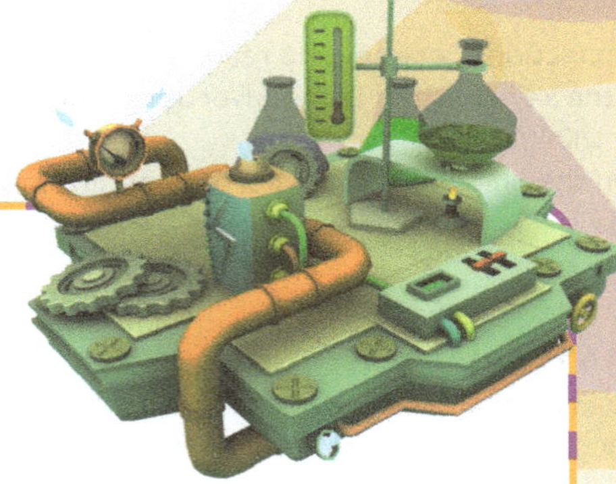

Unit Overview

Themes

The beauty of numbers, shapes, and symmetry

The role numbers play in our daily life

Synopsis

In this unit, students will look at numbers in a different way and think about the beauty that lies in numbers, shapes, and symmetry. They will learn about the sun and solar eclipses. They will discuss how math links to our lives and how it can help them solve problems. Students will prepare and write a biography. They will also give a presentation using visuals and trying to motivate their audience.

Language Book

Vocabulary

angle, divide, even number, hexagon, multiply, odd number, prime number, sequence, spirals, symmetry

Pronunciation: Consonant Clusters

p. 160

Explore Language

Passives: Present and Past

p. 161

Global Citizenship

How does math link to different aspects of our lives?

average, chart, data, fall, percentage, reach a peak, rise, statistics, stay stable, trend

p. 162

Explore Language

Passives: Future Forms *Will*, *Going to*

p. 163

Write About It

A Biography

Writing Chronologically and Supporting a Point with Examples

p. 164

Take the Stage

Presentation: Engaging and Motivating Your Audience; Using Visuals

p. 165

Think It Over

Review and Reflection: 3–2–1

p. 166

Think Together
Why are numbers important in our lives?
p. 173

Visible Thinking
Think, Pair, Share
p. 167

Literacy Book

Fiction
Story: *The Binary Life*

Words in Context: *outcome, free up, symmetrical, fractions, approached*
p. 171

Nonfiction
Biography: *Ada Lovelace*

Words in Context: *Industrial Revolution, punch cards, thread, algebraic, formulas*
p. 168

Reading Skill
Recognizing Story Structure
p. 170

Literary Term
Open Compound
p. 169

Language and Literacy Connections

The connecting theme for Unit 8 is numbers and how they form part of our lives.

	Language	Literacy
Vocabulary	**Set 1:** numbers, shapes, and symmetry **Set 2:** statistics descriptors	**Fiction:** divide, percentage, problem solving, sequence, symmetry
Grammar	**Passives: Present and Past** It's called a total eclipse. It was taken by a professional. You can be blinded by it. The sun has been covered completely. **Passives: Future Forms** Data analysis is going to be used more and more. The data will be analyzed to help them decide. How will the data be collected?	**Nonfiction** At the age of 17, Lovelace was introduced to Charles Babbage. … how technology could be used in the future. Unfortunately, the complete Analytical Engine was never built, so Lovelace's program was never tested. They were published again 100 years later. All computer programs today are based on the ideas suggested by Ada Lovelace. **Fiction** Many of my decisions have been made in this way … This time problem solving couldn't be done by the flip of a coin.
Skills	**Pronunciation:** consonant clusters **Process Writing:** writing chronologically and supporting a point with examples	**Reading:** recognizing story structure **Literary Term:** open compound
International English	analyzed/analysed	

Vocabulary

Lesson Objectives

- to learn vocabulary for numbers, shapes, and symmetry: *angle, divide, even number, hexagon, multiply, odd number, prime number, sequence, spirals, symmetry*
- to read and say a poem about numbers
- to recognize and practice consonant clusters

Materials
Audio Tracks 87 to 91; Video

Warm Up

Explain that you are going to say a word and students must write whatever that word brings to mind. Say *Ready? The word is … math!* Give students ten seconds to write down their first thought. Elicit ideas.

A TRACK 87 TB p. 224 **Listen. Which three photos does the group talk about?**

- This activity introduces the new vocabulary in context. Have students look at the picture and find Ludka from Unit 6 (the girl with short hair on the rug). Then have them discuss in pairs where the children are and what they are doing. Elicit ideas.
- Tell students they are going to listen to the teacher, Ms. Nair, and the children talking about the photos. Ask the question and play the audio. Then check the answer.

Answer
the pictures of the butterfly, the honeycomb, and the shell

- Ask the Unit 7 teaser question: *What beautiful designs are there in nature?* Discuss answers. Play the audio again if necessary (the pattern on the butterfly wings; the shapes in the honeycomb; the circles in the shell; the shapes in the cobweb; the tortoise's shell; the patterns in the snowflake). Then ask further comprehension questions (see **ETB**).

B TRACK 88 TB p. 224 **Find and number the words in A. Then listen and check.**

- Ask students to look at the words and phrases. Elicit whether they already know some of them from math class. Then point out the example (1) and have students find the hexagon in the picture. Have students work in pairs to find and number the other words in the picture.
- Play the audio for them to listen and check. Check pronunciation and drill the words or phrases if necessary.

Answers
1 *hexagon* 2 spirals 3 multiply 4 symmetry
5 angle 6 divide 7 odd number 8 even number
9 prime number 10 sequence

C TRACK 89 TB p. 224 **Close your eyes. Listen, visualize, and say.**

- Prepare students for the visualization (see TB p. 21).
- Play the audio for students to visualize the ideas.
- Play the audio again. Then put students in pairs and ask them to discuss the three most interesting visualizations.

D Look and write.

- Ask students to look at the definitions and the example. Have them read the sentences in pairs and decide on the correct word or answer. Then check answers.

Answers
1 *an angle* 2 odd number 3 Symmetry
4 even number 5 sequence 6 multiply
7 prime number 8 divide 9 hexagon 10 spirals

E TRACK 90 TB p. 225 **Listen and choose. Then watch and say.**

- Have students read the poem silently and think about the answer options. Some of the answers can be guessed by meaning and others from rhyming sounds.
- Play the audio for students to check their ideas and complete the poem. Check answers as a class.
- Play the audio again for students to read along. Encourage them to mime actions for *I have numbers on my mind. / Two lines joined. / Bring it on! / Come and see.*

Answers
1 *Symmetry* 2 multiply 3 even 4 prime
5 An angle 6 hexagon 7 Spirals

F TRACK 91 TB p. 225 **Pronunciation. Listen and say. Copy the consonant clusters. Find other words with consonant clusters in the poem.**

- This task raises students' awareness of consonant clusters in English, particularly of *pl, pr,* and *tr.* Before you play the audio, explain what a consonant cluster is. (when two or more different consonants meet in a word and we say the consonant sounds together). Point out the three example words and elicit the consonants in each cluster. Ask students to find an additional cluster in *multiply* (*lt*).
- Play the audio once for students to listen and say the words, focusing on the consonant clusters.
- In pairs, have students find other words with consonant clusters in the poem. Elicit answers and have students practice saying the words in pairs. Monitor and check.

Answers
numbers, mind, find, patterns, sequence, apply, just, itself, angle, spiral, point, bring, sunflowers, insects

Cool Down

Write these tongue twisters on the board: *I scream, you scream, we all scream for ice cream. / How can a clam cram in a clean cream can? / A big black bear sat on a big black rug.*

Say the tongue twisters and have students repeat. Then put them in pairs to practice.

Practice Student's App: Vocabulary Practice; Spoken Word Video

Explore Language

Lesson Objectives

- to learn how to use passives: present and past
- to practice numbers, shapes, and symmetry vocabulary

Materials
Audio Tracks 92 and 93; information about space to project on the board (F)

Warm Up

Write *Sp* ... on the board and elicit words students know that start with this consonant cluster. If students don't mention *space*, elicit it with a definition. Have students brainstorm in pairs what they know about space. Elicit ideas.

A TRACK 92 TB p. 225 **Listen and read. What information does Adam give Ludka about eclipses?**

- Have students look at the picture or display it using the TTL. Invite students to say what Adam and Ludka are talking about (eclipses).
- This activity is a presentation of the grammar in context. Tell students they are going to listen to Adam giving Ludka information about eclipses. Have them predict in pairs what he is going to say. Elicit ideas and play the audio. Students follow in their books and check their guesses.
- Ask the question and have students look at the dialogue again in pairs and find the answer. Check with the class.

Answer
that solar eclipses happen when the moon passes in front of the sun, what you see depends on where you are on Earth, and you shouldn't look directly at them

- Ask *What kinds of eclipses does Adam talk about?* (partial and total solar eclipses) Then ask further comprehension questions (see **ETB**).

B Look at A. Complete the table. Which verb is in all passive sentences?

- Display the table using the TTL. Tell students to scan the dialogue in A in pairs and complete the table with the missing words. Have them compare answers in pairs.
- Students should now have the skills and strategies to be able to discuss the grammar forms and notice patterns by themselves. When they have completed the table, discuss the word order, form, and patterns together, but let your class guide the discussion. If you feel that students need more guidance, use the notes in the **ETB**.

Answers
's; taken; be; blinded; has; been
The verb *be* is in all passive sentences.

- Refer students to the Grammar tip *Remember.* Point out that the verb *be* is used in the same verb form as the main verb in the active voice.

C Think and discuss. Then choose.

- This activity focuses on the usage of passives. Ask students to refer back to the table in B to discuss the sentences and answer options in pairs. Then check answers.
- Point out that we often leave out the *by* agent when we aren't interested in who did the action, when it's easy to understand who the *by* agent is, or when we don't want to say who the *by* agent is, e.g. *The window's been broken.* (Someone broke it, but we don't know who or we don't want to say who did it.)

Answers
1 True 2 True

D TRACK 93 TB p. 225 **Listen and say.**

- Tell students they're going to practice saying sentences with the passive voice to help with pronunciation in fluent speech and so that they begin to internalize the structure. Play the audio and have students repeat each example chorally. (See TB p. 23, Making Language Drills Fun.)

E Complete the sentences using the correct form of the passive.

- This activity provides controlled practice of different forms of the passive voice. Read the example sentences and discuss why the *by* agent isn't included. (The agent *people* is not specific or important to the sentence.)
- Have students complete the sentences on their own and then compare their answers in pairs.
- To check answers, invite students to read the sentence in the active voice, identify the tense, and then read the sentence in the passive voice. Then display the answers. Discuss where the *by* agent is interesting or useful to include.

Answers
1 *has been studied for centuries* 2 was measured accurately (by scientists) 3 can be seen from Earth without a telescope 4 is used (by astronauts) to practice before the launch 5 A new observatory might be built in Australia.

F Think and discuss. What do you know about space?

- This activity provides freer oral practice of passives. Point out the examples and have students brainstorm ideas in pairs. Allow them to do a quick search if possible. If students can't come up with enough ideas, then project some information on the board. You can include true facts or a combination of true and false pieces of information and ask students to discuss them.
- Invite students to share information about space with the class using the passive voice.

Cool Down

Play *Disappearing Sentences* (see TB p. 25) with sentences from E and F.

Practice **Practice Resource Bank:** Grammar Printout
Student's App: Grammar Practice

Global Citizenship

Lesson Objectives

- to learn vocabulary related to statistics: *average, chart, data, fall, percentage, reach a peak, rise, statistics, stay stable, trend*
- to explore how math is part of everyday life
- to practice listening for gist and details

Materials
Audio Tracks 94 to 96; Audio Track H

Opening Question

Ask the opening question: *How does math link to different aspects of our lives?* Give students 30 seconds to think on their own before discussing ideas in small groups. Elicit ideas.

A TRACK 94 TB p. 225 **Listen to Jung-mi and Hiroki talk about a research project. What information surprises them?**

- Tell students they are going to listen to Jung-mi and Hiroki talking about a project. Play the audio once and elicit what the project is about (children learning languages).
- Ask the gist question, replaying the audio if needed, and check. See the **ETB** for more comprehension questions.

Answer
that a lot of British school children stop learning any language after secondary school / high school

B TRACK 95 TB p. 225 **Look at the pictures and definition in A and write. Then listen and check.**

- Have students look at the pictures and definition. Have they encountered any data in math class or out of class?
- Look at the example. Then have students match the words and phrases to the pictures and definition in A and discuss in pairs. Play the audio for students to check answers.

Answers
1 *data* 2 rise 3 fall 4 chart 5 reach a peak 6 stay stable 7 percentage 8 average 9 statistics 10 trend

TRACK H TB p. 225 **Visualization**
The TTL includes an optional visualization audio track for this vocabulary set. (See TB p. 21)

C Read and complete using the information in the chart.

- This activity provides contextualized controlled practice of the vocabulary. Discuss what the bar charts show (fitness levels of children around the world in 1975 and 2013). Point out the key at the bottom of the chart and the arrows in the text boxes, as these will help students interpret the information.
- Then read the example. Elicit the second answer and where to find it (the blue bar in the 2013 chart).
- Have students complete the rest of the sentences. Check answers, eliciting the feature that indicates the information.

Answers
1 *chart*; fall 2 stayed stable 3 statistics; rise 4 reached a peak 5 percentage 6 average

D TRACK 96 TB p. 225 **Now listen to a radio program. Why does Ms. Pérez say that math is everywhere?**

- Listening for gist: tell students they're going to hear a teacher, Ms. Pérez, talk about math. Ask the question and have students guess in pairs.
- Play the audio and have students listen and check their guesses. Elicit answers.

Answers
because math is used in everyday life, e.g. supermarkets use math to track what we shop; math helps us decide how many homes, schools, and buses we need

E Listen again. Answer these questions.

- Listening for details: encourage students to answer any questions they can before listening again.
- Play the audio and have students complete their answers. Check answers, then discuss if they are surprised by any of the uses of math mentioned by Ms. Pérez.

Answers
1 *When she goes shopping and buys things.* 2 They can calculate what/how much stock they need 3 No, if they run out, they've calculated incorrectly. 4 It can help calculate how many new houses might be needed. 5 In Cambodia, the majority of people live in the country, but in Brazil the majority live in towns. 6 because there will be more children who need to go to school there

Discussion Questions

- Draw students' attention to the discussion questions: *How is math useful in your life? How can math be used to help solve problems in your community?* Have students discuss each question in pairs or small groups (see **ETB**). Encourage students to recognize that measurement, time, counting, and calculating are all based on math, and that math plays an essential part in our lives.
- Return to the opening question to ask again *How does math link to different aspects of our lives?* Review the ideas discussed at the beginning of the lesson and then encourage students to share any new ideas.

Cool Down

Ask students to list three ways in which they use math in their everyday life. Encourage them to think of ways they hadn't realized up to now. Have students compare their lists in pairs. Then elicit ideas from the class.

Practice **Student's App:** Vocabulary Practice; Listening Practice

Explore Language

Lesson Objectives

- to learn how to use passives: future forms
- to practice vocabulary related to statistics

Materials
Audio Tracks 97 and 98

Warm Up

Write questions on the board: *How often do you use your phone, and what do you use it for? Do you think using your phone is safe? Why or why not?* Put students in pairs to discuss and then elicit ideas.

A TRACK 97 TB p. 226 **Listen and read. Why is data important?**

- This activity is a presentation of the grammar in context. Tell students they are going to listen to Adam from Lesson 2 talking to his friend Vincent. Draw their attention to the picture and ask them to guess what they are talking about.
- Play the audio. Have students follow the dialogue in their books and check to see if their predictions were correct.
- Ask the question *Why is data important?* First, elicit a definition or synonym for *data* (information collected from surveys, studies, etc.) and then have students discuss the question in pairs. Check the answer.

Answers
It's used by companies to send people targeted advertisements and to decide which products to make and sell.

International English

Point out the different spellings in *analyzed* and *analysed*. Elicit other verbs with a –*z* and –*s* spelling (*realize–realise*; *summarize–summarise*; *apologize–apologise*; *organize–organise*; *recognize–recognise*). Remind students that despite the spelling change, the pronunciation is the same.

B Look at A. Complete the table. Which verb form do we use for the main verb?

- Display the table using the TTL. Give students a time limit to scan the dialogue in A and find the missing words in the table. Have them work individually and then compare answers in pairs.
- Students should now have the skills and strategies to be able to discuss the grammar and notice patterns by themselves using the examples. When they have completed the table, discuss the word order, form, and patterns together, but let your class guide the discussion. If you feel that students need more guidance, use the notes in the **ETB**.

Practice **Resource Bank:** Grammar Printout
Student's App: Grammar Practice

- Draw students' attention to the Grammar tip *Look*. Remind them to always check the form of the main verb when transforming a sentence from active to passive voice. Point out that we often don't include a *by* agent because we don't know who did the action or it isn't important.

Answers
used; will; analyzed; will; be
We use the past participle of the main verb.

C Think and discuss. Then choose.

- Ask students to read the statements on usage and refer to the examples in the table in B. Have them choose the answers individually and then compare in pairs.
- Check answers, eliciting whether the examples in B are objective or personal and how they know.

Answers
1 objective 2 can't

D TRACK 98 TB p. 226 **Listen and say.**

- Tell students they're going to practice saying sentences and questions with future forms in the passive to help with pronunciation in fluent speech and to consolidate what they've learned. Play the audio and have students repeat chorally. (See TB p. 23, Making Language Drills Fun.)

E Read the report. Write the sentences or questions with a future form of the passive voice.

- This activity provides controlled practice of future forms in the passive. Look at the example together. Point out the extra words (*will be* and *by*) and the transformation of the verb in the past participle form.
- Give students time to write the sentences individually and compare them in pairs. Display answers using the TTL.

Answers
1 *More white sneakers will be bought by girls than by boys next year.* 2 Which video games will be played the most? 3 Jeans are not going to be worn as much. 4 Homework will be corrected by robots not (by) teachers. 5 Big computers won't be bought in the same numbers as today. 6 More apps are going to be designed by teenagers.

F Think about current trends. Make predictions about the future. Talk with a friend.

- Review the meaning of *trends* and elicit current trends related to video games and transportation. Then look at the examples. Tell students to think of things that might change in the future. Have pairs discuss their predictions using the passive voice with *will/won't*, giving reasons for their opinions if possible. Discuss as a class.

Cool Down

Divide the class into teams to play a *Chain Game* (see TB p. 25) using their predictions from F. Demonstrate first with a few volunteers. Then have them play in their teams.

Write About It

Lesson Objectives

- to plan and write a biography
- to learn how to write chronologically and support a point with examples

Materials

Support Writing printouts from the Resource Bank (G)

Warm Up

Draw students' attention to the heading *The Games Master: John Horton Conway* on p. 108. Find out whether students know anything about this mathematician. Then have them guess why the writer describes him as the "games master."

A Read the biography. What's unusual about the mathematician?

- This lesson corresponds with the biography of Ada Lovelace in Unit 8 of the **Literacy Book**. Elicit what a biography is (a text about a person's life). Have students read the text and check their ideas from the Warm Up.
- Ask the gist question *What's unusual about the mathematician?* and have students discuss in pairs. Check as a class. Ask more comprehension questions (see **ETB**).

Suggested Answer

He invented an extraordinary computer game.

B Look at the structure of the biography. Read and write why each feature is important.

- Tell students they're going to look at the structure of the biography. First, have them look at the first feature and the example.
- Then ask students to look at the rest of the features and think of ideas individually for a few seconds. Have them compare ideas in pairs and then write their answers. Check answers.

Suggested Answers

1 *To give the reader a purpose for reading.*
2 so the reader understands where the person is from
3 so the reader understands the sequence of events
4 to give a picture of the person or something relating to the person's life 5 so the reader can see the contribution the person has made 6 so the reader gets a personalized view to follow up / conclude

C Look at the language of the biography. Complete the table with examples from the biography.

- Read the prompts and the example. Have students find examples for the rest of the facts individually. Then ask them to compare answers in pairs. Check answers.
- Discuss whether the language is formal or informal (neutral, but friendly).

Answers

1 *He invented an extraordinary computer game.*
2 It helped create a new type of math. 3 It is used in computer programs and coding today. 4 He has written lots of books. He has received several prizes for his work. 5 Students' own answers

D Think and discuss. Choose a subject for a biography. What do you need to know about this person? Use one of the Generating Ideas techniques.

- In this lesson, students decide which techniques they want to use to generate ideas, plan, and draft/revise. They can refer back to the lessons on pp. 140–142. Encourage them to choose the technique they think will work best.
- Have students think about whose biography they would like to write and what they would need to know about this person, making notes using a Generating Ideas technique.
- Have students compare their notes in pairs or small groups. Encourage them to give their partner(s) more ideas to add to their notes. Monitor and help with ideas if necessary.
- Invite students to share who they are going to write about. Discuss where they'll find the information they'll need. Encourage them to ask other students for information. Allow students time to collect this information.

E Plan your biography. Use your notes in D and one of the Planning techniques.

- Have students plan individually. Encourage them to refer to the text in A for ideas on how to order the information.

F Write a first draft, then revise it. Use a checklist.

- Have students write a draft of their biography in their notebooks, referring to their notes in E. They should read their drafts and make any corrections or improvements.
- Provide a checklist on the board or elicit it as a class, e.g. *Is the information in chronological order? Did I list the most important achievements and explain why they're important? Is my opinion clear? Did I use a variety of narrative tenses?*

G Now write your revised biography.

- Have students write their final versions neatly on paper or on the Support printout.
- In pairs, students read each other's biography and say whether they think the information is ordered logically.

Cool Down

Ask students to imagine they are 100 years old and someone is going to write their biography. Have them list four important facts that should be included. These can be from their childhood, but they can also imagine what they're going to achieve in their lifetime. Then have them role-play in pairs giving their biographer the information. Invite the "biographers" to share what they found out.

Practice **Resource Bank:** Writing Game, *Mystery Guest*
Student's App: Writing Practice

Take the Stage

Lesson Objectives

- to practice giving a presentation using visuals
- to engage and motivate the audience

Materials
Video

Warm Up

Ask students to think about three numbers that have meant something in their day so far. Give an example: *I had two cups of coffee this morning.* Have students share their numbers and ideas in small groups. Elicit some of their ideas and write them on the board. Leave them on the board to refer back to in A.

A TB p. 240 **Watch and listen. Which number surprises Wade?**

- Tell students they are going to watch a video of Wade giving a presentation about numbers in his day. The video provides a presentation of the functional language needed for engaging and motivating your audience.
- With books closed, play the video for students to watch, listen, and see if he mentions any similar numbers to the ones they discussed in the Warm Up. Elicit ideas.
- Ask the comprehension question *Which number surprises Wade? Why?* If necessary, play the video again and then allow some time for students to discuss the answer in pairs. Check the answer. Ask more comprehension questions (see **ETB**).

Answer
He is surprised by the number of steps he took because he didn't think he was so active.

B Watch again. What effect do the phrases have in the presentation? Check (✔).

- Tell students they are going to focus on the functional language Wade uses in his presentation and what effect it has on the audience. Look at the effects as a class, making sure students understand each heading. Have students look at the example and ask them how the phrase engages the audience (it asks them to imagine a situation that they would find difficult and captures their interest).
- Play the video again and have students notice the phrases and what effect they have on them. Give students time to complete the table and compare their answers in pairs. Check answers.

Answers
Engage the audience: *1*; 2
Motivate and incentivize: 7; 8
Encourage reflection: 4; 5; 6
Create interest in a fact: 3

C Think about the numbers in your day. Use these ideas and your own. Think and plan.

- Tell students they are going to give a presentation about numbers in their day, but first they must brainstorm ideas. Allow them to use their ideas from the Warm Up, from the box, and their own.
- Put students in pairs to compare their ideas and discuss how to organize them in a logical way. Draw their attention to the example list and ask them to think about which phrases they are going to use from B. Monitor and provide help if needed.

D Practice with your friends. Then share with the class. Take notes and give feedback.

- Tell students they are going to practice their presentation in small groups. Give them a minute to get ready and think about what they are going to say and how they are going to give the presentation. Have them practice in their groups. Monitor and provide help as needed.
- Students take turns giving their presentations to the rest of the class. If you have a large class, invite volunteers to give their presentation. Ask students to make notes about how they feel while they are listening, using the effects in B as a guide.
- Ask students to analyze their performance, thinking about whether they encouraged the audience to reflect.

Cool Down

Ask students to work in small groups and discuss whether their attitude toward numbers and math has changed. They should compare their attitude now to what they thought at the beginning of the unit. Do they now see numbers in a different way? Do they feel more positive or negative about math and why? When they've had time to discuss, elicit ideas and opinions as a class.

Practice **Student's App:** Speaking Skills Practice; Speaking Video

Think It Over

Lesson Objectives

- to review what has been learned in the unit
- to reflect on the unit and their own progress
- to think about learning strategies and how to continue learning at home

Warm Up

Write a few numbers on the board that mean something to you, e.g. the number of the street you live on, your child's age, your shoe size, the number of the month you were born in. Put students in pairs to guess what the number could mean to you. Elicit ideas and give them the answers. Then have students think of 4–5 numbers for themselves and take turns guessing each other's numbers in pairs.

How well did you meet the challenge of Unit 8? Read and respond.

3–2–1

- Tell students they are going to review what they learned in the unit and also think about their own learning.
- Have students work in small groups to brainstorm different categories related to the unit and make mind maps of what they learned, e.g. words, grammar, numbers, designs and shapes, things I learned about numbers and nature, things I learned about eclipses, graphics and diagrams, data, biography. They can also include ideas from the **Literacy Book**. Then have students display their mind maps on the wall. Have groups go around the classroom and look at each other's maps.
- Refer students to the graphic organizer in the book and the prompt sentences: *3 new facts I learned in this unit; 2 "Ah-ha!" moments I had; 1 big question I still have.* Have students talk in pairs about the different sections. Encourage them to focus particularly on the second and third sections. Elicit what "ah-ha" moments are and explain that the big question can be related to math, science, or any other topic that was discussed in the unit.
- When you feel they have enough ideas, have students work individually to fill out the organizer. Remind them that they should write their own responses about themselves. Monitor and help as necessary. Look at what students are writing so you can tailor your classes and any additional practice to their needs.
- If you feel it is appropriate for your class, have students share their ideas with a friend. Encourage them to think together of how they can find the answer to the big questions they have. They can take guesses as to what the answers are as well.

Looking Forward

Draw students' attention to the character at the bottom of the page. Have students say who he is and what they remember about him. (Vincent appears in Lesson 1, p. 100, and Lesson 4, p. 106. He talks to Adam about online data collection.) Have students look at the speech bubble and make predictions about what Vincent's big decision is and what will help him make it. Tell students they will find out the answer in Lesson 1 of the next unit.

Put It Together

To further review and recycle the language in Units 7 and 8, play the game, *Word Scramble Race*, on pp. 112–113. See TB p. 209 for teaching notes.

Practice **Resource Bank:** Unit Test
Student's App: Vocabulary and Grammar Review

Literacy

Get Ready to Read

Lesson Objectives

- to activate prior knowledge about numbers and math
- to guide inquiry and deepen understanding through a Think, Pair, Share VTR
- to preview the reading skill of recognizing story structure

Materials

VTR printout from the Resource Bank (A, B, C); photo of a sunflower (WU)

Warm Up

Draw a sunflower on the board or display a photo of one. Elicit the compound name: *sunflower.* Put students in pairs to explain why they are called sunflowers and what they know about them. You can also share facts with students or ask them to guess first, e.g. *Where did sunflowers originate?* (in the Americas) *How many hours of sun do they need a day?* (6–8 hours or more) *What do sunflowers do as the sun moves in the sky?* (They follow it, and this is called heliotropism.) *What do we get from sunflowers?* (edible seeds, oil, flour)

Think, Pair, Share

A Look at the picture. What patterns do you see? What does the picture remind you of? Think about it.

- This VTR encourages individual students to participate and gives students time to think independently before contributing their ideas about the image of the sunflower and the patterns it shows.
- Start by having students look at the picture for one minute and say what they see. Encourage them to turn their book around and look at the picture from different angles, as well as close-up and from a distance. Then ask *What patterns do you see? What does the picture remind you of?* Encourage students to make a list and draw pictures if they don't know the exact word. Monitor and provide language help if needed.

B Talk with your partner.

- Divide the class into pairs and have students share their ideas about the picture. Encourage them to discuss any questions they might have and to think of possible answers together.

C Share with the class.

- Ask pairs to decide which ideas they would like to share with the class. Ask them to choose at least two and practice how they are going to explain them.
- Invite pairs to share their ideas about the picture with the class. Encourage students to use *we*, as they are talking on behalf of their partner, too. Encourage the class to respond to the ideas, talking with each other, and not just to you. Keep a record of students' ideas from the VTR to revisit in the Think Together lesson.

Here's an example of this part of the routine.

Teacher: What did you and your friend say about the picture?

Student A: We think it looks a lot like a wheel of a car or of a bike. The seeds go around in a spiral.

Student B: The sunflower reminds us of a wheel and a pineapple. The seeds look like the brown part of the pineapple. And the inside of the pineapple is yellow, too.

Student A: Does anyone think it looks like something different?

Student C: We think it looks like ice cream. It's a round ice cream scoop with lines in the middle. And it also reminds us of the sun. The seeds in the middle look like flames.

Teacher: That's interesting. Any other ideas?

Student D: We think the sunflower seeds look like strawberry seeds. They both go around in a spiral.

Student E: Like a snail or a shell.

Transition

Ask *What do you think mathematicians see in the sunflower? Why do scientists study nature? What can we learn from it?*

D Think and discuss. Where can you see examples of math in the world around you?

- Give students one minute to look around the classroom and see if they can find any examples of math. Encourage them to look for patterns and shapes, as well as numbers. Elicit ideas.
- Then ask students to think about where they can see math in other places, including nature. Have students discuss their ideas in pairs. Elicit ideas from the class.

Answers

Students' own answers

E Think and write. Scan *Ada Lovelace*. What main events do you expect the author to include in the biography?

- This activity previews the skill of recognizing story structure. Ask students to look at the pages of *Ada Lovelace* and identify the text type (biography). Have them scan the reading and discuss what kind of information they find in pairs.
- Elicit ideas from the class and accept all opinions. Students will check their ideas in the next lesson.

Suggested Answers

when she was born, when she died, what she accomplished

Now read **Ada Lovelace**

Nonfiction: *Ada Lovelace—* Biography

Lesson Objectives

- to activate prior knowledge about computer programming
- to make a personal connection to the reading

Materials
Audio Tracks 34 and 35

Warm Up

Look at the pictures on pp. 122–123 or display them using the TTL. Ask students what the people's hairstyle, clothes, posture, and so on tell them about that time in the past. Discuss when Ada Lovelace lived. Accept all ideas.

TRACK 34 TB p. 235 Reading Approach

First Reading: Engage with the Text

- Ask students to look back at their predictions in E on p. 121. Play the audio and have students follow along in their books and check their predictions in E and the Warm Up.
- Elicit the main events in the biography and discuss which events students found most interesting. Then look at the Words in Context.

TRACK 35 TB p. 236 Words in Context

- Brainstorm strategies on the board for students to use with the words: *knowledge of L1/other languages, separate parts of word, pictures, knowledge of similar words, surrounding words and sentences, world knowledge.*
- Have students work in pairs to find and discuss each word. Remind them that words may not be in the main body of the text but could be in captions or callouts and that different combinations of strategies will be needed for different words.

Industrial Revolution (p. 123, noun) This can be broken down, and surrounding words tell us it's a time period. Surrounding sentences give clues about what was happening at that time. Strategies to use: surrounding words and sentences, separate parts of a word

punch cards (p. 124, noun) This can be broken down. Surrounding sentences show that they're used in a machine, and connect them with the picture by referring to *holes in the cards*, and this in turn gives us visual clues. Strategies to use: surrounding words and sentences; separate parts of a word; pictures

thread (p. 124, noun) The caption shows that the word is something that is used when the punch card has holes. It can be inferred that the *thread* goes through the holes. The context is the weaving looms. Strategies to use: surrounding words and sentences; pictures; world knowledge of weaving

algebraic (p. 124, adjective) The sentence shows that the word is an adjective, as it is followed by the noun *patterns*. This shows it describes a type of pattern that the Analytical Engine follows. This machine is referred to on p. 125 in relation to an article written by a mathematician, so we can guess that this word is related to math. Strategies to use: surrounding words and sentences; world knowledge of math; L1 cognates

formulas (p. 125, noun) The sentence shows that this is something that Ada included in her article, as well as notes and diagrams. The picture on the following page shows Ada writing this article and examples of what she included. Strategies to use: surrounding words and sentences; pictures; L1 cognates; world knowledge of math

- Have students change partners and discuss strategies they used and which worked best or didn't work so well. Play the audio to practice the pronunciation.

Second Reading: Analyze the Text and Features

- Have students read the text on their own. Ask them to think about the writer's opinion of Ada as they read.
- Have them discuss the writer's opinion in pairs, then as a class. See the **ETB** for comprehension questions.
- Discuss the questions in the blue boxes.
  - **Personalization** (p. 122): *Do you know how to write a computer program?* Have students share in groups. If any students answer yes, elicit information. If nobody knows, have them do research and bring in information.
  - **Fun Fact** (p. 123): Read the information about Charles Babbage and have students discuss in small groups what they know about Isaac Newton and Stephen Hawking.
  - **Critical Thinking** (p. 125): *Why do you think Lovelace wanted to hide her identity on her published article?* Ask students to discuss ideas in pairs and then share with the class. (Probably because people would not take her seriously if they knew she was a woman.)
  - **Personalization** (p. 127): *What subject fascinates you?* Ask students to think about the question individually for a few seconds and think of reasons why. Have them compare ideas in pairs. Elicit opinions from the class.

Third Reading: Interact with the Text

- Draw a timeline on the board and title it *Ada Lovelace*. Ask students to work in pairs and create their own timeline in their notebooks. Ask them to skim the biography and add the important events in Ada's life on their timelines. Invite students to add information to the timeline on the board.

Cool Down

Tell students they are going to travel back in time and tell Ada Lovelace how important her work has been. Students discuss in pairs what to tell her and role-play the discussion. The student acting as Ada can react showing surprise and ask further questions. Invite pairs to act out their role-play.

Practice **Student's App:** Story Player

Explore the Reading

Lesson Objectives

- to understand and analyze *Ada Lovelace* through reading comprehension activities
- to learn through CLIL (history): computer science
- to make a personal connection to the reading

Warm Up

Have students play *What's the Next Word?* (see TB p. 27) in small groups. They take turns reading a sentence aloud from *Ada Lovelace*.

A Answer the questions.

- Ask students to do a five *Ws* and one *H* routine to recap the main events of Ada Lovelace's biography. Write *Who? What? Where? When? Why? How?* on the board. Elicit questions for each word, then have students ask and answer questions in pairs.
- Have students discuss the questions on p. 128 in pairs.
- Then have them work individually to read the biography and write their answers. Have them compare answers again in pairs.

Answers

1 because she didn't want her to develop her father's creativity and imagination / She thought it would be good for her character. 2 the Difference Machine; It was a huge mechanical calculator. 3 The Analytical Engine and weaving looms both used punch cards to create patterns. 4 because it combined science and creative thinking 5 They contained what is believed to be the first computer program and inspired mathematicians working on the first modern computers.

B Think and write. Find these numbers in the reading. Explain the significance of each number.

- Write the numbers on the board and ask students if they remember what each one refers to in the reading.
- Have them race to scan the reading for the numbers and write their answers. Check answers by saying a number and inviting students to explain the significance. Alternatively, display the answers using the TTL.

Answers

17: At the age of 17, Lovelace was introduced to Charles Babbage.
1842: In 1842, Lovelace translated and published an article about the Analytical Engine, adding her own detailed notes, formulas, and diagrams.
1815: Lovelace was born in 1815.
36: Lovelace died at the age of 36 in 1852.

C Think and discuss. How might things be different now if Babbage and Lovelace had built the complete Analytical Engine in the 19th century?

- Students are going to make hypotheses drawing on their knowledge of the CLIL history focus on computer science.
- Ask students to think about what they know about modern computers (e.g. when they first started being used in companies and schools; what important things they are used for). Then ask them to relate this information to the Analytical Machine. Point out that Lovelace's notes disappeared for 100 years. Encourage students to think about how much technology can change in 100 years.
- Have students discuss ideas in pairs or small groups. Then elicit ideas as a class.

Suggested Answer

Computers, as we know them today, would have been built many years earlier because Babbage and Lovelace's work was forgotten for 100 years. So, technology today would be more advanced and there would be more breakthroughs in medicine, space exploration, art, and so on.

Literary Term: Open Compound

Underline the open compounds.

- Read the information about open compounds and compare them to closed compounds with an example, e.g. *living room* and *sunflower.*
- Have students underline the open compounds individually and compare answers in pairs. Then check answers.

Now find more open compounds in the reading.

- Have students scan the reading to find more open compounds.
- Ask students to compare answers in pairs, then check answers as a class.

Answers

1 full moon 2 post office 3 washing machine
4 swimming pool
Open compounds in reading: flying machine, Industrial Revolution, social life, Difference Engine, Analytical Engine, weaving loom, punch card, poetical science, scientific thinking, computer program

Cool Down

Have students write four ages and dates that have a special significance in their life. Ask students to exchange numbers in pairs and guess what they could mean. Students check their guesses and give explanations.

Practice **Resource Bank:** Literary Term Printout
Student's App: Reading Practice; Literary Term Practice

Get Ready to Read

Lesson Objectives

- to activate prior knowledge of mathematical symbols and terms
- to practice the reading skill of recognizing story structure

Warm Up

Write on the board *A good story has* … Ask students to brainstorm ideas in pairs. Encourage them to refer to good stories in the **Literacy Book** they have already read to base their ideas on. Invite students to share ideas with the class and see if they mention the story structure.

A Look back at *The Boy Who Drew Cats* in Unit 5. Match the main events of the story to the different stages in the story structure.

- Students are going to practice the reading skill of recognizing story structure, which students previewed on p. 121. Have students look at the timelines they made in the reading lesson and notice how the biography is structured in chronological order, after beginning with an introduction.
- Show students the opening pages of *The Boy Who Drew Cats* in Unit 5 (pp. 80–85) and have them recall the main events in pairs. If necessary, students can skim it in order to remember.
- Have students read the reading skill box about story structure. Then ask them to look at the diagram on p. 129 and match the main events to the stages in the story structure. Have them do this individually and compare answers in pairs. Check answers.

Answers

2; 4; 5; 1; 3

B Think and discuss. Why is each stage of the story important? What would happen without each stage?

- Have students think about the questions referring to the stages and the events in A. Do an example with the class by asking *What information does the introduction give us? What would be missing if we didn't have the introduction?* (information about the time, place, characters, setting, etc.).
- Have students discuss the questions in pairs. Then invite students to share ideas with the class.

Answers

Students' own answers

C Think and write. Find these sentences and phrases in the reading. Replace the symbols with mathematical words.

- This activity activates students' prior knowledge of common mathematical words. Draw students' attention to the symbols and see if they know the mathematical word for any of them. Ask students when they usually use these symbols and what they mean. Have some students write examples on the board.
- Ask them to scan *The Binary Life* and find the words to complete the sentences. Have students compare answers in pairs before you check answers as a class.
- Ask students if they use these words outside math classes, e.g. *My friend shared his candy bar with me, so he broke it into two pieces and gave me half / 50%; I divide my free time between playing sports and reading.* Elicit that we also use fraction words to tell the time.

Answers

1 percentage 2 divide 3 half; quarter; eighth
4 binary

Cool Down

Ask students to think of a simple story with a sentence for each stage 1–5 in A. Allow them to make notes, but explain that they are going to draw a simple picture for each event/ stage. Ask them to draw the pictures in random order. Students can do this individually or in pairs. When ready, have them exchange drawings with a partner or another pair. Have them number the pictures in order and retell the story in pairs or groups.

Now read **The Binary Life**

Fiction: *The Binary Life—Story*

Lesson Objectives

- to read a story about a math genius
- to make a personal connection to the reading

Materials
Audio Tracks 36 and 37

Warm Up

If you are using the TTL, project the answers to C on p. 129 or ask students to look at them in their books. Have them guess what the story is going to be about in pairs.

TRACK 36 TB p. 236 Reading Approach

First Reading: Engage with the Text

- Play the audio and have students follow along in their books. Give them time to think about the title and why it fits the story. (Dexter has a binary life because the decisions he makes are a choice between two things.) Then look at the Words in Context.

TRACK 37 TB p. 236 Words in Context

- Give students a few minutes to find and highlight each word and to identify the kind of word it is.
- Write these strategies on the board for students to use with the words: *surrounding words and sentences, contrasting ideas, synonyms, parts of speech, word families, world knowledge, sentence structure, understanding main ideas.*
- Have students work in pairs to discuss the words. Remind them that different words will require different combinations of strategies to figure them out.

outcome (p. 130, noun) The sentence and the one that follows contrast *way more than two* with *only two*. This suggests that *outcomes* and *results* have the same meaning. Strategies to use: surrounding words and sentences; contrasting ideas; synonyms

free up (p. 131, verb) The previous paragraph gives the contrasting idea (Dexter is always thinking). The sentence shows that in not having to make decisions, Dexter can use his brain to concentrate on more important things. Strategies to use: surrounding words and sentences; parts of speech (adjective *free*; verb *free*); contrasting ideas

symmetrical (p. 132, adjective) The subject *it's* tells us that the word is an adjective that describes the sequence of musical notes. The following sentence provides a different form (noun) of the word. Strategies to use: word families; surrounding words and sentences

fractions (p. 133, noun) The following sentence provides examples of fractions. Strategies to use: world knowledge of music theory and math; surrounding words and sentences

approached (p. 133, verb) The sentence shows that this is the past participle form of a verb in the passive. The whole text describes the ways in which Dexter makes decisions. One of these ways is choosing between two options (a binary decision). Strategies to use: sentence structure; surrounding words and sentences; understanding main ideas

- Go through each word in turn to elicit the meaning and how they know. Play the audio to practice the pronunciation.

Second Reading: Analyze the Text and Features

- Have students read the story silently and underline three sentences they like. Have students compare sentences in pairs and explain why they like them.
- Ask *How does Dexter change throughout the story? Why?* Have students discuss in pairs and then elicit ideas from the class. See the **ETB** for more comprehension questions.
- Discuss the questions in the blue boxes. Then look at the text focus.
  - **Critical Thinking** (p. 130): *How do you think someone who is brilliant at math might see the world?* Have students discuss ideas in pairs. Then invite students to share their answers.
  - **Fun Fact** (p. 131): Read the information about probability. Do an example by flipping a coin. Before you flip it, elicit the probability of getting heads or tails (1/2, or 50%). Discuss in what situations it's useful to know the probability of an outcome (weather forecast, sports, etc.).
  - **Critical Thinking** (p. 133): *Do you think there is a connection between mathematical and musical ability?* Ask students to think about the story again and discuss ideas in pairs. Elicit ideas.
  - **Text Focus** (p. 130): Read the information and elicit how Dexter is an anti-hero. (He doesn't look cool or handsome and his behavior might seem strange to other people.) Have students brainstorm anti-heroes from other stories or movies they know.

Third Reading: Interact with the Text

- Have students read the text again and list all the problems Dexter faces in the story (breakfast and lunch, clothes, what to study, etc.). Ask them to think what advice they would give Dexter for each problem.
- Have students compare their ideas in pairs or small groups.

Cool Down

Ask students to work in pairs and imagine Dexter's first day at college. Help them brainstorm ideas with a few questions: *Who did Dexter meet? What decisions did he have to make? What did he enjoy?* Elicit ideas as a class.

Practice **Student's App:** Story Player

Explore the Reading

Lesson Objectives

- **to understand and analyze *The Binary Life* through reading comprehension activities**
- **to practice the reading skill of recognizing story structure**
- **to explore the SEL competency of responsible decision-making through making decisions based on moral, personal, and ethical standards**
- **to make a personal connection to the reading**

Warm Up

Ask students to scan *The Binary Life* and find numbers. Have them write them down individually. Then have them discuss in pairs what each number means or refers to.

Answers

10 steps; 75% cheese in sandwich; 25% tomato in sandwich; 35,000 decisions a day; 2^{35000} ways Dexter's day could go; 1 in 6,000 chances of a coin landing on its edge; 90% chance of Dexter getting into the program

A How does Dexter use numbers and math in the story? Match the two sentence halves.

- Give students time to read through the sentence halves and check they understand the key words.
- Have them match the sentences individually and then compare answers with a partner, looking back at the reading to confirm their answers. Check answers as a class.

Answers

1 c 2 d 3 e 4 a 5 b 6 f

B Think, write, and discuss. Which of Dexter's decisions do you think are binary? Why? What binary decisions have you made?

- Elicit that *binary* means that Dexter has two choices. Have students scan the story and find the binary decisions Dexter had to make.
- Then ask *What binary decisions have you made?* Give students time to think before having them discuss in small groups. Invite students to share with the class.

Suggested Answers

cheese or chicken, tomato or lettuce, apple or banana, what to wear to school, whether to study music or math at college
because there are two options
Students' own answers

C Imagine what happens to Dexter after *The Binary Life*. Write the story structure for the next chapter.

- Before students do the task, point out the story structure and elicit what happens in each part of the story.
- Put students in pairs to brainstorm what happens to Dexter next. You can give them a time limit, e.g. *What happens to Dexter the next week/month/year?* (The longer the period, the more challenging the task.)
- When students have discussed ideas, ask them to write the stages for the next chapter of the story. Ask them to do this individually and tell them it's OK if they include different ideas than the ones they discussed. Monitor and provide language help if needed.
- Ask students to place their books (or notebooks) face-up on their desk and walk around reading other students' stories. Then have them sit in pairs and discuss which events they found interesting.

D Think and write. What do you do when you have a difficult choice to make? Why?

- Students are going to explore the SEL competency of responsible decision-making: make decisions based on moral, personal, and ethical standards.
- Ask students why they think Dexter makes binary decisions (having two options is a more simple decision—having more options may be overwhelming for Dexter). Then ask students if they find it easier to choose between two things or more than two things.
- Give students time to think of a difficult choice they've had to make and how they dealt with it. Then have them share their examples in pairs and explain if their solution is typical. Encourage them to ask each other more questions.
- Then have students write their answers individually.

Cool Down

Ask students to think of a difficult choice and write it on a piece of paper. This can be a serious or silly choice, e.g. *There's X and Y movie on TV at the same time. How do you decide which to watch?* Have students pass around the pieces of paper and discuss each dilemma with a partner.

Practice **Student's App:** Reading Practice

Think Together

Lesson Objectives

- to make connections between the readings
- to explore the key concept: Why are numbers important in our lives?
- to reflect on the unit and provide personal thoughts and opinions

Warm Up

Play a variation of *Chain Game* (see TB p. 25) with the readings from the unit. Call out *Ada Lovelace*. Student A says a word he/she associates with the reading, then Student B says another word. They continue until one of the students can't think of a word. The last pair to stop wins. Then call out *The Binary Life* and repeat, e.g.

Teacher: Ada Lovelace
Student A: Charles Babbage
Student B: Analytical Engine
Student A: Computer program
Student B: Coding
Student A: Punch card
Student B: Weaving loom
Student A: Um …

A Compare and contrast Ada from *Ada Lovelace* and Dexter from *The Binary Life*. Complete the Venn diagram.

- Ask students to work in pairs and for each student to think of facts about a character. Then have them share their ideas and find similarities and differences.
- Display the Venn diagram using the TTL and elicit how to complete it. Students can complete the diagram on their own or in pairs. Monitor and provide language help if needed.
- Check answers as a class or project them on the board if you're using the TTL.

Suggested Answers
Ada: girl, tutored privately, lived a long time ago, she was a real person, she created the first computer program
Dexter: boy, went to school, lives in modern times, he's a fictional character, writes music
Both: loved numbers/math, both were creative/mixed math with creativity, studied math, intelligent, did something unusual, followed their passion

B What are some ways you use numbers in your daily life? Do an Inside-Outside Circle.

- Students are going to do an Inside-Outside Circle routine (see TB p. 21) to make connections to the key concept in the unit: *Why are numbers important in our lives?*
- Give students time to think about how they use numbers on their own first. Then have them stand in circles for the routine. Encourage them to listen and react to what their partner says and to ask further questions if appropriate.
- After the routine, put students in pairs to discuss interesting things they heard. Have volunteers share.

C Think and write. Do you prefer numbers or words, or do you prefer both? How does that have an effect on your daily life?

- Read the questions and give an example for yourself. You can also compare yourself to someone who's different from you. Then ask students to think about their own answers and examples.
- Students compare ideas in pairs or groups, then as a class.

My Reading Journal

Do you think any of the characters from the readings are remarkable? Why?

Did this unit make you think differently about math? Why or why not?

These questions encourage students to personalize what they have learned and relate this to their own life.

Give students time to look through the unit and answer the questions. Have them share ideas in pairs before eliciting a few examples with the from the class.

Example Answers
I think Ada Lovelace was remarkable because (she accomplished a lot even though she died so young).
I (still don't like math a lot, but now I know that it's part of my daily life. So I'll try to understand it more.).

Go back to page 121. What new thoughts do you have to share?

Have students look back at the VTR picture on pp. 120–121 and elicit what they discussed in the Get Ready to Read lesson (use your notes to remind them). Ask them how they think the picture connects to the two readings in the unit. Draw their attention to the concept question: *Why are numbers important in our lives?* Encourage students to think how numbers help us understand the world around us and interact with nature and other people. Encourage them to share any new thoughts they have about the picture.

Cool Down

Play *Test the Teacher* (see TB p. 26). Students work in groups to write questions about the two readings. Make sure students write the answer next to the question. Each group then takes turns asking you a question. The teacher must answer the question from memory! If you answer correctly, you get one point. If the answer is incorrect, the group gets one point.

Practice **Resource Bank:** Unit Test
Student's App: Key Concept Practice

UNIT 9

Make Up Your Mind

Unit Overview

Themes

Strategies for making decisions

The impact of our choices on our future and on other people

Synopsis

In this unit, students will explore decision-making skills and collaborative decision-making. They will think about different ways of making decisions, and they will reflect on how their current decisions affect their future. They will also think about how their decisions affect people around them. Students will prepare and write an instructional article. They will also have a conversation about a day out inviting others to contribute with their ideas.

Language Book

Vocabulary

brainstorm the options, consider the consequences, decide on a solution, define the problem, evaluate your ideas, learn from your mistakes, make a decision, regret

Pronunciation: Connected Speech: Linking

p. 176

Explore Language

Third Conditional: Statements

p. 177

Global Citizenship

How do the decisions we make affect other people?

be fair, control your emotions, fit in with, get your own way, have your say, independence, individual identity, peer pressure, pros and cons

p. 178

Explore Language

Third Conditional: Questions

p. 179

Write About It

An Instructional Article

Organizing Information and Engaging the Reader

p. 180

Talk About It

Conversation: Inviting Contributions to a Conversation

p. 181

Think It Over

Review and Reflection: My Favorite Mistakes

p. 182

Literacy Book

Think Together
How do we handle difficult choices?
p. 189

Visible Thinking
Step Inside
p. 183

Fiction
Story: *It's Not OK*
Words in Context: *notification, shoved, deafening silence, guts, selfies*
p. 187

Nonfiction
Instructional Text: *Making Decisions*
Words in Context: *on the bench, stick with, pressure, cut down, human nature*
p. 184

Reading Skill
Identifying Internal and External Conflict
p. 186

Literary Term
Oxymoron
p. 188

Language and Literacy Connections

The connecting theme for Unit 9 is making decisions and handling difficult situations.

	Language	Literacy
Vocabulary	**Set 1:** decision-making **Set 2:** collaborative decision-making	**Nonfiction:** brainstorm the options, consider the consequences, decide on a solution, define the problem, evaluate your ideas, make a (careful) decision, peer pressure, pros and cons
Grammar	**Third Conditional: Statements** If you had/'d come earlier, we wouldn't have waited in line so long. If I hadn't come, I would have regretted it. **Third Conditional: Questions** What would you have done if you'd fallen? If someone had told you to do something dangerous, would you have done it? If I'd asked you to come with me, what would you have said?	**Nonfiction** If we had made a different decision, the outcome might have been better. **Fiction** If she'd had the guts, she would have told James to be quiet and leave Penny alone. But if the photo had been of me, what would I have done? If I'd been brave, I would have said something before.
Skills	**Pronunciation:** connected speech: linking **Process Writing:** organizing information and engaging the reader	**Reading:** identifying internal and external conflict **Literary Term:** oxymoron
International English	middle school/high school/secondary school; schedule/timetable	

Vocabulary

Lesson Objectives

- to learn vocabulary for decision-making: *brainstorm the options, consider the consequences, decide on a solution, define the problem, evaluate your ideas, learn from your mistakes, make a decision, regret*
- to read and say a poem about making decisions
- to recognize and practice connected speech: linking

Materials
Audio Tracks 99 to 103; Video

Warm Up

Point out the unit title and elicit its meaning (make a decision). Brainstorm the kinds of decisions students have to make.

A TRACK 99 TB p. 226 **Listen. What decision does Annette want to talk about?**

- This activity introduces the new vocabulary in context. Have students find Vincent (the boy in the wheelchair). Explain it's Information Day for middle school students moving on to high school and Annette is talking to a guidance counselor. Ask the question, then play the audio and elicit the answer. See **ETB** for more questions.
- Ask the Unit 8 teaser question *What will help Vincent with his decision?* and check (the same steps Annette took: brainstorm options, evaluate them, consider consequences)

Answer
She wants to talk about whether to study computing or study a language so that she can travel and live abroad.

International English

Draw a line across the board with numbers 5 to 18 representing students' ages. Above the line, write *kindergarten* (5–6), *elementary school* (6–11), *middle school* (11–14), *high school* (14–18). Below the line, write *primary school* (5–11) and *secondary school* (11–16). (See the **ETB** for more information.)

B TRACK 100 TB p. 226 **Find and number the words in A. Then listen and check.**

- Point out the example (1) and have students find it in the picture, then find and number the other words in pairs.
- Play the audio for students to check their answers.

Answers
1 *evaluate your ideas* 2 brainstorm the options
3 consider the consequences 4 learn from your mistakes
5 decide on a solution 6 define the problem 7 regret
8 make a decision

C TRACK 101 TB p. 226 **Close your eyes. Listen, visualize, and say.**

- Prepare students for the visualization (see TB p. 21).
- Play the audio, allowing students to visualize the ideas.
- Ask students to make notes about what they visualized and then explain to a partner.

D Look, choose, and write. Then read and write the letters.

- Students are going to contextualize the new vocabulary by analyzing an example and putting the steps in a logical order. Have students read steps a–e. Look at the example and elicit what the next step is. Students order the rest of the steps, writing the letters in the boxes.
- Have students compare answers and then write the word or phrase from A for each step. Check answers.

Answers
1 *define the problem; e* 2 brainstorm the options; a
3 evaluate your ideas; d 4 consider the consequences; b
5 decide on a solution; c

E TRACK 102 TB p. 226 **Listen and write. Then watch and say.**

- Play the video or audio for students to listen and enjoy.
- Have students look in their books and complete the blanks. Play the audio for students to check answers.
- Play the audio or video again for students to join in with the poem. Encourage them to copy the rhythm and pronunciation.

Answers
1 *problem* 2 options 3 ideas 4 consequences
5 solution

F TRACK 103 TB p. 226 **Pronunciation. Listen and say. Copy the linking. Think of other examples of linking like these.**

- Explain that we often link words in English in different ways, e.g. we can introduce a new sound between words, combine sounds, leave out sounds, or move sounds.
- Play the audio once. Have students listen and say the linking phrases. Elicit the way each one links.
- Have students work in pairs to find other phrases in the poem with similar linking. Elicit answers and write them on the board. Drill the linking.

Suggested Answers
the_(y)_options: do_(w)_I, so_(w)_I (intrusion of /j/ or /w/)
evaluate_your: the *t* is not heard, so there's a slight pause before the *y* (glottal stop)
I can'(t)_decide: C an(d) D, bes(t) decision (elision of /t/ or /d/)
decide_on: define_it, bad_or (consonant-vowel linking)

Cool Down

Have students role-play in pairs using the vocabulary. Student A chooses two clubs from the picture on pp. 114–115, and Student B must help Student A decide which to join.

Practice **Student's App:** Vocabulary Practice; Spoken Word Video

Explore Language

Lesson Objectives

- to learn how to use third conditional: statements
- to practice vocabulary for decision-making

Materials
Audio Tracks 104 and 105

Warm Up

Have students look at the pictures on p. 116 (or display them using the TTL) and guess what's going on in pairs. Then put them in different pairs to compare ideas. If needed, provide some language, e.g. *amusement park*, *bumper cars*, etc.

A TRACK 104 TB p. 226 **Listen and read. What did Annette learn? Did she enjoy her day?**

- This activity is a presentation of the grammar in context. Tell students that they are going to listen to Annette and Yousef talking during their day out. Play the audio and have students follow the dialogue in their books. Have them discuss their guesses from the Warm Up.
- Ask the questions *What did Annette learn? Did she enjoy her day?* Have students look at the dialogue again in pairs and discuss the answers. Check with the class.

Answers
She learned not to be late and to pack her own lunch.
She enjoyed her day.

- Ask *Why does Annette pause and say "um … fun!"?* Elicit ideas from students. Point out that she's being sarcastic as the rides were probably scary experiences for her (judging from her expression in the pictures). Then ask further comprehension questions (see **ETB**).

B Look at A. Complete the table. What verb form comes after *if*?

- Display the table using the TTL. Tell students to scan the dialogue in A and complete the table with the missing words. Have them compare answers in pairs.
- Students should now have the skills and strategies to be able to discuss the grammar forms and notice patterns by themselves. When they have completed the table, discuss the word order, form, and patterns together, but let your class guide the discussion. If you feel that students need more guidance, use the notes in the **ETB**.

Answers
'd; have; brought; would; hadn't; regretted
Past perfect comes after *if*.

- Refer students to the Grammar tip *Look* and drill the sentences. Discuss whether students feel confident using any of the three. You could point out that the third sentence is the least formal and would typically only be spoken, rather than written.

Practice Resource Bank: Grammar Printout
Student's App: Grammar Practice

C Think and discuss. Then choose.

- This activity focuses on the usage of the third conditional. Ask students to refer back to the table in B and discuss the sentences and answer options in pairs. Then check answers.
- Elicit the third conditional structure on the board: *if* + past perfect → *would* + *have* + past participle. Compare it to the first and second conditional structures. Leave the structure on the board for students' reference.

Answers
1 didn't happen 2 imagined result 3 True

D TRACK 105 TB p. 226 **Listen and say.**

- Tell students they're going to practice saying sentences with the third conditional to help with pronunciation in fluent speech and so that they begin to internalize the structure. Play the audio and have students repeat each example chorally. (See TB p. 23, Making Language Drills Fun.)

E Read the regrets and considerations. Complete with the correct form of the verbs.

- This activity provides controlled practice of third conditional statements. Read the example and point out that the *if* clause can come at the beginning of the sentence or in the middle.
- Have students complete the sentences and compare their answers in pairs.
- To check answers, invite students to read a sentence aloud or display answers with the TTL.

Answers
1 *hadn't worked; 'd have failed* 2 hadn't gotten up; wouldn't have missed 3 would have sent; 'd remembered 4 would have learned; 'd lived 5 'd known; would have painted 6 hadn't joined; wouldn't have met 7 would have called; 'd remembered 8 'd gone; would have felt

F Write new sentences for the *if* clauses in E. Then compare with a friend. Whose sentences are the most interesting?

- This activity provides freer oral practice of third conditional statements. Look at the examples and have students identify the sentences in E (1 and 2).
- Give students time to think of a different *if* clause for at least three or four sentences in E. Encourage them to be as creative as possible.
- Students compare ideas in pairs. Invite students to share ideas with the class.

Cool Down

Play *Chain Game* (see TB p. 25) with third conditional sentences. Start with a prompt: *If it hadn't rained* yesterday … See how many *would(n't) have* clauses students can come up with.

Global Citizenship

Lesson Objectives

- to learn vocabulary for collaborative decision-making: *be fair, control your emotions, fit in with, get your own way, have your say, independence, individual identity, peer pressure, pros and cons*
- to explore how our decisions affect other people
- to practice listening for gist and details

Materials
Audio Tracks 106 to 108; Audio Track 1

Opening Question

Ask the opening question: *How do the decisions we make affect other people?* Give students a time limit (e.g. 30 seconds) to discuss ideas using a Think, Pair, Share routine (see TB p. 20).

A TRACK 106 TB p. 226 **Listen to Fatima talk to Lily about decision-making in her family. What kinds of decisions do Fatima's family make?**

- Tell students they are going to listen to Fatima talking to Lily about the decisions her family makes. Invite students to make guesses about what these decisions could be.
- Play the audio for students to check their guesses in pairs.
- Ask the gist question and nominate students to answer. Then ask *Does Fatima usually agree or disagree with her parents?* (both). Ask further comprehension questions (see **ETB**). Then discuss whether students make decisions like these as a family. If not, who makes the decision?

Answer
They make decisions about what to do and where to go on vacation.

B TRACK 107 TB p. 226 **Look at the pictures and definitions in A and write. Then listen and check.**

- Look at the example together and elicit what *fit in with* means (be accepted by a group of people). Refer students to the vocabulary box in B and have them match the words and phrases to the pictures and definitions in A. Allow them to work in pairs and discuss their answers.
- Play the audio for students to check answers. Then play it again to practice the pronunciation, pausing after each word or phrase for them to repeat.

Answers
1 *fit in with* 2 pros and cons 3 individual identity
4 control your emotions 5 independence 6 be fair
7 have your say 8 peer pressure 9 get your own way

TRACK 1 TB p. 227 **Visualization**

The TTL includes a visualization audio track for this vocabulary set. (See TB p. 21.)

C Read the school poster and complete.

- This activity provides contextualized controlled vocabulary practice. Discuss the phrases around the sentences and their meaning. Then have students read the sentences.
- Have students complete the sentences and compare answers in pairs. Check answers.

Answers
1 *independence* 2 fair 3 pros; cons 4 pressure; identity 5 emotions; way 6 say; fit

D TRACK 108 TB p. 227 **Now listen to Professor Jackson. How does the brain affect how 11- to 13-year-olds feel and act?**

- Ask students to listen to a professor talk about the brain. Invite students to share what they know about the brain.
- Listening for gist: ask the question and play the audio. Students discuss in groups. Elicit answers from volunteers.

Answers
It can change the way they think and make decisions.
It makes them more self-conscious and emotional.

E Listen again. Write *True* or *False*.

- Listening for details: have students read the sentences before they listen again. Encourage them to write the answer for any sentences they remember, but then listen carefully to check.
- Play the audio and let students write the answers. Check as a class and discuss any answers students disagree on. Elicit which, if any, information was new or surprising. Ask students if they heard any reasons why it might not be a good idea for Fatima in A to make big decisions.

Answers
1 False 2 *False* 3 True 4 False 5 False 6 True

Discussion Questions

- Draw students' attention to the discussion questions: *How do you make decisions in your family? How can children be involved in decisions about their community?* Have students discuss the questions in pairs or small groups (see **ETB**). Encourage them to remember what Fatima said about decision-making in her family. Focus on the concept of decisions on different scales from family decisions and community decisions to nation- or world-related decisions.
- Return to the opening question to ask again: *How do the decisions we make affect other people?* Review the ideas discussed at the beginning of the lesson and then encourage students to share any new ideas.

Cool Down

Have students discuss in groups how the world would be a better place if children had their say in important decisions. Prompt them by asking *Would people be less poor? Would the environment be better protected? Would animals be safer?* Ask students to make a list and then share their ideas in class.

Practice Student's App: Vocabulary Practice; Listening Practice

Explore Language

Lesson Objectives

- to learn how to use third conditional: questions
- to practice vocabulary for collaborative decision-making

Materials
Audio Tracks 109 and 110

Warm Up

With books closed, write the first sentence from the dialogue with a blank on the board: *Last week, I decided to ________ to everything that people asked me to do.* Students discuss what the two missing words are. Elicit ideas and what students think the conversation is about.

A TRACK 109 TB p. 227 **Listen and read. What new experience did Grace have last week?**

- This activity is a presentation of the grammar in context. Tell students they are going to hear three friends, Grace, Ana, and Tony, talking in a café. Have them look at the pictures and say where they are.
- Play the audio. Have students follow the dialogue in their books and check to see if their predictions from the Warm Up were correct (the answer is *say "yes"*).
- Ask the question *What new experience did Grace have last week?* Invite students to discuss the question in pairs before you elicit the answer from the class. Check students understand what zip-lining is by referring them to the second picture. Ask if any students have tried zip-lining and, if not, if they would like to try it. Then ask further comprehension questions (see **ETB**).

Answer
She went zip-lining.

B **Look at A. Complete the table. Is the position of the *if* clause always the same?**

- Display the table using the TTL. Give students a time limit to scan the dialogue and find the missing words in the table. Have them work individually and then check answers in pairs.
- When they have completed the table, discuss the word order, form, and patterns together, but let your class guide the discussion. If you feel that students need more guidance, use the notes in the **ETB**.
- Draw students' attention to the Grammar tip *Watch Out*. Point out that this is a common mistake and students need to think carefully before making a sentence or question with the third conditional.

Answers
would; if; fallen; told; would; have; 'd; would; said
No—it can be positioned at the beginning or middle of the sentence.

C **Think and discuss. Then choose.**

- Ask students to read the statements on usage and refer to the examples in the table in B. Have them discuss the statements in pairs.
- To check answers, read the sentences and have the class call out *true* or *false*. Elicit that although we use past verb forms (past perfect), we are not talking about the past but about a situation that hasn't actually happened.

Answers
1 False 2 True

D TRACK 110 TB p. 227 **Listen and say.**

- Tell students they're going to practice saying questions with the third conditional to help with pronunciation in fluent speech and to consolidate what they've learned. Play the audio and have students repeat each example chorally. (See TB p. 23, Making Language Drills Fun.)

E **Read the situations and complete the questions. Sometimes there is more than one answer. Then ask and answer.**

- This activity provides controlled practice of third conditional questions. Read the example and check the meaning of *regret*. Look at the question together and point out that the same verb phrase *go to the beach* has been used in both the prompt and the question.
- Give students time to complete the questions individually and then compare with a partner.
- Check answers by inviting pairs of students to read an exchange aloud.

Answers
1 *if you hadn't gone to the beach* 2 if you'd known I was waiting for you 3 how would you have felt / would you have felt better? 4 if you hadn't hurt your leg 5 what would you have bought / would you have bought anything

F **Think about three decisions you made this year. What would have happened if you had made a different decision? Talk to a friend.**

- For this freer oral practice, students use their own experiences to elicit questions in pairs. Read the example prompt and elicit how to complete the question.
- Give students time to think about three decisions they made and make notes. Monitor and help with ideas if necessary.
- In pairs, students take turns sharing a decision and answering their partner's question. Monitor and check for grammatical accuracy. Invite students to report on their partner to the class.

Cool Down

Divide the class into groups of three and have them act out the dialogue (or part of it) in A. Invite groups to perform for the class.

Practice **Resource Bank:** Grammar Printout
Student's App: Grammar Practice

Write About It

Lesson Objectives

- to learn how to edit and publish (Process Writing Step 4)
- to plan and write an instructional article
- to organize information and engage the reader

Materials
Examples or pictures of weekly schedules (WU); Support Writing printouts from the Resource Bank (G)

Warm Up

Display the schedules you brought in. Have students discuss in groups why people use these schedules and whether they use one. Elicit ideas from the class.

A Read the article. Check (✔) the points the article mentions.

- This lesson corresponds with the instructional text in Unit 9 of the **Literacy Book**. Draw students' attention to the title of the article. Elicit on the board what vocabulary students think will be included in the article.
- Have students read the article once to check their ideas. and to check the points mentioned in the article. Check answers. Then ask comprehension questions (see **ETB**).

Answers
1; 2; 4

International English

Drill the words and elicit in which other contexts these words are used (e.g. for trains and buses). *Timetable* usually refers to a written plan that is the same each week or month. To talk about plans, *schedule* can also be used in British English.

B Look at the structure of the article. Read and complete.

- Students are going to look at the article's structure. Look at the features and example. Elicit how the list makes the article clear. (It's easy to see how many points there are.)
- Have pairs discuss and complete the rest of the table. Check answers as a class, eliciting different opinions.

Suggested Answers
1 "Keep Your Eye on the Clock: Time Management for Kids"; It has a catchy phrase to introduce the topic and explains what the topic is about. 2 It helps the reader see how many points there are / where each point starts and ends. 3 "Here are some tips to help you." "Make it a work of art!" "So, no more excuses."; The author's advice and opinions are easy to understand. 4 "Your life will be more efficient: you'll have the time to do what you need to do and what you want to do."; It's clear why the author makes these suggestions to the readers.

C Look at the language of the article. Match the features to the examples.

- Students are now going to focus on the language used in the article. Have students match the features to the examples in pairs. Check answers.
- Read the text in the pink box and elicit other genres where short sentences and bullet points may be used (e.g. recipes and instructions).

Answers
1 c 2 a 3 b

D Think and discuss. You're going to write an article called *How Can You Make Good Decisions in Your Life?* Use one of the Generating Ideas techniques.

- This lesson focuses on checking your work after writing, i.e. editing it.
- Write the title of the article on the board. Have students choose a Generating Ideas technique and use it to note down ideas, either individually or in pairs. Monitor and provide language help if needed.
- Then have students share their ideas in small groups.

E Plan your article. Use your ideas in D and one of the Planning techniques.

- Tell students they are going to plan their instructional article. Point out each section in the colored notes.
- Have students organize their ideas in D using a suitable Planning technique. Allow them to work in pairs.

F Write a first draft. Then review it using a checklist.

- Have students write a draft of their article in their notebooks, referring to their plan in E. They should read their drafts and make any corrections or improvements using a checklist.
- Ask students to turn to p. 143 to learn about **Process Writing Step 4: Editing and Publishing** (see TB p. 214). Students will need to do this step before they do G.

G Now write your article. Re-read and edit it. Then publish it.

- Have students write their articles on paper or on the Support printout.
- Ask them to read it once more and edit it for spelling and grammar errors. Then they make a final version. You can display the articles in class at the end of the lesson.
- Ask students to work in pairs, read each other's article, and follow the instructions.

Cool Down

Ask students to make a schedule for next week with things they have to do. Have them compare their schedules in small groups and explain what they can do to make sure they do everything on time.

Practice **Resource Bank:** Writing Game, *How Do You Do That?*
Student's App: Writing Practice

Talk About It

Lesson Objectives

- to have a conversation about spending a day with friends
- to invite contributions to a conversation

Materials
Video

Warm Up

Write on the board *Our Perfect Day*. Give students 30 seconds to think about what would happen on a perfect day for them. When time is up, have students compare ideas in pairs. Then elicit ideas and write them on the board. Leave them on the board for students to refer back to later in the lesson.

A TB p. 240 **Watch and listen. What does Wade think is an important decision?**

- Tell students they are going to watch a video of three friends, Wade, Maria, and Veronica, talking about a perfect day. The video provides a presentation of the functional language needed for inviting contribution to a conversation. With books closed, play the video for students to watch, listen, and see if any of the ideas from the Warm Up are mentioned. Check answers.
- Ask the comprehension question *What does Wade think is an important decision?* If necessary, play the video again and then allow some time for students to discuss the answer in pairs. Check the answer. Ask more comprehension questions (see **ETB**).

Answer
Wade thinks it's important to decide on the meals.

B Watch again. Put the phrases in the order you hear them.

- Tell students they are going to focus on the functional language the friends use to invite each other to contribute. Have them read the phrases and look at the example number.
- Play the video again and have students order the phrases. Have students compare their answers in pairs before checking with the class.
- Ask students why Veronica asks Maria a question. Elicit that she wants to know Maria's opinion and is trying to encourage her to participate in the discussion. Point out that some people, like Maria, are quieter than others and sometimes they tend not to speak up without being prompted, especially in group situations. Explain that it is important to involve everyone in a conversation and that sometimes we might need to nudge people by asking questions.

Answers
1 e 2 b 3 d 4 f 5 a 6 c

C Imagine you're going to spend a day with two friends. What do you want to do and why? Think and plan.

- Students are going to brainstorm ideas on their own before they plan their perfect day.
- Have students plan individually. Encourage them to think of as many details as possible, including what activities they will do, what and where they will eat and drink, and so on. Students can use some of the ideas they had in the Warm Up. Although students will have their conversation in groups, they don't need to plan together. An element of surprise will make the conversations more realistic and encourage more spontaneous responses. Monitor while students are making their notes and help with language if needed.

D Talk with your friends using phrases from B. Plan your perfect day together.

- Put students in groups of three. Tell them they are going to discuss and plan a perfect day together like the friends in the video did.
- Give students time to have their conversations and discuss their ideas from C, using phrases from B. Encourage them to also use phrases for summarizing points (see Unit 3). Tell students that they don't have to mention all their ideas from C—it is more important that they respond to their group's ideas.
- Then invite students from each group to present their decisions to the class. Set up a class vote on the best "perfect day."
- Have students work with one person from their group in D and discuss whether everyone was included in the conversation. If they weren't, encourage them to review the things they could do to make sure everyone is included next time.

Cool Down

Ask students to write a short text message to another friend telling them about their perfect day. Have students compare messages in their groups and see whether they wrote different things. Invite volunteer students to read their message to the class.

Practice **Student's App:** Speaking Skills Practice; Speaking Video

Think It Over

Lesson Objectives

- to review what has been learned in the unit
- to reflect on the unit and their own progress
- to think about learning strategies and how to continue learning at home

Materials

Packs of sticky notes

Warm Up

With books closed, write *MISTAKES* down the board and elicit the acrostic poem from p. 125. Give students definitions and synonyms to help them find the words. Then discuss what they think about the meaning: Do mistakes mean they are starting to acquire knowledge, experience, and skills? Elicit opinions.

How well did you meet the challenge of Unit 9? Read and respond.

My Favorite Mistakes

- Tell students they are going to think about what they learned during the unit and how they can improve. Point out that making mistakes is a natural part of learning and it can actually help you improve. Tell students that they are going to think about the mistakes they made in the unit, as well as what they have learned. Let them know that it's important that they don't worry about what other people think or say, as different students will have made different mistakes. Point out that everyone can find some way of improving, even if they think they didn't make any mistakes!
- Have students work in groups to think about the activities they did during the unit. Give each group a pack of sticky notes and have them write an idea on each one. Encourage students to think about the different things they studied or remember from the unit, e.g. third conditional, how to make decisions, contributing in a conversation, interesting ideas, things that made me think. Then have students stick their notes onto a board or a poster and display them on the wall. Have groups go around the classroom and look at each other's sticky note board.
- Draw students' attention to the graphic organizer. Refer students to the different sections: *Two mistakes I made in this unit that moved my learning on are …; Two things (knowledge) I learned about decision-making are …; Two things (experience and skills) I learned to say or do in English are …* Have students talk in pairs about the different sections. Encourage them to focus particularly on the first section and to discuss how they are going to avoid making these mistakes in the future and when they will use their experience and skills again.
- Ask students what they would like to work on to improve. Refer students to the final section in the graphic organizer, *One thing I want to work on next month is …*, and the notes below it. Have students think about their ideas and then discuss them with a friend.
- When you feel they have enough ideas, have students work individually to fill out the organizer. Remind them that they should write their own responses about themselves. Monitor and help as necessary. Look at what students are writing so you can tailor your classes and any additional practice to their needs.
- Ask if anyone has the same goals as their friend. Point out that goals should be personal and each student should choose those they think they would benefit from most. Remind students that everyone learns differently, so they will all have different answers.

Looking Forward

Draw students' attention to the characters at the bottom of the page. Have students say who they are and what they remember about them. (Ana and Tony Moreno appear in Lesson 4, p. 120. They are talking to their friend Grace about her experience with zip-lining.) Have students look at the speech bubble and make predictions about which country they are going to next. Tell students they will find out the answer in Lesson 1 of the next unit.

Practice **Resource Bank:** Unit Test
Student's App: Vocabulary and Grammar Review

Literacy

Get Ready to Read

Lesson Objectives

- to activate prior knowledge about decisions and consequences
- to guide inquiry and deepen understanding through a Step Inside VTR
- to preview the reading skill of identifying internal and external conflict

Materials

VTR printout from the Resource Bank (A, B, C)

Warm Up

Write *Safe* and *Risky* on either side of the board. Say different activities or situations and have students call out *Safe!* or *Risky!* according to their opinion. Elicit reasons why.

Step Inside

A Look at the picture. Choose a person or a thing. What can they see?

- This VTR encourages students to step inside a person or object they can see and imagine their point of view. Start by asking what they see in the picture of people choosing different paths. Provide vocabulary where needed.
- Ask students to imagine they can step inside the picture and become a person or thing in it. Encourage them to think about what they can see, hear, and feel and to be imaginative!
- Have students discuss their ideas in pairs, then as a class.

Here's an example of this part of the routine.

Teacher: Who or what are you?
Student A: I'm the Risky sign.
Student B: I'm this person who's going inside the dark castle.
Teacher: What can you see?
Student B: I can see the door to the castle. It's very big and heavy.
Teacher: Can you hear anything?
Student B: I can hear the bats flying above me and a noise behind the door.

B What do you think they believe?

- Tell students to think about the person or thing they chose. Ask them to think about what they believe about themselves and other people, about what they see, and so on.
- Have students discuss ideas in pairs, then as a class. Encourage other students to ask questions and contribute ideas to the discussion.

Here's an example of this part of the routine.

Teacher: What do you believe?
Student A: I think this woman believes that risky decisions are a bad idea if you have children.
Student B: I agree. But I also thinks she believes that some risky decisions are fun. She used to make them when she didn't have children.

C What do you think they care about?

- Ask students to think about what's important to the people or things they chose to be. Have students discuss their ideas in pairs, then as a class. Make notes to revisit in the Think Together lesson.

Here's an example of this part of the routine.

Teacher: What does the person or thing care about?
Student A: I think the man with the flashlight cares about success. He wants to be successful, so he doesn't mind taking risky decisions.
Teacher: What does the flashlight tell you?
Student A: Maybe that he cares about his safety. The flashlight shows he's prepared.

Transition

Ask *Is anyone in the picture making a difficult decision? Why? What do you think the decision is?*

D Think and discuss. What is a decision? What decisions do we make every day?

- Tell students they are going to think about decisions. Elicit the meaning of *decision* and if anyone made any decisions today. Encourage them to think of small, insignificant choices they make, as well as more important ones. Let students think and then discuss the questions in pairs.

Suggested Answers

A decision is when we make a choice. Every day, we choose what to eat or wear, what music to listen to, etc.

E Think and predict. Then write. Look at the picture from *Making Decisions*. What do you think the girl is feeling? Why might she be feeling that way?

- This activity previews the skill of identifying internal and external conflict. Look at the picture together. Ask students to describe it.
- Give students time to think about their answers to the questions, as well as reasons. Then discuss as a class.

Answers

Students' own answers

Now read **Making Decisions**

Nonfiction: *Making Decisions—* Instructional Text

Lesson Objectives

- to activate prior knowledge about making decisions
- to make a personal connection to the reading

Materials
Audio Tracks 38 and 39

Warm Up

Play *Stand Up, Sit Down* (see TB p. 26). Use statements based on the reading, e.g. *It's a good idea to make decisions quickly.* (False) *It's OK to ask people for advice before you make a decision.* (True) Don't check answers at this stage.

TRACK 38 TB p. 236 Reading Approach

First Reading: Engage with the Text

- Ask students to look at the text and graphic features on pp. 138–139 and think about the genre. Elicit ideas but don't confirm yet.
- Play the audio and have students follow along. Pause at the end of p. 139 and elicit the genre (instructional text).
- Play the rest of the audio and discuss the answers from the Warm Up. Then look at the Words in Context.

TRACK 39 TB p. 237 Words in Context

- Give students a few minutes to find and highlight each word and identify the kind of word.
- Write these strategies on the board for students to use: *sentences, separate parts of word, positive/negative, pictures, prefixes, world knowledge, contrasting ideas.*
- Have students work in pairs to discuss the words. Tell them there is one strategy they can't use: they may not actually use all the strategies to figure out the words, but there is one strategy that can't be used at all.

on the bench (p. 138, noun phrase) The sentence shows that she isn't playing from here. Knowledge of team games will help with this phrase. Strategies to use: separate parts of word; surrounding words and sentences; pictures; world knowledge of team sports

stick with (p. 138, phrasal verb) The earlier part of the sentence shows that *drop down* is a move from A to B team. Later it contrasts the two verb phrases, showing that *stick with* is the alternative option to *drop down.* Strategies to use: separate parts of word; surrounding words and sentences; contrasting ideas

pressure (p. 139 / p. 140, noun) The first sentence shows that *pressure* is something that makes us decide quickly. The surrounding sentences tell us it has negative connotations. The second instance provides an example, and the callout includes the phrase *peer pressure.* Strategies to use: surrounding words and sentences; positive/negative

cut down (p. 139, phrasal verb) The following paragraph provides context and an explanation of the heading. Clues are given in *too many choices, remove the ones that don't help,* and *fewer things to pick from.* Strategies to use: surrounding words and sentences; separate parts of word

human nature (p. 140, noun) This can be broken down and the following sentence provides a definition. Strategies to use: surrounding words and sentences; separate parts of word

- Go through each word in turn to elicit the meaning and how they know. Ask students which strategy on the board can't be used and why (prefixes). Play the audio to practice the pronunciation.

Second Reading: Analyze the Text and Features

- Allow students to read the text again silently at their own pace. To keep them focused, ask them to find out what decision Lena made at the end. (She decided to change to B team and try A team again next season.)
- Ask some questions to check comprehension: *Why did Lena want to leave A team?* (because she hardly plays) *Why didn't she play in A team?* (because the other players are better) Discuss if students think she made a good decision and why or why not. See the **ETB** for more comprehension questions.
- Discuss the questions in the orange boxes.
  - **Personalization** (p. 138): *How do you make decisions?* Have students reflect on a couple of decisions they made recently and explain the process they followed to a partner. Invite students to share ideas.
  - **Fun Fact** (p. 140): Ask students to brainstorm in pairs situations when children their age may feel peer pressure, both face-to-face and online. Elicit ideas and discuss why peer pressure can be dangerous.
  - **Personalization** (p. 141): *When was the last time you had to make a decision in a hurry? What did you decide?* Give students time to think on their own and then share experiences in pairs.

Third Reading: Interact with the Text

- Tell students they are going to use the information from the reading to make a decision. Give them time to think of a real or imaginary decision they have to make.
- Have students look at the reading again and follow the steps to making decisions on p. 140. Encourage students to make a pros and cons list like Lena did. Prompt them to think about the consequences and then make a decision. Have students share their thoughts in pairs.

Cool Down

Have students think about a time when they made a wrong decision. Have them discuss it in pairs and reflect on what they learned from it. Elicit ideas.

Practice Student's App: Story Player

Explore the Reading

Lesson Objectives

- to understand and analyze *Making Decisions* through reading comprehension activities
- to learn through CLIL (social studies): ethics
- to make a personal connection to the reading

Materials
Pieces of paper (WU); a coin (B)

Warm Up

With books closed, ask students to remember what they read about in *Making Decisions*. Then put them in groups of five or six and hand out a piece of paper to each group. Students write one thing they remember from the text on the paper and pass it around to the next person. At the end, one student reads aloud the information on the paper. Have groups trade papers and discuss them.

A Think and write. Choose the strategy that matches each sentence.

- Display the headings from the reading and have students discuss in pairs or small groups what they remember about each strategy.
- Then give students time to read the sentences and match them to the strategies individually.
- Put students in pairs or small groups to compare their answers. Check answers (or display them using the TTL).
- Have students work in pairs to put the strategies in order. Then have them check their answers by looking back at p. 139.

Answers
1 Big or Small? 2 Cut Down Your Choices
3 It's Good to Talk 4 Pros and Cons List
5 Stop and Think!

B Think and write. Imagine you have a difficult decision with two choices. A friend says you should just flip a coin. Is that a good strategy? Why or why not?

- Put students in pairs. Demonstrate flipping a coin. Tell each student to choose *heads* or *tails*. Then flip the coin. Tell students that the winners get to choose whether they want to start the conversation or have their partner start.
- Give students time to discuss their opinion and reasons in pairs. Before they begin, remind them of Dexter in *The Binary Life* (Unit 8). To help them generate ideas, encourage them to discuss the situations in which he flipped a coin and whether it worked well for him.
- Put students in different pairs to share their ideas. Invite volunteer students to share ideas with the class. Accept all opinions.

C Think, discuss, and write. Do you agree with Lena's decision? What would you have done in her position?

- Write a prompt on the board: *If Coach Williams had asked me to choose between the A team and B team, I would have …* Ask students to put themselves in Lena's shoes and think about what they would have decided and why.
- Have students write their answers and compare their ideas in pairs. Invite students to explain their opinion.

D Think and discuss. What do each of these people think about in each situation?

- Students are going to use a Think, Pair, Share routine (see TB p. 20) to discuss the questions and explore the CLIL social studies concept of ethics.
- Have students read the information about the three people. Ask a prompt question to help them think about what beliefs these people might have: *What do each of these people think is right or wrong in each situation?* Elicit ideas for the first person, e.g. *I should study a bit every day. I shouldn't go out the day before the test.*
- Have students think about the question on their own and then compare in pairs.

Cool Down

Play *Board Basketball*. Students are going to play in two teams. Draw a simple basketball court on the board with five symbols for each team. These should be placed in varying positions from the defense area to the scoring area. Use a different color for each team. Students have to answer questions correctly in order to advance from their basket to the opposing team's basket and score a point. Draw a line or color in the symbols to show the team's advancement across the court. You can ask questions about the reading or read sentences from the reading, leaving out a word and having students call it out, e.g. *You have to cut … your options.*

Practice Student's App: Reading Practice

Get Ready to Read

Lesson Objectives

- to activate prior knowledge about conflict when having to make a tough decision
- to practice the reading skill of identifying internal and external conflict

Warm Up

Write *Conflict* on the board and give an example. Say, for example, *My best friend told me about a new multiplayer game he/she has joined and he/she wants me to join, too. I've just checked online reviews, and they all say the game isn't very good. I don't know what to do.* Elicit what a conflict is (opposing opinions, ideas, or facts that confuse us) and examples of conflicts students have had.

A Read, think, and write. List two of the conflicts Pia faces in *Urgent Message*. Describe these conflicts.

- This lesson practices the skill of identifying internal and external conflict, which students previewed on p. 137. Have students look at the picture, or display it using the TTL. Elicit what story it is and what students remember about it (*Urgent Message* is the first reading in Unit 1).
- Ask students to read the extract and find two conflicts. Then have them write a few sentences describing the conflicts.
- Check answers as a class or display them on the board. Discuss any different opinions students might have.

Suggested Answers

Pia received a strange message, but her dad tells her it's a trick.
Her mom tells her not to reply to strange messages, but Pia feels anxious.
Pia is worried about her friend Helen and wants to help, but she thinks her parents won't understand.

B Read and write. Are these conflicts external (*E*) or internal (*I*)?

- Have students read the skills box. Then invite students to explain the difference between an external and internal conflict in their own words.
- Give students some time to read the sentences and decide if they're describing an external or internal conflict. Have them do this individually and compare answers in pairs. Check answers.

Answers

1 I 2 E 3 E 4 I

C Think and write. Look at the first picture from *It's Not OK*. Do you think the girl is facing an internal or external conflict? Why?

- Ask students to look at the picture on p. 144, or display it using the TTL. Ask *Is she facing an internal or external conflict? Why?* Have students discuss ideas in pairs, giving reasons for their ideas.
- Invite students to share their ideas with the class. Encourage students to take charge of the discussion, addressing their comments to each other; only join in to prompt when necessary.

Suggested Answer

The girl is probably facing an internal conflict because she isn't talking to anyone or arguing with anyone. Maybe she received a message and she doesn't know what to do. The look on her face shows she is unsure.

D Think and discuss. Think of a time when you faced a tough decision. What happened?

- Elicit synonyms of *tough* in this context (*difficult, hard*). Invite students to give examples of tough decisions people often have to make throughout their life. List these on the board.
- Give students time to think about their answers and make notes. Then put students in small groups to share their experiences.

Answers

Students' own answers

Cool Down

Write the story title on the board: *It's Not OK*. Brainstorm things or situations that aren't OK, e.g. *It's not OK to arrive late for a meeting. It's not OK to cheat in board games.* Then put students in pairs to discuss why these behaviors or actions aren't OK. Elicit ideas on the board, e.g. *It's not OK to arrive late for a meeting because it's rude to make other people wait. It's not OK to cheat in board games because you aren't showing respect for the other players.*

Now read **It's Not OK**

Fiction: *It's Not OK*—Story

Lesson Objectives

- to read a story about bullying
- to make a personal connection to the reading

Materials
Audio Tracks 40 and 41

Warm Up

Ask students to look just at the first picture of the story (display it if using the TTL). Read the first two lines in the story and have students guess in pairs what the message was. Encourage them to brainstorm ideas based on Miral's facial expression. Elicit ideas but don't check answers.

TRACK 40 TB p. 237 Reading Approach

First Reading: Engage with the Text

- Play the audio and pause at the end of p. 145. Elicit whether students' guesses in the Warm Up were correct.
- Continue to play the audio and pause again at the end of p. 147. In pairs, have students discuss what Miral should do.
- Play the rest of the audio. Elicit whether Miral did what they suggested she should do. Then look at the Words in Context.

TRACK 41 TB p. 237 Words in Context

- Give students a few minutes to find and highlight each word and to identify the kind of word.
- Write these strategies on the board for students to use with the words: *surrounding words and sentences, word families, world knowledge, positive/negative, L1 cognates, pictures.*
- Have students work in pairs to discuss the words. Remind students that different words will require different combinations of strategies to figure them out.

notification (p. 144, noun) The sentence shows that this is related to a cell phone and there's a noise (*beeped*). The paragraph implies that when you receive this, you open an app. Strategies to use: surrounding words and sentences; word families; world knowledge of cell phones

shoved (p. 144, verb) The sentence shows that *shove* is a way of putting an object into something quickly. The second part of the sentence gives a reason for this action and tells us that it has a negative connotation. Strategies to use: surrounding words and sentences; positive/negative; world knowledge

deafening silence (p. 145, noun) This phrase can be broken down into its two parts, and the core word in *deafening* can help. The two words can then be contrasted. Knowledge of difficult situations and how uncomfortable a silence between friends is will help. Strategies to use: word families (deaf); surrounding words and sentences; world knowledge

guts (p. 146, noun) The sentence structure (third conditional) tells us that Miral doesn't have this, but it would be a good thing if she did. Knowledge of peer pressure situations will help infer that a synonym is *brave*, which appears on p. 149. Strategies to use: surrounding words and sentences; world knowledge

selfies (p. 147, noun) The verb *take* gives us a clue that this is a type of photo and the picture illustrates the meaning. Strategies to use: possible L1 cognates; word families; picture

- Go through each word in turn to elicit the meaning and how they know. Play the audio to practice the pronunciation.

Second Reading: Analyze the Text and Features

- Have students read the story silently to consolidate understanding.
- Ask some questions to check comprehension, e.g. *Who did some students make fun of?* (Penny) *Why did they make fun of her?* (because she had new braces on her teeth) See the **ETB** for more comprehension questions.
- Discuss the questions in the orange boxes. Then look at the text focus.
  - **Critical Thinking** (p. 144): *Why are some decisions hard to make?* Have students discuss in pairs. Then invite students to share their answers. Discuss as a class what can help with making a difficult decision.
  - **Critical Thinking** (p. 147): *Why did the phone feel hot in Miral's hands?* Give students time to read that part of the story again and discuss their ideas in pairs. Elicit ideas (probably because she felt embarrassed and angry to receive the donkey message, so it resembles her feelings).
  - **Personalization** (p. 149): *Who would you talk to if you or someone you knew was being bullied?* Have students discuss the question in pairs. Invite students to share their answer.
  - **Text Focus** (p. 145): Have students read the explanation of *antagonist*. Review who the protagonist is (the main character; students looked at this in Unit 1, *Urgent Message*). Elicit who the antagonist is (Dana and/or the bullying).

Third Reading: Interact with the Text

- Have students act out one of the scenes between Miral and Penny or Miral and Mr. Costa in groups of three. One of them takes on the role of the narrator.
- Invite pairs of students to perform their scene for the class.

Cool Down

This activity promotes students' critical thinking. Put students in pairs and have them choose the most important piece of advice from the text. Explain it should be something everyone should know about. Elicit ideas from pairs.

Practice Student's App: Story Player

Explore the Reading

Lesson Objectives

- to understand and analyze *It's Not OK* through reading comprehension activities
- to practice the reading skill of identifying internal and external conflict
- to explore the SEL competency of responsible decision-making through reflecting on how current choices affect the future
- to make a personal connection to the text

Warm Up

With books closed, give pairs a minute to make notes about *It's Not OK*. Encourage them to note down as many details as they can. Elicit ideas on the board.

A Complete the story mountain with the main events from *It's Not OK*.

- Draw or display the story mountain on the board and elicit the parts of the story from students. (They should remember this from Unit 8 of the **Literacy Book**, p. 129.)
- Let students skim the story to remember more details. Then in pairs, have them discuss each section and complete the diagram. Provide language help if necessary.
- Invite students to come up and complete a section of the story mountain on the board. Alternatively, display answers using the TTL. Elicit any variations students have.

Suggested Answers

1 **Introduction** Main characters: Penny, Miral, Dana; Main setting: Penny, Miral and Dana's school 2 **Conflict** Bullying and cyberbullying of Penny because of her new braces 3 **Climax** Miral goes to see Mr. Costa. 4 **Falling action** Miral talks to Penny in class. Miral admits she was wrong and apologizes to Penny. 5 **Resolution** Miral and Penny are friends. They agree to play badminton together after school.

B Think and write. What internal conflict do you think Dana might be having at the end of the story?

- Have students find Dana in the story (the girl with red hair). Then put them in pairs to discuss how she feels in each scene
- Have students write their answers individually.

Suggested Answer

Dana's internal conflict is that she knows that bullying is wrong, but she enjoyed making some of her friends laugh. I think Dana is wondering whether to apologize to Penny.

C Think and discuss. Why do you think going to see Mr. Costa was such a difficult choice for Miral to make?

- Ask students to skim the first four pages of the story. Tell them to look for clues about how Miral feels and what thoughts she has.
- Have students discuss the question in small groups. Ask if they have ever felt an internal conflict like this and what they did in the end. Was it the right decision? Have students share their experiences with the class.

Suggested Answers

If she goes to see Mr. Costa, the other students might know it was her. Maybe she doesn't want to get bullied herself. This might be the first time Miral speaks to Mr. Costa on her own, so maybe she's nervous of his reaction.

D Think and discuss. What do you think might have happened if Miral had decided to take action about the bullying when it started?

- Students are going to explore the SEL competency of responsible decision-making: reflect on how current choices affect the future.
- Have students think how the story would be different if Miral had stopped the bullying at the start. Remind students that these are hypothetical ideas and encourage them to use the third conditional if they can. Write the structure on the board to help: *If … had/hadn't …, … would / wouldn't have (happened).*
- Have students discuss in pairs and then share as a class. Encourage students to think of ways to prevent such a situation in their future. See the **ETB** for further discussion of the SEL competency.

Literary Term: Oxymoron

Underline the oxymorons.

- Draw students' attention to the information about oxymorons. Read the first sentence and elicit the words with opposite meanings (*clearly, confused*).
- Have students underline the oxymorons in the rest of the sentences individually and compare answers in pairs. Then check answers.

Now find three pairs of oxymorons in the reading.

- Have students scan the reading to find more oxymorons.
- Ask students to compare answers in pairs, then check answers as a class. Ask students if they can think of any oxymorons that are used frequently in their language.

Answers

1 clearly confused 2 bittersweet 3 seriously funny 4 love/hate

Examples of oxymorons found in the reading: deafening silence, old news, open secret

Cool Down

Put students in pairs to do a role-play between Penny and Dana. Explain that Dana is apologizing to Penny. Allow students to decide how Penny will respond. Students can discuss the dialogue and write it down before they act it out. Invite students to perform for the class.

Practice **Resource Bank:** Literary Term Printout
Student's App: Reading Practice; Literary Term Practice

Think Together

Lesson Objectives

- to make connections between the readings
- to explore the key concept: How do we handle difficult choices?
- to reflect on the unit and provide personal thoughts and opinions

Warm Up

With books closed, have students work in pairs to remember the six steps from *Making Decisions*. Give them a minute and then elicit ideas on the board. Ask students to open their books and check their answers.

A Think and write. How could Miral from *It's Not OK* have used Lena's six steps from *Making Decisions* to decide what to do?

- Have students work in pairs to adapt Lena's notes so they are true for Miral. Monitor and provide language help if needed.
- Invite students to share ideas with the class.

Suggested Answers

1 Miral is trying to decide what to do about Dana's bullying. 2 Tell a teacher or the principal; not say anything; tell Penny; ask a friend what to do. 3 Everyone knows about the pictures; Dana and others think the pictures are funny; Penny already knows about the pictures; Penny is embarrassed; Penny is on Miral's badminton team. 4 Miral might get in trouble. They might not stop bullying Penny anyway. Miral will know she did something to help Penny. 5 Tell the principal. 6 This was a good decision because Miral and Penny are still friends.

B Make a list. What kinds of decisions do you have to make in your life? Think of an example for each kind. Do a Think, Pair, Share.

- Students are going to do a Think, Pair, Share routine (see TB p. 20) to discuss different kinds of decisions they have to make in their lives.
- Ask *What kind of decisions do you have to make in your life?* and ask students to think of ideas and examples on their own. If necessary, elicit an example from the class: *I have to decide how to organize my time. I have to decide what to do first when I get home—do my homework or help my dad make dinner.*
- Invite students to share ideas in pairs before they share with the class.

C Choose one of the decisions from your list in B. Choose a decision-making strategy and make a decision. What might the consequences of your decision be?

- Students are going to think about the different decision-making strategies they learned about in this unit and make connections to the key concept question at the top of the page: *How do we handle difficult choices?*
- Ask students to choose one of their decisions from B and then choose a decision-making strategy they think would work well. Give them time to complete the strategy and think of how their decision will affect their future.
- Have students discuss their ideas in pairs. Invite students to share their ideas with the class.

My Reading Journal

Has this unit helped you in any way? Why or why not? Write a review of the unit.

These questions encourage students to personalize what they have learned in the unit and relate this to their own life.

Give students time to look through the unit and answer the questions with their ideas. Have them share ideas in pairs before eliciting a few examples with the class.

Example Answers

Yes, it has helped me to understand which decisions are important and which aren't.

In this unit, we learned about decision-making strategies and that it isn't always easy to make decisions. We also learned that it's OK to make mistakes because we can learn from them.

Go back to page 137. Do the routine again.

Have students look back at the VTR picture on p. 137 and elicit what they discussed in the Get Ready to Read lesson (use your notes to remind them). Discuss how they think the picture connects to the two readings in the unit. Ask *Do you think the people making the risky decisions are thinking about how these will affect their future? What would you tell the people going down the safe path? And those going down the risky path?*

Then guide students to do the Step Inside VTR again. They could do this for the same person or thing they chose, focusing on how their thoughts and beliefs are different now. Alternatively, they could choose a different person or thing to step inside.

Cool Down

Ask students to look through the pictures in the unit and choose the one they think best illustrates the unit topic of decision-making. Have students compare in pairs and then elicit ideas. Accept all opinions.

Practice **Resource Bank:** Unit Test
Student's App: Key Concept Practice

UNIT 10

Take the Lead

Unit Overview

Themes

What makes a good leader

What influences us in our daily lives

Synopsis

In this unit, students will learn about leaders and leadership skills. They will think about how confident they are taking the lead and work on projects that inspire them to lead others. They will discuss the importance of leadership and write a blog post proposing a school program or event. Students will practice giving a presentation in pairs (with slides) giving causes and effects and sounding positive.

Language Book

Vocabulary

can-do attitude, encourage, gut feeling, inspire, mentor, positive influence, respect, role mode

Pronunciation: Sentence Stress: Influencing Meaning

p. 192

Explore Language

Future Progressive

p. 193

Global Citizenship

Can anyone be a leader?

commitment, focus, honest, motivate, organizational skills, passionate, set a good example, support

p. 194

Explore Language

Review: Future Forms

p. 195

Write About It

A Blog Post

Features of a Blog; Informal Language and Ellipses

p. 196

Take the Stage

Presentation: Using Cause-and-effect Reasoning; Sounding Positive

p. 197

Think It Over

Review and Reflection: Looking Back

p. 198

Literacy Book

Think Together
How are we influenced by things around us?
p. 205

Visible Thinking
See, Think, Wonder
p. 199

Nonfiction
Informational Text: *Recycle Runway*
Words in Context: *individuality, aluminum, upcycled, outfits, commissioned*
p. 203

Fiction
Play: *Click to Follow*
Words in Context: *formulaic, take me seriously, ethically, authentic, influential*
p. 200

Reading Skill
Summarizing Readings
p. 202

Literary Term
Assonance
p. 201

Language and Literacy Connections

The connecting theme for Unit 10 is influencing and leading other people.

	Language	Literacy
Vocabulary	**Set 1:** positive values **Set 2:** influencing and leading	**Fiction:** motivated, set a good example **Nonfiction:** committed, encourage, influence, inspire, passionate
Grammar	**Future Progressive** Who will we be following in the future? I'll be feeling inspired by the end of this trip! People won't only be following "celebrities" in the future. **Review: Future Forms** I'm going to find out how many students are interested. I'm having a meeting with the group later today. How much will this cost? I hope it'll be a great success.	**Fiction** But will people take me seriously? StyleGuru says that next season we'll be wearing yellow. But I'll be wearing green. That means I'll only buy clothes that are ethically produced. Today, I'm going to review a brand that creates clothes that are stylish. **Nonfiction** Maybe in the future we'll all be wearing sustainable clothing, recycling more, and creating less waste. When people see it, they'll remember.
Skills	**Pronunciation:** sentence stress: influencing meaning **Process Writing:** features of a blog	**Reading:** summarizing readings **Literary Term:** assonance
International English	regular people / ordinary people; buddy/mate	

Vocabulary

Lesson Objectives

- to learn vocabulary related to positive values: *can-do attitude, encourage, gut feeling, inspire, mentor, positive influence, respect, role model*
- to read and say a poem about the future
- to recognize and practice sentence stress: influencing meaning

Materials
Audio Tracks 111 to 115; Video

Warm Up

Write on the board *Emma took the lead in organizing the school trip and made all the difficult decisions.* Elicit the meaning of *took the lead* in this context (to accept responsibility and deal with a situation) and invite students to talk about a time when they took the lead in doing something.

A TRACK 111 TB p. 227 **Listen. What's the students' end-of-year project about?**

- Display the picture using the TTL or ask students to look at it in their books. Have students work in pairs to identify as many characters from previous units as they can.
- Ask the Unit 9 teaser question *Which country are we going to next?* Have students look to find the answer (Egypt).
- Explain to students that they are going to listen to Mrs. Moreno (in the pink jacket) talking to two of her students. Ask the question *What's the students' end-of-year project about?* Then play the audio and elicit the answer. Then ask further comprehension questions about the scene (see **ETB**).

Answer
people and things that are inspiring

B TRACK 112 TB p. 227 **Find and number the words in A. Listen and check.**

- Ask students to look at the list of words and phrases and discuss in pairs what they could mean.
- Then point out the example (1) and have students find the mom encouraging her son. Have students work in pairs to find the other words in the picture and to write the numbers in their books.
- Play the audio for students to check their answers.

Answers
1 *encourage* 2 can-do attitude 3 gut feeling
4 positive influence 5 respect 6 inspire 7 mentor
8 role model

C TRACK 113 TB p. 227 **Close your eyes. Listen, visualize, and say.**

- Prepare students for the visualization (see TB p. 21).
- Play the audio for students to visualize the ideas.
- Have students choose one of the questions from the visualization and discuss it in pairs. Invite students to report something interesting they found out about their partner.

D Look and write. Then complete the column for you.

- Students are going to contextualize the new vocabulary by completing the sentences and providing a personal response. Give students time to complete the missing words and phrases in the first column. Check answers.
- Explain that they are now going to think of a person for each sentence. It can be anyone they want, including a fictional character. Give an example if necessary. Monitor and encourage them to think of reasons.
- Have students compare ideas in pairs and explain their reasons.

Answers
1 *role model* 2 mentor 3 respect 4 encourages
5 inspires 6 positive 7 can-do 8 gut
a–h: Students' own answers

E TRACK 114 TB p. 228 **Listen and write. Then watch and say.**

- Have students look at the title and guess words or phrases that might be in the poem. Then play the audio or video, allowing students to listen and enjoy the poem.
- Have students look at the lines in their books and fill in the blanks. Play the audio again and have students check.
- Ask students to stand up in two groups, facing each other. Play the audio again and have students join in. Both groups read the first verse together and then each group reads one verse.

Answers
1 *role* 2 encourage 3 mentor 4 respect 5 inspire

F TRACK 115 TB p. 228 **Pronunciation. Listen and say. Copy the sentence stress. How does it change the meaning?**

- Draw students' attention to the sentence and the dots over the stressed words. Play the audio for students to listen and notice the stress pattern in each sentence.
- Have them discuss how the meaning changes in each sentence. Play the audio again if necessary. Elicit that each stressed word shifts the focus onto a different concept or meaning, i.e. *best* (quality), *you* (the person), *ever* (concept of time).
- Play the audio again for students to repeat. Then, in pairs, have them practice saying the sentence aloud for their partner to point out the stressed word.

Cool Down

Ask students to work in small groups to discuss a school trip they've been on. Elicit ideas. Then ask them to choose a country or place they think would make a good destination for a school trip.

Practice **Student's App:** Vocabulary Practice; Spoken Word Video

Explore Language

Lesson Objectives

- to learn how to use the future progressive
- to practice vocabulary related to positive values

Materials
Audio Tracks 116 and 117

Warm Up

Look at the picture on p. 128 or display it using the TTL. Ask students whether they recognize the people in the pictures inside the thought bubble. Elicit ideas and write them on the board, but don't give answers. Have students discuss in small groups what they know or can guess about each person.

A TRACK 116 TB p. 228 **Listen and read. What kind of people is Sofia talking about?**

- This activity is a presentation of the grammar in context. Tell students to listen to Mr. Moreno and Sofia talking about people. Play the audio and have students follow in their books and check their guesses from the Warm Up.
- Ask the question and have students look at the dialogue again in pairs and discuss the answer. Confirm whether their guesses about the people in the picture were correct. Then ask further comprehension questions (see **ETB**).

Answer
She is talking about great leaders, including scientists and a pharaoh. She also talks about celebrities.

International English

Point out the American English phrase *regular people* and the British English phrase *ordinary people*. Discuss what the adjectives mean in this context (normal, not unusual) and which collocation they think will be easier to remember.

B **Look at A. Complete the table. What verb form comes after *will be*?**

- Display the table using the TTL. Tell students to scan the dialogue in A in pairs and complete the table with the missing words.
- Students should now have the skills and strategies to be able to discuss the grammar forms and notice patterns by themselves. When they have completed the table, discuss the word order, form, and patterns together, but let your class guide the discussion. If you feel that students need more guidance, use the notes in the **ETB**.

Answers
will; following; be; feeling; won't; be
The *–ing* form comes after *will be*.

- Refer students to the Grammar tip *Look* and elicit the adverb in the sentences in the table (*only*).

Practice **Resource Bank:** Grammar Printout
Student's App: Grammar Practice

C **Think and discuss. Then choose.**

- This activity focuses on the usage of future progressive. Ask students to refer back to the table in B and think about the sentences and answer options. Have them compare ideas and decide in pairs. Then check answers.

Answers
1 an action in progress at a point 2 in progress

D TRACK 117 TB p. 228 **Listen and say.**

- Tell students they're going to practice saying questions and sentences with the future progressive to help with pronunciation in fluent speech and so that they begin to internalize the structure. Play the audio and have students repeat each example chorally. (See TB p. 23, Making Language Drills Fun.)

E **Read and complete.**

- This activity provides controlled practice of future progressive forms. Read the example together and elicit again the structure of the future progressive.
- Have students complete the sentences and compare their answers in pairs.
- To check answers, invite students to read a sentence aloud or display them on the board. Point out the time expressions that are usually used with the future progressive: *in the future, this time next week/year, when I'm older, by the time …*

Answers
1 *'ll be working* 2 'll be swimming 3 won't be living
4 won't be studying 5 will; be doing 6 'll be living
7 Will; be singing 8 won't be making

F **Read the prompts and make sentences for yourself. Then talk to your friend.**

- This activity provides freer oral practice of the future progressive. Look at the prompts together. Then have two students read the example exchange. Point out that the time phrase is used in the question and the answer.
- Give students time to think or write sentences for themselves for each prompt. Monitor and provide language help if needed.
- Put students in pairs to ask and answer questions. Monitor while students do the task and check for correct use of the future progressive and the time expressions.

Cool Down

Have students choose one of their questions from F and conduct a class survey. Have them mingle in class and make notes of their classmates' answers in a notebook. Set a time limit and then ask students to sit down and share their results in pairs. Elicit any interesting information from students' surveys.

Global Citizenship

Lesson Objectives

- to learn vocabulary related to influencing and leading: *commitment, focus, honest, motivate, organizational skills, passionate, set a good example, support*
- to explore leadership qualities
- to practice listening for gist and details

Materials
Audio Tracks 118 to 120; Audio Track J

Opening Question

Ask the opening question: *Can anyone be a leader?* Put students in small groups and have them share their ideas. Encourage them to give reasons and examples for their opinions. Then have them decide as a group what qualities, skills, and abilities a leader needs to have.

A TRACK 118 TB p. 228 **Listen to André talk to his mentor, Patrick. Does André believe he can be a good leader? Why?**

- Tell students they are going to listen to André and his mentor, Patrick, talk about leadership skills. Play the audio and have students check their ideas from their discussion of the opening question. Elicit some leadership skills, e.g. show passion, make people feel they are part of a team.
- Ask *Does André believe he can be a good leader? Why?* Have students discuss in pairs. Play the audio again if necessary and elicit ideas. Discuss whether students think they are like André. Would they make a good leader? Then ask further comprehension questions (see **ETB**).

Answer
Yes, he does because he thinks he has all the qualities Patrick mentions.

B TRACK 119 TB p. 228 **Look at the pictures and definitions in A and write. Then listen and check.**

- Look at the example together and have students point out other words and phrases in the box heard in the audio.
- In pairs, have students match the words and phrases to the pictures and discuss their answers.
- Play the audio for students to check their answers. Then play it again to practice the pronunciation.

Answers
1 *set a good example* 2 passionate
3 organizational skills 4 motivate 5 focus
6 support 7 commitment 8 honest

TRACK J TB p. 228 **Visualization**
The TTL has a visualization audio track for this vocabulary set. (See TB p. 21.)

C **Read and complete the advice.**

- This activity provides contextualized controlled vocabulary practice. Read the title and the first sentence. Check the meaning of *enthusiasm* with a synonym (e.g. *excitement*).
- Have students complete the advice in pairs. Display answers using the TTL or have students call them out.
- Give students time to read the advice again and decide which they think is the most important tip. Elicit ideas.

Answers
1 *passionate* 2 set a good example 3 motivate
4 support 5 Focus 6 commitment 7 honest
8 organizational skills

D TRACK 120 TB p. 228 **Now listen to Dev talk about Will Lourcey. What did Will do to help in his community?**

- Listening for gist: explain that students are going to listen to Dev talk about an inspiring teenager named Will Lourcey who helped his community. Have students guess what Will did by looking at the picture and play the audio.
- Check the answer as a class. Did anyone guess correctly?

Answer
He helped hungry children by collecting and providing food for them.

E **Listen again. Put the events in order.**

- Listening for details: have students read the events before they listen again. Allow them to discuss the order in pairs.
- Play the audio and have students order the events. Check answers as a class and discuss what students think about Will Lourcey and his projects. Encourage students to make connections with A by eliciting which of the skills that Patrick mentioned were displayed by Will in his project.
- Ask students if they think Will's project is for a good cause. Have them discuss ideas in pairs, then share with the class.

Answers
1 *d* 2 b 3 e 4 a 5 c 6 f

Discussion Questions

- Draw students' attention to the discussion questions. Write or project the questions onto the board. Have students discuss each question in pairs or small groups (see **ETB**). Encourage students to recognize that anyone can be a leader as long as they have a good cause that they believe in and the right attitude. Elicit some local and global causes that students are interested in helping.
- Return to the opening question to ask again *Can anyone be a leader?* Review the ideas discussed at the beginning of the lesson and encourage students to share new ideas.

Cool Down

Have students think about someone they know who would be a good leader. Encourage them to think of reasons why and discuss in pairs. Invite students to share with the class.

Practice **Student's App:** Vocabulary Practice; Listening Practice

Explore Language

Lesson Objectives

- to review future forms
- to practice vocabulary related to influencing and leading

Materials
Audio Tracks 121 and 122

Warm Up

Ask students to look at the picture on p. 132 or display it using the TTL for 30 seconds. Then remove the picture and say true or false sentences about it. Have students stand up for the false sentences and correct them.

A TRACK 121 TB p. 228 **Listen and read. What does Lucas want to do?**

- This activity is a presentation of the grammar in context. Tell students they are going to listen to Lucas talking to Mr. Hussein, the principal of the school in Alexandria, about a project. Have students find Mr. Hussein on pp. 126–127 (the man on the stage). Elicit ideas on what the project could be.
- Play the audio. Have students follow the dialogue in their books and check to see if their predictions were correct.
- Ask the question *What does Lucas want to do?* Invite students to discuss the question in pairs before you elicit the answer from the class. Then ask further comprehension questions (see **ETB**). Discuss whether students have an exchange program in their school and if they would like to go on one.

Answer
He wants to arrange and lead next year's student exchange program.

B Look at A. Complete the table. Which verb form doesn't use an infinitive?

- Display the table using the TTL. Tell students to scan the dialogue in A and find the missing words individually or in pairs.
- Students should now have the skills and strategies to be able to notice the grammar patterns by themselves using the examples. When they have completed the table, discuss the word order, form, and patterns together, but let your class guide the discussion. If you feel that students need more guidance, use the notes in the **ETB**.

Answers
'm; going to; will; cost; 'll; be
The present progressive doesn't use an infinitive.

- Draw students' attention to the Grammar tip *Look*. Point out that both sentences are correct and we usually drop the second *go* for speed and because the meaning stays the same.

Practice **Resource Bank:** Grammar Printout
Student's App: Grammar Practice

C Think and discuss. Then match.

- Ask students to match the uses to the verb forms and refer to the examples in the table in B. Have them do the task individually and then compare in pairs. Point out that one function matches two verb forms. Check answers.

Answers
1 d 2 a; b 3 c 4 a

D TRACK 122 TB p. 228 **Listen and say.**

- Tell students they're going to practice saying sentences and questions with different future forms to help with pronunciation in fluent speech and to consolidate what they've learned. Play the audio and have students repeat chorally. (See TB p. 23, Making Language Drills Fun.)

E Read the email. Underline the time phrases. Then complete with the correct future form.

- This activity provides controlled practice of future forms. Have students read the email once and underline time phrases that will help them choose the correct future form. Point out that *hope* is also a key word.
- Ask students to complete the email with the correct future form. Point out that in some cases more than one answer is possible. Students can work in pairs.
- To check answers, invite students to read a sentence aloud and explain why they chose that future form. Elicit different answers from students and then confirm. Discuss the difference in meaning of *will be* in number 6. (It's more a matter of fact than a prediction.)

Answers
Time phrases to underline: *last year*, tomorrow, on Friday, On Sunday, after
1 *'ll make* 2 are/'re going to finish, are/'re finishing 3 will/'ll ask 4 is/'s going to go / is/'s going 5 cooking / going to cook 6 are/'re going to be / 'll be

F Think about your life in the next six months and make notes. Then talk with a friend.

- For this freer oral practice, students have a conversation about their own near futures. Have two students read the example sentences. Point out that the examples are for the near and more distant future.
- Have students write their sentences individually using each future form at least once. Monitor and provide language help if needed.
- In pairs, students take turns saying a sentence. Encourage them to ask follow-up questions. Monitor and make a note of the sentences.
- Read students' sentences to the class and encourage students to guess who wrote/said them.

Cool Down

Play *Chain Game* (see TB p. 25) in two teams. Each time, have students use a different future form. Demonstrate first with a few volunteers. Then have them play in their teams.

Write About It

Lesson Objectives

- to plan and write a blog post
- to identify the features of a blog post
- to use informal language and ellipsis

Materials

Support Writing printouts from the Resource Bank (G)

Warm Up

Remind students of the interviews they did in Unit 7 (Talk About It). What skills did they discuss? Then discuss whether their school has a student council, how members are chosen, and what their responsibilities are. If there isn't one, discuss what changes a student council could bring to their school.

A Read the blog post and comments. What does the writer of the blog post want to achieve? Does everyone agree to help?

- This lesson corresponds with the fiction reading in Unit 10 of the **Literacy Book**. Tell students they are going to read a blog post from a member of a school's student council. Ask students to read the post once for gist.
- Ask the questions and have students discuss their answers in pairs. Invite volunteers to share answers with the class. Ask more comprehension questions (see **ETB**).

Answers

The writer wants to set up a new online collaborative group between schools to help with the following: helping with the school play, training sports teams, mentoring younger kids, and exchanging ideas and plans for how to persuade teachers when they want to do something new. Two people agree to help but one doesn't.

B Look at the structure of the blog post. Match the features to the reasons.

- Tell students they're going to look at the structure of the blog post. First, ask them to look at the list of features and reasons. Elicit or explain what *chatty style* means (e.g. informal, friendly, similar to speech).
- Have students match the features and reasons individually, then compare answers in pairs. Check answers.

Answers

1 c 2 d 3 a 4 b 5 e

C Look at the language in the blog post. Read and respond.

- Have students do the two tasks in pairs. Check answers.
- Point out the ellipsis in the blog post. Explain that these three dots are called an ellipsis and ask students to think about what it means and how it's used. (It indicates we haven't completed a thought, or that we're hesitating).

Suggested Answers

1 a Hey, classmates! b Well, if we're all willing to help, … c How about we set up a new club?
2 a ~~Do you~~ (think this is a) good idea? b ~~Please do~~ send (your) comments. c ~~We~~ don't have (enough) time. ~~I'm~~ sorry.

D Think and discuss. You're going to write a blog post about a project or event. Choose a project or event that you'd like to organize and lead. Brainstorm lots of ideas using one of the Generating Ideas techniques.

- Tell students that in this last writing lesson, they can choose how to carry out each stage of the writing process, using their experiences from the year. They can refer to the lessons on pp. 140–143 for ideas.
- Have students read the instructions and then ask *What project or event would you like to organize and lead?* Give students time to think of ideas on their own and record them using a suitable Generating Ideas technique.
- Have them share ideas in pairs and encourage students to suggest other ideas that would be suitable for their partner's project or event.

E Plan your blog post. Use some of your ideas in D and one of the Planning techniques.

- Have students review their ideas in D and choose those they would like to include. Remind students to think about how they can write their ideas in a logical order and to include three or four paragraphs.
- Then allow enough time for students to plan their blog post in note form, using a suitable Planning technique.

F Now write a first draft of your blog post. Then review it using a checklist.

- Have students write a draft of their blog post in their notebooks, referring to their notes in E.
- Ask students to think of their own checklist and elicit ideas on the board. Students can refer to these as they revise.

G Write your blog post. Then check it using the Editing and Publishing questions. Publish it.

- Have students write the final draft versions neatly on paper or on the Support printout, referring to the checklist.
- Have students check their final draft using the questions on p. 143.
- In pairs, have students read each other's blog post and write a suitable comment in response.

Cool Down

Display students' blog posts in class, on the walls, or on students' desks. Have students walk around and read a few blog posts. Encourage them to write a comment in response. Students can then look at the responses they received.

Practice **Resource Bank:** Writing Game, *Guess What?*
Student's App: Writing Practice

Take the Stage

Lesson Objectives

- to give a presentation about a student program or club
- to use cause-and-effect reasoning and sound positive

Materials
Video

Warm Up

Ask students to think about their first day at school next year. Ask *What do you worry about? What do you think will be challenging?* Have students discuss ideas in pairs. Elicit ideas on the board. If students won't be changing schools, have them think about how they could help a new student on their first few days of school.

A TB p. 240 **Watch and listen. How will *Buddies 4U* help new students?**

- The video provides a presentation of the functional language needed for using cause-and-effect reasoning. Tell students they are going to watch a video of two students, Linda and Gene, talking about a program called *Buddies 4U*. Elicit what *buddy* means (friend) and what students think the talk is going to be about.

International English

Point out the American English *buddy* and the British English *mate*. Discuss whether students have ever seen or heard these words. Compare them with words students use in L1. Ask students if they know any other informal synonyms of *friend*, e.g. *bestie* or *BFF* (best friends forever—commonly used on social media).

- With books closed, play the video for students to watch, listen, and check their guesses (*Buddies4U* is a mentoring program for new students).
- Ask the comprehension question *How will Buddies 4U help new students?* If necessary, play the video again and then allow some time for students to discuss their answer in pairs. Check answers. Ask more comprehension questions (see **ETB**).

Answers
It helps students with any worries and helps them cope with new responsibilities like getting to the right classroom, keeping up with homework, and making decisions about joining new clubs. It also provides students with someone to talk to if they are unhappy.

B **Watch again. Check (✔) the phrases you hear. Then write *R* (cause-and-effect reasoning) or *SP* (sounding positive).**

- Tell students they are going to focus on phrases students used in their presentation. Point out the two categories: cause-and-effect reasoning and sounding positive. Look at the example together.
- Play the video again and have students check the phrases they hear. Then give them time to label them *R* or *SP*. Have them compare their answers in pairs before checking with the class.

Answers
1; 2; 3; 4; 5; 6; 8; 9; 10
Cause-and-effect reasoning: 2; 4; 6; 7; 10
Sounding positive: *1*; 3; 5; 8; 9

C **You're going to talk to your class about a new student program or club in your school. Plan your presentation with a friend.**

- Tell students they are going to discuss and plan a presentation about a new student program or club for their school. Draw their attention to the list of things they need to think about.
- Put students in pairs to discuss ideas for possible programs and clubs and make notes using phrases from B. Monitor and provide language help if needed.

D **Practice with your friends. Then share with the class. Take notes and give feedback.**

- Tell students they are going to give their presentation in class, but first they are going to practice in pairs. Give students time to decide who is going to say what by referring to their notes. Encourage them to practice using their slides if they have prepared any.
- Invite volunteer students to give their presentation in class. Ask students to make notes while they are listening. They should think about the presentation itself (e.g. slides, how students speak to the class) as well as the language they use.
- Have pairs analyze their performance, focusing on whether they used suitable phrases to show cause-and-effect reasoning and to sound positive.

Cool Down

Ask students to vote on the top two or three ideas they heard about. Invite them to give reasons why they think a particular program or club would be a success at their school.

Practice **Student's App:** Speaking Skills Practice; Speaking Video

Think It Over

Lesson Objectives

- to review what has been learned in the unit
- to reflect on the unit and their own progress
- to think about learning strategies and how to continue learning at home

Materials

Large sheets of paper

Warm Up

Ask students to look at the pictures around the organizer (not the characters at the bottom of the page) and think on their own about what each picture shows and represents. Give them a minute for this and then ask them to compare ideas in pairs. Elicit ideas from different students, focusing on the concept of achievement and progression.

How well did you meet the challenge of Unit 10? Read and respond.

Looking Back

- Tell students they are going to review what they learned in the unit and also think about their own learning. *Looking Back* encourages students to remember enjoyable moments in the unit and in the course. By sharing ideas with friends, they will remember more activities and things they learned, and they may also be encouraged to go back and review things they had forgotten.
- Have students do a Chalk Talk routine (see TB p. 20) to recap as many things that they have done during the unit as possible. Elicit categories from the class (e.g. words, grammar, leaders, leadership skills, things I learned about school programs, interesting ideas, things that made me think) and write each one in the middle of a large sheet of paper. Give students a couple of minutes to do each stage of the Chalk Talk routine.
- When students have finished adding ideas to the Chalk Talk posters, have them stick the posters on the wall for reference. Then refer students to the graphic organizer in the book and the prompt sentences: *My favorite activity was …; One thing I learned is …; I'll never forget when …; The funniest moment this month was when …* Have students talk in pairs about the different sections. Remind students to give reasons for their answers by explaining why they have chosen these things. Ask students what they particularly remember from the unit. Making connections between the material, activities, and personal emotions can help students remember what they have learned. Encourage them to focus particularly on the last section and elicit some funny moments students had this month.
- When you feel they have enough ideas, have students work individually to fill in the organizer. Remind them that they should write their own responses about themselves, and encourage them to write extended answers. Monitor and help as necessary. Look at what students are writing so you can tailor your classes and any additional practice to their needs.
- If you feel it is appropriate for your class, have students share their ideas with a friend. As this is the last unit in the book, encourage students to think about the progress they have made over the course of the whole school year. Ask them what they enjoyed most in the book. They can discuss in small groups, and then ask the groups to report back.

Reflection

Draw students' attention to the characters at the bottom of the page. Have students identify them and elicit what they remember about each character (they appear in various units throughout the book). You can also ask them to discuss in pairs who their favorite character is and why.

Put It Together

To further review and recycle the language in Units 9 and 10, play the game, *Solve a Problem!*, on pp. 138–139. See TB p. 210 for teaching notes.

Practice **Resource Bank:** Unit Test; End-of-year Test **Student's App:** Vocabulary and Grammar Review

Get Ready to Read

Lesson Objectives

- to activate prior knowledge about influences around us
- to guide inquiry and deepen understanding through a See, Think, Wonder VTR
- to preview the reading skill of summarizing readings

Materials
VTR printout from the Resource Bank (A, B, C)

Warm Up

Draw a mind map on the board with *Environment* in the circle and lines for ideas branching out. In pairs, have students fill in a mind map of their own, then exchange and compare ideas with another pair. Elicit ideas on the board.

See, Think, Wonder

A Look at the picture. What do you see?

- This VTR encourages students to make predictions, observations, and interpretations about the image of people in the park. Ask *What do you see?* and give students up to a minute to look at the picture and think silently.
- Guide students to focus their answers on what is visible, not how they interpret it. Have students share in small groups or pairs. Then bring the class together to discuss. Note their ideas to revisit in the Think Together lesson.

Here's an example of this part of the routine.
Teacher: What do you see?
Student A: I see a park in the city.
Student B: There are lots of people in the park.
Teacher: What else do you see, Student B?
Student B: I see two children painting pictures and children playing basketball.

B What do you think?

- Ask students to think about the picture on their own for a few seconds. Then have them discuss their thoughts in pairs before sharing as a class.

Here's an example of this part of the routine.
Teacher: What do you think?
Student A: I think it's the weekend because there are so many people in the park.
Student B: I think it's spring or summer because the people are wearing summer clothes.
Student C: I agree. And I think the people want to take care of the park to keep it beautiful.
Student D: I think that the children who are collecting the trash have to do it.
Teacher: Can you explain?
Student D: Maybe their teacher asked them to do it.

C What do you wonder?

- Have students work in pairs again to explore what questions they have about the picture.
- Elicit an idea from each student and encourage further discussion.

Here's an example of this part of the routine.
Teacher: What do you wonder, Student A?
Student A: I wonder how big this park is. We don't have parks that are this big in our town.
Student B: Yes, I wondered that, too. I also I wonder what else people like to do in this park.
Student C: I wonder what the squirrel is thinking.
Teacher: Why do you wonder that?
Student C: Because he's looking at the people.

Transition

Ask *What kinds of things do you think are popular with the children in the picture? What do you think is fashionable in their world? Do you think the smaller kids look up to the bigger kids?*

D Think and discuss. What are the latest trends and fashions for you and your friends?

- Ask students to think about their answers and then discuss the questions in pairs. Encourage students to talk about clothes, toys, video games, actions and gestures, language, and so on and to think about where these trends come from.

Answers
Students' own answers

E Read and write. Read the author biography of Jed from *Click to Follow*. Then write one sentence to explain what you read.

- This activity previews the skill of summarizing. Explain that students are going to read a play titled *Click to Follow* and one of the characters is named Jed. Give students a minute to read Jed's biography and write one sentence to explain what they read.
- Have students compare sentences.

Suggested Answer
Jed Anwar writes a very successful weekly fashion and lifestyle blog called Friday Fashion Fix, which has a huge following.

Now read **Click to Follow**

Fiction: *Click to Follow—Play*

Lesson Objectives

- to activate prior knowledge about fashion icons
- to make a personal connection to the reading

Materials
Audio Tracks 42 and 43

Warm Up

With books closed, hold up the pictures on pp. 154–155 or display them using the TTL. Elicit who students think Jed is and why. Ask pairs to brainstorm ideas about what happens in the story. Elicit ideas but don't confirm.

TRACK 42 TB p. 238 Reading Approach

First Reading: Engage with the Text

- Play the audio and have students follow. Alternatively, use the Story Player in the TTL. Pause at the end of p. 157. Ask *What do you think Jed's idea is, and do you think it's going to be a success?* Have students discuss in pairs for a minute. Then play the rest of the audio.
- Check if students' guesses about Jed's idea were correct. Then look at the Words in Context.

TRACK 43 TB p. 238 Words in Context

- Brainstorm strategies on the board for students to use with the words: *surrounding words and sentences, word families, remembering other contexts, knowledge of similar words, separate parts of word, synonyms.*
- Divide the class into pairs and assign two words to each pair (assign each pair either the first two words, the second two words, or the third two words). Have students find and discuss their words.
- Have pairs get together with two other pairs (groups of six) and explain their words to each other, saying which strategies they used.

formulaic (p. 154, adjective) The use of *it* and *that* before the adjective shows that the subject has been referred to earlier and we need to read the previous sentence, which provides an explanation. Strategies to use: surrounding words and sentences; word families

take me seriously (p. 157, verb phrase) The sentence shows that this is an action that other people might do when Jed shares his idea. Strategies to use: knowledge of similar words; separate parts of word

ethically (p. 158, adverb) The following sentence uses the word *sustainable* (Level 5) as an example of *ethically produced.* The previous page implies that Jed is concerned about the conditions in factories. Strategy to use: surrounding words and sentences

authentic (p. 159, adjective) The sentence uses the synonym *real.* Strategies to use: surrounding words and sentences; synonyms

influential (p. 159, adjective) The superlative structure shows that the word is an adjective. Students may have previously encountered *influence* (**Language Book**). Strategies to use: word families; remembering other contexts

- Bring the class together to discuss which strategies worked or didn't work. Play the audio to practice the pronunciation.

Second Reading: Analyze the Text and Features

- Play the audio again to consolidate students' understanding of the play.
- Invite students to find the climax of the story (scene 4). Ask some questions to check comprehension: *Why was Jed worried about writing blog posts on ethical fashion?* (because it was different from his style and he was worried he would lose his audience) *How did people first react to Jed's new content?* (They didn't like it. He lost his audience.) See the **ETB** for more comprehension questions.
- Discuss the questions in the pink boxes. Then look at the text focus.
    - **Personalization** (p. 154): *Do you write or follow a blog?* Have students discuss in small groups and then invite students to share experiences with the class.
    - **Language in Context** (p. 158): *What do you think "Wanna" is short for?* Ask students to find the phrase. Elicit that it is informal and is short for *Do you want to?*
    - **Critical Thinking** (p. 159): *Do you know where your clothes come from?* Ask students to look at the labels on their clothing and identify the brands. Have them look at where they are made and what they're made of. Discuss whether they think their clothes are made ethically or not and why.
    - **Text Focus** (p. 156): Have students work in pairs to read the heading for each scene and discuss where it takes place.

Third Reading: Interact with the Text

- Divide the class into five groups and assign one scene to each group. Have students act out their scenes. Encourage students to use actions and gestures as they read together. (See TB p. 23.)
- Invite groups to act out their scene for the class.

Cool Down

Have students think what Jed's next blog post is going to be about. Ask them to brainstorm ideas in pairs or small groups. Elicit ideas from the class.

Practice **Student's App:** Story Player

Explore the Reading

Lesson Objectives

- to understand and analyze *Click to Follow* through reading comprehension activities
- to explore the SEL competency of relationship skills through resisting inappropriate social pressures
- to make a personal connection to the reading

Materials
Audio Track 44

Warm Up

Draw a story structure diagram on the board (like the story mountain on p. 129) and discuss the main events of *Click to Follow*. Elicit events for each stage of the story.

A Read, think, and write. What is inferred by these statements? Write the meaning.

- Review what *inferring* is (drawing conclusions from textual or visual evidence). Elicit who said each of the statements.
- Discuss what can be inferred from the first statement as an example. Then ask students to discuss the rest in pairs.
- Check answers by inviting different students to give their opinion for each statement.

Suggested Answers
1 He used to like writing about clothes and brands, but his feelings have changed. 2 He thinks people might do what he says even if it is really silly. 3 The important thing is that people like the blog and are following him, not what he actually writes about. 4 He's going to start wearing clothes that are ethically produced. 5 Now he is happy to be writing about something he believes in.

B Think, write, and discuss. Describe Jed's character and write the evidence for each description.

- Look at the example and elicit evidence that proves Jed is a creative person. Encourage students to look back at the reading to find examples.
- Ask students to brainstorm two or more adjectives that describe Jed and evidence to support their opinion. Monitor and provide language help if needed.
- Have students write their answers. Check answers by eliciting adjectives and evidence from different students.

Suggested Answers
creative: He's a writer / creates styles.; **hard-working**: He wants to write something good / works late into the night.; **funny**: He has funny ideas like the superhero look.

C Think and discuss. What should you think about before you click to follow a blog?

- Students are going to connect the reading to the SEL competency of responsible decision-making: resist inappropriate social pressures.
- Ask students if they follow any blogs or vlogs. Elicit what made them start following them. Have students discuss the question by doing a Rally Robin or Think, Pair, Share (see TB p. 20).
- Bring the class back together to compare ideas.

Suggested Answers
Think about the author and his/her goal. Maybe do some research and find out his/her background and why he/she is writing the blog. Think about how often you are going to get notifications and if that's going to be annoying. Think about whether your personal information might be given to third parties through the blog.

Literary Term: Assonance

TRACK 44 TB p. 238 **Listen. Then underline the assonance. Then write three sentences or phrases using assonance.**

- Read the information about assonance. Play the audio once and have students underline the assonance. Point out that there are more than one example of assonance in sentence 1. Check answers.
- Have students write three sentences of their own using assonance. Allow them to work in pairs. Monitor and provide help if needed. Students can also use examples they have heard in advertising slogans.

Now find more examples of rhyming in the reading.

- Have students scan the reading to find more rhyming sentences.
- Ask students to compare answers in pairs, then check answers as a class.

Answers
1 You don't have to have the latest, greatest clothes to look good. 2 That woman has the top job in the company. 3 Their store sells cool shoes.
4–6 Students' own answers
Examples of assonance in the reading: "You tell people what's hot and what's not!"; Speed Feet sneakers

Cool Down

Play *Who Said It?* (see TB p. 27) using sentences from the play. Invite students to read a sentence for the class to call out the character's name.

Practice **Resource Bank:** Literary Term Printout
Student's App: Reading Practice; Literary Term Practice

Get Ready to Read

Lesson Objectives

- to activate prior knowledge about upcycling in fashion
- to practice the reading skill of summarizing readings

Warm Up

Ask students to read *Click to Follow* again quickly and choose their favorite exchange. Ask them to compare exchanges in pairs and say why they like what the characters say in that excerpt. Elicit ideas from students.

A Complete the table. Read the main ideas from *Click to Follow*. Look back at the play. Find at least one important supporting detail for each main idea.

- This lesson practices the skill of summarizing, which students previewed on p. 153. Have students read the first main idea in the table. Encourage them to look back through the play to find any supporting details. Elicit suggestions for the answer.
- Put students in pairs to find supporting details for the other main ideas. Monitor and provide help if necessary. Check answers as a class and invite discussion if they have different ideas.
- Have students read the skills box. Draw their attention to the table above and elicit that the *Supporting Details* column shows us ideas that have a common theme, which we can summarize as the main idea. (e.g. choosing which details are important and which aren't, especially with longer texts).

Suggested Answers

Jed doesn't feel inspired by his work. He doesn't have any ideas for this week's Friday Fashion Fix blog post. / He doesn't find the clothes people send him interesting anymore.

He tries to make his work more fun. He gives his readers some crazy styles to try and he's amazed when they like his ideas.

He hears bad news about the conditions in clothing factories. He hears about a clothing factory that collapsed and a chemical leak from a sneaker factory.

He decides to write about more important things. He says he's going to review a brand that creates clothes that are sustainable. / He thinks people should know where their clothes come from and where they're going.

B Read, think, and write. Complete the table.

- Give students time to read the text about fashion. Then have them find at least three important details in the text.
- Put students in pairs to compare their findings and to summarize the main idea.
- Then have students find the minor details or unimportant examples for each important supporting detail. Check answers as a class.

Suggested Answers

Main Idea: Fashion is powerful.

Important Supporting Details: Wearing a red coat can give us confidence. / Many people in the real world will never look like models in the same clothes. / People dream of looking like fashion models.

Minor Details/Unimportant Examples: Clothes made for fashion shows are different from clothes sold in stores. / Models are often tall and thin.

C Read and write. Read the first paragraph of *Recycle Runway*. Write one sentence to summarize the paragraph.

- Tell students they are going to practice their summarizing skills with the first paragraph of the text. If using the TTL, display the opening paragraph. Ask students to read it and discuss the main idea in pairs.
- Have students write their sentence summarizing the paragraph individually. Monitor and provide language help if needed. Invite students to read their sentence to the class.

Suggested Answer

Clothes can deliver important messages.

D Think and discuss. Look at the pictures of *Recycle Runway*. What do you think Nancy Judd's job is? Why?

- Ask students to look at the pictures of *Recycle Runway*, or display them using the TTL. Have students say what they see and predict what each clothing item is made from.
- Have students discuss in pairs what Nancy Judd's job is and think of reasons.

Answers

Students' own answers

Cool Down

Write on the board *For me, fashion is …* Ask students to complete the sentence giving reasons and examples. In small groups, students read their sentence(s) and ask each other follow-up questions.

Now read **Recycle Runway**

Nonfiction: *Recycle Runway—* Informational Text

Lesson Objectives

- to read a text about using recycled materials in fashion
- to make a personal connection to the reading

Materials
Audio Tracks 45 and 46

Warm Up

Draw a mind map on the board. In the circle, write *Fashion* and draw lines for ideas branching out. Have students brainstorm the topic of fashion in small groups. They can include words relating to fashion, opinions about fashion, or things they know about the topic. Elicit ideas and write them in the mind map. Leave it on the board and refer to it again after the second reading.

TRACK 45 TB p. 238 Reading Approach

First Reading: Engage with the Text

- If you are using the TTL, display the spreads or use the Story Player to reactivate students' predictions from D on p. 161. Have students recall what they think Nancy Judd's job is.
- Play the audio once and have students follow along in their books. Give them time to think about what they read, then ask students to say what Nancy Judd does.
- Then look at the Words in Context.

TRACK 46 TB p. 238 Words in Context

- Brainstorm strategies on the board for students to use with the words: *word families, contrasting ideas, pictures, world knowledge, L1 cognates, prefixes/suffixes, surrounding words and sentences.*
- Have students work in pairs to find and discuss each word in the text. Remind them that different words will require different combinations of strategies to figure them out. Some key words appear more than once in the reading, so students should read all the instances to help them.

individuality (p. 162, noun) The sentence includes contrasting ideas: *the same as everyone else* and *express our individuality.* This is shown with the use of *or.* Strategies to use: word families; contrasting ideas

aluminum (p. 162, noun) The pictures of the dress and the information later in the sentence (*metal pieces*) tell us what material the dress is made of. Strategies to use: pictures; world knowledge of materials; L1 cognates

upcycled (p. 163, adjective) This contrasts with *recycled* in the previous sentence. The different prefixes suggest that there is a slight difference in meaning. Strategies to use: parts of words; prefixes; contrasting ideas

outfits (p. 163, noun) The caption points students toward the picture, which shows whole sets of clothes and accessories worn together. Strategy to use: pictures

commissioned (p. 164, verb) Later in the paragraph, *They paid Judd to create this sculpture* is an explanation of the word. Strategy to use: surrounding words and sentences

- Have students change partners and discuss which strategies they used and which worked best. Play the audio to practice the pronunciation.

Practice **Student's App:** Story Player

Second Reading: Analyze the Text and Features

- Have students read the text silently. Allow them to choose the order in which they read the texts, depending on what interests them most. Ask them to find the answer to this question to keep them focused: *Why does Nancy Judd make all these clothes?*
- Have students discuss ideas in pairs. You can also ask students to add one more idea inspired by the text to the mind map from the Warm Up. See the **ETB** for more comprehension questions.
- Discuss the questions in the pink boxes.
  - **Critical Thinking** (p. 162): *How do you think fashion affects the environment?* Have students discuss ideas in pairs or small groups. If possible, allow them to do some research into environmental problems caused by the textile industry.
  - **Critical Thinking** (p. 163): *Why do you think the designs are displayed in airports, museums, and shopping malls?* Have students discuss in pairs. Then invite students to share their answers (so they have a bigger impact; more people will see them).
  - **Fun Fact** (p. 164): *More than 1 billion car tires are trashed each year.* Encourage students to share anything they know about car tires and suggest how car tires could be upcycled.
  - **Personalization** (p. 165): *Have you ever created something new with recycled materials?* Give students thinking time and then have them discuss in pairs. If they haven't, encourage them to come up with an idea together.

Third Reading: Interact with the Text

- Have students read the text again and think of three questions they would like to ask Nancy Judd.
- Have students compare their questions in pairs or small groups. Then invite students to share their questions with the class.

Cool Down

Write *Our Eco-Pledges* on the board. Elicit a synonym of *pledge* (*promise*) and ask students to think about an eco-pledge they'd like to make. Have them compare ideas in pairs and then elicit them on the board.

Explore the Reading

Lesson Objectives

- **to understand and analyze *Recycle Runway* through reading comprehension activities**
- **to practice the reading skill of summarizing readings**
- **to learn through CLIL (science): ecology**
- **to make a personal connection to the reading**

Warm Up

Play *Stand Up, Sit Down* (see TB p. 26) using statements about the text. Suggested sentences: *The Aluminum Drop Dress is made from a shower curtain and pieces of tire.* (False) *Nancy Judd organizes exhibitions in airports, museums, and shopping malls.* (True) *Nancy's workshops are only for children.* (False) You can have students compete in two teams.

A Answer the questions. Find the evidence for each answer. Write the page where you found the answer.

- Give students time to read through the questions. Point out that they need to find the information in the text and note down the page number. Do an example if necessary.
- Have students do the task individually and then compare answers. Check answers as a class.

Answers

1 a way to be the same, a way to be different, important messages; "a way to be the same as everyone else or a way to express our individuality … deliver a more important message" (p. 162) 2 to teach people about the environment, make them think differently about waste, change the way they live; "teach us about the environment … getting people to look differently at waste and to change the way they live on Earth" (p. 162) 3 at a recycled fashion contest, at exhibitions in airports, museums, and shopping malls; "a recycled fashion contest … exhibitions … shown in airports, museums, and shopping malls" (p. 163) 4 because the clothes attract a large audience and could be a good advertising opportunity; "have received worldwide media attention, generating interest from big companies" (p. 163)

B Think and write. Which sentences express important details (*I*) that can be used to give a summary of the reading? Which ones express minor details (*M*)?

- This activity provides further practice of summarizing. Ask students to read the sentences from the text and decide whether they express important details or minor details. Have them complete the activity individually and then compare answers in pairs. Check answers.

Answers

1 I 2 I 3 M 4 I 5 M 6 M

C Complete the table with details about the fashion sculptures.

- Draw students' attention to the headings in the table and elicit an example answer for each column.
- Ask students to complete the table individually and compare answers in pairs. To check answers, draw the table on the board and invite students to come and complete a row. Alternatively, display the answers on the board using the TTL.

Answers

Aluminum Drop Dress; shower curtain and recycled soda cans; Recycling aluminum cans reduces the use of natural resources and chemicals.
Jellyfish Dress; plastic bags; Plastic bags harm marine life.
Tireless Couture; the inside of car and bicycle tires; People should drive less to reduce greenhouse gas emissions.
Faux Fur Coat; second-hand coat and video and audiotape; Electronic waste can be recycled and reused.
Sol Man; trash from energy-efficient building projects; You can save energy in the home.

D Think and discuss. What is the difference between recycling and upcycling?

- Students are going to explore the CLIL science focus of ecology by thinking about the difference between recycling and upcycling.
- Write *Recycling* and *Upcycling* as two headings on the board. Elicit an example of each and write them under the headings, e.g. recycling plastic bottles and using plastic bottles to make a chair.
- Ask students to discuss the question in pairs and to brainstorm their own examples. Then elicit ideas on the board.
- Ask students how recycling and upcycling are both good for the environment. Encourage an open discussion, getting them to think about the benefits of each. Have them think about what things they themselves could do more of and how.

Suggested Answers

Recycling: giving things to a charity shop, using old clothes as cleaning rags, putting clothes in a recycling bin to be turned into rags or fibers to make other stuff
Upcycling: altering or improving an item of clothing, such as changing buttons on a jacket, reshaping, or using the fabric to make a different item, like a rug or a bag.

Cool Down

Play *Disappearing Words* (see TB p. 25) with words from the text.

Practice **Student's App:** Reading Practice

Think Together

Lesson Objectives

- to make connections between the readings
- to explore the key concept: How are we influenced by things around us?
- to reflect on the unit and provide personal thoughts and opinions

Warm Up

Play *Correct the Teacher* (see TB p. 25) with sentences from the two readings in the unit. You can also invite students to take on your role.

A Compare and contrast *Click to Follow* and *Recycle Runway*. Complete the Venn diagram.

- Display the Venn diagram using the TTL or draw it on the board. Tell students they are going to look for similarities and differences in the two readings. If necessary, do an example as a class first. Then have students complete the diagram on their own or in pairs. Monitor and provide language help if needed.
- Project answers on the board or invite students to come up and complete the diagram.

Answers

Click to Follow: a fictional story about a fictional blog; reviews new brands that are affordable and sustainable
Both: about fashion; about somebody who cares about ethical issues / has a strong voice; about people who want to inspire and influence people; share the same message that we should think more about what we are buying, where it comes from, and its environmental impact
Recycle Runway: makes sculptures out of existing materials; is about a real person and project

B Who or what influences what you buy, how you think, and what you do? Do a Rally Robin. Make a list.

- Students are going to make connections to the key concept question at the top of the page: *How are we influenced by things around us?* Have students discuss the questions using a Rally Robin routine (see TB p. 20). Give them time to make a list during or after their discussion.
- Invite students to share their ideas with the class, encouraging them to give examples of how they have been influenced. Make a list on the board to use in C.

Suggested Answers

TV advertisements, shows, friends and family, books, bloggers, singers, media messages, video games, music, technology, social media, celebrities, advertising

C Look at the list in B. What are the most positive influences in your life? Are there any negative influences?

- Ask students to look at the list of influences on the board and categorize them into positive and negative influences. Encourage them to think about this on their own and then discuss in pairs. Ask students to explain why.
- Invite students to share ideas with the class.

My Reading Journal

Imagine you are Nancy Judd. Sketch a design for a fashion sculpture and present it to the class.

How did the readings in this book influence you? Is there anything you will change or do in your life as a result of reading them?

These questions encourage students to personalize what they have learned in the unit and relate this to their own life.

Give students time to think of their fashion sculpture and draw their design. Point out that they can design accessories as well as clothes, e.g. shoes, bags, hats. Monitor and provide help if needed. Invite students to present their design to the class.

Ask students to discuss the questions in pairs and then write down their ideas. Invite students to read their sentences to the class.

Cool Down

Tell students that they have now finished the **Literacy Book**. They should give themselves a round of applause for finishing! You could have students evaluate their progress throughout the year. How happy are they with what they have learned? You could create a class poster with information and drawings from all the different readings.

Practice **Resource Bank:** Unit Test; End-of-year Test
Student's App: Key Concept Practice

Know It, Win It (Units 1 & 2)

Lesson Objectives

- to review vocabulary from Units 1 and 2: online safety and healthy food
- to review grammar from Units 1 and 2: verbs of thinking, simple and progressive forms, present perfect, and present perfect progressive
- to practice communication and fluency skills

Materials

Color Spinner printout from the Resource Bank (one spinner per group); *Question Cards* printout from the Resource Bank (one per group); Counters (one per player)

Warm Up

Put students into groups of three or four and hand out a Question printout to each group. Have them discuss which set of questions is more challenging and why. Elicit ideas.

How to Play

- To save time, download and cut out the spinner and counters before the lesson.
- Students are going to play a game in which they move around a board and answer questions. The goal of the game is for students to go around the board once and then return to the center.
- Go through the instructions on p. 35. More detailed instructions on how to play are given here.
- Put students into groups of four. They only need one book to play. Each student has a counter, which they should color in a different color from those of their teammates. Have them place the counters in the center of the board.
- Students take turns spinning the spinner and moving around the board. When they stop on a square, another player chooses a question from the corresponding colored category on the Question Sheet. The player whose turn it is answers the question and can spin again if the answer is correct. If the answer is wrong, the turn passes to the next player.
- If the spinner lands on Open Play, all the players have the chance to answer the question. The student whose turn it is chooses a question from the Question Sheet or invents a new one. The first player to answer correctly has the next turn.

Note: for personal or opinion questions, a correct answer should be fluent and extended. You can give a time requirement for these answers, e.g. speak for at least 30 seconds.

- When students have gone around the board once and have returned to the center of the board, they have to answer a Time To Speak question. They must talk for one minute to win the game.

Here is an example:

Student A: Four. One, two, three, four. Red. Computer Cool.
Student B: OK. I'm choosing this question: "What's important to remember when choosing your username?"
Student A: Well, it's important to remember that you shouldn't use your real name. It's better to make a funny username like "chocolateman24."
Student B: That's a good answer, isn't it?
Student C: Yes, correct.

Answers

Computer Cool: password—combination of numbers, uppercase and lowercase letters, and special characters; save to favorites—so you can find the website again easily; padlock symbol—to show a website is safe; download—articles/reports, music, movies, blog posts, photos/pictures; username—it's not your real name; devices—students' own answers
Thinking Time: Students' own answers
Fun with Food: in season food—it's better for the environment and it'll taste better; junk food—processed food and convenience food or burgers, fries, fried chicken, sodas, candy, etc.; being late—it's rude; healthy diet—to eat a balance of vegetables, protein, whole grains, and foods that are high in fiber. Don't eat too much red meat or foods that are high in salt or saturated fat.; processed food—lots of salt and saturated fats; local produce—students' own answers
You've Done It!: Students' own answers
Time to Speak: Student's own answers

Cool Down

Have students think of one more question for each category. Then put them in pairs to ask and answer their questions. Invite students to share questions and answers with the class.

Chatter Boxes (Units 3 & 4)

Lesson Objectives

- to review vocabulary from Units 3 and 4: dreams and ambitions, mysteries and illusions
- to review grammar from Units 3 and 4: second conditional, *wish* + past forms, modals of deduction, and modals of obligation
- to practice communication and fluency skills

Warm Up

Ask students to look at the pictures and categories on pp. 60–61. Have them discuss in pairs which category they find most interesting and why. Elicit ideas.

How to Play

- Students are going to play a question and answer game in order to win points. Go through the instructions on p. 60. More detailed instructions on how to play are given here.
- Put students in pairs. Have them fold their books in half so they can see only one page: Student A looks at p. 60; Student B looks at p. 61.
- Have students write their names at the top of the Points Charts. For each question they answer, they color in the squares with the points they get. Their partner will award them 0, 1, or 2 points depending on how well they answer.
- Students take turns choosing a Chatter Box category and answering a question, e.g. Student A chooses a picture box and reads out the title. Student B chooses a question from the text box with the same heading. If Student A answers correctly, Student B can award 1 or 2 points. If the answer is incorrect or poor, Student B should give 0 points.
- The turn then passes to Student B, who chooses a picture box category from p. 61 and the process is repeated.
- Monitor and help with evaluating answers as necessary. Encourage students to be honest in awarding points, pulling on their skills of evaluation and reflection. They can also check back in the units to help justify their decisions.
- The first student to complete their Points Chart, or the student with the most points after answering all of the questions, wins.

Here is an example:

Student A: Fascinating History!
Student B: OK. Ready? What is the period of very early history called?
Student A: Could you repeat the question, please?
Student B: Sure. What is the period of very early history called?
Student A: Um… I think it's called "historic."
Student B: Are you sure?
Student A: No, but I don't really know the answer.
Student B: I think it's called "prehistoric." Let's check. Yes, it's here on page 53.
Student A: You're right. OK. Do I get any points?
Student B: Well, part of the word is right, so I'll give you one point.

Answers

My Dreams: Students' own answers; fresh start; hero
That's Strange: nonfiction; optical illusion; students' own answers
Life Might Be Different: Students' own answers (x3)
Obligations: Students' own answers (x3)
Fascinating History: Stonehenge, Easter Island moai statues, or students' own answers; clue; prehistoric
I Wonder: Students' own answers (x3)
Good Qualities: Students' own answers; confidence; wealth
If Only: Students' own answers (x3)

Cool Down

Have students look at the pictures again and in pairs say what the people are saying or thinking. Elicit ideas from different pairs of students.

Yesterday's Vacation Fun (Units 5 & 6)

Lesson Objectives

- to review vocabulary from Units 5 and 6: describing art, playing traditional board games and video games
- to review grammar from Units 5 and 6: past perfect simple, past perfect progressive, narrative tenses, indirect questions, defining and non-defining relative clauses
- to practice communication and fluency skills

Warm Up

Ask students to work in pairs and tell each other what they did on Saturday morning and afternoon. Invite students to report what their partner did to the rest of the class.

How to Play

- Students are going to do a variation on a find-the-differences game and then tell a story.
- Put students in pairs. Have them fold their books in half so they can see only one page, p. 86 or p. 87.
- Students describe the a. pictures (Yesterday morning) to their partner and find the differences. The scenes are very different, so they should explore them from all angles, going beyond the obvious. Encourage them to ask questions and find at least ten differences.
- Then they describe and discuss the b. pictures (Yesterday afternoon) and again find at least ten differences. Encourage them to find different things from what they found in picture a.
- Now have students tell the story of the day's activities from the perspective of the two children in the first picture a., keeping their pictures hidden from each other. Using the times of day in the labels, they can figure out what happened first and develop the story. Encourage them to be imaginative and embellish the story with details.
- Finally, have them look at all the pictures to see if they felt they told a good story. You could have them write their story out either as a dialogue/play or a narrative.

Here is an example:

Student A: There's a boy and girl who are playing a video game.

Student B: Oh! In my picture, there are lots of boys and girls and two adults. What do your children look like?

Student A: The boy has short brown hair and the girl has short orange hair.

Student B: OK. I have those children in my picture, too, but they're doing a craft activity, making a collage, I think. What are the boy and girl wearing?

Suggested Answers

Picture a. 9:00 a.m. / 10:30 a.m.: indoors/outdoors; two people / nine people; only children / seven children and two adults; playing a video game / doing craft activities; sitting on cushions / standing or sitting on stools; sunny day / windy day; the girl is wearing a pink T-shirt, pink pants, and green striped socks / the girl is wearing a yellow sweater; the boy is wearing a yellow T-shirt, orange pants, and blue-and-purple striped socks / the boy is wearing a blue sweater; a red table with four yellow chairs / a pink table with four yellow stools; a TV / no TV; a game of chess / craft paper and crayons

Picture b. 5:15 p.m. / 1:45 p.m.: indoors/outdoors; two people / nine people; only children / seven children and two adults; raining / sunny; playing Ping-Pong / playing a puzzle game; the girl is wearing a green and yellow T-shirt, pink pants, and green striped socks / the girl is wearing a pink T-shirt, pink pants, and green and white sneakers; the boy is wearing a blue and yellow T-shirt, orange pants, and blue-and-purple striped socks / the boy is wearing a yellow T-shirt, orange pants, and black and white sneakers; a TV and video game controls / no TV or video game; two cushions and four yellow chairs / a pink table with three yellow stools on top; a game of chess in a box / no game of chess; two cushions in the corner / no cushions

Cool Down

Have students work in different pairs, A and B again. Have students look at a set of pictures for a few seconds. Then have them close their books. One of the students in each pair keeps their book open and asks questions about the pictures their partner was looking at. Their goal is to test their partner's memory. Then students change roles and repeat with the other set of pictures.

Word Scramble Race (Units 7 & 8)

Lesson Objectives

- to review vocabulary from Units 7 and 8: advertising and numbers
- to review grammar from Units 7 and 8: reported statements, commands, and questions; passives
- to practice communication and fluency skills

Materials

Playing Cards printout from the Resource Bank (one per group); envelopes (one per team, with the cut-up word cards)

Warm Up

Play *Stand Up, Sit Down* (see TB p. 26) to review facts from Unit 7 and Unit 8 (but not the sentences used in the game). Suggested sentences: Unit 7—*Gabriela watched an ad about a gray toothpaste.* (black toothpaste) *Packaging is often used to make a product more attractive. Jugaad means fixing things and selling them again.* (fixing them and reusing them in new forms) Unit 8—*The sun is 4,000 times bigger than the moon.* (400 times) *In a solar eclipse, the moon passes in front of the sun. In Conway's Game of Life there is only one human player.* (There are no human players.)

How to Play

- Before the lesson, download and cut out the word cards for each group. Jumble them up and place them inside an envelope. Label each envelope A or B.
- Students are going to race to make sentences with sets of word cards and then decide which sentence is false.
- Go through the instructions on p. 133. More detailed instructions on how to play are given here.
- Put students in groups of four with two pairs playing against each other: Team A and Team B. Hand out the envelopes and have each team use one book as the board.
- The teams race to make four sentences from the words in their envelope, using the size of the bricks on the board as clues. At this point, they just have to construct grammatically correct sentences—they shouldn't worry about factual accuracy. Award points or rank the teams on the board for speed in making the sentences.
- When both teams have finished making their sentences, give them a few minutes to discuss (quietly) which sentence is false.
- The teams then trade sentences (i.e. turn their books) and decide which sentence from the other team is false. The team to identify it first wins. Award points and combine these with the sentence-making points to have an overall winning team.
- Have students discuss all the sentences as a group. Encourage them to say what they remember about the facts and look back through the unit to check them. You can also discuss any grammar queries resulting from the ordering activity.

Here is an example:

Student A: OK, we've put all the sentences in order. Which one is false?

Student B: I think it's number 4—you should read the small print before buying something, not building it.

Student A: I agree.

...

Student C: So what do you remember about the Fibonacci sequence?

Student A: I remember that you find it in sunflowers and other things in nature.

Student B: Yes, and if you count the spirals, it follows the sequence.

Answers

Team A

1 He told me that the Fibonacci sequence starts with the numbers: 0, 1, 1, 2, 3.
2 A billboard ad will be remembered by 89% of its target market.
3 Spirals are often found in shells and flowers.
4 You should always read the small print before building (buying) something.

Team B

1 The teacher explained that the hexagon had six angles of 120°.
2 Ads are used to persuade people to buy products.
3 A prime number can only be multiplied (divided) by one or itself.
4 One of the largest target markets for fast food is teenagers.

Cool Down

In their groups, have students choose words from their sentences and ask the other pair to explain what each word means. If students can't explain the word, the other pair must try and do so. Monitor and provide help if necessary.

Solve a Problem! (Units 9 & 10)

Lesson Objectives

- to review vocabulary from Units 9 and 10: decision-making and leadership
- to review grammar from Units 9 and 10: third conditional statements and questions, future progressive, and mixed future forms (*will*, *going to*, present progressive)
- to practice communication and fluency skills

Warm Up

Write *Super Sports Club: Special Training Day* on the board. Ask students to imagine that a day like this is going to take place at their school. Have them discuss in pairs what they expect to see, hear, and do on a day like this. Elicit ideas.

How to Play

- Students are going to play a problem-solving game.
- Go through the instructions on p. 139. More detailed instructions on how to play are given here.
- Put students in groups of four. Have students read the introduction paragraph in the How to Play panel and look at the pictures. Give them time to evaluate what went wrong, looking carefully at the details of both pictures. Point out that the top picture shows the organizers planning the event, and the bottom one shows the event itself. Let them make notes if they want to.
- Have students choose a role card from p. 139, and ask them not to look at the others. Point out that each role card says what that student thinks was the *main* problem of the event. This is now their point of view as one of the event organizers.
- Give students time to think about how they are going to explain the problem, consequence, and future solution to the other organizers. Point out they should use examples from the picture to help them explain and justify their arguments and give them time to make notes. Tell them they have to persuade the rest of their group that their solutions are the best, so they will need to come up with lots of ideas.
- Have students discuss and share their ideas with their groups. Point out that their goal is to agree what went wrong in the past and agree on how they are going to manage a similar event in the future. Encourage them to listen and respond to each other and to make up details during their discussion. Monitor and help move the discussion forward if necessary.
- At the end of the discussion, have students vote on the best solution. Share decisions as a class to see if all the groups chose the same solution.

Here is an example of how the discussion might start:

Student A: OK, so I think the biggest problem was that we had poor leadership. If we had had someone to lead us and to inspire us, then more people would have taken part.

Student B: Yes, that was a problem, but we also made the wrong decisions about which sports to offer. Tennis and soccer were offered, but we didn't have enough space to play both.

Student A: Yes, but someone with good organizational skills would have prevented that from happening. The leader we had couldn't make up his mind.

Student C: I see your point, but …

Answers

Students' own answers

Cool Down

Have students look at the pictures again. They take turns describing a person from one of the pictures for their partner to identify.

Process Writing

Generating Ideas

Lesson Objective

- **to learn about process writing: generating ideas**

This is the first in a series of lessons that help students develop their writing skills and become better writers. Process writing breaks down the stages of writing into carefully scaffolded steps. Process writing encourages students to write with better organization, structure, and accuracy.

In this lesson, students are going to learn different ways of generating ideas.

- Have students read the Generating Ideas explanation box. Elicit from students how they brainstorm ideas inside and outside of class.
- Then elicit topics students would like to talk about and write them on the board. Give students time to brainstorm talking points about the topic(s) in pairs or groups, then elicit ideas. Group the ideas as you write them on the board, if you can.
- Guide students to reflect on how they brainstormed ideas, encouraging them to describe what went on in their head. Ask *Did you have lots of ideas right away? Did you have to think about different parts of the topic? Did you remember what other people have told you about this topic? Did you see any images in your head? Did you need to write something down? Did you think in English or in your own language?*

A Think and discuss. Look at the different ways we can get ideas. Which one(s) could be helpful for each type of writing? (a–e)

- Have students look at the different ways of getting ideas and choose the ones they use. Then have them compare with a friend and give reasons. Elicit ideas from students and advantages/disadvantages of each technique.
- Draw students' attention to the five types of writing. Ask a few questions to check if students understand or remember the features of each type of writing: *Which of these types of writing are formal? Which are informal? Which ones try to persuade the reader? Which entertain or inform the reader?*
- Then have students look at each Generating Ideas technique and discuss in pairs how useful it is for each type of writing. When you check answers, highlight that more than one technique can be used for each kind of writing. Point out that there are other kinds of techniques not included in this section, such as story maps.

Suggested Answers

a Research: question words; Flow chart; Categories
b Discovery; Categories
c Mind map; Flow chart; Categories
d Research: question words; Mind map
e Discovery

B You're going to write an article called *The Good and Bad Points About Getting Older*. Choose two ways from A to get ideas. Make notes.

- Write the title of the article on the board and find out how students feel about this topic.
- Ask students to choose two Generating Ideas techniques from A and brainstorm ideas on their own. Point out that there's no right or wrong answer. This task will help them see how effective a technique is depending on the topic.
- Before they start, check that they understand the words in the second technique, *Discovery*, and how these actions help with brainstorming ideas. You may wish to point out that *Apply* here means how the point relates to themselves and to a situation they are familiar with.
- Monitor while students do the task, and make sure they are taking notes. When they finish, put them in pairs to compare ideas. Ask them to discuss which of the techniques was the most effective, i.e. which produced the most ideas. Elicit ideas from students.

Answers

Students' own answers

C Think and discuss with a friend. Which way do you prefer? Why?

- When they've finished, have them compare their ideas with another pair of students.
- Then have some students explain why they liked (or didn't like) the different ways of getting ideas and taking notes.

D Write a paragraph for the article on the good points about getting older. Use your notes from your preferred method in B.

- Give students time to write their paragraph using their notes. Remind them that they only need to write about the good points. They do not need to include all their ideas. Point out they should only write a maximum of 70 words.
- Draw students' attention to the brainstorming callout. Discuss whether any of the techniques that they didn't use would work well for an article about the advantages and disadvantages of getting old.

Answers

Students' own answers

Planning

Lesson Objectives

- to learn about process writing: planning
- to practice generating ideas

Materials
Sticky notes and large pieces of paper (C)

This is the second in a series of lessons that help students become better writers. In this lesson, students are going to learn how to plan their writing.

- Draw students' attention to the first two sentences in the planning explanation box. Tell students that once they have lots of ideas, they need to choose the best ideas to include in their writing. They will then need to think about how to organize their ideas.
- Then have students read the third sentence. Students are familiar with different types of texts from this tier: letter of complaint, email, essay, diary entry, flyer, acrostic poem, biography, story, infographic, article. Choose one or two of these and ask students who the readers are and what kind of information they need to know for each.

A You're going to write a story called *A Time When I Changed My Mind*. Choose a way from p. 140 to develop ideas and make notes.

- Write the title of the story on the board and elicit what *change my mind* means. Have students remember the different ways of getting ideas and choose the one they are going to use. Give students a few minutes to brainstorm ideas, either individually or in groups. Remind them to choose a method of noting their ideas and organize their ideas in three sections: Setting, Characters, and Problem.
- Ask students which ways of generating ideas they used and if they think they made the right choice. Tell students they can change the way of generating ideas during a brainstorming activity if they feel that it is not working for them.

Answers
Students' own answers

B Look at your notes and choose ideas or events you want to include. Discuss your decisions with a friend. Give reasons why these ideas or events are important.

- Remind students they will not be able to fit everything in and ask them to decide which ideas or events they noted down are important and should be included in the story. Have students cross out any they don't want to include.
- Then have students discuss their ideas with a friend. They should try to explain why these ideas or events are important, and why they decided not to use others. Encourage students to ask each other questions and make suggestions to improve their partner's story, e.g. *I think it would be funny to include this idea.*

Answers
Students' own answers

C Think about the best order for your ideas. Choose two ways to help you plan your story. Which method do you prefer?

- Draw students' attention to the planning callout. Discuss why planning is so important, e.g. it can save time in the drafting stage; it can help students think of interesting language to use; it ensures students express their ideas in a clear order.
- Point out the three different ways of planning. Ask students to choose two methods and plan their story using their notes from B. Hand out sticky notes and big pieces of paper as needed.
- Have students compare their notes in pairs and discuss which method they preferred and why. Invite students to share with the class.

Answers
Students' own answers

D Now think about your reader. How can you help him/her understand the order and importance of the events and how the characters feel? Look at your story plan so far and make notes.

- Ask students to think about who their target reader is. Ask *Are you writing for your friends? Are you writing for people the same age as you, younger, or older? Are you writing for people who live in a different country and might need further information?*
- When students have decided on their target reader, ask them to think about how they can help him/her understand the story better. Remind them to think about what a reader needs to know at the beginning of a story. Have them look at their story plan from C and complete the table in D.

Suggested Answers
Time phrases: *then*, after that, suddenly, in the end, finally
Adjectives showing feelings and reactions: *surprised*, disappointed, angry, upset, happy, excited

E Write the first paragraph of your story.

- Give students time to write the first paragraph of their stories or have them write them for homework. This can include the beginning and middle parts of the story. They should write a minimum of 50 words.
- Then ask students if they think the planning helped them write a better story.

Answers
Students' own answers

Drafting

Lesson Objectives

- to learn about process writing: drafting
- to practice generating ideas and planning

This is the third in a series of lessons that help students become better writers. In this lesson, students are going to learn how to write a draft.

- Draw students' attention to the first two sentences in the drafting explanation box. Tell students that sometimes we plan some good ideas but realize that they don't fit when we do our writing. Point out that a draft is like a practice run and is always followed by a revision stage where we can cross out any ideas we don't like, or move them to a different place, insert new ideas, or change words and expressions. Point out that the revision stage is not an editing stage; rather, it's a chance to make changes to the content.
- Then have students read the last sentence and elicit that a draft does not have to be neat and tidy; in fact, their writing will probably be better if the revision has lots of changes!

A You're going to write an essay called *Why It's Important to Try New Things*. Think of ideas and make notes on these two different points of view.

- Draw students' attention to the title of the essay and elicit one or two examples of new things people can try, e.g. new food, a new sport.
- Have students read the two different points of view. Point out that in both cases the conclusion is the same, i.e. it's important to try new things. Then refer students to the Generating Ideas techniques on p. 140. Ask them to choose one and make notes of their ideas.
- Have students compare their notes in pairs. Invite students to share ideas with the class. You could organize the ideas on the board.

Answers
Students' own answers

B Plan your essay like on p. 141. Then write a draft conclusion for point of view 1 and a draft conclusion for point of view 2.

- Have students use a planning technique from p. 141. Give students time to decide which ideas to include and organize their ideas.
- When students are ready, ask them to write two conclusions: one for point of view 1 and one for point of view 2. They should write a maximum of 50 words for each paragraph. Point out that these are draft conclusions and they will have the chance to revise them later.

Answers
Students' own answers

C Choose one of your conclusions from B. How can you improve it? Think and discuss with a friend.

- Ask students to choose one of the two conclusions that they would like to improve. They can either choose the conclusion they think is strong or the one they think needs more work.
- Draw students' attention to the list of things they can consider in order to improve the conclusion. Go through the questions and check understanding.
- Put students in pairs. Have them take turns talking their partner through their plan and reading out their conclusion. They should answer the questions in the boxes to help them analyze their paragraphs. Their partner offers them ideas on how to improve the conclusion. Monitor and provide help if necessary.

Answers
Students' own answers

D Revise and rewrite your conclusion from C.

- Ask students to rewrite their conclusion based on the discussion they had in B. Make sure they rewrite the whole conclusion and not just make changes to their draft. If possible, allow them time to read each other's conclusion in the same pairs and discuss them further.
- Draw students' attention to the drafting callout. Point out that a draft is the basis for their final writing and the reader won't see it. So, they are free to cross out words, make notes on the side, and so on. You can also discuss with students that even though they may feel they don't have enough time to follow all the steps (brainstorming, planning, drafting), practice will help them complete these steps faster each time. Stress the importance of following these steps every time they are asked to do a writing task.

Editing and Publishing

Lesson Objectives

- to learn about process writing: editing and publishing
- to practice generating ideas, planning, and drafting

This is the last in a series of lessons that help students become better writers. In this lesson, students are going to learn different ways of editing and publishing their writing.

- Draw students' attention to the editing and publishing explanation box. Read the information and point out that this is the stage at which they can add, delete, reorder, and replace words, as well as rephrase sentences to make them clearer or more complex. Explain that to check their work, it's important to think differently—as though they were the reader, not the writer. Highlight the importance of handing in a final draft that's neat and tidy. This is the piece of writing they will share with their readers.

A You're going to write a blog post called *What I've Learned This Year*. Think of ideas and make notes on these things.

- Write the title of the blog post on the board and elicit ideas from a few students.
- Then look at the four points together. Give students a minute to make notes for each point. Ask them to use a Generating Ideas technique from p. 140. Allow them to compare ideas in pairs as they finish.

B Plan and then write a first draft of the beginning of your blog post. Trade with a friend. Check the content and structure of your friend's writing. Think and discuss.

- Tell students they are going to write the beginning of their blog post using the planning and drafting steps of process writing to help them create a good piece of writing. If necessary, quickly review ways of planning (p. 141) and drafting (p. 142).
- Give students plenty of time to follow the steps. They should write around 70 words.
- Ask students to exchange their writings in pairs. Have them read their partner's beginning and check the content and structure. They must also look at the spelling, punctuation, and grammar. Point out the questions in the table. Ask students to make notes on the writing using a different colored pen if possible.

C Revise the beginning of your blog post. Then trade with your friend again. Put on your editor's hat and answer the questions.

- Have students look at their own writing again, with their friend's comments. Give them time to revise the beginning of their blog post.
- Ask students to exchange their writings again. Tell them to imagine they are an editor looking at someone else's writing. Draw their attention to the questions and give them time to respond.
- Have students discuss their answers in different pairs. Invite students to share ideas with the class.

D Look at your friend's notes. What type of mistakes did you make? What type of mistakes do you make most? Think and discuss.

- Ask students to look at their partner's notes and reflect on their mistakes. Encourage them to think whether these are mistakes they often make and why, if appropriate. What other mistakes do they often make?
- Ask students to discuss their ideas in pairs and then share with the class.

E Now, edit the beginning of your blog post. Have you dealt with the problems your friend identified?

- Ask students to edit the beginning of their blog post, bearing in mind their partner's notes.
- When they finish, you can ask them to exchange writings again and check how their partner improved their text. Invite students to explain to the class what corrections or changes they made.
- Draw students' attention to the editing and publishing callout. Ask students whether having a friend read their writing was beneficial and how so. Who else could they ask to read their writing before publishing it?

F Make a final copy of the beginning of your blog post. Think about how to make your writing look professional and attractive to the reader. Publish your work!

- Ask students to write one final copy of the beginning of their blog post. Discuss how they can make their writing look professional and attractive, e.g. by writing the title in larger letters, not splitting words at the end of a line. You can also discuss other things they should consider when making a final copy, such as the size of the text, whether it should be typed or handwritten, and whether it should have illustrations. You could also discuss different ways of publishing their work—would a hard copy or digital version be more appropriate for example?
- When they have finished, help students display their writing in class. Invite them to walk around and read other people's writings and notice what they did differently.

Audio Scripts

Language Book

For the vocabulary drills, where an alternative exists in British English, this is noted in parentheses next to the corresponding American English word/phrase. Audio recordings of the British English pronunciation and words/phrases are available through the **Teacher's App** on **Navio**.

Language Review

TRACK 1

Language Review

A Listen and write. How did all the children feel?

Daniel: I'm so happy I went to the "Get to Know Everyone" day, Mom—it was a really good way to start the school year, and it was really fun!

Mom: What did everyone do, Daniel?

Daniel: We did all kinds of things. Chen was confused at first about how to put the tent up—it took him ages! And Leila was enthusiastic about everything as always and especially loved trampolining. Giulia didn't do much—she was upset about something and spent the whole afternoon swinging in the hammock! Jane was a bit worried because she had to build a shelter under the trees with rope. She did it in the end, though! And Michael learned how to dive, but Amari was furious because he got completely soaked!

Mom: And what about you, Daniel? What did you do?

Daniel: I was delighted because I had the best time of all—I went rappelling. Bouncing down a wall on a rope is awesome.

TRACK 2

Language Review

A Listen and complete.

Girl: Have you tried to play these instruments yet?

Daniel: No, I haven't, but I'd like to.

Girl: These drums were made in Ghana.

Daniel: They're great, aren't they?

Boy: I've just eaten this Indian food. It's delicious!

Girl: I haven't tried it yet, but I've already eaten some Japanese food.

Boy: I was taught how to make sushi at the Japanese stall.

Girl: Yes! It was fun, wasn't it?

Girl: Have you seen these? They're the Pyramid of the Sun and the Pyramid of the Moon in Mexico.

Boy: Only in pictures. You've been there, haven't you?

Girl: Yes, they're amazing. They were built about 2,000 years ago.

Boy: Wow! I'd love to go to Mexico!

Unit 1

TRACK 3

Unit 1, Vocabulary

A Listen. What information does Daniel want? How does he find it?

Daniel: Kate, can you help me?

Kate: What's up, Daniel?

Daniel: You know our class blog, *One World*, and this week's blog post, "The School Day"? Well, I want to search for facts about how a school day in Ghana is different from our school day. Can you help me?

Kate: Yes, sure. It's an interesting project, isn't it?

Daniel: Yes, it is. Sorry, I only have half an hour. The first person to get three facts will be the person to write the post, and I really want to do it! Sofia and I found a good website yesterday, but I can't find it now.

Kate: Did you use "save to favorites"?

Daniel: No.

Kate: You could email or message Sofia to see if she remembers the website.

Daniel: I did. But she hasn't answered yet and time is running out!

Kate: Um, we can look in your search history.

Daniel: Of course! Why didn't I think of that?

Kate: OK. Let's have a look at the list of websites you visited recently. Hey, that's a really bad website—don't use that! Oh! Do you like pandas?

Daniel: Yes …

Kate: Ah, I think this is the website you want.

Daniel: Oh, thanks so much, Kate. Right, I'm going to do this as fast as I can!

TRACK 4

Unit 1, Vocabulary

B Find and number the words in A. Then listen and check.

1 crash
2 upload
3 email
4 message
5 search history
6 blog
7 blog post
8 comment
9 save to favorites
10 download

TRACK 5

Unit 1, Vocabulary

C Close your eyes. Listen, visualize, and say.

You turn on your laptop. You're going to start a new blog. What's it going to be about? Who's going to read it? Say "blog." Think about your first blog post. What do you want to write about today? What's the title of your post? Say "blog post." You find some photos you want to upload to your blog post. How long will they take to upload? Say "upload." Someone has made a positive comment on your first blog post. How will you respond? Say "comment." Now that you've written a post for your blog, you remember a video you saved to favorites. Why is it a favorite? Click on "favorites." Say "save to favorites." Hmm. The video isn't in favorites. Go to "search history" and look at the list of websites you've visited. Say "search history." You find the video. You start to download it. How long does it take to download? Say "download." You try to open the video, but suddenly, your computer crashes! How do you feel? Say "crash." You decide to use your cell phone to email a friend who can help. What will you put in the subject line? Say "email." Oh, hold on! A message will be quicker. Write it on your cell phone. What does it say? Did you use any emojis? Say "message."

TRACK 6

Unit 1, Vocabulary

E Listen and write. Then watch and say.

Search the Net

Search the net, search the net.
My turn to search and write the blog post!
Search the net, search the net.
Facts—who can find the most?

Search the net, search the net.
Save to favorites now!
Search the net, search the net.
Upload your photos—wow!

Search the net, search the net.
Don't download that—it's trash!
Search the net, search the net.
My computer's going to crash!

TRACK 7

Unit 1, Vocabulary

F Pronunciation. Listen and say. Copy the sentence stress. Find other sentences in the poem and notice the stress patterns.

My turn to search and write the blog post! (x2)
Save to favorites now! (x2)
My computer's going to crash! (x2)

TRACK 8

Unit 1, Explore Language

A Listen and read. What's different about a school day in Ghana?

Daniel: Hey Deepak—I have a lot of facts about Ghana for our blog! Did you know that the official language is English?

Deepak: Interesting. What else did you find out?

Daniel: Well, I read on one boy's blog that schoolchildren can get up between 5:30 and 6 o'clock—before it's too hot. This boy I read about gets up at 4:30.

Deepak: 4:30! I wonder if he always wakes up on time—I don't know if I could do that.

Daniel: Before school, children usually clean the house, go get water, or help prepare the evening meal. They make their own breakfast, too.

Deepak: Wow! Do you know how they get to school?

Daniel: Most children walk—sometimes for an hour. When it's time for class, drums start playing.

Deepak: Drums? I don't understand why they have drums.

Daniel: To get everyone excited about the school day, I guess! But I don't remember if the children play them. Let's look … Oh, I forgot which website it was.

Deepak: Did you save it to favorites?

Daniel: Yes … here it is! I wonder whether we'll go into class playing music someday.

TRACK 9

Unit 1, Explore Language

D Listen and say.

1 I forgot which website it was.
2 He doesn't remember how to do it.
3 I wonder what we'll do today.
4 They don't know if they can come tomorrow.
5 I don't think I understand.

TRACK 10

Unit 1, Global Citizenship

A Listen to an online video tutorial. What information does the tutorial give?

Meg: Mom, I want to do some research about citizen science projects. That's where people can do things that help scientists, like counting local birds to see if their numbers are going up or down. I'll need to sign up via a website, so I've found a video tutorial about registering for a website safely.

Mom: OK. Let's take a look.

Tutor: When you register for a website, the system will take personal information, such as your name and date of birth, so it can recognize you every time you log on. When you've registered, you can create a profile with more personal information and often a photo.

This video shows you how to register safely on any of your devices—computer, laptop, tablet, or phone—and how to create a profile. You need to know what personal information is safe to give and understand who can access it—your online privacy and online safety are very important.

Before entering any personal information, check if the site is secure—does the website exchange data or information safely? Look at the website address in the search bar. Does it start with *https*? The *s* stands for "secure." Also look for a padlock symbol next to the search bar. This shows the site is probably safe.

When you know a site is safe, you can enter your personal information. Think of a username that's different from your real name. You also need a password—make yours a phrase you can remember, and use a combination of numbers, uppercase and lowercase letters, and special characters if you can. Oh, and don't tell anyone your password!

Mom: Apart from me!

TRACK 11

Unit 1, Global Citizenship

B Look at the pictures and definitions in A and write. Then listen and check.

1 register
2 online privacy
3 online safety
4 create a profile
5 personal information
6 devices
7 secure
8 username
9 password
10 uppercase letters
11 lowercase letters
12 special characters

TRACK A

Unit 1, Global Citizenship

Close your eyes. Listen, visualize, and say.

First, choose which device you're going to use—computer, laptop, tablet, or cell phone. Say "devices." Stop! Are you on a safe network at home or at school? Say "online safety." Log on to the internet and open the website you want to register for. Say "register." Stop! Look at the website address. Can you see the padlock symbol and s for "secure"? Say "secure." Find the place where it says you can create a profile. Click on it. Say "create a profile." Think. What personal information will you give online? Say "personal information." What information do you want to keep private? Say "online privacy." Think of a username. Is it different from your real name? Say "username." Now think of a password between 8 and 12 characters long. Shhh, don't tell anyone! Say "password." What uppercase letters does your password have? Choose four. Say "uppercase letters." What lowercase letters does your password have? Choose four. Say "lowercase letters." Include two special characters in your password. What are they? Say "special characters." Now you can submit your form!

TRACK 12

Unit 1, Global Citizenship

D Now listen to Pablo and Mari presenting a podcast. What's the podcast about?

Pablo: Hi and welcome to Teen World. I'm your co-host Pablo.

Mari: And I'm Mari. Welcome to the second installment of our *Technology Today* podcast.

Pablo: Last week, we talked about online safety and some of the negative aspects of technology.

Mari: Today, we're talking about the benefits of technology for learning. The first thing is research. There's so much information out there on the internet, and that's great! We can learn so much.

Pablo: That's right, Mari. We can learn about black holes or how to change a tire. We can find anything …

Mari: But, as we learned last week, we need to be careful about the websites we use.

Pablo: Second, you can find study groups online. You can connect with people studying the same thing as you, or with the same special interests, like music. We met Olivia from Singapore who composed her own song. Then she went online and found other teenagers who helped her record it.

Mari: Third, there are online projects that can help people around the globe. One example is the charity Shout It Out Kids Foundation, which connects children and creates communities across the world, giving children a voice by letting them tell their stories to others. We can learn from children all over the world, and see what different things affect them. It's interesting to find out how children have different ideas about solving problems.

Pablo: Yes, like Priya, who started her own vegan snack business. Those snacks looked so good!

Mari: We've even started a project of our own, called Teen World Connects. We believe that you can use technology to do something individually and then use that information to come together and exchange ideas.

Pablo: There's more detail about the project on our blog for you to read. We hope you like it and want to register.

Mari: That's all we have time for now. Until next time on Teen World, the podcast for global teens.

TRACK 13

Unit 1, Explore Language

A Listen and read. What does Sofia want? Can she have them?

Sofia: Deepak, did you know you can get selfie shoes? You put your phone in a special shoe and use your foot to take a selfie!

Deepak: Really, Sofia? Are you sure that's true?

Sofia: Yes! Daniel told me about it. When he was looking for information yesterday on how to take the best selfie, he found an article about it. He wasn't joking!

Deepak: Do you remember what Miss Goran said about checking for fake news?

Sofia: Oh, yeah—I forgot.

Deepak: Do you have the website there?

Sofia: Yes, I'm taking a look right now. What did Miss Goran tell us to check? Oh, yeah! Is anyone else reporting it?

Deepak: Yes. And also to check for things like bad spelling or grammar—is it bad quality?

Sofia: Well, yes, it is. While I was reading it, I found a lot of mistakes.

Deepak: Wait a minute. Look, it says here that the reports are fake!

Sofia: Well, I still want some. They'd be a great invention!

TRACK 14

Unit 1, Explore Language

D Listen and say.

1 I'm taking a look right now.
2 He saw you do it.
3 Do you remember what she said?
4 How often do you check your email?
5 Why were you checking your phone?

Unit 2

TRACK 15

Unit 2, Vocabulary

A Listen. What are the rules for the sports club?

Cathy: So, Ben, is this your first time at sports' practice? I haven't seen you here before.

Ben: Yes, it is! I don't know many people here, apart from Coach García.

Cathy: Don't worry, everyone is really nice. I can tell you who everyone is. There's Sofia and her brother Diego just coming in the door. They're late for practice. Sofia is always late! Mrs. Perry looks annoyed. She likes everyone to be punctual so we can start on time.

Ben: Oh, yes, I recognize her. And who's that, with his hand up?

Cathy: The boy with the blond hair and green tracksuit? That's Sam. He's always very polite.

Ben: And who's that boy behind him? He looks so messy.

Cathy: That's Tom. He loves playing soccer, so his tracksuit is ripped and he has mud on his pants. He does look really messy! And those girls beside us are Jen and Emily.

Ben: They look like they're arguing about something.

Cathy: Yeah, you're right. They're really good friends, but they must be having a fight.

Matias García: OK, listen up, everyone! Thanks for coming. We're going to play lots of fun sports today. First though, I want to tell you the sports' club rules. I want you all to be here on time. You also need to work out often—at least three times a week—so that you can keep fit. It's good for your mind and body! And lastly, no junk food! I want you to think about what you're eating and try to have a healthy diet.

Ben: I guess I can't eat my candy bar now.

TRACK 16

Unit 2, Vocabulary

B Find and number the words in A. Then listen and check.

1 be late
2 sleep late
3 punctual
4 healthy diet
5 work out
6 junk food
7 polite
8 messy (British English: untidy)
9 argue
10 rude

TRACK 17

Unit 2, Vocabulary

C Close your eyes. Listen, visualize, and say.

Imagine yourself lying asleep in bed. You wake up suddenly and realize what the time is. You're late! How do you feel? Say "sleep late." You get up quickly, but you trip over lots of things lying on the floor. What are they? You can't find your clean clothes! Say "messy." You need to get to sports practice, but you're on the bus and the traffic is bad. How do you feel? Say "be late." Someone bumps into you on the street. They don't say "sorry"—what do you think about them? Say "rude." Imagine being late for class. How do you think the teacher feels? What should you say to the teacher? Say "polite." Phew! You arrive at class at exactly the right time. What's the time? Say "punctual." Oh, no! Two friends of yours are shouting at each other. Why are they shouting? Say "argue." Oh, dear—you're hungry already! Think about your favorite type of fast food. How often do you eat it? Say "junk food." You know you should really eat more fruit and vegetables. Think of some different types—how many different colors are there? Choose one fruit and one vegetable. How do they taste? Say "healthy diet." But you play sports every day, so that's good. What sports do you play on Tuesdays and Wednesdays? What are your sneakers like? Say "work out."

TRACK 18

Unit 2, Vocabulary

E Listen and write. Then watch and say.

You Can Do Better

My brother said it wasn't great
That my room's a mess and I'm sleeping late.
He tells me that I'm always rude.
And I'll get sick from all that junk food.

My brother says, "Don't argue, keep it cool,
You can do better, don't be a fool."
So I guess I have to try
To wave my bad habits all goodbye.

So I have a plan—but keep it quiet
Work out often, have a healthy diet,
Be punctual, polite—I agree
To be the best that I can be.

TRACK 19

Unit 2, Vocabulary

F Pronunciation. Listen and say. Copy the weak forms. Find other examples in the poem.

You can do better. (x2)
I have to try. (x2)
To be the best. (x2)

TRACK 20

Unit 2, Explore Language

A Listen and read. Do Ziad and Isabella agree?

Ziad: Look at this debate, Diego. Have you ever been in one? I'm going to take part because I think the way we use technology has made us rude.

Diego: Do you think so? Has technology really changed the way we communicate?

Ziad: Yes, it has! People argue more now because they just say what they want online. Because they don't say it face-to-face, they don't think about the effect their words have on people.

Isabella: Well, I haven't become ruder. I think we've gotten better at communicating because technology lets us stay in touch. Like messaging someone to say happy birthday.

Ziad: OK, Isabella, but we've just seen someone being pretty rude, haven't we?

Isabella: What do you mean?

Diego: Well, when Coach García posted a notice about practice a few minutes ago, someone wrote "That's crazy! Do we have to start SO early?"

Isabella: OK. That doesn't sound very polite … Is Coach García angry?

Ziad: I don't think so. He's already responded with "You snooze, you lose!"

TRACK 21

Unit 2, Explore Language

D Listen and say.

1 Have you ever been in one?
2 I've just arrived.
3 Has he gone to work out? Yes, he has.
4 We haven't eaten healthily since Monday.

TRACK 22

Unit 2, Global Citizenship

A Listen to Victor talk to his dad. What changes is Victor's dad making to their meals?

Victor: What's for dinner tonight, Dad?

Dad: Well, I know you were learning about healthy food last week, Victor …

Victor: Yes …

Dad: And you told me all about whole grains—food like brown rice—and making sure we don't eat food that is too high in salt or sugar …

Victor: Yes …

Dad: Well, I'm going to make a really healthy meal … I bought some vegetables in the market and they're local produce so I know they're fresh … and some red meat from the farmers' market!

Victor: I'm not sure we need to eat red meat that often. And we've already had burgers this week.

Dad: They were homemade chicken burgers!

Victor: Oh, yeah! Well, dinner sounds great, and it means we'll be eating food that's in season: spring vegetables! It'll taste better …

Dad: Yes—but it does take more time to prepare! That's why people use convenience food—everything's ready to serve.

Victor: I know, but in class we learned that it's more expensive and has a lot of packaging that's bad for the environment when you throw it away. I can help you cook. I could find some healthy recipes and plan them out for the week. And I can cook pasta on the day I have sports practice, as that's good for energy.

Dad: Wow—you are serious. I'll just sit back then …

TRACK 23

Unit 2, Global Citizenship

B Look at the pictures and definitions in A and write. Then listen and check.

1 in season
2 saturated fat
3 convenience food
4 local produce
5 red meat
6 white meat
7 packaging
8 whole grains
9 high in salt and sugar
10 high in fiber
11 processed food

TRACK B

Unit 2, Global Citizenship

Close your eyes. Listen, visualize, and say.

You decide to buy some fruit and vegetables at a market near your house. Say "local produce." Think about what fruit tastes best at this time of year. Say "in season." You consider buying some beef to make burgers. Say "red meat." You buy some chicken to make a casserole tomorrow. Say "white meat." After all that shopping, you're feeling tired and you decide to get some food that is already prepared at the market. Say "convenience food." The food you bought that was already prepared isn't homemade—it was made in a factory. Say "processed." Finally, you get home with all the shopping. Take all of the food out of its packaging—is there a lot? Say "packaging." You decide to have some brown rice for your dinner. Say "whole grains." Hmm, you bought some sauce for the rice, but now you realize it's very unhealthy. Say "high in salt and sugar." While you're cooking, you decide to add some lentils and beans to your dinner. Say "high in fiber." And to make up for the unhealthy sauce, you decide not to have any butter on your toast tomorrow. Say "saturated fat."

TRACK 24

Unit 2, Global Citizenship

D Now listen to the fitness instructor. Why is she talking about diet?

Hi, I'm Coach Kim. Before our workout today, I want to focus on what you're putting into your body because this can have a positive—or negative—effect. Having the right kind of diet can actually help you achieve your goals—in study or in sports. And it isn't difficult to make changes that'll make a real difference. Now, it's important to understand that eating for fitness doesn't require any special diets. It's all about making sure you eat the right foods in the right amounts. Eat a varied and balanced diet so you get all the minerals you need—like calcium from milk and cheese, and vitamins from vegetables and fruit. If you do work out regularly, you might need more calories than your classmates.

Carbohydrates are an excellent source of fuel that you can get from whole grains and other foods that are high in fiber. And don't forget everyone needs a certain amount of fat each day, but avoid unhealthy saturated fats or any food that's high in salt or sugar. And remember to drink lots of water, not juice. Juice and smoothies have a lot of sugar in them! So, they're really bad for your teeth too. Get your moms and dads on board and you'll all feel better. After a couple of weeks, you'll really begin to notice the difference. OK, let's get started …

TRACK 25

Unit 2, Explore Language

A Listen and read. Are Samuel and Uncle Matias talking about food for physical health, for mental health, or for both?

Samuel: Can I ask your advice, Uncle Matias? I've been studying for my exams but I have a terrible memory.

Matias García: Well, exams are tough. Have you been sleeping well?

Samuel: No, I haven't. I've been waking up a lot at night.
Matias García: Hmm—maybe it's your diet.
Samuel: I guess I haven't been eating healthy food.
Matias García: Well, you know, the right kind of food can be good for your brain as well as your body. And what have you been doing to work out?
Samuel: I've been running a lot with my friend—he's been helping me.
Matias García: OK, that's good. Also, think about doing things that will help you sleep, like taking a bath. And make sure any screen time you have is way before bedtime.
Samuel: OK, no cell phone or tablet before bed.
Matias García: Exactly. Well, I have to go. I'm off to the theater, again.
Samuel: Looks like you haven't been sleeping too much either, Uncle Matias!

TRACK 26
Unit 2, Explore Language
D Listen and say.
1 My friend's been helping me.
2 I've been running a lot.
3 What's she been eating?
4 What have they been studying?
5 They've been learning about healthy diets.

Unit 3

TRACK 27
Unit 3, Vocabulary
A Listen. What's different about this theater experience?
Actor: Welcome to *Life Is a Theater*! You will see a number of interesting doors leading to some amazing rooms. You need to decide which room to go into to participate in your theater experience. Every door leads to a different play, and you will star in that play with other actors. Choose carefully because—remember—you will *be* that person while you're in the room. You could be an astronaut, a famous athlete, or the president of a country!
Matias García: A president! Ooh! That sounds like fun!
Actor: Do you have goals that you want to achieve? Do you want to be better than anyone else? You could try the Ambition room.
Matias García: Sounds great, doesn't it, Camila?
Camila: Hmm …
Actor: You might also like the Success room. Do you want to have a positive result for everything you do? Or the Wealth room, where you will act in a play and you will be as rich as you want!
Matias García: You'd like that, wouldn't you?
Actor: Don't decide yet, because there's more! In the Pride room, you'll get a feeling of deep satisfaction about your achievements.
Matias García: Ooh, go for that one!
Actor: There's more, so hang on. What about the Determination room? This is where you'll find the strength in you to keep going so you can achieve what you want. Or the Confidence room, where you can have total belief in yourself.
Matias García: Camila, you should do all of them!
Camila: Dad!
Actor: Remember, everyone—you can only choose one. What's your main aim in life? What's your dream? And remember, it's *your* dream, it's *your* decision. *You* decide what *you* want and what play you will act in!

TRACK 28
Unit 3, Vocabulary
B Find and number the words in A. Then listen and check.
1 ambition
2 health
3 success
4 happiness
5 pride
6 determination
7 confidence
8 wealth

TRACK 29
Unit 3, Vocabulary
C Close your eyes. Listen, visualize, and say.
Think of a goal you want to achieve. Why is it important to you? Say "ambition." Think about your ambition. What will you do? How can you be sure you're going to achieve it? Say "determination." Picture yourself with success in the future. What is "success" for you? Say "success." Think about how you will feel about yourself when you're successful. What gives you the most pride? Say "pride." Picture yourself with double the confidence you have now. What can you do with this confidence? How does it feel? Say "confidence." Picture yourself with wealth in the future. What does "wealth" look like to you? What things do you have? Say "wealth." Imagine not feeling well. What can you do to make yourself feel better? Breathe deeply. How do you feel now? Imagine feeling really healthy. Say "health." Think about what gives you happiness. What's your happiest moment? Say "happiness."

TRACK 30
Unit 3, Vocabulary
E Listen and write. Then watch and say.
My Dreams
I have a dream of ambition
I have a lot to do
I'm full of determination
I'm ambitious, through and through!

I have a dream of success
To get right up to the top
I'm full of love and happiness
I'm strong, I'll never stop!

I have a dream of wealth
I want to work with pride
I'm full of energy and health
Live life! Enjoy the ride!

TRACK 31
Unit 3, Vocabulary
Pronunciation. Listen and say. Copy the linking. Find other examples in the poem.
have a dream (x2)
full of love (x2)

TRACK 32
Unit 3, Explore Language
A Listen and read. Which doors do Elise and Ji-su choose? Why?
Elise: If you could be anyone, who would you be?
Ji-su: Hmm, if I were someone famous, I'd be a famous athlete—you know, someone with real determination. My sister and I both love sports. She'd be a famous gymnast if she could choose! But if I had the choice, I wouldn't be a gymnast, I'd be a track star because I love running. I'm determined to be a professional track star and go to the Olympics. If I could have anything, I wouldn't have a lot of money, I'd have an Olympic gold medal!
Elise: So, which door are you going to choose?
Ji-su: I can't decide between "Success" and "Pride."
Elise: If I were you, I'd choose "Pride"—imagine how your amazing achievements would make you feel. You would have the satisfaction of going to the Olympics and, who knows, maybe even winning an Olympic medal!
Ji-su: I think I'm going to choose that, too! Let's go.

TRACK 33
Unit 3, Explore Language
D Listen and say.
1 If you could be anyone, who would you be?
2 She'd be a famous gymnast if she could choose!
3 If I were you, I wouldn't worry about it.
4 If you could live anywhere in the world, where would you live?
5 If we could live anywhere, we'd live in Australia.

TRACK 34
Unit 3, Global Citizenship
A Listen to Kamala interviewing three of her teachers. How can adults learn from children?
Host: Welcome to our show, Kamala.
Kamala: Yes, thank you for having me. I'm excited to be here.
Host: So, you interviewed your teachers for a school project. Tell us a little bit about that. Students don't often get to ask teachers interview questions.
Kamala: It was great! I was doing research for a school project about how we learn throughout our lives in different settings. So I chose the question, How can adults learn from children?
Host: OK, let me play the interview for our listeners. Ready?
Kamala: Sure! … Hello, I'm here with Mrs. Taylor, my math teacher. Mrs. Taylor, how do you think adults can learn from children?
Mrs. Taylor: Well, Kamala, children see every day as a fresh start. Most children move on quickly when they experience failure, so when they make a mistake, they are soon ready to try again. Because of this, I think they have much less fear of the unknown than adults.
Kamala: Thank you. Mr. Addison?
Mr. Addison: When I was a child, my mom always said to me, "Be the hero of your own story." Many adults have forgotten that. Children are much better at being the center of their own lives and focusing on themselves. But friends are important, too, and children spend a lot of time nurturing friendships. We can learn a lot from that.
Kamala: Yes! Ms. Asal, what about you?
Ms. Asal: I think we can also learn from children's creativity. Children are often great inventors because they find joy in spending hours doing things for fun. When your brain is free, you create new things without realizing it. Children notice the small things—the color of a flower, how big the moon is—that adults are often too busy to notice. But really, it's the small things which are important in the end. Adults sometimes forget that.

TRACK 35
Unit 3, Global Citizenship
B Look at the pictures in A and write. Then listen and check.
1 fresh start
2 experience failure
3 fear of the unknown
4 notice the small things
5 nurture friendship
6 do things for fun
7 find joy in
8 be the hero

TRACK C

Unit 3, Global Citizenship

Close your eyes. Listen, visualize, and say.

You decide to join a club which you've never been to before. Imagine your first day. What are you worried about? Say "fear of the unknown." You have a test, but you didn't study. You fail. How do you feel? Say "experience failure." You decide to be healthy from today. You'll work out and eat well. What do you do? Say "fresh start." Think about a friend. What do you do for your friend? What does your friend do for you? Say "nurture friendship." Think of something you like doing a lot. Is there something specific that makes it so enjoyable? Say "find joy in." Think of something you did just for fun recently. Why was it fun? Say "do things for fun." Think of a time recently when you stopped to notice the small things. What did you notice? What did you learn? Say "notice the small things." Say to yourself, "I'm the hero of my own story!" What are you doing? How do you feel? Say "be the hero."

TRACK 36

Unit 3, Global Citizenship

D Now listen to Feliks. How successful were the children in the soccer tournament?

Host: We now move on to our feature, "Inspiring Stories from around the World." Feliks is going to talk about his inspiring story.

Feliks: I watched an incredible story online about some children in Thailand who made a huge difference their community. People in their village, Ko Panyi, loved watching soccer on TV but nobody played it. They couldn't play because there was no space at all in their village. The buildings in Ko Panyi are all built on stilts in the shallow water next to a large rock in the sea, so there is no spare dry land.

But the children there really wanted to play and they thought of a brilliant idea—to build a floating soccer pitch. At first, the adults laughed at them—but the children were determined. They collected pieces of wood and made the pitch. It was pretty small, the surface wasn't very flat, and sometimes they fell into the water. But they loved playing soccer on their new pitch, and they got better and better.

After a lot of practicing, they decided to enter a tournament. The villagers loved having a community soccer team, so they gave the children special uniforms for the tournament and came to the matches to cheer them on. The team didn't win, but the players were proud of getting to the semifinals. And the whole village was proud of their determined and creative children, who ended up playing soccer really well! I bet those children felt like heroes!

TRACK 37

Unit 3, Explore Language

A Listen and read. How does Juan feel about joining the softball club?

Max: Hi, Juan. Do you want to join the softball club?

Juan: Hi, Max. Yes, but I wish I could play it better. I'm just not very good!

Max: Just play more! Joining a club is a great place to start. My cousin wishes she was better at photography, but she's getting better. She joined a club, and now, she works as a photographer on weekends.

Nella: Everyone has to start somewhere. You know, one of Einstein's teachers didn't think he would do anything with his life, but he kept working hard. And look what he became! I wish I didn't find math so hard, but I just keep trying.

Juan: Yes, but I wish softball wasn't so difficult!

Max: Nella's right. It's all about practice and hard work—but we can help you with that.

Nella: Do you wish you were a great athlete?

Juan: Yes, but …

Max: I wish you'd stop saying "yes, but …" and just join. You won't regret it.

Juan: OK. Yes!

TRACK 38

Unit 3, Explore Language

D Listen and say.

1 Do you wish you were a famous athlete?
2 I wish I were better at art.
3 I wish I didn't find science so hard.
4 I wish I could invent things.
5 I wish you'd stop saying that.

Unit 4

TRACK 39

Unit 4, Vocabulary

A Listen. What mystery are Sachin and his friends discussing?

Sachin: Hey, Julia, you should come outside!

Julia: Why? There's a big storm coming.

Sachin: Exactly! I just saw something amazing. A kind of ball of light in the sky. It had a tail on it. Did *you* see it, Max?

Max: No. Are you sure it wasn't just lightning?

Sachin: It wasn't just lightning! This was like a ball made of light.

Julia: Hmm. Maybe you're seeing things which aren't there. Sorry, I don't believe you, Sachin. I think you're just making it up!

Sachin: No, I definitely saw it! We've been studying different types of weather in class, but I've never seen anything like this.

Kasia: I wonder what it was.

Max: It was probably something called "ball lightning", Kasia. It's also called a fireball. You can see ball lightning in a thunderstorm, and it has a strange glow or light around it.

Sachin: Yes, that's exactly what I saw! It only lasted a few seconds. What makes it happen?

Max: Well, it's a bit of a puzzle because there's no specific explanation of why we see that strange light. It might be just an optical illusion—you know, when something looks very different from what it really is.

Julia: Yes! I think Sachin's seeing things that aren't there because of all the candy he's been eating this evening. Look at the wrappers around the trash can! I've found real evidence right there!

Kasia: Well, I have a feeling we're going to see the biggest storm ever. The weather's so exciting tonight. So maybe Sachin *did* see it!

Sachin: Thanks, Kasia!

TRACK 40

Unit 4, Vocabulary

B Find and number the words in A. Then listen and check.

1 evidence
2 make up
3 play a trick
4 optical illusion
5 fact
6 see things
7 puzzle
8 have a feeling

TRACK 41

Unit 4, Vocabulary

C Close your eyes. Listen, visualize, and say.

You and your friends from the photography club are staying in a large house. You learned some interesting facts about the history of photography today. Say "fact." It's five o'clock in the evening, and it's getting dark. Now you're all sitting by the fire telling stories. Say "make up." One of your friends stands up and goes out. You go to look for her. Her bedroom door is open and the room's empty. You think she's gone out. Say "have a feeling." You walk to the front door, but it's locked from the inside. Say "puzzle." On the floor by the front door is your friend's scarf. Say "evidence." You hear a noise behind you. You turn and see a shadow, but when you walk over, there's nothing there. Say "seeing things." You look out the window for your friend. It's raining hard, and it looks like someone's moving in the trees. You unlock the door and run outside to look closely. It's just the leaves. Say "optical illusion." Suddenly your friend jumps out from behind you. Boo! You jump. Say "play a trick."

TRACK 42

Unit 4, Vocabulary

E Listen and write. Then watch and say.

My Friend Oscar

Well, my friend Oscar, just for kicks,
Likes to play a lot of tricks
He likes to cause great confusion
By setting up an optical illusion.

Let me tell you I have a feeling
He finds mysteries very appealing.
He tells us "facts," but then we see
He's just made them up, entirely.

He makes us think we're seeing things
He spends hours and hours preparing things.
But really the only great big puzzle
Is why Oscar goes to all this trouble.

TRACK 43

Unit 4, Vocabulary

F Pronunciation. Listen and say. Copy the linking. Find other examples of linking in the poem.

just for kicks (x2)
great confusion (x2)
let me tell you (x2)

TRACK 44

Unit 4, Explore Language

A Listen and read. What do all the photos have in common?

Jenna: Look at this photo. It's weird, isn't it? Her feet look really big!

Max: It's an optical illusion, Jenna! They must have put the shoes by the camera, then the photographer must have lain down on the ground.

Noor: Hmm. This one with two people is a bit of a puzzle. They might have put two photographs together.

Jenna: But they're in the same room, Noor. Could they have done it with a computer, do you think? That's cheating!

Max: They must have used Photoshop because the person on the right is really big!

Noor: Oh look, in this one it looks like his head's a flower pot!

Max: No—look. He pulled his sweater over his head then sat in front of the pot. But you can still see his hair! They can't have spent very long on that one!

Noor: Oh, I want to try it! Come on, let's take some trick photos!

TRACK 45
Unit 4, Explore Language
D Listen and say.
1 They must have put the shoes by the camera.
2 Could he have seen it? No, he can't have.
3 They may have come up with a theory.
4 She might not have seen the trick.

TRACK 46
Unit 4, Global Citizenship
A Listen to Fairuza and Theo watch a TV documentary about Stonehenge. Why is Stonehenge a mystery?

Fairuza: Hey, Theo, do you want to watch a documentary with me? I have to work on a homework assignment about an ancient monument from prehistoric times, so something that's thousands of years old. I chose Stonehenge, so I want to watch this documentary.
Theo: Sure, let's watch it.
Voice on TV: Stonehenge is a series of stones built on flat land in the southwest of England. This means the giant stones can be seen from far away. Archaeologists who have studied it think that Stonehenge is over 5,000 years old.
Theo: Wow, that's really old!
Fairuza: Shhh, Theo!
Voice on TV: Nobody is sure why these stones were put there, but there are several theories—some experts say it could be a temple. Or maybe it's an ancient calendar—in the summer, on the longest day of the year, you can see the sun rising through the stones. But it really is a mystery. There isn't any real evidence, and there aren't any good clues to help understand how the stones were put there or why. So no one has solved the mystery. The huge stones are so fascinating that people have made up stories about them which have become legends. One of these is that dancing giants were turned into stone.
Theo: The stones are huge! How did they get there, Fairuza?
Fairuza: It's impossible to know. They didn't even have wheels back then, but they must have used something.
Theo: And they look far too heavy to be lifted. Hmm ...
Fairuza: Isn't it amazing? I think it's important to try to figure out the mystery. It might help us understand the past and how we've changed. Plus, it's so interesting! I mean, how did they move those massive rocks?!
Theo: You're right! It is interesting. I wonder how they did it ...

TRACK 47
Unit 4, Global Citizenship
B Look at the pictures and definition in A and write. Then listen and check.
1 prehistoric times
2 archaeologist
3 legend
4 expert
5 solve
6 clue
7 theory
8 ancient monument

TRACK D
Unit 4, Global Citizenship
Close your eyes. Listen, visualize, and say.
You've just arrived at an ancient monument. You're an archaeologist working at the site. Which country are you in? What are you searching for? Say "archaeologist." You're walking around the monument. How old is it? What does it look like? Say "ancient monument." As you walk around, you imagine the monument during prehistoric times. Imagine prehistoric people painting on the walls. What do the pictures show? Say "prehistoric times." You see something interesting that tells you what life was like in the past. What is it? Say "clue." There are a lot of other experts working with you. You want to talk about what you've found. What do you say to each other? Say "expert." Looking at the clue has reminded you of an old legend about the monument. What was it about? Say "legend." Hmm, you're putting the clues and the evidence together and you've thought of an explanation for one of the mysteries. What is it? Say "theory." You're sure that you're the first person to solve the mystery of this monument. How do you feel? Who will you tell? Say "solve."

TRACK 48
Unit 4, Global Citizenship
D Now listen to Fairuza's classmate Yasin. Which site is his presentation about? Do experts know all the facts about this place?

Teacher: OK, everyone, quiet down. Yasin is going to talk to us now about something very interesting. Yasin?
Yasin: Thank you. Everyone knows about the legends of the Loch Ness Monster and Bigfoot. They're fun, but after doing some research in the school library, I got more interested in ancient history. We can learn so much from how people lived in different societies, such as when they only used stones as tools, and we can think about whether any of these ideas from the past are useful for today's society. Have you seen this picture of an underwater city, on the southern coast of Yonaguni Island, Japan? Like Stonehenge, some experts think this city was built thousands of years ago. The ruins cover a huge area. The structures include a castle, an arch, and five temples. Some scientists think the structures were created by the ocean, but others say this is impossible when you look at the different parts of the "city." For example, there's an enormous pyramid-like structure. Some people think the city became buried after a huge tsunami. So, what do you think? Was this place built by humans or made by the ocean? We definitely have more questions than answers, but now I'll try to answer any questions you have ...

TRACK 49
Unit 4, Explore Language
A Listen and read. What do you think the children see in the park?

Inez: Mrs. Lewis! We just saw the Yeti or Bigfoot in the woods!
Mrs. Lewis: Are you sure, Inez? There isn't any evidence that they exist. Is someone just playing a trick?
Kayla: No, it's true! We didn't have to stay late at school, so we went to the park. We wanted to take some photos for our club competition. Then we heard a strange noise coming from a group of trees. We went nearer and saw a dark shape. We had to get pretty close to see it better.
Mrs. Lewis: You shouldn't have gotten too near, Kayla. Weren't you scared?!
Inez: We wanted to solve the mystery.
Mrs. Lewis: Well, what did it look like? You should've taken some photos as evidence for your theory!
Kayla: We tried to take a photo—but then suddenly it disappeared!

TRACK 50
Unit 4, Explore Language
D Listen and say.
1 We had to get pretty close.
2 I had to go and visit my grandma.
3 You didn't have to give me a present!
4 We should've said sorry.
5 They shouldn't have believed him.

Unit 5

TRACK 51
Unit 5, Vocabulary
A Listen. Which two paintings does Tyler like? Why?

Mrs. Lewis: Are you enjoying the Art Club Exhibition, Tyler?
Tyler: Yes, very much, thank you.
Mrs.Lewis: Which paintings do you like?
Tyler: I like this one of a family and their cat. It's serious—look, the colors are dark, and they have serious looks on their faces. They aren't smiling at all, but the cat is very cute!
Mrs. Lewis: Yes, I agree. I also like this one of the boy with the brown hat. I love the colors: the combination of the white shirt, green leaves, and red sky is very powerful. The way the boy is staring straight at us is pretty powerful, too. I also like the other portrait—it's very playful, as part of the face looks normal and the other part is really strange. Look at his green lips!
Tyler: I like it, too. And this one—with the bright colors and just a few shapes. The painting is simple, but I like the way Aaliyah has used the colors—she's made it different and interesting.
Mrs. Lewis: Yes. Which ones do you like, Katia?
Katia: I prefer more abstract art—similar to Aaliyah's—not pictures of people or well-known objects, but pictures like this one with the straight lines and circles. I also like the one with the colorful dots over at the back and the other one with the white squiggles.
Tyler: Really? I don't think the squiggles show that you can paint. It's the same as the painting with the simple doodles. That looks like something I'd draw in my schoolbooks! Surely anyone can draw that? I mean, it isn't really art, is it?
Mrs. Lewis: Hmm. I don't think you can say that. Just because you don't like it doesn't mean it isn't art!

TRACK 52
Unit 5, Vocabulary
B Find and number the words in A. Then listen and check.
1 doodles
2 dots
3 squiggles
4 powerful
5 complex
6 playful
7 serious
8 simple
9 abstract shapes
10 lines

TRACK 53
Unit 5, Vocabulary
C Close your eyes. Listen, visualize, and say.
You're walking around an art gallery, studying the paintings. The first picture you see is a simple painting of a house. How does it make you feel? Say "simple." The next picture has a lot of yellow and red dots on it. What do you think it's meant to show? Say "dots." You see a picture with a lot of abstract shapes. Is it nice to look at? Say

"abstract shapes." The lines on this painting seem to lead into the distance. Where do you think they're going? Say "lines." The next picture is a powerful painting of a big black horse. What's the horse doing? Why is the painting powerful? Say "powerful." You see a picture covered in squiggles. Follow the squiggles with your fingers. What do you think they're supposed to be? Say "squiggles." Here's a sketchbook that an artist used. She drew doodles to get her ideas. Do they look like finished paintings? Say "doodles." You see a picture showing a man sitting in a café. The colors are dark, and it looks very serious. What's the man thinking about? Say "serious." The picture in front of you is full of shapes, colors, people, and animals. It's very complex, and you look at it for a long time. What story is it telling? Say "complex." The last picture shows some children flying kites. It's a playful picture, and the children look happy. Does it remind you of when you were younger? Say "playful."

TRACK 54

Unit 5, Vocabulary

E Listen and write. Then watch and say.

The More I Look

I can see colors—bright and clear.
The more I look, the more they appear.
Red dots dance before my eyes,
An abstract shape? A black bird flies.

I can see squiggles—messy and free.
The more I look, the more I see.
A simple face with a powerful stare.

Doodles of dogs. And a big yellow square.
I can see lines—in front and behind.
The more I look, the more I find.
A playful painting. What does it mean?
I'm not sure. But I like the green.

TRACK 55

Unit 5, Vocabulary

F Pronunciation. Listen and say. Copy the sentence stress. Think of other sentences like these.

The more I look, the more they appear. (x2)
The more I look, the more I see. (x2)

TRACK 56

Unit 5, Explore Language

A Listen and read. How did Kofi's paintings change when he came back from Paris?

Mrs. Lewis: Hi, Kofi!

Kofi: Hey, Mom, thanks again for taking me to Paris! Before we went there, I hadn't realized it was so cool!

Mrs. Lewis: I know, it's great, isn't it?

Kofi: I loved those amazing paintings in the street. I'd never seen anything like them before.

Mrs. Lewis: Yes, they were beautiful and so realistic, weren't they? Had you heard of the artist Patrick Commecy before we went to Paris?

Kofi: No, I'd read about a lot of artists in the Louvre art gallery but I hadn't heard about that street artist before. I'd already been thinking about different ways of painting and he's really inspired me to make my paintings bigger.

Mrs. Lewis: Oh, really?

Kofi: *Yes, I'd never thought about art in that way before.* Come and see what I've done!

Mrs. Lewis: What? Where are we going?

Kofi: I want to show you something in the yard. Here! Look! Ta-da!

Mrs. Lewis: Oh, wow! That's amazing! I love it!

TRACK 57

Unit 5, Explore Language

D Listen and say.

1 I hadn't realized it was so cool.
2 He'd read about the artists before he went.
3 Had you seen the picture before?
4 She'd been thinking about going to Paris.
5 We hadn't been planning to finish so late.

TRACK 58

Unit 5, Global Citizenship

A Listen to Eugene ask Felicity about the Statue of Liberty. Do they think the Statue of Liberty is a work of art?

Felicity: I'm going to talk about the Statue of Liberty in New York in class next week—it's an amazing piece of art. Look at this photo I took on my trip to New York.

Eugene: Nice photo, Felicity. But the Statue of Liberty isn't art—it's a statue!

Felicity: But a statue is art. It has become iconic—it's an image that people immediately associate with New York City. It also symbolizes important aspects of the USA—about the history and the people.

Eugene: What do you mean?

Felicity: It's a symbol. When you see it, you think of the USA and the idea of being able to live freely in this place.

Eugene: How does it show that? I just see a statue.

Felicity: Well, it's 93 meters tall, so not just any statue. It's a large-scale statue. But there are also a lot of small details which depict, or show, different things. For example, her crown has seven spikes on it, representing the oceans and continents in the world and showing that liberty, being free, is a global ideal.

Eugene: That's interesting!

Felicity: And look at the things in her hands in this other photo—the tablet symbolizes law, and the torch symbolizes understanding and learning.

Eugene: Oh, I love this photo! It's a masterpiece! It looks like a famous artist took it! And it really shows your creativity.

Felicity: Thank you, Eugene! I'm not sure it's that good. I wanted to show the contrast between the green color of the statue and the blue of the sky behind.

Eugene: Your style is so clean and powerful, Felicity. I love the way you photograph colors!

TRACK 59

Unit 5, Global Citizenship

B Look at the pictures and definitions in A and write. Then listen and check.

1 symbolize
2 masterpiece
3 large-scale
4 contrast
5 style
6 creativity
7 iconic
8 depict

TRACK E

Unit 5, Global Citizenship

Close your eyes. Listen, visualize, and say.

You're a famous artist in your studio. You're going to paint a picture that will be your best ever. Use as much of your creativity as you can. Say "creativity." You usually paint small pictures. This time you decide to make a very large painting. Say "large-scale." What will your painting depict? Will you paint from real life? Say "depict." Perhaps you'll paint something more abstract. You'll use shapes to symbolize something important. Say "symbolize." Look at the colors—they're all the same. Add some more contrasts in color. That's better. Say "contrast." How would you describe the style of your piece? Say "style." Your painting looks great. It's the best painting you've ever done—it might be your masterpiece! Say "masterpiece." Your painting's finished! It belongs in a museum. Do you think it could become iconic? (Why?) Say "iconic."

TRACK 60

Unit 5, Global Citizenship

D Now listen to Bo, the art gallery guide. How were kites used in the past?

Hello, everyone, welcome to our art gallery. My name's Bo and I'll be your tour guide today. Please follow me. Our first exhibit focuses on leisure activities in art. As you can see, this painting depicts some Chinese children flying kites. I love this picture! Flying kites is a popular pastime in China, and my parents and grandparents have many old kites that they used to play with when they were younger. In fact, it was the Chinese people who invented kites, about 2,500 years ago. The legend says that the first kite was invented by a Chinese farmer who tied string to his hat to stop it blowing away in the wind. After some time, kite-flying spread outside of China to Korea and east to India. The kites had different styles in each area, and each culture had a different purpose for flying the kites. In the 16th century, kites became popular children's toys, and in the 17th century, they even became useful for scientists!

During the last 1,000 years, people have developed many different styles of kites, including simple paper ones, beautiful painted ones, and even ones which play music when they fly.

In the 1900s, large kite festivals started in China which show off a huge range of kites. Have you ever seen a large dragon kite? Some of them are 300 meters long—they're amazing! But to be honest, although those kites are great, I love the simple ones in the painting here, because it's really fun playing with kites with your friends on a windy day.

TRACK 61

Unit 5, Explore Language

A Listen and read. Describe Aaliyah's self-portrait.

Aaliyah: I'm going to enter the Art Club portrait competition with this selfie.

Hugo: A selfie? Is that allowed?

Aaliyah: Yes, I think it's an interesting way of doing a portrait. Isn't a selfie just a modern self-portrait? While I was looking at some old paintings, I was thinking about how things are now. In the past, artists painted self-portraits because they didn't have cameras. They often included objects in their paintings to show details about their lives. I decided to take a selfie and also include something I like doing. So I took a photo of me playing chess. What were you thinking of doing?

Hugo: I was wondering about it this morning and I'd decided to take a photograph. But now I'm going to do a traditional painting. I'd been thinking of doing a self-portrait but I'd rather do someone else. Maybe I could paint a portrait of you and your selfie. So there's art inside art!

TRACK 62
Unit 5, Explore Language
D Listen and say.
1 In the past, artists painted self-portraits.
2 While they were waiting, she was looking at her phone.
3 She was talking, when suddenly she stopped.
4 After he'd taken the photo, he showed it to me.
5 They'd been painting for hours.

Unit 6

TRACK 63
Unit 6, Vocabulary
A Listen. Which game is Simon most interested in playing: chess, Go, or backgammon? Why?
Aaliyah: Welcome to the Games Club, Simon. You can play different board games here. There are modern board games, like the one over there. You have to spin the spinner, take your counter, and move it until you land on the winning square. Or you can play traditional board games. We play Go, chess, and backgammon.
Simon: Sounds great! Hi, Marge! What are you playing?
Marge: Hey, Simon! I'm playing Go. It's really fun, but it's quite complicated! You have to cover as much of the board as possible with your pieces.
Boy 1: This is chess. There are two players. One has black pieces, and the other has white. The point of the game is that you have to get your pieces to the other side of the board by taking the other player's pieces.
Simon: And what about this game?
Boy 2: Oh, this is backgammon. It isn't as complicated as chess or Go. There are two players, and you take turns to throw the dice until one player, the winner, doesn't have any pieces left. And you must always play—you never miss a turn.
Simon: Oh, I like games that have an element of chance where you can't plan or control what happens.
Boy 2: Me, too! I was losing, but look, I've just thrown a double six and won!
Aaliyah: But backgammon's also a game of strategy because you have to plan what to do next. Would you like to play any of these games?
Simon: Thanks, Aaliyah—I think I'll take my chances with backgammon.

TRACK 64
Unit 6, Vocabulary
B Find and number the words in A. Then listen and check.
1 strategy
2 miss a turn
3 players
4 pieces
5 board game
6 chance
7 throw the dice
8 lose
9 win
10 land on

TRACK 65
Unit 6, Vocabulary
C Close your eyes. Listen, visualize, and say.
It's raining outside. You and your friends decide to play a board game. Choose a board game you like. What does the board look like? Say "board game." How many players can play this board game? Can all your friends play? Say "players." Think about what the pieces in this board game look like. What color do you want? Say "pieces." You throw two dice. What number do you want to land on? Say "throw the dice." Now move your piece. How many squares did you move? Say "land on a square." You throw the dice again. This time you land on a square where you have to miss a turn. How do you feel? Say "miss a turn." This is a game of chance. Are you lucky when you throw the dice? Say "chance." This game also has some strategy in it. What's going to be your next move? Do you know what the other players are going to do? Say "strategy." One of your friends beats you. How do you feel when you lose? Say "lose." You play the game again. This time, you're the winner. How do you feel when you win? Say "win."

TRACK 66
Unit 6, Vocabulary
E Listen and write. Then watch and say.
Fun and Games
A game of chance. Which is my square?
I take my turn. Don't land on there!
I move my piece. I count to eight.
I move again. Oh, that's great!

My turn again. I'll move on now.
I have two twos. I don't know how.
I move my piece. I count to four.
I miss a turn. Oh, are you sure?

I take my piece. I throw the dice.
I got a five. I got it twice.
I move my piece. I count to ten.
I miss a turn. Oh, not again!

Win or lose, it's fun to play.
Another game? Well, yeah, OK!

TRACK 67
Unit 6, Vocabulary
F Pronunciation. Listen and say. Copy the intonation. Think of other phrases like these.
Oh, that's great! (x2)
Oh, not again! (x2)

TRACK 68
Unit 6, Explore Language
A Listen and read. What activities are Simon and Marge doing?
Simon: Great! I can do my puzzles in peace and quiet.
Marge: I'm going to play a word game! Do you know how to play, Simon?
Simon: No, I don't.
Marge: I have to find two opposites for each word. Can you tell me what the opposites of "light" are?
Simon: Dark. Heavy.
Marge: Yes! And I wonder whether you know the two opposites of "lost."
Simon: Found. Won.
Marge: Oh, you're good at this! I wonder if you can answer this one.
Simon: Marge, I'm trying to do my puzzle.
Marge: Yes, but I'm not sure what the two opposites of "right" are …
Simon: That's easy, but what about this one? Do you have any idea what the opposite of "noisy" is?
Marge: Yes, it's "quiet!" Oh, you mean *me* … ha, ha!

TRACK 69
Unit 6, Explore Language
D Listen and say.
1 I wonder if you can answer this one.
2 Can you tell me how to play?
3 I wonder why he's losing.
4 I'm not sure what you want to play.
5 Have you any idea what the rules are?

TRACK 70
Unit 6, Global Citizenship
A Listen to Kendra help her brother Malik to choose an online game. Can you describe the game?
Malik: Miss Gomez said we can use a video game to help with our homework. Kendra, can you play with me? This is the list of games Miss Gomez said we could choose from.
Kendra: Video games? Wow, your teacher likes gaming! That's great! OK, let's see. This one looks good—*Whyville*. It's great because it covers a lot of topics like math, science, art, and geography. Your teacher will like that. Are you going to collaborate and work with your classmates?
Malik: Um—yeah.
Kendra: OK, good. Let's look at the instructions for how to play. *Whyville* is multiplayer—so you play with other people. First, you create your own character, your avatar, and you choose how your avatar looks. *Whyville* is a role-playing game, so you get to choose whether your avatar will be a builder or a traveler, or something else. Also, you interact with different players in the Whyville community. You never meet them in person because the community is virtual, but you still get to play with them. Let's go to the website. See, you can design your own look!
Malik: The graphics are beautiful. I love the colors. It looks really fun.
Kendra: I know! OK, so there are over 100 games and other activities that cover a lot of different subjects. You can play a game, for example, which involves solving math problems, to gain points. You have fun and learn at the same time! And, look, you collect points called "clams." You can use clams to buy things and improve or level up your avatar. You can even make your avatar fly if you get enough of them!
Malik: So can we work together and share information with each other? That'll make the homework easier!
Kendra: Yes, it's about building communities in a made-up world. It isn't like the games where you only score points. There's also a "newspaper" every week, so if have a question, you can post it to get people's comments. Let's give it a try …

TRACK 71
Unit 6, Global Citizenship
B Look at the pictures and definitions in A and write. Then listen and check.
1 avatar
2 collect points
3 instructions
4 gaming
5 virtual
6 graphics
7 multiplayer
8 collaborate
9 level up
10 role-playing game

TRACK F
Unit 6, Global Citizenship
Close your eyes. Listen, visualize, and say.
Everyone's talking about a new online video game. You decide to give it a try. It's a role-playing game. Say "role-playing game." First, you have to create and design your avatar. Say "avatar." Now it's time to play! Step into the virtual world. Say "virtual." The virtual word looks so cool! Say "graphics." Hmm, you're not sure where to start. Find the instructions. Say "instructions." Ah, you see that you can play online with other people. That sounds fun! Say "multiplayer." You go online with your mom and start playing the game. Say "gaming." You're getting good at this now. You collect some

points. Say "collect points." You want to level up your character and get some new abilities. Say "level up." A new mission is taking place. For this one, you'll need to work together with another player in order to win. Say "collaborate." You did it! Good job!

TRACK 72

Unit 6, Global Citizenship

D Now listen to Mr. Suvlu, an Inupiat teacher from Alaska. What's special about this game?

Mr. Suvlu: Malik, Luisa—you know we've been looking at how we can learn about different cultures? Did you know you can sometimes do this through gaming?

Malik: Really?! That's great, Mr. Suvlu!

Mr. Suvlu: Yes. I want you to try playing *Never Alone*. It's a game that's based on stories told by the Inupiat about my culture and you can learn about our way of life. It's multiplayer, so you can have friends watch and play at the same time. You play as a young Inupiat girl or an arctic fox. You have to get across the icy world of the Alaskan Arctic together to stop the winds that are destroying the land. As you travel, you get to learn about my people and our history, and it has short videos of real people who talk about growing up in the Arctic. And because you're playing in the virtual world, you get a good sense of what the problems are.

Luisa: What—like living in the dark a lot of the time and how the cold affects you?

Mr. Suvlu: Exactly. And our relationship with the stars! The other thing that you can see is different ways that cultures can tell their history, not just through books. It isn't the same as actually being there, but it will help you see a way of life that's very different from your own.

TRACK 73

Unit 6, Explore Language

A Listen and read. What does a team have to do to win The Name in the Hat game?

Boy: This is fun.

Girl: Oh, I got a good one.

Guan: OK, kids—Let's play a game.

Boy & Girl: Can't we play a video game?

Guan: No—let's do something we can play together ... This game should be fun!
OK, so these are the instructions.
1 Get into two teams.
2 Each team member writes down the name of a famous person on a piece of paper. It must be someone who you all know.
3 Fold all the pieces of paper up and put them in a hat, which you put in front of everyone.
4 A member from each team takes turns to take a piece of paper out of the hat—the person whose name has the most letters starts first.
5 Each team member has one minute to try to help *their* team guess the name. You can use mime or say something about the person, like "He lives in the place where a lot of actors live," but you can't say the name.
6 The other team has to try to guess the name first.
7 The team that guesses the most names correctly, wins!

Girl: You're never going to guess!

Guan: You see ... I told you this was going to be fun!

TRACK 74

Unit 6, Explore Language

D Listen and say.

1 It must be someone who you all know.
2 This is the game which we played all last summer.
3 The player whose turn it is throws the dice.
4 Is it a game that we can all play?
5 He was hiding in the bedroom, where it was very dark.

Unit 7

TRACK 75

Unit 7, Vocabulary

A Listen. Why is advertising important?

Guan: Welcome to the China Global Advertising Agency here in Shanghai—a city full of design. Congratulations on winning the advertising competition.

Sami: Thank you, Mr. Guan. Wow! There are so many fantastic advertisements!

Guan: Yes, Sami. Nowadays, the streets are full of advertisements—there are ads everywhere.

Sami: Mmm, the donuts on that billboard over there look good!

Guan: They do, Sami. Imagine you have a donut company. In order to succeed, you need to make enough money. How do you do that?

Sami: You need to sell a lot of products—donuts! And you need to make more money than you spend.

Guan: Yes, exactly. When you make more money than you spend, that's called making a profit—and a lot of your spending will be on advertising. Why?

Gabriela: Because you need to persuade people to buy your product—people should think they need your donuts even if they don't!

Sami: That's easy! Donuts are delicious!

Guan: Maybe, but there are a lot of donut companies, and people have to look after their health, too. So, companies need to be creative and persuade their customers to choose their product; to show that their donuts offer great quality and great value—quality because they're the most delicious donuts and value because they have good price. Advertising keeps prices low because companies offer discounts—selling for less than the usual price. And bargains—which are really, reaaaaally low prices or special offers, like two for one.

Sami: Two donuts for the price of one! Yes, please! I'm sold!

TRACK 76

Unit 7, Vocabulary

B Find and number the words in A. Then listen and check.

1 discount
2 bargain
3 customer
4 persuade
5 products
6 quality
7 value
8 profit
9 advertisement (British English: advert)
10 billboard

TRACK 77

Unit 7, Vocabulary

C Close your eyes. Listen, visualize, and say.

You're in a store looking at what to buy. You're the customer. What will you buy? Say "customer." What shower products does your family always buy? Why? Imagine buying some different ones. Are they better or worse? Say "products." Think of one your favorite advertisements in a magazine or on TV. What is it about? Why is it your favorite? Say "advertisement." Where are there some billboards in your town? Which one do you like best? Why? Say "billboard." Think of a time when someone persuaded you to do something. What was it? Did you agree quickly? How did you feel? Say "persuade." You have a company, and you made a big profit this year. What will you do with the money? Say "profit." Would you rather have good quality or something cheap when you're buying clothes? How long will the clothes last? Say "quality." Have you ever bought something that was very good value? What was it? Why was it good value? What did you like about it? Say "value." You see a product with a 50% discount. It's nice, but you don't need it. Do you buy it? Say "discount." These video games have an 80% discount. You have to buy them! How do you feel about getting such a bargain? Say "bargain."

TRACK 78

Unit 7, Vocabulary

E Listen and write. Then watch and say.

Why Buy?

Bargains, bargains!
Come and spend.

Products, products!
Buy for a friend!

Discounts, discounts!
The ad—it's true!

Profits, profits!
More for you!

Billboards, billboards!
We want them, yes!

Come and buy,
We sell happiness!

TRACK 79

Unit 7, Vocabulary

F Pronunciation. Listen and say. Copy the intonation. Find three more sentences like these in the poem.

Come and spend. (x2)
Buy for a friend! (x2)

TRACK 80

Unit 7, Explore Language

A Listen and read. What products do the girls describe?

Guan: So you've watched different ads. What were they for?

Gabriela: Ours was for black toothpaste!

Ludka: And ours was a puzzle alarm clock.

Guan: Right! And what can you remember about these products?

Ludka: Well, the girl in the ad said you had to complete a puzzle to stop the alarm going off! She said she was getting up on time every day because the puzzle was challenging, and this made her feel wide awake.

Gabriela: Our ad told us to try this amazing new toothpaste. They said that it would remove stains from your teeth, even though the toothpaste is black!

Guan: Would you like to try these products out?

Ludka: We're not sure—what if you can't find the pieces to turn off the alarm clock! In my group, we thought that the puzzle should be easier, too.

Gabriela: I think it sounds fun! In our ad, people told the presenters that they'd never used a better toothpaste. Sami told us not to use it because it's so black! But I'd like to try it—the color wouldn't put me off. I'd have to warn my mom, though!

TRACK 81
Unit 7, Explore Language
D Listen and say.
1 We thought that the puzzle should be easier.
2 He said we had to watch the ads carefully.
3 She said she'd found a real bargain.
4 She told me she was brushing her teeth.
5 Mom told them not to shout.

TRACK 82
Unit 7, Global Citizenship
A Listen to Naomi talk to her mom. What does she learn about advertising strategies?
Naomi: Mom, look at this ad for running shoes. The girl looks amazing!
Mom: Let's see! Hmm—you know what they've done—they've altered the photo. They've used software like Photoshop to make the image "perfect": hair, skin, everything! They shouldn't do that to promote their products.
Naomi: Why not? I'd buy them. She looks great!
Mom: Exactly! But it creates a false impression. Real people don't look like that. Not even the girl in the ad looks like that in real life. The ad's saying "Buy our brand of shoes and you'll look like this." You'll see a lot of images have been altered like that. Most of the big-name companies and brands do it, because they want their product to look the best.
Naomi: But that's really wrong! Their slogan "Run fast, run cool" works really well. But then they say "You can look better in our shoes." Are they allowed to say that?
Mom: Well, yes, because it says you "can" and that isn't a 100% guarantee. Read the small print—that really tiny writing, there at the bottom. It gives some statistics on that and other claims, but they've only asked 20 women! I think it's worse for young people like you—you're their target market—because they know you worry about what you look like and you might believe their claims. But what they say is true often isn't true at all!
Naomi: You know, I'm going to post an article on the school blog about this.

TRACK 83
Unit 7, Global Citizenship
B Look at the pictures and definition in A and write. Then listen and check.
1 promote
2 brand
3 slogan
4 claims
5 target market
6 image
7 small print
8 false impression

TRACK G
Unit 7, Global Citizenship
Close your eyes. Listen, visualize, and say.
You see a competition in a magazine to create an ad for your favorite product. What product is it? You want everyone to love it so it becomes one of the best. Say "brand." Who will buy your product? How old are the people it's aimed at? Say "target market." What kinds of pictures will you use for your ad? Will the image be modern or more traditional? Say "image." Are your pictures real? Will you change them in any way? Be careful not to lie to people. Say "false impression." Think! You need a short phrase to sell your product—something people will remember. Say "slogan." Why is your product good? What specific things are you going to say to help sell it? Say "claims." What extra information do you want to give the customer, to be sure you're being truthful? Imagine this information at the bottom of the page of your ad. Say "small print." Where will you put your ad so people see it? What else can you do to advertise the product? Say "promote." You're done. It's time to enter the competition. Good luck!

TRACK 84
Unit 7, Global Citizenship
D Now listen to Gail's podcast. What problems and solutions does she mention.
Did you know that the average person sees thousands of ads a day? Companies are constantly pushing products at us and urging us to buy things we don't actually need. Think about it—do you really need that new pair of shoes and also the box they come in? And when you throw these things away, where does it all end up? Some packaging is unnecessary, and its only purpose is to make the product more attractive. On top of that, a lot of packaging doesn't decompose like food or paper does, and it can't even be recycled—which is why our oceans are filling up with plastic.
Our waste mountain is such a concern that we need to be thinking hard about how we can reduce and recycle more. Some organizations like cafés and supermarkets are changing their packaging options, and they arrange to give leftover food to homeless people at the end of the day. You can get involved too by reusing your trash! For instance, in India it's very common for parts of products that are broken to be reused in new forms. These parts might fix a broken wall or make a vehicle powered by water! This way of fixing things that are broken using your creativity is called *jugaad*. So, when your bike breaks, could you use any of the parts for something else? Could you actually make a new product? You really should try!

TRACK 85
Unit 7, Explore Language
A Listen and read. What's the TV quiz about?
Boy: Go, Ludka!
Quiz host: Welcome to Ask the Experts! Today's show is about ads. OK, so, Ludka, you're in the final round. Can you guess the answers to the questions we asked our experts? Are you ready? First, the questions:
Number 1: We asked how many marketing messages a person received every day.
Number 2: We asked what people thought the most annoying ads were.
Number 3: We asked which product was top in the sports and outdoors category.
Number 4: We asked where in the world 50% of the total advertising budget is spent on digital media.
Number 5: We questioned whether people remembered the advertising messages.
Number 6: We wanted to know if people knew how much money is spent on advertising in one year worldwide.
OK, those are the questions. Now, Ludka, are you ready to answer?
Ludka: Yes, I think so.
Quiz host: Here we go …! Let's play Ask the Experts!

TRACK 86
Unit 7, Explore Language
D Listen and say.
1 I questioned whether they thought the slogan was effective.
2 He asked me how true the claims were.
3 She wanted to know if I was going to buy the shoes.
4 They asked her why she'd advertised so many things.
5 She wondered if they'd be banning ads for candy.

Unit 8

TRACK 87
Unit 8, Vocabulary
A Listen. Which three photos does the group talk about?
Ms. Nair: We're here to see how nature is *full* of amazing mathematical patterns. Let's look at some examples in these pictures, then we'll explore to find more. Nature is big on symmetry—for example, the pattern on a butterfly's wings is exactly the same on both sides. And can you see a shape with six sides here? A hexagon? Ludka?
Ludka: The honeycomb, Ms. Nair.
Ms. Nair: That's right. For us to draw something absolutely symmetrical, we'd need to measure the angles—that's the point where two straight lines join or cross each other. But look at the honeycomb—it's perfect! Bees make hexagons naturally. Right, what about spirals going round and round in circles? Vincent, can you see a spiral?
Vincent: Yes, inside that shell!
Ms. Nair: Yes! The inside of the nautilus shell grows in a perfect spiral. The way it grows is mathematically calculated—but the shell doesn't know that! No, it does it naturally.
Vincent: How do we know it's a perfect spiral, then?
Ms. Nair: Mathematicians use something called the Fibonacci sequence of numbers to explain it. Look at these numbers: 1, 1, 2, 3, 5, 8. Dexter, can you show us how it works?
Dexter: Yes, you need to look at the numbers in pairs and add them together: so, 1 and 1 is 2, 2 and 3 is 5, 3 and 5 is 8 … can you see the pattern? What's the next number in the sequence?
Ludka: 40!
Dexter: No, don't multiply it—just add.
Ludka: Oh, yes! 13.
Ms. Nair: Excellent! Nature uses numbers all the time to help it grow and survive. Now, let's go and look at the sunflowers!

TRACK 88
Unit 8, Vocabulary
B Find and number the words in A. Then listen and check.
1 hexagon
2 spirals
3 multiply
4 symmetry
5 angle
6 divide
7 odd number
8 even number
9 prime number
10 sequence

TRACK 89
Unit 8, Vocabulary
C Close your eyes. Listen, visualize, and say.
Think of a butterfly. What's the pattern like on its two wings? Notice how both wings are the same. Say "symmetry." How many things have six sides? Think of a beehive. Imagine the pattern on a soccer ball. What about the end of your pencil? Say "hexagon." Draw a triangle in the air with your finger. Look at one of the angles—is it wide

open, or small? Say "angles." Think of a snail shell, a chameleon tail, and a galaxy of stars. Trace the pattern going round and round with your finger. Say "spiral." Think. 10, 20, 30, 40 … Now, circle, square, triangle; circle, square … Say "sequence." Think of a number. Multiply it by 3. What number do you have? Say "multiply." Think of a number. Divide it by 2. What number do you have? Say "divide." Think of an important date that's an odd number. Why is it important? Say "odd number." Think of an important year that's an even number. Why is it important? Say "even number." How old are you? Is your age a prime number? Say "prime number."

TRACK 90

Unit 8, Vocabulary

E Listen and choose. Then watch and say.

I Love Numbers

I have numbers on my mind
Symmetry's in patterns I find.
In my sequence, multiply
Odd and even, then apply!

Numbers, numbers!

My number's prime. What's the rule?
Divide just by itself and one. That's cool!
Two lines joined. What did you get?
An angle at the point they met.

Numbers, numbers!

Math in nature? Bring it on!
A honeycomb is a hexagon.
Sunflowers, insects, a galaxy?
Spirals in nature, come and see.

Numbers, numbers!

TRACK 91

Unit 8, Vocabulary

F Pronunciation. Listen and say. Copy the consonant clusters. Find other words with consonant clusters in the poem.

symmetry (x2)
multiply (x2)
prime (x2)

TRACK 92

Unit 8, Explore Language

A Listen and read. What information does Adam give Ludka about eclipses?

Adam: Did you know that the sun is about 400 times bigger than the moon, and it's also about 400 times further away?

Ludka: Really?

Adam: Yes, that's why they look the same size when they're seen from Earth.

Ludka: Right! And the angle of light from the sun affects how much light and shade we get, doesn't it?

Adam: Yeah. But during a solar eclipse, the moon passes in front of the sun so it goes dark, see? The sun has often been covered completely—it's called a total eclipse.

Ludka: Doesn't what you see depend on where you're positioned on Earth?

Adam: Yes, in most places it's only a partial eclipse. They're amazing to see. But you can't look directly at the eclipse as you can be blinded by it.

Ludka: Oh, that's bad! How did you get this photo then?

Adam: Oh, that's not mine. It was taken by a professional, with an expensive camera.

TRACK 93

Unit 8, Explore Language

D Listen and say.

1 It's called a total eclipse.
2 The last eclipse was seen by millions of people.
3 New information about the sun has been discovered.
4 That photo was taken by my friend!
5 No number can be divided by zero.

TRACK 94

Unit 8, Global Citizenship

A Listen to Jung-mi and Hiroki talk about a research project. What information surprises them?

Hiroki: Writing up our research project is really difficult! I don't know where to start!

Jung-mi: I know! But let's see if we can break it down. So, we're looking into learning languages in high school. These are the facts, and here we have a lot of information organized as numbers—they're called statistics. So altogether, this is our data.

Hiroki: Yes. Right, so we've analyzed the numbers and we have the results. We now need to show the statistics clearly.

Jung-mi: Well, I made this chart with colored sections. This shows which languages are taught most in schools around the world. You can see that most children learn English—no surprise there!

Hiroki: And children learning a modern language in England, for example, mostly learn French, German, or Spanish. Can we convert each one into a percentage—how many for every 100?

Jung-mi: OK. We can do that. Hmm, here it says that after secondary school, you know, high school, a lot of British children *stop* learning French or *any* language. That seems surprising!

Hiroki: Yes, it does!

Jung-mi: I'm going to draw a line up to show a rise in people learning English, and this line going down to show a fall in learning other languages. I wonder why that is? Perhaps a lot of the children know *we're* learning languages, so they don't have to!

Jung-mi: I wonder how *long* it takes to learn a language?

Hiroki: Ha—well, I tried to find out what the average time would be for someone to learn a language, but not all the statistics match. But I guess that's because there are so many factors to consider: the language, where you live, the education system, the language spoken at home, other languages you speak, and so on.

Jung-mi: Well, we've been studying English for five years … Let's do some more research to check …

TRACK 95

Unit 8, Global Citizenship

B Look at the pictures and definition in A and write. Then listen and check.

1 data
2 rise
3 fall
4 chart
5 reach a peak
6 stay stable
7 percentage
8 average
9 statistics
10 trend

TRACK H

Unit 8, Global Citizenship

Close your eyes. Listen, visualize, and say.

Imagine you're in a huge theme park. It's packed with people. How many people attend every day? Every year? Say "statistics." You remember a few years ago, theme parks weren't so popular. That's changed. Say "trend." You're waiting in line for a roller-coaster ride. You have to measure yourself against a height chart. Are you tall enough? Say "chart." What do you think is the average age of the people in the line with you? Say "average." Is there a higher percentage of tall people or short people, do you think? Say "percentage." Think about getting onto the ride. The train starts to move. Imagine the shape of the whole track. The train travels upwards along the track. Say "rise." It reaches the top and stops. It's a long way down! Say "reaches a peak." Then there's a sudden drop! How do you feel? Down you go! Say "fall." You travel along horizontally for a while. Say "stay stable." You reach the end of the ride. How do you feel? When you leave, you're asked to give feedback on the theme park. What kind of feedback do you give? How will they use the data? Say "data."

TRACK 96

Unit 8, Global Citizenship

D Now listen to a radio program. Why does Ms. Pérez say that math is everywhere?

Host: Today we're talking all things numbers! I'm here in the studio with someone who just loves math! Ms. Pérez, welcome!

Ms. Pérez: Thank you! I do love math and you should, too—it's all around us!

Host: Yes, I use math when I go to the store to buy something, but all around us—how?

Ms. Pérez: The store is a good example—you use math to calculate how much to buy and to pay. But how does the store know, for example, how many bananas they'll need to keep their customers happy?

Host: Oh, yes, it's really irritating when a store runs out of stock, or I have to wait in line …

Ms. Pérez: That's when the store hasn't used their statistics well. It's basic supply and demand. Supermarkets can track what products their customers buy by looking at what they put in their shopping baskets. The receipt you receive has information that is important to them: the products, how many, the place, the date, the time, and so on. This is important data that can help stores figure out what they need to stock. The more information they can get about their customers, the more they can ensure they are stocking correctly. Bananas are a great example. Statistics from 2012 say that worldwide more than 100 billion bananas are eaten every year, so a store that runs out of bananas has messed up their math!

Host: OK, here's another example from my life—there are lots of new houses being built near me. How do they know how many houses to build, and where?

Ms. Pérez: Well, we can collect data on things like how many people are getting married and how many babies are being born, and then we can estimate the number of new families who will need new homes. To know where, we can look at trends: for example, in Cambodia, the majority of people live in the country, whereas here in Brazil the majority of people live in towns! So you'd build houses in towns in Brazil, but in the country in Cambodia.

Host: And with houses, you need the right number of schools, buses, parks …

Ms. Pérez: Exactly! And we can work out how many schools and buses we need using math! It's brilliant!

Host: Well, you've certainly convinced me, and I'm sure our listeners, too. Now, can you help me with my math assignment …

TRACK 97

Unit 8, Explore Language

A Listen and read. Why is data important?

Vincent: Adam—you're using your phone AGAIN!

Adam: What? I'm just looking up train times …

Vincent: You know, I read recently that every time you search a website online, data is being collected—data about you! Companies use the information to send you targeted advertisements about things you like—your favorite jeans or video games. Some companies collect data on the TV shows people watch. The data will be analyzed to help them decide whether to make another series or not, or which characters to change. They're saying that data analysis is going to be used more and more.

Adam: That sounds good, doesn't it? In the future, TV shows I like won't be canceled if they've analyzed my data!

Vincent: But it's like everything we do is being watched.

Adam: True. I guess I do use my phone for everything. Hmm, so, now we know we're being watched, how will the data be collected? And what do you think the results will be?

Vincent: Good questions …

Adam: Well, after this, I'm going to be sent a ton of ads about trains from this station!

TRACK 98

Unit 8, Explore Language

D Listen and say.

1 The data will be analyzed.
2 You're going to be sent an ad.
3 Data won't be used by everyone.
4 The way we shop is going to be affected.
5 Will data be used by teachers, too?

Unit 9

TRACK 99

Unit 9, Vocabulary

A Listen. What decision does Annette want to talk about?

Vincent: Hey, look, Annette. Why don't you ask that man at the desk with the glasses for some advice about making your big decision?

Annette: Yeah, good idea. Hi. I wonder if you can help me with an important decision I need to make. It's really worrying me.

Expert: Sure. What's the problem?

Annette: Well, I can't decide which subjects to study next year in high school. I'm good at computer programming. But I want to live abroad, so should I learn a language?

Expert: OK, so let's think about your options. We can brainstorm the options now, if you like.

Annette: Great. OK. Well, I could study computing but do a language course outside of school. And there's a language club at school during lunch. Or I could study languages and then take a programming course after school. Or maybe I could ask my friend Oscar to teach me. He programmed an app.

Expert: Right—so you need to evaluate your ideas—decide which ones are best.

Annette: OK—for example—computing is fun and easier for me, so I won't have to spend hours in the evening studying.

Expert: Now, consider what happens if you don't study a language at school. What's the consequence?

Annette: Well, I won't be able to learn it so quickly.

Expert: Right … and if you don't take computing?

Annette: Urm … I might not get such good grades. I need to think about this …

Expert: So, what's your solution? Have you decided?

Annette: I'm going to choose computing and sign up for a language club.

Vincent: Great. So, now you just need to decide which language to choose!

TRACK 100

Unit 9, Vocabulary

B Find and number the words in A. Then listen and check.

1 evaluate your ideas
2 brainstorm the options
3 consider the consequences
4 learn from your mistakes
5 decide on a solution
6 define the problem
7 regret
8 make a decision

TRACK 101

Unit 9, Vocabulary

C Close your eyes. Listen, visualize, and say.

You have an important job to do or an important decision to make. What exactly do you have to do? Say "define the problem." Think about three different possible solutions to your problem. Say "brainstorm the options." Think about your options. In what ways are each of your ideas good? Say "evaluate your ideas." For each of your ideas, what are the possible consequences? Say "consider the consequences." Which of your three ideas is the best? Say "decide on a solution." Do you think you've made a good decision? Why? Say "make a decision." You do what you decided to do. It doesn't work the way you planned. Do you feel bad? Say "regret." There's no reason to feel bad. You'll use this experience and try to do better in the future. Say "learn from your mistakes."

TRACK 102

Unit 9, Vocabulary

E Listen and write. Then watch and say.

Make Up My Mind

Define the problem—yes or no?
Define it logically—where shall I go?

Brainstorm the options—one, two, three.
Brainstorm—A, B, C, and D.

Evaluate your ideas—bad or good?
Evaluate—do I think I should?

Consider the consequences—nothing to regret?
Consider them carefully—I can't decide yet!

Decide on a solution—it's now or never!
Decide so I can say—it's my best decision ever!

TRACK 103

Unit 9, Vocabulary

F Pronunciation. Listen and say. Copy the linking. Think of other examples of linking like these.

the options (x2)
evaluate your ideas (x2)
decide on (x2)
I can't decide (x2)

TRACK 104

Unit 9, Explore Language

A Listen and read. What did Annette learn? Did she enjoy her day?

Annette: Phew! That was a long wait, Yousef.

Yousef: If you'd come earlier, Annette, we wouldn't have waited in line so long.

Annette: I know! I'm sorry. I hope we like it after all that! Lunch was so expensive!

Yousef: If you'd brought your own lunch, it would have been cheaper.

Annette: I know. Your lunch looks really nice! Well, I've learned from my mistakes today. Don't be late and pack my own lunch!

Yousef: But you still had a good time, didn't you?

Annette: Sure. If I hadn't come, I would have regretted it. I would have missed all this, um … fun!

TRACK 105

Unit 9, Explore Language

D Listen and say.

1 If you'd come earlier, we wouldn't have waited in line so long.
2 If you'd studied more, the exam would have been easier.
3 If we hadn't come, we would have regretted it.
4 If they'd had the time, they would have come.
5 If she'd known, she would have waited.

TRACK 106

Unit 9, Global Citizenship

A Listen to Fatima talk to Lily about decision-making in her family. What kinds of decisions do Fatima's family make?

Fatima: In my family, we make decisions together. I always have my say, and even my seven-year-old brother gives his opinion.

Lily: But he's too young to make good decisions, isn't he?

Fatima: Well, he just gives his opinion. My parents still make the decision. It isn't always about getting your own way or getting what you want, but my parents think being fair is important. That means sometimes I win and sometimes he wins. Of course, there are pros and cons—sometimes it takes a *long* time to decide things.

Lily: Does it give you a feeling of independence?

Fatima: Yes, it can. It makes us feel that our opinions are important. Giving our opinions lets us express our individual identity, I think. You learn to think for yourself and not always go with peer pressure, you know, not do what all our friends do.

Lily: Yes, but it's nice to fit in with your friends sometimes, too. Do you ever disagree with your parents?

Fatima: Well, for smaller things, like a family day out, I might have a different opinion. My parents might suggest doing something, but I might prefer to do something else. Sometimes we do what my brother wants one week and what I want another week. I don't always like it. I get really annoyed when we get to go to the movies but have to watch something that's too young for me, but you have to learn to control your emotions sometimes and accept some things you don't like.

Lily: What about the bigger decisions, like vacations?

Fatima: I always give my opinion, but sometimes I want my parents to decide. They have a lot more experience!

TRACK 107

Unit 9, Global Citizenship

B Look at the pictures and definitions in A and write. Then listen and check.

1 fit in with
2 pros and cons
3 individual identity
4 control your emotions
5 independence
6 be fair
7 have your say
8 peer pressure
9 get your own way

TRACK 1

Unit 9, Global Citizenship

Close your eyes. Listen, visualize, and say.

A friend asks you to go to the movies. Another friend asks you to go to the park. What are the pros and cons of each one? Say "pros and cons." A lot of friends at school are watching a TV series which your parents don't want you to watch. But your friends want you to watch it. How do you feel? Say "peer pressure." Your dad asks what you want for dinner. Tell him what you want. Does your dad want the same? Say "have your say." Your friend suggested a race, but she started before you. Will you say anything or just run faster? Say "be fair." You feel that your little sister always gets her way. You don't think it's fair because you always have to do what she wants. Say "get your way." Your friends are going to the shopping mall. You don't want to go, but you want to spend time with them, so you go anyway. Say "fit in with." You got angry at your little brother yesterday. Do you think you could have controlled yourself better? Say "control your emotions." You always do everything with your best friend, but you'd like to be able to make more decisions for yourself. Will you say something to your best friend? Say "independence." You'd like to not always follow the ideas of your friends. You're going to do what you want to do from today. Say "individual identity."

TRACK 108

Unit 9, Global Citizenship

D Now listen to Professor Jackson. How does the brain affect how 11- to 13-year-olds feel and act?

Did you know that the brain changes hugely around the ages of 11 to 13 and that these changes affect the way we think, and particularly the way we make decisions? The changes at this age are due to the brain starting to prepare the child for adulthood. One of the changes is that the pre-teen brain becomes much better at scanning the environment for different types of information: other people's emotions, information from their senses, cultural norms, values, etc. Because their brain is getting so good at noticing and analyzing details in their environment, pre-teens naturally become more self-conscious than before. Suddenly, it seems that other people are noticing and judging everything about them—their actions and their appearance. And of course this can make it easier to feel peer pressure. However, this is a really exciting time in a pre-teen's life because as they are analyzing the culture and people around them, they are also continuing to develop their individual identity.

Another major change for pre-teens is that their brain is now much better at seeing different points of view at the same time. This allows them to have ambiguous thought patterns: they no longer see things as black or white. This is great because as they become older and gain more independence, they will need to look at situations from different angles to make good choices. However, when you see things from different points of view, you can feel overwhelmed or confused. So decision-making can become more difficult.

At this age, the emotional part of the brain often takes over from the logical part of the brain. This means that although children can identify risks, they may make decisions based on strong emotions rather than logic. If something is risky but fun to do and they feel peer pressure, pre-teens will often do it. It's natural for them to feel the need to fit in with their peers, so it's important to develop strategies to handle risks responsibly. Being aware of these changes in the brain can be a great help in dealing with these issues calmly, so children can have fun and stay safe, too.

This time in a child's life involves a lot of change, and change can be difficult and confusing. But these changes in the brain ultimately help teenagers become smarter. To any children going through these changes, just know that you are not alone and that everyone will go through this time in their life. Talk to your friends and your family—they will be there to help!

TRACK 109

Unit 9, Explore Language

A Listen and read. What new experience did Grace have last week?

Grace: Last week, I decided to say "yes" to everything that people asked me to do.

Ana: That's exciting! But if someone had told you to do something dangerous, would you have done it?

Grace: Of course not! Nobody asked me to do dangerous stuff and I wouldn't have taken any silly risks. I just did it for fun.

Tony: And was it?!

Grace: Well, there were pros and cons. Sometimes I felt nervous, but it made me do things that normally I wouldn't have done. Like going zip-lining.

Ana: But what would you have done if you'd fallen?

Grace: Oh, I wore the right equipment so I was safe. It's a bit scary, though.

Tony: You're brave ...

Grace: Honestly, it's fun. If I'd asked you to come with me, what would you have said?

Ana: I'm afraid I'd have said "No!"

Tony: Me too! I like adventures but not heights!

Grace: But ...

Ana: No way. I like to keep my feet on the ground!

TRACK 110

Unit 9, Explore Language

D Listen and say.

1 What would you have done if you'd fallen?
2 If you'd known about it, would you have gone?
3 What would have happened if you'd said no?
4 If she'd been there, what would she have said?

Unit 10

TRACK 111

Unit 10, Vocabulary

A Listen. What's the students' end-of-year project about?

Seif: This has been such a great trip, Mrs. Moreno. I'm really sad that it's nearly over!

Aaliyah: Yeah, so am I!

Mrs. Moreno: I'm so glad you've both enjoyed it.

Aaliyah: Definitely! We just need to do our end-of-year project before we go. I really don't know what to write about for that!

Mrs. Moreno: What do you have to write about?

Aaliyah: We need to write about someone or something that inspires us. I'm not sure who I should choose. Do you have any ideas?

Mrs. Moreno: Well, try and think about who has a positive influence on you. It should be someone who has a good effect on your life.

Seif: So do you think it should be someone famous or someone who we know?

Mrs. Moreno: I don't think it has to be someone famous. There are lots of different ways people can be inspired in everyday life. Like look at that little boy over there who's just learning how to ride a bike. He has a can-do attitude; he's been trying for ages and now he can do it!

Seif: That's true. I'd say it helps that he has his family cheering him on. His mom clearly encourages him a lot!

Mrs. Moreno: Exactly! And look at Daniel talking to that famous athlete.

Seif: He's Daniel's role model. Daniel said he thinks he's an amazing athlete and he wants to be just like him.

Mrs. Moreno: Different people can inspire in different ways. Think about whether you have a mentor—someone who can teach you and show you how to do lots of different things like play basketball or value your friends and family.

Aaliyah: Mrs. Lewis told us that art really inspires her. I can see her admiring that painting over there. Perhaps she'll paint one like that herself!

Mrs. Moreno: That's a good point. It doesn't have to be a person; it could be something like music or art.

Aaliyah: Well, I *was* thinking of writing about my grandma. She always listens to me and gives me advice. She encourages me to trust my instinct—my gut feeling—and follow my heart. Like when I wanted to choose art, even though my parents weren't sure about it, she was very supportive. And now I'm so happy I chose art, I might even want to be an artist one day!

Mrs. Moreno: Yes, your grandma sounds perfect for your project. Write about her!

TRACK 112

Unit 10, Vocabulary

B Find and number the words in A. Then listen and check.

1 encourage
2 can-do attitude
3 gut feeling
4 positive influence
5 respect
6 inspire
7 mentor
8 role model

TRACK 113

Unit 10, Vocabulary

C Close your eyes. Listen, visualize, and say.

Who's your role model? What quality do you want to copy from them? Say "role model." Who would you choose as your mentor? How would they help you? Say "mentor." Who encourages you to do good things in your life? Think of a time when you were encouraged to do something. Say "encourage." Who inspires you? What do they inspire you to do? Say "inspire." Who has had a positive influence on you? How have you changed? Say "positive influence." Which famous person do you respect? Why do you respect them? Say "respect." Which of your friends has a can-do attitude? How do you feel when you're with them? Say "can-do attitude." When was the last time you did something because you just knew it was the right decision? Was it right? Say "gut feeling."

TRACK 114

Unit 10, Vocabulary

E Listen and write. Then watch and say.

Let's Look to the Future

I believe in myself.
I believe in you.
Let's look to the future.
Wow! What a view!

You're my role model.
You're so clever.
You encourage me.
You're the best friend ever!

You're my mentor.
I respect you, too.
You do your best.
And inspire me, too!

TRACK 115

Unit 10, Vocabulary

F Pronunciation. Listen and say. Copy the sentence stress. How does it change the meaning?

You're the *best* friend ever. (x2)
You're the best friend ever. (x2)
You're the best friend *ever*. (x2)

TRACK 116

Unit 10, Explore Language

A Listen and read. What kind of people is Sofia talking about?

Mr. Moreno: So, who do you think are great leaders, Sofia?

Sofia: Well, in the past, there were some great leaders in Egypt like Hatshepsut, the second female pharaoh. And scientists can also be leaders, like Dr. Ali Moustafa Mosharafa. He even corresponded with Albert Einstein!

Mr. Moreno: What about now? And who will we be following in the future?

Sofia: Hmm, people like Roger Federer and Beyoncé. Some celebrities have millions of followers on social media …

Mr. Moreno: Do you think celebrities are good role models?

Sofia: Some can be. But some people are famous just for being famous—they haven't really *done* anything inspiring.

Mr. Moreno: You're right. I hope people won't only be following celebrities in the future. I hope they'll be learning more about regular hard-working people who do amazing things.

Sofia: Well, I'll be feeling inspired by the end of this trip, I'm sure! This time next week I'll be looking to discover what amazing things I can achieve.

Mr. Moreno: Good for you!

TRACK 117

Unit 10, Explore Language

D Listen and say.

1 Who will we be following in the future?
2 I'll definitely be wearing bigger shoes next year.
3 He won't be posting many updates on Sunday.
4 I'll be thinking about the next project by the time you finish that one.

TRACK 118

Unit 10, Global Citizenship

A Listen to André talk to his mentor, Patrick. Does André believe he can be a good leader? Why?

André: I think it'd be great to set up a Young Persons' Business Club next year, Patrick, but I'm not sure I can do it. I have some good ideas, but I'm not sure anyone will listen to me.

Patrick: People will listen if you get their attention. You need to show people your commitment to what you want to do, really show them that you're determined to do what you say you'll do. Then people will see your passion, you know, that you really care, and they'll become interested and passionate about it, too. But you need to lead, André. Let's list what makes a good leader. Then you can check what your strong points are.

André: OK—well, you have to have good organizational skills so you know what to do and when to do it.

Patrick: Yes—and something that's really important is being honest. Saying what's good as well as what's bad, and thinking about how to improve is essential. This is how you motivate other people to be part of what you're doing. If they feel like they're really part of a team, then they'll be determined to achieve the team's goals.

André: Great.

Patrick: Also, a leader should be good at listening to people so they can offer support to anyone who needs help and encourage them.

André: OK—I think I can do all these things.

Patrick: You can, but remember, you need to listen to people and take their advice, too. The big thing to remember is to set a good example—then they'll learn from you. By this time next year, I'm sure you'll be leading a very successful Young Persons' Business Club!

André: Thanks! I'll try to do everything you've said. You're a great mentor!

TRACK 119

Unit 10, Global Citizenship

B Look at the pictures and definitions in A and write. Then listen and check.

1 set a good example
2 passionate
3 organizational skills
4 motivate
5 focus
6 support
7 commitment
8 honest

TRACK J

Unit 10, Global Citizenship

Close your eyes. Listen, visualize, and say.

Think of something you feel really strongly about. Say "passionate."
Think of somebody who sets a good example in your class. Say "set a good example."
Who motivates you to do things that you might not do otherwise? Say "motivate."
Think of something you want and how you're going to achieve it. Say "determined."
Do you always tell people the truth? Say "honest."
Think about someone who needs your help. How will you help them? Say "support."
Think about something you've promised to do. How will you stop yourself from giving up? Say "commitment."
Think about something you have to organize in your life. Say "organizational skills."

TRACK 120

Unit 10, Global Citizenship

D Now listen to Dev talk about Will Lourcey. What did Will do to help in his community?

My name's Dev. I'd like to show you how *everyone* can make a difference by telling you the story of Will Lourcey. He's a teenager who started a charity to help fight hunger when he was only seven years old. One day, on his way home from a baseball game, he saw a man on a street corner holding a sign that said, "Need a Meal." This really worried him, so he went away and thought about how to solve the problem. He went to the local food bank and found out about the work they were doing. Then he talked to his friends at school and on his baseball team. Together they came up with the idea of FROGs—Friends Reaching Our Goals—an organization run by children to help the hungry, particularly hungry children, in their own community. They decided on a goal of collecting 1,000 cans of food for the food bank. Then, when they'd done that, Will started FROGs Dinner Clubs, places where hungry children could come and eat a healthy meal once a month—he persuaded restaurants in his area to donate the food. The example set by Will and his friends has inspired a lot of other children to volunteer and have fun while helping others.

Will saw a problem he cared about, he had an idea about how to solve it, and he managed to get other kids involved. It shows anything's possible with the right commitment. Will's message is simple: "See a need, make a plan, gather friends, and change the world." So if you think you're good at motivating people and you have good organizational skills, find something you feel passionate about and act!

TRACK 121

Unit 10, Explore Language

A Listen and read. What does Lucas want to do?

Mr. Hussein: Tell me your ideas for next year's student exchange program, Lucas.

Lucas: Well, I think the students from both schools will really benefit from it. We can schedule two weeks in the spring semester for students from your school to visit us next year. The students will attend classes at our school and they'll experience how we spend our free time. I'm going to find out how many students are interested. I think there'll be a lot. I'm having a meeting with the group later today.

Mr. Hussein: It sounds great, but how much will this cost?

Lucas: I'm not sure yet, but I'll be asking students to organize a fundraising event, which will support the program and help pay for the travel costs. I'd like Aaliyah to help me with this, if you agree?

Mr. Hussein: Yes, agreed. She has excellent organizational skills and will support you.

Lucas: Good. We'll also need to figure out where the students can stay.

Mr. Hussein: There's a lot to think about. But I'm sure you'll make it work.

Lucas: Thank you. I'm determined to make sure other children have an exchange experience like this one. I hope it'll be a great success.

Mr. Hussein: Great. Now, let's say goodbye to this year's exchange students. We have cake!

TRACK 122

Unit 10, Explore Language

D Listen and say.

1 I'm having a meeting with the group later today.
2 Do you think it'll be worth it?
3 I'm going to talk about fundraising.
4 I think he'll be very good!
5 She isn't going to help organize it.
6 We're leaving tomorrow!

Literacy Book

Literacy Review

TRACK 1

Literacy Review, Fiction, *The Secret Way to Petra*

Boy: Hey, there!

Narrator: said a young boy in long shorts.

Boy: Come this way. I can show you a secret way in!

Narrator: Zac followed the boy into a cave. It was cool and quiet away from the hot desert sun and the crowds of tourists who were waiting at the entrance to the Lost City. The boy ran off through a long tunnel, jumping over stones and disappearing around corners.

Zac: Wait for me!

Narrator: Zac's voice echoed. The tunnel opened out into a narrow passage between smooth pink and red rocks. The boy stopped to show Zac some beautiful ancient carvings in the rock, but then he looked up and smelled the air.

Boy: I smell rain!

Narrator: he shouted and dashed off.

Zac: I didn't know it rained in the desert,

Narrator: said Zac, chasing after the boy. Soon it was raining hard and water splashed around his ankles.

Boy: Up here!

Narrator: called a voice. Zac looked up and saw the boy sitting high up on a rock.

Boy: Hurry! This is an old water tunnel. If it floods, we might drown!

TRACK 2

Literacy Review, Nonfiction, *Machu Picchu*

The city of Machu Picchu was built by the ancient Inca civilization in the 15th century. At more than 2,400 meters above sea level, the Inca constructed huge steps in the mountains for farming and making their homes. Their engineering skills were good and they developed ways to transport water to the fields and houses. Then, in the 16th century, the Incas left the city. They may have died from diseases. Plants grew around Machu Picchu and it disappeared into the jungle. Consequently, this helped to preserve the site. When the Spanish people came to Peru, they didn't find Machu Picchu and it remained hidden from the world. Eventually, in 1911, it was rediscovered by an American historian named Hiram Bingham. About 200 buildings were found around a square.

In order to protect Machu Picchu for future generations, it was named a UNESCO World Heritage Site and is the most visited tourist site in Peru. Some of the buildings have been rebuilt. The area has grasslands, forests, and tropical rainforests, so it's an important area for conservation, too. Machu Picchu must be safely passed on to future generations.

Unit 1

TRACK 3

Unit 1, Fiction, *Urgent Message*

Narrator: Pia lifted her head off the pillow. Instant message alert. She stared at the clock. 6:00 a.m.

Pia: *Who could be sending messages this early?*

Narrator: Pia wondered. Pia looked at her laptop screen. There was the message. But no username or personal information. This was weird. She'd never seen a message without a username before. Pia got up and showed her parents.

Dad: It's a trick.

Narrator: said Dad with a yawn.

Dad: Soon they'll ask you for money.

Mom: Never reply to strange messages, you know better than that.

Narrator: said Mom.

Pia: OK.

Narrator: agreed Pia. But she couldn't help feeling a little anxious. The second message arrived later that day while Pia was playing a video game online. No name, no ID. The message gave Pia the heebie-jeebies.

Pia: *-oat s-nk?*

Narrator: Pia didn't understand.

Pia: *Goat stink? Float sank? Was the first word boat? Boat sank!*

Narrator: Her friend Helen was on a boat right now, sailing with her parents for vacation. Just the other day, Helen sent Pia some photos. Was Helen in trouble? Pia knew she shouldn't reply, but she and Helen had a secret code made from the letters of their names. She quickly typed. Pia needed to be sure. Pia waited and waited. It seemed like forever. She started to wonder if this was someone's bad idea of a joke. Then it came. When she got the message, Pia's heart beat faster. *Phil* was the correct response. It was Helen. This was no joke. Somehow Helen was sending messages—maybe she still had a phone? But why didn't Helen contact the coast guard? Maybe she couldn't.

Pia: *Maybe I'm her last chance,*

Narrator: thought Pia.

Pia: Where are you?

Narrator: Pia typed. She sat by her laptop, staring at the screen. Pia needed to do something. She had to find out more, then perhaps she could convince her parents that this wasn't a prank.

Pia: *What clues do I have?*

Narrator: She remembered Helen's family kept their boat at Costa del Sol.

Pia: *Where were they going? Isla Punta Zacate, wasn't it?*

Narrator: Pia searched for a sailing map tool online, and found Costa del Sol. Then she found the islands. Using the tools, she drew a line between the two places. The map told her the distance was 154 km. Pia knew that boats didn't always travel in a straight line, so she circled the whole area. Pia looked at her circle. Helen was stuck somewhere in there.

Pia: *What did Helen say?* "Small island."

Narrator: On the map there were quite a few islands. How was she going to find them?

Pia: *The photos Helen emailed me!*

Narrator: Pia opened up the messages from Helen. The last one was sent just two days earlier. It was of Helen sitting on the deck of the boat pointing at a small island. The message said "Isla Garrobo rocks!" Pia enlarged the map and looked closely at the details. Isla Garrobo, there it was. Helen was on an island between Isla Garrobo and the Isla Punta Zacate. Pia drew a smaller circle and studied it. There was only one piece of land inside her circle that made sense. Isla Violín!

Pia grabbed her laptop and ran with it into the living room. She took a deep breath and calmly told her parents everything. She showed them all the evidence she'd collected: the messages, the photo, and the map. Mom didn't say anything. Then with a nod she reached for her phone and dialed.

Mom: Coast guard, please. It's urgent.

TRACK 4

Unit 1, *Urgent Message*, Words in Context

Find these words in the reading. What do you think they mean?

instant message
weird
coast guard
prank
enlarged

TRACK 5

Unit 1, Literary Term, Register

1 What's up? Have you started your homework yet?
2 That car chase in the movie was so awesome.
3 Cut it out! I can't concentrate with all that noise.
4 Just take it easy and don't think about tomorrow.

TRACK 6

Unit 1, Nonfiction, *Communication Time!*

Narrator: Since the earliest days of humanity, communication has allowed people to share ideas, feelings, and thoughts and to exchange information.

People are always looking to improve the way they communicate. Communication technology has grown from the first cave paintings, through the invention of written language, to today's cell phones and wireless internet.

Let's look at some important moments in the history of communication.

600s: The Chinese use woodblocks covered in ink to print on paper.

1440s: The printing press is invented. For the first time, copies of books can be made in large numbers.

1844: The first message is sent along telegraph wires by Samuel Morse using his code.

1876: Alexander Graham Bell makes the first telephone call to his assistant: "Mr. Watson—come here—I want to see you."

1890s: The radio arrives.

The invention of radio is a big step on the communication timeline. Radio technology provides a way to communicate without wires. People can make easy contact over great distances, connecting the world.

Who invented radio communication? There isn't an easy answer.

Guglielmo Marconi versus Nikola Tesla

Tesla: 1884: Electrical engineer Nikola Tesla arrives in the United States from Europe.

1890: Tesla succeeds in transmitting energy through the air—the beginning of wireless power.

1894: As a result of his experiments with sending and receiving radio signals, Tesla works out a way to make wireless signals stronger. He patents an electromagnetic coil, known as the Tesla coil, so that no one can copy it and sell it.

Marconi: 1895: Italian inventor Guglielmo Marconi experiments with using electromagnetic waves to send signals without using wires. He sends and receives a signal over a distance of 2.4 km.

Tesla: 1895: Tesla prepares to send a signal over a distance of 80.5 km., but a fire in his workshop destroys all his work.

1898: Tesla plans to build a worldwide wireless system. But his project later runs out of money.

Marconi: 1899: Marconi sends a signal across the sea between England and France.

Tesla: 1900: The United States Patent Office recognizes Tesla as the inventor of the radio.

Marconi: 1901: Marconi transmits a message across the Atlantic Ocean. The signal is the letter S in Morse Code.
Tesla: 1904: The United States Patent Office reverses its decision and gives Marconi the patent for inventing the radio. (This decision was later reversed in Tesla's favor in 1943.)
Marconi: 1909: Marconi wins the Nobel Prize. He becomes known as the "father of wireless."
Narrator: While people might argue about who should be known as the real inventor of radio, the story of communication technology doesn't end there ...
1906: The first voice and music is transmitted over radio waves. Radio becomes a way of sharing news, information, and entertainment with a huge audience.
1926: John Logie Baird sends a picture wirelessly. This is the first demonstration of television.
1962: The first active communications satellite, *Telstar 1*, is launched.
1969: Scientists create a way of sending messages from one computer to another.
1971: The first demonstration of a wireless computer network happens. This is the early beginnings of wi-fi!
1973: The first cell phone call is made. The world takes a step toward wireless phones!
1989: Tim Berners-Lee creates the World Wide Web, a way of sharing information across the planet. This was the beginning of the internet as we know it.
2004: Online social media service Facebook is launched. It became the first social media site to reach 1 billion users.
2014: An estimated 7 billion people across the world use cell phones.
2018: Close to 2.7 billion people around the world use social media.
2040: ...?
Communication technology has grown since the first words were printed on paper. Scientists and inventors build on ideas that came before.
Communication technology is always changing. What do you think will be next?

TRACK 7
Unit 1, *Communication Time!*, Words in Context
Find these words in the reading. What do you think they mean?
wireless
telegraph
patents
reverses
demonstration
wi-fi

Unit 2

TRACK 8
Unit 2, Fiction, *My Stay at Camp Karma* by Cathy Rosales
Sunday, June 27
Excuse my writing! In the car on the way to Camp Karma. Mom's idea of a great family vacation! She says that Dad needs to exercise every day, and that Billy and I have been spending too much time glued to screens and have lost the ability to communicate. As for Mom, she hasn't been sleeping well and is feeling stressed. She got upset when Billy and I started arguing because Billy kept putting his video game in my face! How rude! I'm so stressed I'm biting my fingernails more than ever. Aaargh! I'm dreading it!
Monday, June 28
Survived the first night in our yurt. No, we can't stay in a hotel or a tent like normal people—have to stay in a yurt in the middle of a field! Apparently we'll all sleep better and become nicer people! Mom woke us at dawn for yoga before breakfast. I say breakfast, but there wasn't a sugary cereal in sight, just green smoothies—broccoli and cabbage, cabbage and pear, or broccoli and pear! (Sugar is banned at Camp Karma because it isn't good for you. Billy is NOT happy!) Getting ready for a *gentle* 15 km. hike through the forest with a bunch of other families who are crazy enough to come here.
Tuesday, June 29
Ached all over this morning. Billy and I had a plan. Set off early for the store just outside the entrance to the camp to buy some candy. We were about to escape through the gate when we heard a cheerful "Good morning, kids!"—from Mom and Dad and the Early Bird running group. *Poof* went our plan! Had to join the Early Birds and run around the camp before breakfast! Was so hungry even the green juice tasted good. This afternoon, went to the beach. At last, I thought, a chance to sunbathe! How wrong could I be? Exercising in the sand is even harder than in a gym! I'm exhausted!
Wednesday, June 30
They called today a rest day—that meant a morning of chanting followed by meditation. At first Billy and I couldn't stop giggling, but then we closed our eyes and concentrated on our breathing like the instructor said. Afterwards felt unexpectedly happy and calm. Mom and Dad actually smiled at Billy and me over our healthy lunch of fish and green vegetables. We haven't had a nice family meal like that for a long time! This afternoon we hung out at the yurts. There's no wi-fi so Billy and I were forced to talk to the other weird kids, because there was nothing else to do. Actually had a good time chatting and sharing stories. One of them, Maisie, is really friendly and she can play the guitar, so she played and we sang songs around a campfire in the evening.
Thursday, July 1
No time to write today! Too busy having a wonderful day with Maisie and the gang, hiking to the beach, swimming in the ocean, breathing in the fresh air, and just enjoying being here!
Friday, July 2
Today was our last day and I hate to admit it, but felt kind of sad. Had our last yoga class on the beach (I'm actually quite good at yoga now!), drank our last smoothies (I asked for the recipes!), and said goodbye to our new friends. Dad plans to have a daily run, I've stopped biting my nails, Billy has developed a love of broccoli, and as for Mom—she's smiling a lot! Billy and I are going to sing campfire songs all the way home! Goodbye Camp Karma and thank you!

TRACK 9
Unit 2, *My Stay at Camp Karma*, Words in Context
Find these words in the reading. What do you think they mean?
glued to
fingernails
dreading
meditation
forced to

TRACK 10
Unit 2, Literary Term, Dropped Subjects
Hey Maisie,
Today isn't going well. Billy got up late. Said he couldn't get to sleep last night. Went to school as usual but got stuck in traffic. Was late for first class and my teacher gave me an unhappy look. Never asked why I was late. I was so embarrassed! Can't wait for this day to be over. How's your day going?

TRACK 11
Unit 2, Nonfiction, *Why Do We Sleep?*
Why do we sleep? It's a difficult question to answer. We spend about a third of our lives asleep—that's 30 years for a person who lives to be 90—but nobody knows exactly why. Are we wasting our time lying in bed doing nothing when we could be doing something useful? Scientists don't think so. All mammals and birds sleep, even though while they sleep they are easy prey for predators. Fish, reptiles and insects rest too, so there must be a good reason.
What are the scientific theories?
When we sleep enough we feel better and more energetic; it's easier to concentrate and make decisions. After a good night's sleep, we solve problems and think of new ideas better. We're generally healthier and happier. Scientists have developed several theories for why we sleep. Our bodies rebuild and replace energy we've used in the day. Muscle grows, tissue is repaired, and hormones, chemicals our bodies need, are produced while we're sleeping.
Our brains recover from the day, store information, and process experiences and memories while we are asleep. Our brains also clear away anything we don't need to remember.
What happens if we don't sleep?
Without sleep, parts of our brains become inactive. We get confused and forget things; we can't concentrate. Tiredness, stress, and difficulty following directions are all results of not getting enough sleep. Also, lack of sleep weakens the immune system, so it can't fight illness very well and we may become sick.
Why do we dream?
When we sleep we may have amazing adventures in our dreams that seem real. We all dream at night, but we don't always remember our dreams. Nobody really knows why we dream, but it might be part of organizing our memories and emotions.
How is modern life affecting sleep patterns?
Before the light bulb was invented, people usually went to bed when it was dark and got up when it was light. In today's world, we go to sleep about two hours later and get up two hours earlier than we used to. Technology has made it harder for us to sleep, so we are more tired. Looking at brightly lit screens before bed, whether they are TVs, cell phones, or computers, is making it harder for people to get to sleep and harder to wake up in the morning, too.
Why can't I sleep sometimes?
Worrying about something can keep us awake, but there may be several things keeping us from sleeping. Here are a few tips to help:
Don't look at a screen just before bedtime.
Don't eat junk food. Eat a healthy diet, but don't eat just before bed.
Sleep in a cool, dark, quiet room.
Go to bed at the same time every night.
Work out regularly, but not late in the evening.
Don't drink anything with caffeine in it, like soda, coffee, or tea, before bed.

Am I getting enough sleep?
Feeling sleepy or annoyed and having difficulty concentrating and making decisions are signs that we're not getting enough sleep. Most children need between 8 and 10 hours of sleep a night. Keeping a sleep diary noting what time we go to bed, wake up, and how we feel during the day can help us to find out whether we're getting enough sleep. Taking a daytime nap, or a power nap, can help boost energy for studying and playing.
Along with water, food, and oxygen, we also need sleep in order to survive. So falling asleep on the sofa in the middle of the day isn't really lazy. Don't feel bad—instead, consider how much good it's really doing!

TRACK 12
Unit 2, *Why Do We Sleep?*, Words in Context
Find these words in the reading. What do you think they mean?
hormones
process
clear away
weakens
caffeine
power nap

Unit 3

TRACK 13
Unit 3, Nonfiction, *Communities Making Dreams Come True*
Cash Flow Problems
Rupa is a hardworking tea farmer in northeast Bangladesh. To help make her business grow, she needed to borrow money.
But Rupa doesn't have a phone or internet access, so she had to go to the nearest bank herself. It took her a day to travel there by bus. At the bank, Rupa eventually saw someone. Before they gave her a loan, the bank wanted something to guarantee that they would get their money back. Unfortunately, she didn't have anything valuable, so she left empty-handed.
Microloans
Rupa was determined to reach her goal, and didn't give up. She heard about organizations giving loans of small amounts of money—microloans—to people who find it difficult to get a bank loan. She decided to talk to a nonprofit microloan organization.
After carefully assessing her application, the organization loaned Rupa the money she needed. Rupa bought a new tiller, hired two employees to help with the harvest, and was able to pay back her loan on time.
When Noam Tep's fishing nets were stolen, he lost his only source of income, but a microloan meant the Cambodian fisherman was able to make a fresh start by buying some new nets.
Today, there are many organizations working in countries all around the world using microloans to help people achieve their dreams.
Crowdfunding
Siblings Jorani and Leap had a great idea for a game app. Together these Cambodian teens planned all of the levels and figured out that if Jorani drew the characters and backgrounds, and Leap wrote the game to work on cell phones and tablets, they would be onto a winner.
But as soon as they wrote their business plan, they realized they didn't have enough savings to purchase everything they needed. So they turned to a crowdfunding site, offered investors a copy of the game once it was complete in return for their help, and gave themselves a month to raise the money. If they didn't meet their goal, they would delay their plan until they could fund it themselves.
At first, only a few people contributed, but just two days before the deadline, their campaign suddenly went viral! Thousands of people saw their campaign, contributed, and they had all of the money they needed. Jorani and Leap worked really hard and one year later, Octopus Knight was released worldwide!
Crowdfunding is when a large group of people give money to help a particular project or dream become a reality. It's usually done over the internet, where crowdfunding websites connect people with projects and dreams to people who have the money that can help. There are many different websites that help with crowdfunding for a variety of purposes.
Crowdfunding can be used for artistic projects, such as publishing a book. It can also help raise money for people who need medical help or for communities who need new equipment or resources.
For more than 20 years, LeVar Burton was the host of *Reading Rainbow*, a television show that focused on teaching children about books and reading. In 2014 he launched a crowdfunding campaign on a site called Kickstarter. His dream was to make more *Reading Rainbow* videos, classroom materials, and apps for children all over the world to use for free. The campaign reached its goal in just one day. Today, Burton's dream is real and children everywhere can use the *Reading Rainbow* Skybrary!
Whether it's microloans or crowdfunding, people from all walks of life can use a helping hand to achieve their dreams.

TRACK 14
Unit 3, *Communities Making Dreams Come True*, Words in Context
Find these words in the reading. What do you think they mean?
cash flow
nonprofit
tiller
campaign
went viral
walks of life

TRACK 15
Unit 3, Fiction, *Dreams*
Narrator: A dream is another way of saying ambition or wish.
It says so in the dictionary.
Something you really want, and hope will happen one day.
A dream. Right there on page 23.
It's tough grasping hold of a dream.
Dreams slip through the air like notes from a guitar, the ringing of the bell, the whoosh of a roller coaster.
Falling, spinning, floating.

Until they find a home, dreams are almost out of sight.
You need those special dream eyes.
But dreams are there, it's true.
And every dream needs a dreamer.
Boy: Faisal dreams of making a stop-motion movie.
He wants to shoot it on his phone and post it online for his friends. Just for fun.
Super Max to the Rescue!

Faisal paints the scene, and shapes the hero out of clay.

Move, click, move, click! The process takes forever, but at last it's done! Success!
100 likes already! And it's only been online for a few hours.

Every dream needs a dreamer
with special dream eyes.
Girl: Winning the 100 meters is what Isabel wants most of all.
She's never won before. Third place is her best so far.
Isabel wishes she could feel the string break and know she's won.
She wants a blue ribbon pinned to her chest.
But she needs determination.

After school, Isabel stays behind at the track.
She gulps a mouthful of water and starts to dash, around and around, her legs warming up.
Then she practices her starts: Ready, set, go!

Every dream needs a dreamer
with special dream eyes.

Sofia's dream is for a bedroom, a space to call her very own.
Whisper quiet when she wants to read, really noisy when she feels like tuning out the world.
She wishes she could paint the walls blue and have a shelf full of books.

Sofia knows this dream won't happen. Not yet. Not for years.
There isn't a spare room in the house,
not unless you count the closet under the stairs.
But she can dream all the same.

Every dream needs a dreamer
with special dream eyes.

Lilly dreams of snow. She wishes she could feel it, just once.

She wants to lie on her back and move her arms.
Then throw big snowballs at Mom and Dad, and zoom down a hill on a sled, stopping for hot chocolate.

Lilly plans a mountain trip: the journey, the clothes, the stay.
She shows her parents. "Can we please, please, go?"
"Maybe," Mom smiles. "If you get good grades at school."
So Lilly works hard. She needs those grades.
She wants the happiness of snow!

Every dream needs a dreamer
with special dream eyes.
Boy: Seth has a dream. Well, he calls it a goal.
He wishes he had a rabbit. A Flemish Giant—one of the biggest there is.
They have huge ears that stick up, and noses that twitch.
He promises he'll look after it really well.

Seth saves all his money, for weeks and weeks and weeks.
He helps his mother build a big rabbit pen.
They cut wood, pound nails, and fill the bottom with hay.
Then they bring home Buttons. What a happy day!

Every dream needs a dreamer
with special dream eyes.
Narrator: So you see, you can grab hold of a dream.
It's not always easy, and sometimes it doesn't happen at all.
But like a superhero, a blue ribbon, and a very large rabbit, it's only impossible if you don't put your mind to it.

TRACK 16
Unit 3, *Dreams*, Words in Context
Find these words in the reading. What do you think they mean?
stop-motion movie
gulps
tuning out
twitch
hay

Unit 4

TRACK 17
Unit 4, Nonfiction, *The Sci-Files*
Case Study 1: Sliding rocks in Death Valley
How can rocks move on their own?
The mystery
The Racetrack is a playa, or dry lake bed, in Death Valley National Park, California, USA. Years can pass without a drop of rain falling here. But it has become famous for a geological mystery. Rocks that are stuck in the dry mud have long tracks behind them. They appear to have moved hundreds of meters on their own.
Possible theories
1 Hypothesis: It could have been a trick. Someone might have moved the rocks.
Argument against: They couldn't have done this without leaving evidence of a truck or footprints.
2 Hypothesis: Strong winds might have moved them.
Argument against: Many of the rocks are extremely heavy.
Investigation
The problem was that nobody ever saw the rocks moving, but a team of scientists had an idea. They fitted rocks with GPS trackers and used time-lapse photography to record any movement. It was going to be a long experiment taking up to 10 years. But only two years later, when scientists visited the site to collect information in 2013, by coincidence, the rocks started to move while they were there. It was icy after some rain and the mystery was solved!
Conclusion
Sometimes rain falls in winter, creating a shallow pond in the playa, half covering the rocks. At night, the temperature drops suddenly. The top of the pond freezes into a thin but strong sheet of ice. On sunny mornings, the ice starts to melt and break up. Light winds cause the floating ice sheets to push the rocks slowly across the playa, leaving tracks in the mud. In spring, the ground dries up and the rocks are left at the end of their tracks.
This rare sequence of events has to happen to start the rocks moving. Because it's dry 99% of the time in Death Valley, this might not happen for many years.
Case study 2: Fairy circles in the Namib Desert
Where do these amazing patterns in the desert come from?
The mystery
The grasslands of the Namib Desert in Africa are covered with large circles that are uniform in size. They are known as fairy circles and have puzzled the local Himba people for generations. What might have created these bare patches of ground?
Possible theories
1 Hypothesis: Termites were seen in the fairy circles, so the circles might have been caused by termite nests.
Argument against: It didn't explain why the circles are so regular in size.
2 Hypothesis: Dying plants might have poisoned the soil.
Argument against: It couldn't have been caused by this, as there was no evidence of poison in the soil.
3 Hypothesis: Thicker grass grew around the circles, so they could have been caused by plants competing for water.
Argument against: It hadn't been proven by any tests.
Investigation
Termites look for food in a circular area around their nest. If they meet another colony of a similar size, they don't go any fu rther. Ecologists, who study how plants and animals live together, created computer software to investigate the result of termite colonies surrounded by other colonies of a similar size eating the roots of plants above their nests. This caused the plants to die. They also investigated plants living close together that create natural shade for each other but grow long roots. These roots take water from the soil further away, causing the plants there to die. The software predicted regular patterns would be formed of big circles created by the termites eating the plants' roots, and small circles because of the plants competing for water. The team then took aerial photos of the fairy circles.
Conclusion
The aerial photos confirmed the predictions of the software and showed small circles between the large circles. So two of the three theories were correct. Nobody noticed the small circles before because everyone was interested in the big circles. They couldn't see the forest for the trees!

TRACK 18
Unit 4, *The Sci-Files*, Words in Context
Find these words in the reading. What do you think they mean?
geological
GPS trackers
uniform
termites
colony
ecologists
aerial

TRACK 19
Unit 4, Fiction, *An Enlightening Journey*
Nora: I'm no expert, but we're lost, aren't we?
Narrator: asked Nora.
Eddy: It's all part of the adventure. But, yes, we're lost,
Narrator: answered Eddy.
Eddy: We'll just have to float until we see land.
Nora: Go to sleep, Josh, we'll be home soon.
Narrator: Nora whispered.
Josh: I have bad dreams when it's dark,
Narrator: mumbled Josh.
Nora: There's nothing to worry about.
Narrator: replied Nora.
Josh: But there's something outside. There's a light.
Eddy: It's probably just an optical illusion.
Narrator: Eddy said. They went outside to investigate. Josh pointed at the water.
Josh: The sea is on fire!
Nora: No, it isn't fire, but it's beautiful and very strange.
Narrator: said Nora.
Eddy: I can see land,
Narrator: shouted Eddy suddenly.
Eddy: Look! That must be a town.
Narrator: They could hear the sound of thunder in the distance.
Eddy: Where's the town?
Narrator: Eddy was disappointed.
Eddy: I saw lights. I can't have imagined them. But look at the sea!
Narrator: The children watched the sparkling waves dance along the beach. Josh jumped.
Josh: Did you hear that? I think there's something following us.
Eddy: No there isn't, but there's a storm coming.
Narrator: said Eddy.
Eddy: We should keep moving.
Narrator: A single light hovered in front of Josh's face.
Josh: What's that? Its tail is flashing.
Eddy: It's a firefly.
Narrator: replied Eddy.
Eddy: Look. There are lots of them!
Narrator: As they walked, the ground became softer and wetter.
Josh: I don't like this place. It smells bad.
Narrator: Josh said.
Nora: We're in a swamp, Eddy,
Narrator: whispered Nora.
Eddy: I know, but I think we should follow the lights.
Narrator: Eddy pointed to the glowing path.
Eddy: It's OK, Josh, I'll carry you.
Josh: There's something following us. Listen!
Narrator: sobbed Josh.
Eddy: He's right. I can hear it.
Narrator: Eddy looked up to see a swirling dark shape approaching from the distance.
Eddy: Run!
Josh: It's like the monster from my dream!
Narrator: cried Josh. The dark shape followed them, pulling trees out of the ground as it chased them through the swamp. Nora tripped and fell.
Nora: Eddy! Help!
Josh: Get away from her!
Narrator: Josh picked up a branch and threw it as hard as he could. It swallowed the branch whole. A crack of thunder and lightning came from the sky as Eddy grabbed Nora's hand. They ran until they were exhausted.
Nora: A cave. Quick, get inside!
Narrator: shouted Nora. Outside, the tornado rushed past the entrance of the cave, hurling branches and pieces of rock in anger. Inside, the cave was quiet.
Eddy: This is unbelievable.
Narrator: whispered Eddy. Looking closely at the strings of light, they could see they were made of threads of silk.
Eddy: All this must have been made by insects.
Narrator: Josh felt safe in the cave.
Josh: I saved you from the monster, didn't I, Nora?
Nora: You were very brave, Josh,
Narrator: Nora replied.
Nora: You can go to sleep now. Look, the lights are on!
Narrator: In the morning, the sun was shining outside.
Nora: Where are you going?
Narrator: said Nora, rubbing her eyes.
Eddy: Now that it's daylight maybe we can find clues to help us get home,
Narrator: answered Eddy.
Eddy: Let's all go outside.
Nora: We must have walked a long way last night. Just think, we might have been blown away by that tiny tornado!
Narrator: shuddered Nora
Eddy: But those beautiful lights led us to the cave,
Narrator: said Eddy.

Eddy: They kept us safe and we only saw them because we got lost!
Nora: Look. I can see over the whole island. Come on. I have a feeling it's this way. Look, Eddy, Josh, here's a path.
Narrator: Things felt different that day as they found their way home in the sunshine. Back home, Nora pulled the blanket up over her little brother.
Nora: Do you want me to leave the light on, Josh?
Josh: No. I'm not scared of the dark anymore,
Narrator: he answered as he fell asleep.

TRACK 20
Unit 4, *An Enlightening Journey*, Words in Context
Find these words in the reading. What do you think they mean?
hovered
firefly
swamp
glowing
swirling
hurling

Unit 5

TRACK 21
Unit 5, Nonfiction, *Cave Painting*
Cave Person: Oil burned in the bowl carved from stone. Dark smoke rose to the roof of the cave. The smoke made the young woman choke and cough a little, but she needed the light of the lamp. Deep down in this cave, there was no daylight.
The artist had laid out her tools the day before: pieces of charcoal she'd saved from the fire, flint, twigs, and tiny bones. She stared at them and the cave walls. Her paintings covered the cave with giant bulls, deer, and horses. This spot was still empty, ready for a new piece of art. What would she paint?
Modern Artist: To recreate the art made in a cave 15,000 years ago, today's artists can work with digital tools. Instead of a cave wall and charcoal, there are design programs and styluses.
To begin working, the digital artist switches on her desktop computer and monitor. The artist opens up Illustrator, a design program, and makes sure her drawing tablet is connected. Next, she creates a new file and saves it as cave_ painting.ai.
Cave Person: The artist picked up a piece of charcoal. She began to draw simple lines, a few squiggles. With a thicker piece of charcoal she sketched some powerful shapes, the neck of the horse and the dark mane. When she liked what she saw, she smudged the lines with her finger to create shadows.
Modern Artist: With the file ready to use, the digital artist touches her stylus to the tablet and selects a brush tool. She chooses its thickness. She starts with a thinner brush type.
Next, pressing gently, the artist moves the stylus over the surface of the tablet. The stylus acts and feels just like a pencil. On screen, the artist follows her stylus strokes as she sketches the outline of the horse.
If the artist makes a mistake, there is also an eraser tool that can correct any errors.
Now that the outline is finished, she selects some of the shapes and applies a filter—this creates a smudge effect that matches the messy lines of the original.
Cave Person: She wanted to choose a color for the horse's body. She had painted many of her animals in black or charcoal. She wanted this one to stand out, so she chose a contrasting color, something brighter than all the other animals. The woman found her powdered red clay, and mixed it with some water, adding more powder to get it just right. Then, with a brush she had made from horsehair, she started painting.
Modern Artist: The digital artist opens up the color picker in her program. To get the red of the cave paint, which came from iron oxide, the artist uses the slider tools to mix red, green, and blue.
With the color chosen, a few more touches and the shape of the horse is filled with red.
Cave Person: The artist smiled. *Now this wall is finished.*
Just one more thing. She filled a hollow bird bone with red paint. She put her hand on the wall beside her art. Then she blew into the bone, spraying the paint over her hand and onto the wall. When she lifted her hand, an outline of her hand was on the wall.
Her print was next to the horse, for everyone to see.
Modern Artist: The drawing stage complete, the artist finds a photograph of a rock surface similar to the cave wall. She opens the photo file and with a few touches she adds her horse drawing to the rock surface. She moves the horse until it's in the best place. It looks like it's painted on rock.
At last, the digital cave painting is finished. The artist saves her file. She posts it in an online gallery, beside a photo of herself. Now, her work is shared for everyone to see.

TRACK 22
Unit 5, *Cave Painting*, Words in Context
Find these words in the reading. What do you think they mean?
charcoal
recreate
stylus
tablet
smudged
strokes
slider

TRACK 23
Unit 5, Fiction, The Boy Who Drew Cats: A Retelling of a Japanese Folk Tale
Narrator: Long ago, in a small village in Japan, there lived a family of farmers: the father Takeshi, the mother Aki, and their four sons. Three of Takeshi's sons followed in their parents' footsteps and sweated beside them harvesting rice. But the youngest son had no interest in farming. His name was Jun, meaning "obedient" in Japanese—that means doing as you are told. But when Jun went to the fields, he spent most of the day drawing in the dirt with a stick. Drawing made him happiest of all. Jun drew cats. Big cats and little cats. Enormous cats and tiny cats. He drew old cats and kittens. There were tabby cats with stripes like a tiger and cats with curious eyes.
Takeshi: What are we going to do with him?
Narrator: grumbled Takeshi.
Aki: He's been drawing since he was a toddler. He never stops.
Narrator: Aki said desperately.
Villager: Send him to Hideaki the Wise,
Narrator: suggested the villagers.
Hideaki had taught the emperor himself! So Jun went to study with Hideaki the Wise.
Hideaki tried to teach Jun to write in the old style and to read the great books. But Jun was only interested in art. When he sketched, it made his heart sing. Drawing made him feel free.
Jun: See this cat, Master Hideaki,
Narrator: said Jun.
Jun: Look how it has a tail like a snake and ears like mountain peaks.
Hideaki: I've failed.
Narrator: sighed Hideaki.
Hideaki returned Jun to his parents after just a week. That winter, a cold wind blew. Snow had been falling for weeks on end, covering the countryside like a quilt. But the frosty wind did more than freeze the bones of the villagers. It drove hundreds of rats from the fields into the village. The rats came in swarms seeking somewhere warm to hide. They tore holes in the walls and ate the grain in the village stores. They stole rice from the kitchens and chewed holes in socks. The villagers didn't know what to do. Only Jun didn't seem bothered. With the ground covered in snow, he started drawing his cats on the walls, using pieces of charcoal from the fireplace. When Jun ran out of room on the walls of his home, he sketched cats on the walls in the village. Huge cats and small cats, striped cats and spotted ones.
Jun's cats soon spread all over the village. His art covered every wall.
Villager: Jun's cats are so playful, so free.
Narrator: said the villagers, smiling.
They forgot about their problems for a while. But the villagers weren't the only ones to notice Jun's cats. One day there came a terrible thunderstorm that made the ground tremble and shiver and shook the rats from their hiding places. Scurrying from place to place, the rats looked up and froze. There above them, an army of giant cats was staring down at them. Monstrous cats with sharp teeth like daggers and claws like rakes. The rats saw there were cats in the grain store and cats in the marketplace. There were cats in the kitchen, cats in the baker's, and cats in the butcher's. They were surrounded by cats! The rats squeaked in terror. It was better to be cold than to be caught by giant beasts. With one last look at the terrifying creatures, they fled back into the countryside as fast as they could.
Villagers: Jun's cats!
Narrator: cried the villagers.
Villager: They've saved us!
Narrator: The very next day, Takeshi and Aki bought a book of drawing paper, a brush, and a pot of ink. From then on, they left Jun to draw as much as he wanted. And it will come as no surprise that he was happy.

TRACK 24
Unit 5, *The Boy Who Drew Cats*, Words in Context
Find these words in the reading. What do you think they mean?
swarms
scurrying
rakes
beasts
fled

Unit 6

TRACK 25

Unit 6, Nonfiction, *The History of Board Games*

As the famous author Roald Dahl said, "Life is more fun if you play games." Go, chess, Snakes and Ladders, and many more board games have been enjoyed all over the world for centuries by people old and young. New games are designed all the time, but traditional games have been part of our cultures for thousands of years and are one of the oldest forms of social interaction. Let's have a look at the history of board games!

Archaeologists have found painted stones and bones that might have been pieces from early board games. These games existed before we had written language! Even the ancient Egyptians enjoyed escaping from daily life by playing Senet—a set of this early board game was found in Tutankhamun's tomb. There is no record of the exact rules, but it was a kind of race across a grid between two players and it may have inspired the game of backgammon.

Go was invented in China more than 2,500 years ago. The rules of this ancient game with black and white pieces are simple, but the game is challenging and requires discipline and strategic thinking in order to carefully plan each step. People still play Go today and after all these years, the game has hardly changed.

Early games of chess were played in India hundreds of years ago, but the pieces were different from those we recognize today. Instead of castles, bishops, knights, and pawns, there were elephants, horses, chariots, and soldiers. Today, over 600 million people play chess and there are tournaments all around the world. Chess requires concentration, as well as logic and strategic thinking. It may also help us to plan ahead and to search for solutions to our real-life problems.

Many board games teach us life skills, such as communicating, following rules, taking turns, and, most importantly, learning how to win and lose gracefully. Snakes and Ladders was originally used to teach important life lessons. The ladders represented positive things people might do, while the snakes represented the negative ones. This reflects the fact that although great things might happen to us in real life, there will also be disappointments. We also learn more than just vocabulary and spelling when we play Scrabble, which requires us to be patient and wait our turn, and the real estate game of Monopoly may even help us to spend our money more wisely.

Today, games like Trivial Pursuit and Pictionary are on the shelves of most board game lovers. Whether players are good at geography, history, art, or science, there are questions for everyone in the general knowledge game of Trivial Pursuit. Creative types enjoy playing Pictionary, in which teammates try to guess what image is being drawn.

Perhaps inspired by the interactive worlds of video games, more modern games involve imaginative settings and intricately designed boards with wonderful details. In Catan, the beautiful board represents an island. Players compete for resources to build cities and roads to colonize the island.

For people who don't like competition, there are cooperative games like Pandemic or Forbidden Island. Instead of competing with other players, everyone must collaborate to win these games. In Pandemic, players work together traveling between cities, treating diseases, discovering cures, and building research stations. Forbidden Island has a team of adventurers racing to collect treasures before the island sinks under the sea.

In these days of digital gaming, it may be surprising that sales of board games are increasing, but many games are timeless as well as ageless. Families and friends still love getting together to move plastic pieces around a piece of cardboard. Perhaps, like the ancient Egyptians, we enjoy the face-to-face interaction and friendly competition that they offer. So, come on everybody, Roald Dahl was right—let's have some fun and play a game!

TRACK 26

Unit 6, *The History of Board Games*, Words in Context

Find these words in the reading. What do you think they mean?

grid
strategic thinking
pawns
gracefully
intricately

TRACK 27

Unit 6, Fiction, *The Game of Life*

Announcer: The atmosphere is electric … There's the whistle … Twenty minutes into the game and it's one-all. Dribbler … Quickfeet … he's going to score! It flies off his boot, past the goalie. Goal! Just one minute to go, the pink team is in real trouble … Quickfeet … Dribbler … Yes! The blue team wins three goals to one.
Will: We won again!
Narrator: The next day at soccer practice …
Tom: Out of my way, Wilfred!
Will: Ouch! And the name's Will …
Tom: Get up! I barely touched you!
Hasan: What's up, Tom? You seemed distracted out there.
Tom: Just … stuff at home. It's nothing. I put on my headset and play SuperSoccer, then I can't hear the arguing.
Hasan: That's a cool game.
Tom: Yeah, I really like it! I'm pretty good but I've lost a lot of games recently. There are two awesome players, Quickfeet and Dribbler.
Will: *No way! We've been playing against Tom!*
Narrator: At Will and Caitlin's house …
Will: Caitlin, you know Tom Taylor from school?
Caitlin: Yeah …
Will: He tackled me really hard today at soccer practice. I didn't even have the ball.
Caitlin: He can sometimes be a bit of a bully, but …
Will: Today, I heard him saying he plays SuperSoccer on his own every evening.
Caitlin: By himself? That's no fun.
Narrator: After dinner …
Will: But get this, he said a couple of players called Quickfeet and Dribbler keep beating him.
Caitlin: Are you serious? That's us!
Will: Yeah! I hope he never wins!
Caitlin: Come on! That's not nice.
Will: Whose side are you on?
Hey, there's a question on the SuperSoccer forum from TacklerTom from Fairview. That might be Tom's username.
Caitlin: OK, let's see if we can help.
Will: What?
Caitlin: It's only a game, Will! Sometimes kids who are mean to others are having problems themselves.
Maybe he's unhappy or something. Can I look at the question?
Will: OK …
Tom: Help!! I keep losing games. It's getting me down. I wonder if you have any tips?
Caitlin: Don't let it get you down. It's only a game. Keep practicing, be patient. Remember, soccer starts in your head. Plan your strategy.
Will: Here's a trick. If you can't get past an opponent, try a rainbow kick to get the ball over their head. Just pull the right stick down, then forward really quickly.
Tom: That's so cool! Thanks, guys.
Caitlin: Do you want to play a game and try it out now? We can talk you through it.
Will: No, Caitlin!
Caitlin: Shh! We'll still beat him! Come on, Will. Just one game …
Will: OK, Just one.
Stop! You can't score from there. Take your time and pass the ball like in a real game.
Caitlin: How about trying a rainbow kick to get past that defender?
Will: Good try, but you weren't fast enough …
Narrator: Tom kept trying…
Tom: That was great!
Announcer: It's five-nil to the pink team! Amazing tactics …
Tom: Yes! Dad? Want to kick a ball around after dinner … if you have time?
Dad: Sounds good, but I promised your mom I'd take the dog to the park …
Tom: Maybe we could take the ball to the park, too?
Mom: Actually, that's a great idea! We can go together.
Narrator: The next day at soccer practice…
Tom: Great goal! Wait a second … was that a rainbow kick?
Will: Yep! I learn a lot playing SuperSoccer. I visualize what my player does in the game, then copy it in real life. Soccer starts in your head, remember?
Tom: Dribbler?
Will: No, that's my sister. I'm Quickfeet! Pleased to meet you, TacklerTom. Come on, let's win this game together.

TRACK 28

Unit 6, *The Game of Life*, Words in Context

Find these words in the reading. What do you think they mean?

headset
tackled
bully
forum
opponent
tactics

Unit 7

TRACK 29

Unit 7, Fiction, *Commercial Break*

Narrator: Cassie leaned against the bus window and stared out at the streets. As she watched the city go by, messages flashed across the lenses of her Insta-Glasses. The bus drove past an airline office, and Cassie's glasses told her that she should "book a flight now." In the park, the trees said: "Love your park. Don't be lazy, grab your garbage!" Cassie stared at the advertisement that popped up when they passed Go Shoes.
Frank: Great, I want some tennis shoes.
Narrator: said her brother Frank, looking at the ad. Cassie hadn't thought about it, but maybe she did need some new shoes. A new message suddenly popped up on Cassie's lenses. "See you this weekend for bargains. Share this message with your friends for 20%

off! Great. Grand. Go Shoes." Cassie blinked and selected her friends. She blinked again. Message sent. As the bus pulled up to their stop, Cassie stared at the ads covering the school building. At the same time, she tried to read the news headlines running down the side of her lenses. Cassie took off her glasses and rubbed her eyes. Lately, all these messages were giving her a headache. Why did everything need to be covered with ads all the time? Cassie looked around, making her eyes wide. It actually felt good with the Insta-Glasses off. Things looked different.

Cassie: *Why not?*

Narrator: thought Cassie. With a shrug, she put the glasses in her bag.

Eva: Thanks for sharing the message about the shoe sale,

Narrator: said Eva when she spotted Cassie at the lockers.

Eva: Hey, where are your glasses?

Cassie: I figured I'd switch off for the rest of the day,

Narrator: said Cassie.

Frank: A whole day?

Narrator: said Frank.

Frank: No way!

Eva: You'll be so out of touch,

Narrator: Eva laughed. Frank asked her how she would get her news and messages.

Cassie: It's just till my headache goes away.

Narrator: said Cassie.

Frank: Of course, sure.

Narrator: said Frank. In science class, Mr. Daunt was teaching the class about how cats' tongues work. Cassie stared at the photo on the screen. Mr. Daunt pointed at the screen.

Mr. Daunt: If you zoom in with your glasses, you'll notice the whitish area is actually rows of backwards-facing barbs. These barbs are made of the same stuff as your fingernails.

Narrator: Cassie looked around the classroom. Her classmates had all zoomed in on the photo, the little red lights on their glasses blinking. She squinted at the photo, trying hard to see what they saw but couldn't see what Mr. Daunt was talking about. Cassie realized that there was no zoom feature when you just used your eyes.

Frank: That tongue looks like my hair,

Narrator: laughed Frank, making the class giggle.

Mr. Daunt: Focus on the lesson,

Narrator: said Mr. Daunt. In art class after lunch, Cassie had fun with a paintbrush. It felt good to hold the brush in her hand. She dripped and swirled paint over her paper, making patterns. The colors seemed so bright, so alive.

Cassie: Check out my painting,

Narrator: she said to Eva.

Eva: You should see what I'm doing with mine.

Narrator: replied Eva. She adjusted her glasses.

Cassie: But you haven't even picked up your brush yet,

Narrator: said Cassie. Eva shrugged.

Eva: I'm using a painting app. Same thing.

Narrator: Cassie thought it wasn't the same. But she didn't say anything.

Eva: The latest Skate Duty album is on sale—my favorite band!

Narrator: said Eva, her glasses flickering. On the ride home after school, Cassie sat beside Frank again.

Frank: How's the headache?

Narrator: her brother asked.

Cassie: It's gone, thanks.

Narrator: said Cassie.

Frank: You should put your glasses back on,

Narrator: said Frank.

Frank: I'm watching a trailer for the new *SuperSoccer* movie.

Narrator: Cassie shook her head and stared out the window. As they passed the park, she saw the bright white swans on the lake. She hadn't noticed them floating there that morning. But now there were no distracting messages to get in the way.

Cassie: *Everyone should try this,*

Narrator: thought Cassie. Before Frank could stop her, Cassie reached over and took off his Insta-Glasses.

Cassie: Time for a commercial break,

Narrator: she said.

TRACK 30

Unit 7, *Commercial Break*, Words in Context

Find these words in the reading. What do you think they mean?

lenses
popped up
lockers
squinted
distracting

TRACK 31

Unit 7, Literary Term, Alliteration

1 Peter Piper picked a pickled pepper.
2 Five fat flamingos flew fast.
3 Round the rocks the rascal ran.
4 I used to yearn for Europe in my youth.

TRACK 32

Unit 7, Nonfiction, *Ad Smart*

A child is watching TV. The cartoon suddenly stops. Now the child is learning about the latest toy. For homework, a student finds a website with good information. Messages about a book she searched for earlier flash on the side of her screen. The judges in a TV talent show are all drinking the same brand of soda. A character in a movie eats at a popular fast-food restaurant. What do all of these have in common? They're all forms of advertising.

Advertising to children

Advertising helps raise awareness about a product, business, or service. Today, advertising is everywhere.

Research shows that the average child in the USA sees about 16,000 television commercials a year. That's almost 45 a day! That's not counting the ads on the internet, ads on billboards, ads in magazines, commercials on the radio, or commercials at the movie theater. Even while watching a movie there's probably product placement, when companies pay to have their products in movie scenes.

In fact, it is thought that companies spend about $17 billion each year advertising to children. Why? Children and teens often have their own money to spend, and they also affect the way their parents spend money. This spending power is worth hundreds of billions of dollars a year.

Why is this an issue?

Some people argue that children younger than eight aren't old enough to understand that ads are selling something. Really young children might find it difficult to tell the difference between a commercial and a TV show because they look and sound the same.

Researchers argue that many ads for children promote junk food using cartoons. This encourages them to buy unhealthy foods, which can add to health problems. This is one example of how advertising can influence the values children are developing at this age.

For these reasons, many countries have rules about advertising for children. In some countries, like Sweden and Norway, there are bans against advertising to children under the age of 12.

Advertising techniques

Advertisers have many different ways to persuade people to buy or do something:

Repetition: A customer is more likely to buy a product the more times they have seen the advertisement. This is why advertisers repeat their ads.

Association: An ad might also use catchy slogans or phrases that people will remember.

Endorsement: Some advertising will use a favorite cartoon character or a celebrity to help sell their product or service.

Promotion: An ad could also offer a discount, free gift, or say that people can save money.

Emotional Appeal: An ad might suggest that the audience will be happier if they buy the product. An ad could also make the audience sad or scared to encourage them to do something.

Internet advertising

Advertisers have different internet tools. For example, when someone visits a website, the website can put a small file on their computer called a cookie. A cookie stores information about how that person uses the internet. Cookies track what sites the person uses, what information they search for, and what things they like.

The next time the person goes online, advertisers can show them ads based on that information. These are called targeted ads.

But advertising can be put to good use, too. To do their work, many charities and community groups depend on donations from the public. Advertising allows these groups to raise awareness about important issues, show the problems they are trying to solve, and tell people about the opportunities they are providing. They can tell stories of people they have helped and ask the public to donate money to support their work.

What can children do to be ad smart?

When looking at an ad, consider what the ad is really saying. Which company is behind the advertising? Who do they want to sell the product to? Who is this ad for? What does the ad want the viewer to think or do? Which technique is the ad using?

When children think critically about ads, they see which parts of the ad don't make sense to them or are not true for them. Then they can make better choices about which products they buy or ask their parents to buy. In a world full of advertising, it certainly pays to be ad smart.

TRACK 33

Unit 7, *Ad Smart*, Words in Context

Find these words in the reading. What do you think they mean?

service
product placement
spending power
catchy
cookie

Unit 8

TRACK 34

Unit 8, Nonfiction, *Ada Lovelace*

Ada Lovelace (1815–1852), born Augusta Ada Byron, led a remarkable life. She was the daughter of Lord George Gordon Byron, the famous poet, and Lady Anne Isabella Milbanke Byron. Her mother, who had studied math, didn't want Lovelace to develop her father's creativity and imagination, as she thought this would be bad for her character. But Lovelace was creative, and she had a brilliant mind.

As a child, she was always trying to invent things. She designed boats and steam-powered flying machines and was so fascinated by flying that she wrote a book called *Flyology*. But it was her mathematical ability that really took off when she was a teenager.

In those days, some people believed that women's minds were not strong enough to understand complicated math, but Lovelace didn't let what others thought stop her. She questioned everything and was curious about all sorts of developments in science and technology. It was the time of the Industrial Revolution when new, faster ways of making things were being invented, so there was plenty for her to be excited about.

Lovelace was born into a wealthy family in 1815 and, through her education and social life, she met many famous people of that time in England, including author Charles Dickens and scientist Michael Faraday. At the age of 17, Lovelace was introduced to Charles Babbage, the inventor of the Difference Engine—a huge mechanical calculator. This fascinated Lovelace, who thought it was like a thinking machine!

Babbage stopped work on the Difference Engine and started to design a more ambitious machine in 1834—the Analytical Engine. Lovelace asked for the plans to this new machine because she was determined to understand how it worked. She and her mother visited factories to look at different machines. Lovelace noticed how weaving looms and Babbage's engine both used punch cards to operate them. The holes in the cards gave instructions to the machine.

Her way of thinking was, in Lovelace's own words, "poetical science." She believed that creativity and imagination were essential in scientific thinking. Lovelace's creative mind allowed her to see the potential of how technology could be used in the future. Her ideas went beyond making calculations. She imagined technology for making music, creating images, and for other practical purposes. She was ahead of her time. She predicted a digital future.

Babbage was extremely impressed with Lovelace's mathematical ability and creativity. It was the start of a long friendship and they worked together to develop the Analytical Engine.

In 1842, an Italian mathematician named Luigi Menabrea wrote an article about the Analytical Engine. Lovelace translated the article into English and published it under the name A.A.L., to hide her identity. She added so many of her own detailed notes, formulas, and diagrams that her article was three times longer than the original. These notes contained what many now believe to be the first computer program.

Unfortunately, the complete Analytical Engine was never built, so Lovelace's program was never tested. She died in 1852, when she was only 36. Her notes have become some of the most important documents in computing history. They were published again 100 years later and inspired many mathematicians working on the first modern computers in the second half of the 20th century. All computer programs today are based on ideas suggested by Ada Lovelace.

Since 2009, there has been an Ada Lovelace Day in October, celebrated every year to help inspire women in science, technology, engineering, and math. She has also had a computer programming language named after her, and has been the subject of many books and films, both fact and fiction.

TRACK 35

Unit 8, *Ada Lovelace*, Words in Context

Find these words in the reading. What do you think they mean?

Industrial Revolution
punch cards
thread
algebraic
formulas

TRACK 36

Unit 8, Fiction, *The Binary Life*

Dexter: I like to count the steps when I walk downstairs. It makes me feel calm. There are 10 …

Mom: What do you want for breakfast, Dexter?

Dexter: The questions start as soon as I get up in the morning.

Mom: Cheese or chicken in your sandwich today? Do you want tomato or lettuce on it? Apple or banana for dessert?

Dexter: I don't like all these questions, but I do like the way Mom cuts my sandwich into four equal triangles. She's good at estimating the percentage of sandwich toppings, too. I like 75% cheese, 25% tomato.

We make an average of 35,000 decisions every day. There are usually way more than two possible outcomes to each decision. But, if there *were* only two possible results, that means there are possibly 2^{35000} ways my day could go. I like to analyze things mathematically. I translate the world into a language I'm comfortable with.

My brain couldn't stop thinking about this, so I had an idea—I could make life easier by flipping a coin to decide everything. Of course, there's a 1 in 6,000 chance of the coin landing on its edge but, if I flip it again, that possibility can be removed from the equation.

Tails. Green T-shirt.

Heads. Red shorts.

Many of my decisions have been made in this way…

Mom: What *are* you wearing, Dexter? It's freezing!

Dexter: This technique doesn't always work well, but at least I don't have to think about it. That frees up my brain to concentrate on music. I play cello, and I like to compose.

It started last autumn …

Ms. Park: You're a natural musician. I'll be disappointed if you don't study music in college,

Dexter: Ms. Park said.

Mr. Diaz: Math is clearly your subject. You'll go far if you major in math,

Dexter: Mr. Diaz told me.

But I already knew this. That was my problem. This time problem solving couldn't be done by the flip of a coin and I was getting more and more stressed. All I wanted was to divide my time between playing cello and doing calculations. Why couldn't they see that?

When I'm stressed I think everything can be solved with math, and I believed I could calculate my way out of this confusion. So I started to write—numbers, equations, formulas. But as I wrote, I started to hear music in my head and forgot about the problem completely. The number sequences poured out of my pen. The hours passed and I wrote through the night.

Ms. Park: No homework? This isn't like you, Dexter. You don't have a choice about homework. Homework *must* be done.

Dexter: Sorry, ma'am.

Ms. Park: What's wrong, Dexter?

Dexter: I'm not sure, but I spent all night writing music.

Ms. Park: Really? Wow! Tell me, who's your favorite composer?"

Dexter: Bach.

Ms. Park: Why?

Dexter: Well, in this piece here the notes go up. Then the same sequence of notes is repeated here, but upside down—it's symmetrical."

Ms. Park: And you like symmetry?

Dexter: Yeah. I like all math.

Ms. Park: So do you think math helps your music?

Dexter: Well, listening to music feels like counting, and when I compose I see numbers, patterns, and waves. Rhythm looks like fractions to me. There are beats and half beats, quarter and eighth notes. You understand what I'm saying, don't you?

Ms. Park: Yes, Dexter, I do. You know, there's a college that teaches computer-based musical composition. I could find the details for you if you want.

Dexter: So this doesn't have to be approached as a binary decision?

Ms. Park: Exactly! Don't think about it like you have to choose.

Dexter: What do you think are the chances of me getting into the program?

Ms. Park: Oh, about 90%!

Dexter: So here I am on my first day at college. I'm nervous, but I have to go now. Class starts in fifteen minutes. I've given up on the coin flipping, but I still have all these steps to count. Wish me luck!

TRACK 37

Unit 8, *The Binary Life*, Words in Context

Find these words in the reading. What do you think they mean?

outcome
free up
symmetrical
fractions
approached

Unit 9

TRACK 38

Unit 9, Nonfiction, *Making Decisions*

Narrator: Lena is a good volleyball player. Her serve is excellent, and she is good at passing. But Lena doesn't get much game time. The rest of the girls on the A team are so strong, Lena spends more time watching on the bench than playing. After volleyball practice, Coach Williams calls Lena over for a chat. The coach offers Lena a choice. This season, she can drop down to the B team where she'll play every game and be one of their better players, or she can stick with the A team. The decision is hers.

What should any of us do when we're faced with making an important decision? What should our strategy be?

Stop and Think!

We want an answer right now. We feel the pressure to decide quickly. But rushing into a decision doesn't allow us time to consider it properly. Next time you have an important decision to make, stop and think first.

Big or Small?

Not every decision is important. What you're going to eat for lunch is a small choice. Which school you go to is a big one. Learn to recognize which decisions are big and need careful thought, and which ones you shouldn't worry about too much.

It's Good to Talk
Ask a friend or adult for advice. They may have a new and different way of looking at the problem.
Cut Down Your Choices
Sometimes, having too many choices makes it a struggle to come to a decision. From a list of options, you can remove the ones that don't help you meet the goal or can't be done. This will give you fewer things to pick from.
Pros and Cons List
One technique to help make a decision is to make a **Pros and Cons List**. Look at your options. For each one, write down all the reasons it's a good choice: the pros. Next, make a list of all the negatives: the cons. A list like this can show you which choice is the one with the most pros and the smallest number of cons.
Steps to Making Decisions
1 Define the problem or decision.
Stop and think about what the problem is. Then consider whether it's a big or small problem.
2 Make a list of your options.
Research and brainstorm the options to solve the problem. You might also ask someone for advice.
3 Evaluate your ideas.
Look at the ideas that you came up with. Cut down your options.
4 Consider the consequences.
From the options still available, think about what the results might be for each one. Make a pros and cons list.
5 Decide on a solution.
Review all of the information you have and decide which option you feel best about. Then take action.
6 Reflect on the results of the decision.
Think about what happened after you made the decision. Were you happy with the results? Sometimes we make the wrong decision, but it's part of human nature. It happens to everyone. What is important is to reflect on why we got it wrong, and learn for the future. We need to recognize that if we had made a different decision, the outcome might have been better. Common reasons for making poor decisions are: We're in a rush.
Child 1: I was late for the bus!
Narrator: We don't think about all of our options.
Child 2: I didn't ask for more time.
Narrator: We feel pressure from other people.
Child 3: My friends made me do it.
Narrator: We don't think through the consequences.
Child 4: Now, I'm way too busy!
Narrator: **Lena's Decision** To make a careful decision, Lena follows the steps.
1 Define the problem or decision.
Lena tells her coach she needs some time to think. She goes home and sits alone.
Lena: *Which volleyball team should I play for this season?*
Narrator: 2 Make a list of your options.
Lena: *I could play for the A team, drop down to the B team, or quit playing volleyball.*
Narrator: 3 Evaluate your ideas.
Lena: *I like volleyball a lot and don't want to quit, so I'll eliminate that option.*
Narrator: 4 Consider the consequences.
Lena makes a pros and cons list to help her look at possible outcomes.
Narrator: 5 Decide on a solution.
Lena: *I'll play for the B team and then try for the A team again next season.*
Narrator: 6 Reflect on the results of the decision.
Lena: *I think I got a lot stronger playing so much and it made me a better player.*
Narrator: Whichever strategy you choose, it's important to have a range of strategies in your decision-making toolbox, ready to pull out when you need them most. And remember, every mistake is an opportunity to learn and grow!

TRACK 39

Unit 9, *Making Decisions*, Words in Context
Find these words in the reading. What do you think they mean?
on the bench
stick with
pressure
cut down
human nature

TRACK 40

Unit 9, Fiction, *It's Not OK*
Narrator: While Miral waited for the school bus, her phone beeped: it was a message notification from Dana. Miral opened the app. The photo stayed on Miral's screen for a moment, then the app made it vanish, as if it had never been there at all. But Miral had seen it. Penny would have seen it, too. It was Penny with the new braces on her teeth. People could be so mean sometimes. Miral shoved her phone back into the pocket of her backpack, trying to pretend the photo had never existed. In school, Miral saw Penny. Miral forced a weak smile.
Miral: What's up?
Narrator: she asked. Penny shrugged.
Penny: Not much.
Narrator: Miral saw the phone in Penny's hands, her fingers wrapped tightly around it. She thought of the photo.
Miral: *What should I say?* Did you do your homework?
Narrator: asked Miral, filling the deafening silence.
Penny: Uh-huh,
Narrator: said Penny.
Miral: Tough, wasn't it?
Penny: Uh-huh.
Narrator: Penny didn't say much at school that day. Miral didn't say much either. It didn't stop there. Over the next few days, there was a photo of a grinning donkey saying "Hee-haw." A photo of train tracks. A photo of Penny with a funny smile. Each time, Miral burned inside.
James: How funny was that donkey?
Narrator: said James at lunch. Miral shook her head. She looked around the lunch room. Penny was sitting by herself.
Miral: *Maybe Penny doesn't care about the jokes,*
Narrator: thought Miral.
Miral: *Dana will get bored with teasing soon, right? It'll become old news, and we can forget it ever happened. It'll go away, right?*
Narrator: Miral gave Penny an embarrassed wave. Penny waved back.
James: Hee-haw,
Narrator: laughed James as he left. Miral felt cold as she finished her lunch. If she'd had the guts, she would have told James to be quiet and leave Penny alone. Later that week, Penny wasn't at badminton. She was always at badminton. Miral helped the other kids set up the nets while Dana took selfies with her friends. Miral's phone beeped. It was Dana's photo.
Dana: Badminton Club! EVERYONE'S here.
Miral: *Not everyone,*
Narrator: Miral thought.
Miral: *I should do something about this.*
Narrator: She sighed and put her phone away. That night, Miral got another message. Someone had saved the donkey message and was sharing it again. Before the photo had a chance to vanish, Miral quickly copied it onto her phone. The phone felt hot in her hands.
Miral: *Now what?*
Narrator: She did nothing, set her phone on her desk, and tried to get to sleep.
Miral: *But if the photo had been of me, what would I have done?*
Narrator: Miral wondered. The next morning, Miral made a decision. Before school started, she went to the assistant principal's office and knocked on the door.
Miral: I need to show you something, Mr. Costa,
Narrator: she said. Miral opened up her phone, her hands shaking.
Miral: It's making fun of Penny—she just got new braces,
Narrator: she explained. Miral watched as the smile dropped from Mr. Costa's face. Miral swallowed.
Miral: It's been going on for a while,
Narrator: she admitted.
Miral: It's kind of an open secret.
Mr. Costa: Would you like to tell me why you're only telling me now?
Narrator: asked Mr. Costa gently. Miral went red. She looked down at the floor.
Mr. Costa: Sometimes it's hard to know what to do, isn't it?
Narrator: said Mr. Costa. Miral nodded.
Mr. Costa: Leave it with me,
Narrator: said Mr. Costa.
Mr. Costa: You've spoken out now. Off you go to class.
Narrator: In class, Miral sat down beside Penny.
Miral: You weren't at badminton yesterday,
Narrator: said Miral. Penny shrugged.
Penny: Didn't feel like going.
Miral: About those photos,
Narrator: said Miral quickly.
Miral: I think they're really mean. Your braces look fine. If I'd been brave, I would have said something before. I'm sorry.
Penny: That's OK,
Narrator: said Penny.
Miral: No, it's not. It's really not,
Narrator: said Miral. As she spoke, she gave Dana a long stare. Dana went bright red.
Miral: Friends?
Narrator: Miral asked hopefully.
Penny: Friends,
Narrator: replied Penny.
Miral: Badminton after school?
Narrator: asked Miral.
Penny: Sounds good,
Narrator: said Penny with a big, beautiful smile.

TRACK 41

Unit 9, *It's Not OK*, Words in Context
Find these words in the reading. What do you think they mean?
notification
shoved
deafening silence
guts
selfies

Unit 10

TRACK 42

Unit 10, Fiction, *Click to Follow*

Narrator: Scene 1: Inside a bright office

Jed: I need something new for this week's Friday Fashion Fix blog post.

Lucie: Just write the same as you always do, Jed—what you're wearing, what celebrities are wearing, what your readers should be wearing, upload a photo, done!

Jed: Does it really sound that formulaic?

Lucie: It's the same with my food blog. Where to eat, what to eat, photo, post! People love it! What's wrong?

Jed: Well, writing about clothes was always my dream, but it's not the same as it used to be.

Lucie: You tell people what's hot and what's not! Those Speed Feet sneakers you blogged about last month—everyone wants them. People buy what you to tell them is cool. Isn't that great?

Jed: No, it isn't! If I told people to wear an actual watermelon on their head, chances are some of them would do it!

Lucie: So?

Jed: I'm known for my blog style, and I've become connected with the brands I write about.

Lucie: I know. I think it's so cool that companies send you products to review.

Jed: Look what came today—aluminum shorts, shoes that look like duck feet, glasses without any glass in them!

Lucie: People love crazy fashion. It's all about clicks, likes, and follows, right? And you have thousands of followers. You add fun to people's lives.

Jed: But I'm not having fun. I'm not excited anymore.

Lucie: So make some fun! Give your readers some interesting styles to try.

Jed: Yeah, maybe you're right, this calls for a photo shoot. Danny!

Danny: On it, Jed!

Lucie: Perfect! Let's livestream it.

Narrator: Scene 2: The photo shoot

Jed: Amazing! People are loving it!

Tamara: How about this? The superhero look—shorts on the outside!

Lucie: I like it!

Jed: … We're all superheroes inside, show us your superhero style.

Narrator: Scene 3: Jed's living room

Reporter 1: … a clothing factory collapsed today injuring 16 workers …

Jed: That's awful.

Reporter 2: … a chemical leak at the Speed Feet sneaker factory has polluted the local water supply.

Jed: Why do things like this happen so often? I wonder … There's so much I didn't know about this … Someone should really say something to raise awareness. I have an idea! But will people take me seriously?

Narrator: Scene 4: In the office

Lucie: "StyleGuru says that next season we'll be wearing yellow. But I'll be wearing green. That means I'll only buy clothes that are ethically produced. Today, I'm going to review a brand that creates clothes that are stylish, affordable, and sustainable …"

Danny: "Is somebody else writing this blog now?"

Jed: I'm losing my audience.

Lucie: Maybe it's not the right audience for you anymore.

Jed: I think I'm OK with that. Before, I just wanted them to like me. Now it feels better to write about something important.

Danny: Hey, look at this comment! "We all love cool clothes and gadgets. But let's think about where our things have come from and where they're going …"

Tamara: Here's another one! "I love this! Wanna start a clothes swap campaign with us?"

Jed: Guys, I just got an email from Green Threads. They make sustainable clothes and they want to have a meeting with me.

Narrator: Scene 5: The office, the next day

Reporter 1: The makers of Speed Feet sneakers announced a plan to review how their products are made.

Jed: I can't believe I used to promote those sneakers.

Lucie: Your message is so much more authentic, this sounds like the real you. You seem so much happier and motivated now.

Tamara: Yeah, and you were invited to attend Fashion Week to report on ethical fashion. They actually called you one of the most influential young voices in fashion.

Jed: Yup, I think I've found my voice, and it feels great to use it to set a good example.

TRACK 43

Unit 10, *Click to Follow*, Words in Context

Find these words in the reading. What do you think they mean?

formulaic
take me seriously
ethically
authentic
influential

TRACK 44

Unit 10, Literary Term, Assonance

1 You don't have to have the latest, greatest clothes to look good.
2 Kniffen has the top job in the company.
3 This store sells cool shoes.

TRACK 45

Unit 10, Nonfiction, *Recycle Runway*

People have been fascinated by clothes and influenced by fashion for as long as we've had mirrors. Clothes offer us a way to be the same as everyone else or a way to express our individuality. But what if they could do much more than that? What if beautiful clothes could help us deliver a more important message?

Nancy Judd creates fashion sculptures from trash. But her purpose isn't just to show us her wonderful designs, it's to teach us about the environment—Judd is an artist and a passionate environmental educator. She is committed to getting people to look differently at waste and to change the way they live on Earth. The Aluminum Drop Dress Judd is wearing in the photo is made from an old shower curtain covered with drop-shaped metal pieces cut out from soda cans. Recycling cans reduces the use of natural resources and chemicals.

Judd started the Recycle Runway project while working as the Recycling Coordinator for the City of Santa Fe in New Mexico, USA. She realized that art and fashion could be a fun and positive way to deliver her message, so she organized a recycled fashion contest. To promote this event, Judd created some upcycled outfits, and this gave her the idea for a special collection of designs.

Exhibitions of these sustainable fashion designs are shown in airports, museums and shopping malls. The clothes have received worldwide media attention, generating interest from big companies to sponsor her work.

Judd runs creative workshops for children and adults, and gives presentations about environmental issues. Many of these outfits are made during public workshop events, so people can take part in creating them. The sculptures are inspiring people all over the world to help care for the planet.

Through her amazing creations, Nancy Judd is showing the world that you don't have to be a dedicated follower of fashion. You can make fashion work for you! Maybe in the future we'll all be wearing sustainable clothing, recycling more, and creating less waste.

The Jellyfish Dress is made of blue, green, and white plastic bags and brings attention to issues about marine conservation. It was created to be displayed in public in a coastal city.

Plastics can seriously harm marine life. Turtles sometimes eat plastic bags, mistaking them for jellyfish, one of their favorite foods. Sea trash such as plastic bottles, plastic bags, and cans are all recyclable.

Tireless Couture is made from the inside of car and bicycle tires. It was commissioned for a city that wanted to encourage people to drive less and use the new pedestrian and cycle paths more. They paid Judd to create this sculpture so that, when people see it, they'll remember to use the car less and bicycle more to reduce their carbon footprint.

Faux Fur Coat uses many meters of old video and audiotape, sewn onto a second-hand coat. Electronic waste often contains glass and valuable metals as well as dangerous chemicals. These materials can be recycled and reused, but the chemicals can get into the soil if electronic waste is thrown away as landfill trash.

Sol Man is a project inspired by 6th grade students that combines art with science to teach about energy conservation. In science they learned about how energy is created and the problems with different energy sources. Then in art they drew their ideas of a superhero character. Judd used their ideas to design the costume for the superhero. The students then helped make the pieces that look like solar panels in their consumer sciences class. They designed and made a new recycled costume called Sol Man. This sculpture is made from trash from energy-efficient building projects. Through this project, the students learned how to save money and energy in their homes.

Judd encourages us all to make eco-pledges. These are promises to help the environment. We make simple decisions all the time that affect the planet.

What eco-pledges can you make?

TRACK 46

Unit 10, *Recycle Runway*, Words in Context

Find these words in the reading. What do you think they mean?

individuality
aluminum
upcycled
outfits
commissioned

Video Scripts

Language Book

The video scripts for the spoken word pieces and chants in the **Language Book** are exactly the same as for the audio scripts and the text on the page. Please refer to the relevant unit in the Audio Scripts on TB pp. 215-238.

Unit 1

CONVERSATION

What Should We Blog About?

Lloyd: We're starting a blog about school lunches. I think we should share our ideas with children in other countries.

Gene: What do you mean? That we should write about the different food we have for lunch?

Lloyd: Yes, exactly! Why don't you do the writing? You're good at that. And you could include some things like what the food is and some recipes.

Gene: So, you're saying I need to find out how to make the dishes?

Lloyd: That's right. And we could ask someone to help by searching online or in the library.

Gene: Yes, maybe Linda could help. There's tons of information out there, and she loves doing that.

Lloyd: Linda can do the research and then email it to you and then you can write the blog post.

Gene: Do you mean it will just be text in the post? I think we need to upload some photos, too; otherwise, it'll look boring.

Lloyd: Well, that's true. Maria could take the photos. She has a great camera!

Gene: OK. And what are you going to do?

Lloyd: Oh, what about me? I forgot! What can I do?

Gene: I think you'd be good at making videos.

Lloyd: Yes! I could eat my lunch on video!

Gene: No … *make* the lunch on the video!

Unit 2

PRESENTATION

Life Is Stressful

Linda: I'm Linda, and I am going to agree with the statement that young people have a more stressful lifestyle than adults today.
Older people think young people like us have a very easy life because we usually have someone to look after us. They think we only worry about our leisure time. But I really believe they're wrong! Think about it. Today we spend our time worrying about getting good grades in all our school subjects, and we also get stressed about how well we are doing on our sports teams.
Some of us are very concerned about who we are friends with and making friends, about what we wear and if we are eating the right things. In summary, I believe that life as a young person is not easy and I would like adults to understand more what our daily life is like.

Veronica: My name's Veronica, and I am speaking against the statement.
I believe that adults have a much more stressful life than young people. They work every day so they have enough money to pay for everything, like rent, bills, food, clothes, and trips. If they have children, they have to plan and organize *their* lives *and* their children's lives. They can't just come home and rest or see their friends. They always have to do something!
For example, in just one day they have to think about work, what they're going to cook, what their children are doing after school, helping out with homework, cleaning the house, and shopping. Apart from the usual worries, they also have to worry so much about us—their children! To summarize, adults have much more stress, so I strongly disagree with the statement.

Unit 3

CONVERSATION

Let's Plan the Day

Maria: Our group needs to think of ideas for the International Day of Happiness. Can we hear your ideas? Lloyd, what about you?

Lloyd: Well, we could send nice things to people. You know, surprising people makes them happy.

Maria: You mean we could send them messages or photos?

Lloyd: Yes, and also maybe things like cards or postcards in the mail.

Maria: Good idea. OK, so wait a sec … send messages

Lloyd: … photos and cards.

Maria: Linda, what ideas did you have?

Linda: Well, more than just messages, we could actually give things to people.

Lloyd: Yes, that's nice. People love getting presents, especially when they're not expecting them.

Maria: OK, what you're saying is, we give presents to people for no particular reason, just to surprise them and make them happy.

Linda: Yes, small things can make a difference. They could be things we've made or pictures we've drawn, as well as small things we could buy.

Maria: Hang on then … give presents.

Linda: Yes, things we make or things we buy.

Lloyd: I think things we make is better—it's more personal and creative.

Maria: Yes, you're right. So, to be clear, we could, one, send things to people, like postcards and photos, and, two, give things to people, like pictures and cakes and other things we've made.

Lloyd: That sounds great. And you know, it'll make us feel good to know we've made someone happy.

Linda: It's win-win!

Maria: That's true!

Unit 4

PRESENTATION

That's Interesting!

Maria: Do you know about the statues on Easter Island called *moai*? I wonder what you know about them. This is one of the biggest world mysteries yet to be solved. When did the first people arrive on Easter Island? Where did they come from? Why did they create such enormous statues? And how did the statues get up onto the platforms? Hundreds of experts claim to have solved the puzzle—but their theories keep changing!

Lloyd: Easter Island is a volcanic rock in the South Pacific Ocean. There are nearly 900 of these ancient monuments on the island, and some are almost ten meters tall. We don't know how the first islanders got there. And we certainly don't know why or how they created and moved these great works of art.

Maria: When people started investigating how the first people got to the island, some thought that they had used the stars to help navigate across huge distances. But others said they couldn't have traveled so far without getting lost! When people examined the statues, some thought that the islanders must have moved them across ancient roads. But others pointed out that wasn't possible, as the roads weren't flat. There is no historical record of why or how the statues were built.

Lloyd: So, what do you think?

Unit 5

PRESENTATION

Welcome to our Exhibition

Gene: Ladies and gentlemen, boys and girls, good evening and welcome to our Fourth Annual School Art Exhibition called "Be Brave, Be Creative!"
We're very pleased to see so many of you here today. I won't say much, as I'm sure you want to look at all the wonderful art here.
But before you start, I'd like to point out three things: one, this year, there is even more variety than usual. You will find fantastic paintings, drawings, photographs, sculptures, and some mixed media pieces. You'll see some powerful pieces and some playful, fun things, as well as serious pieces with a serious message.
Two, the students have been experimenting with the question "What is art?" See what you think of the "Selfies as Art" section and make up your own mind.
And three, we're really proud to be showing the work of two competition winners this year. This is personally my favorite part of the exhibition. Linda Stevens and Veronica García have both won prizes—so make sure you don't miss the exciting work of these talented children.

So, to repeat: variety, experimenting, and competition winners are the three things that are our focus. I wouldn't have thought that the art in last year's exhibition could have been improved, but I was wrong! This year, it's even better!

Thank you to all the artists and thank you for coming. I really hope you enjoy the exhibition, and remember, as our title says, "Be Brave, Be Creative!"

Unit 6

CONVERSATION

Decisions, Decisions

Veronica: The weather's so bad today. Should we play a game?

Linda: Well … I have an idea. I need to finish a class project all about games. One task is to invent a new game. Why don't we do it together? We could invent a new board game.

Veronica: Sure, I'd like to invent a new game, but I'd prefer not to invent a board game. They're boring! I don't get why people play them.

Linda: OK, if you don't like board games, we can invent a new multiplayer video game. The players could design their own levels!

Veronica: But what's the point of that? It's like the game isn't even finished. I think it's better to invent a really simple game that you can play on your phone.

Linda: OK … but a video game would get players to use their creativity, too. You wouldn't just collect points and level up. First, you could choose the location—perhaps there are options like a jungle, different cities around the world, or the moon!

Veronica: Sounds fun. Is this game just for kids?

Linda: I don't think it needs to be a kids' game. If players are designing different worlds, there's a lot of skill and strategy involved. It's almost like art! And once you're finished, you can share it online with other players. That'd be really cool.

Veronica: And players can create their own avatars.

Linda: Of course! That's the most fun part!

Veronica: OK, let's give it a go. We should start by thinking of a name.

Linda: Oh … now … that's difficult!

Unit 7

CONVERSATION

Promote Yourself!

Linda: Have you seen that the school is looking for student community leaders?

Maria: Yes, I'm very excited about it. One of the jobs involves working on the advertising campaign for the summer fair. I'd love to do that!

Linda: I thought you would. What will you say when they interview you?

Maria: I'll probably say that I'm very hard-working and I always give 100% to anything I do. I can say I'm a very committed person, as I always stick with a job right to the end. As well as that, I'm not afraid of hard work and I'm a very good team player.

Linda: That's great! You're good at communicating, too. Why don't you talk about when you were team leader of the basketball committee?

Maria: Oh, yes, I organized social events for them. One of my skills is being able to listen to what everyone wants! Do you think they will be impressed by that?

Linda: Absolutely! You're really organized, too.

Maria: Thanks. I think you're right, being organized is one of my main strengths.

Linda: And remember when you led a group to organize and design a new uniform for the basketball team? Their old uniform was so bad.

Maria: Oh, yeah! My experience in design really helped. I collaborated with art students to design the new uniform. Everyone loved it, and I had a lot of fun being creative and solving problems.

Linda: That showed that you really know how to take initiative, so you should mention that.

Maria: OK, I'm going to use my initiative again now—I'm going to send my application!

Linda: Good luck

Unit 8

PRESENTATION

Numbers in My Day

Wade: Imagine a world with no numbers. No statistics or complicated math problems.
No times or dates. No favorite numbers. Impossible, isn't it? Numbers are a part of our everyday lives. Today, I'm going to share my numbers with you.
My first number is 7:15. This is the time on my alarm clock when I wake up.
Four minutes in the shower. Did you know that roughly 11 liters of water is used for every minute in the shower? So, I used around 44 liters of water. That's quite a lot, but it's important to be clean and hygienic!
Five people in my family. We help each other get ready for school in the morning so we can leave on time.
Seven buttons on my school uniform—six on my shirt, one on my pants. I help my little brother button up. It's good to help people, isn't it? Take a minute to think about a time when you needed help with something.
Forty-three people on the school bus. Twenty-two girls, 20 boys, and one adult. My brothers and I travel a total of ten kilometers by bus every day.
The next numbers come at recess: nine, one, three, and four—I eat nine olives, and I share one bag of potato chips with three friends. After all that, I'm thirsty, so I drink four glasses of water!
Seven is the number on my soccer shirt. I'm a right-winger. I scored zero goals, but we played well as a team, so it was fun.
14,568—the number of steps I walk! This surprises me: I didn't think I'd been very active, but it seems I was. Do you know how active you are?
So, what are your numbers? Let's take on the world of math and connect our lives to numbers!

Unit 9

CONVERSATION

Our Perfect Day

Wade: There's a competition in this magazine: "Win a perfect day for you and two friends. Just write a paragraph describing what you'd like to do on your perfect day, but you must make the decision together. Everyone should have their say."

Veronica: Oh, wow, that's easy! Let's do it. What would you like to do for your perfect day?

Wade: I'd definitely start by going to a café for breakfast—maybe a diner type of place? What do you think?

Veronica: Oh, no! That's a waste of time—we can just have a quick breakfast at home and then go to the beach and maybe take a surfing lesson. Maria, you're very quiet—do you think that's a good idea?

Maria: I'm not sure yet, Veronica. Perhaps we should brainstorm ideas on our own first. Then we can talk about the pros and cons of the ideas and choose the best one.

Veronica: Yes, that's a good idea.

Wade: OK, but I think it's important to decide about the meals—like where we're going to have lunch. Do you agree?

Veronica: Not really. You're always hungry, Wade! I think the activities are more important. Anyway, what do you think of Maria's idea of brainstorming first?

Wade: I don't know … Actually, I think I'd prefer to brainstorm as a group. Is that OK?

Veronica: Yes, fine. Let's make a mind map so we can write our ideas down.

Unit 10

PRESENTATION

Buddy Up

Linda: Welcome to Sunnydays Middle School! We're here to tell you about *Buddies 4U*. We started this mentor program last year, and it had great results, and because of that, we'll be continuing with it this year.

Gene: The idea of this great program is to support and encourage all new students in our school. Some things here are new, and we're here to help so that nobody feels worried or confused about anything.

Linda: We've found that it's a great help if every new student has a specific person who takes time to get to know them. For this reason, every child has a specific mentor, or buddy, assigned to them.

Gene: One of the differences here is that you'll be having classes with lots of different teachers. You'll also be getting more homework and more tests. But don't worry, your buddy will help you with new responsibilities like getting to the right classroom and keeping up with your homework.

Linda: Another benefit of *Buddies 4U* is that you'll always have someone to talk to. We hope you'll never feel unhappy or have problems with other students, but if you do, your buddy will be there for you.

Gene: And we hope you'll be inspired to join some clubs and try out new activities. Sometimes it's hard to choose; therefore, your buddy will take you to the exciting New Clubs Event next week, where you'll see what's on offer.

Linda: We know that starting a new school isn't always easy, but don't worry! *Buddies 4U* will help you have fun and stay on track.

Gene: So, does anyone have any questions?